Safety, Health and Environment Cases

2001

by

Compiled by CMS Cameron McKenna
Environment Law Group

Health and Safety cases edited by
Deborah Lloyd, Herbert Smith

Tolley

A member of the Reed Elsevier group plc

First edition published October 2000, ISBN 0 75450 372-0

Published by
Tolley
2 Addiscombe Road
Croydon, Surrey CR9 5AF
020-8686 9141

Typeset in Great Britain by
Tradespools, Frome, Somerset

Printed and bound in Great Britain by
Hobbs, Totton, Hants

ISBN 0 75450 372-0

About this book

This first edition of Tolley's Safety, Health and Environment Cases 2001 has been compiled and edited by Daniel Chappell, CMS Cameron McKenna with special thanks to Matthew Townsend (formerly at CMS Cameron McKenna).

Deborah Lloyd, Herbert Smith, has edited the health and safety cases.

For ease of reference, the cases within both the health and safety section and environment section have been divided on a subject basis. There is an inevitable overlap between many of these subject areas.

Several cases have been included which do not directly relate to the environment. These are however included as they highlight points of law or practice which have general application and which may be relevant to the practitioner in this field. The cases are also a mixture of civil and criminal and include where relevant, decisions of the European Court of Justice. Environment law must not be simply viewed in a domestic context.

Contents

Part A: Health and Safety

Part B: Environment

Abbreviations and References

The following is a list of abbreviations used frequently throughout the book.

BATNEEC	=	Best Available Techniques Not Entailing Excessive Costs
BPEO	=	Best Practicable Environment Option
COPA 1974	=	Control of Pollution Act 1974
DETR	=	Department of Environment, Transport and the Regions
EA	=	Environment Agency
EA 1995	=	Environment Act 1995
EC	=	European Community
ECJ	=	European Court of Justice
EEA	=	European Economic Area
EIA	=	Environmental Impact Assessment
EPA 1990	=	Environmental Protection Act 1990
EU	=	European Union
HMIP	=	Her Majesty's Inspectorate of Pollution
HSC	=	Health and Safety Commission
HSE	=	Health and Safety Executive
HSWA 1974	=	Health and Safety at Work etc. Act 1974
IPC	=	Integrated Pollution Control
NRA	=	National Rivers Authority
SEPA	=	Scottish Environment Protection Agency
SPA	=	Special Protection Area
The 1957 Treaty	=	Treaty of Rome 1957
WIA 1991	=	Water Industry Act 1991
WRA 1985	=	Water Resources Act 1985
WRA 1991	=	Water Resources Act 1991

Introduction

There have been considerable developments in both health and safety and environmental law over the last decade. These have partly been driven by initiatives from the European Commission and from domestic social and political pressure. Environmental issues continue to gain increasing prominence on the political agenda which are being matched by a recognition from the commercial sector that such issues need to be addressed, both in terms of risk management and as a public relations exercise.

The *Environmental Protection Act 1990* (the *'EPA' 1990*) brought significant aspects of environmental regulation into a more coherent framework. The *EPA 1990* has been followed and preceded by a plethora of EU directives and regulations, legislating on a wide range of areas such as packaging, waste, producer responsibility and water quality to name but a few.

These regulatory developments have been accompanied by an increasing body of case law in this area. As this book demonstrates, such case law has developed in both the civil and criminal courts. Recent cases such as *Blue Circle Industries Ltd v Ministry of Defence (1998)*, in which £6 million in damages was awarded against the Ministry of Defence as a result of the escape of radioactive material from its site in Aldermaston, appear to demonstrate that the courts are willing, in the right circumstances, to make significant financial awards. We await to see what the level of environment related civil claims will be in the next five to ten years.

A similar pattern emerges from the criminal courts. The number of cases brought before the Magistrates' and Crown Courts relating to environmental offences continues to rise. Few would predict this trend is likely to change given the perceived political pressure on the regulatory authorities to bring more successful prosecutions for environmental offences. Nor are the courts reluctant to impose penalties which are seen to reflect the impact of the offence. In January 1999, Milford Haven Port Authority was fined £4 million (plus costs) for a breach of *section 85* of the *Water Resources Act 1985* (the *'WRA' 1985*), following the release of light crude oil from the Sea Empress oil tanker which ran aground off the South Wales coast. This is the largest fine to date under these provisions of the *WRA 1985*.

Health and safety law has followed a similar pattern and to some extent continues to occupy an even more prominent position in the public domain as a result of high profile tragedies such as the Paddington Rail Disaster, the Kings Cross Fire and the Herald of Free Enterprise. Health and safety law has for a considerable time been of crucial importance to the workplace and this is reflected in the extent of primary and secondary legislation now in place.

The case law concerning corporate liability for health and safety offences may also need to be reconsidered in the light of the proposed corporate killing legislation. The proposed law will make UK companies liable for a new offence of corporate killing. This will replace the offence of manslaughter in certain cases where death is caused without intention of death or serious injury. The offence would mean that companies could be convicted of corporate killing and fines would be borne by the shareholders. In addition, if a company is convicted, the court will be able to punish the company severely and will be able to order the company to put right the failings that were the cause of the death. More importantly, the proposed legislation would give courts the power to impose on the senior management of a company, its chairman and managing director an overarching responsibility for the health and safety of its workforce and the general public, thereby preventing senior management from evading responsibility

It is important to note that both environment and health and safety law are moulded by civil and criminal case law as well as by legislation made by the UK and European parliaments. Thus the purpose behind this book is to understand the legal context in which these cases arise. This section provides an overview of the sources of law in health and safety and environment, together with an explanation of the civil and criminal court system in England and Wales.

The subsequent chapters of this book provide a review of the most significant health and safety and environment cases in both the civil and criminal courts in England and Wales. To avoid the reader becoming lost in a legal maze, the book deliberately concentrates on the most important and influential cases. It identifies, at the outset, what the practitioner, student, health, safety and environment compliance officer or other really needs to know. This section gives an introduction to the legal system and legislative, judicial and administrative bodies in England and Wales which have given rise to the health and safety and environment cases reviewed in the following chapters.

The Civil and Criminal Court System

Civil courts

The civil courts in England and Wales consist of the County Court and the High Court (known as courts of first instance) from which there are rights of appeal to the Court of Appeal and, ultimately, the House of Lords.

A County Court's jurisdiction is largely limited to minor civil claims. Where some discretion does exist as to the forum for a case, the parties (and the court) will need to consider the value of the claim, the complexity of the issues and the general public importance of the issues raised.

On 26 April 1999, the civil court system in England and Wales was subject to fundamental reform following a review of the civil system carried out by Lord Woolf. These changes affect a range of procedural matters when bringing a civil claim. The changes are widely referred to as the *'Woolf reforms'* and the new procedural rules are set out in the *Civil Procedure Rules 1998 (1998 No 3132)* ('Rules') together with associated practice directions.

The new Rules and practice directions are the complete procedural code for the County Court, High Court and the Civil Division of the Court of Appeal. The Rules apply to proceedings commenced on or after 26 April 1999. When interpreting the new Rules or exercising any power under them, a court must give effect to the 'overriding objective'.This requires cases to be dealt with justly which includes, so far as is practicable, ensuring that the parties are on an equal footing; saving expense; dealing with the case in a proportionate way; ensuring that the case is dealt with expeditiously and fairly and that an appropriate share of the court's time is allocated to it. The courts are actively encouraged by the new Rules to case manage.

There are now three tracks on which a case may be brought (a small claims track, a fast track and multi-track) and allocation to a particular track is determined in accordance with the Rules.

Criminal courts

The criminal court system operates in parallel to the civil system. It consists of, at first instance, the Magistrates' Court and the Crown Court, with rights of appeal to the High Court (on points of law only), the Court of Appeal and, ultimately, the House of Lords. In practice, the Magistrates' Courts hear less serious cases and this is where most environment and health and safety cases are dealt with.

Whether a case is heard in the Magistrates' Court or Crown Court will depend upon a range of factors. Criminal offences are triable (1) summarily (i.e. in the Magistrates' Court) or (2) on indictment (i.e. in the Crown Court) or (3) either way (i.e. in the Magistrates' or Crown Court). Statutory offences prescribe the mode in which the offence is to be dealt. Most health and safety and environment offences are triable either way.

Employment tribunals

Health and safety law frequently arises in the context of the relationship between an employer and employee. As such, many relevant issues are dealt with in employment tribunals.

Law in England and Wales

The law in England and Wales is largely contained in primary legislation (i.e. Acts of Parliament). However, there is a considerable body of law (particularly in the field of health and safety) contained within secondary legislation (such as regulations). Both the environment and health and safety fields have also tended to generate a considerable amount of statutory and non-statutory guidance issued by the government in the form of circulars, planning policy guidance notes, codes of practice. Such guidance often contains much of the practical detail behind the framework statutory provisions (as can most recently be seen in the statutory guidance to the contaminated land regime).

The common law system in England and Wales means that much law is also judge made. It is in the courts rather than parliament that concepts such as nuisance, negligence and trespass have been developed.

Institutions of the European Union

The main institutions of the European Union ('EU'), formerly known as the European Community ('EC') are the European Commission, the Council of Ministers, the European Court of Justice ('ECJ') and the European Parliament. Each has powers derived from the European Treaties (principally the *Treaty of Rome 1957* as amended by later treaties such as the *Maastricht Treaty 1991*).

European Commission

The European Commission acts as the civil service of the EU and has responsibility for generating proposals for legislation and ensuring its implementation. The Commission is divided into a number of directorates. Directorate-General XVI has responsibility for environment matters (and the current Environment Directorate is Margot Wallström). The Directorate-General XXIV covers health and consumer protection matters.

Council of Ministers

The Council of Ministers is made up of one representative from each member state and is largely a political body. It considers legislation proposed by the Commission and the European Parliament and has a duty to ensure that the objectives of the *Treaty of Rome 1957* are attained. Most proposals must be agreed unanimously although some legislative proposals are subject to qualified majority voting.

European Parliament

The European Parliament does not have legislative power in the same way as a national parliament. It operates mainly as a consultative and advisory body on proposed legislation but it does have certain powers to actively influence legislation. It also exercises some supervisory powers over the Commission.

European Court of Justice

The ECJ is the court of the EU. It consists of fifteen judges which number reflects the number of member states. The court is assisted by Advocates-General which make submissions to the court in each case. The ECJ is the supreme arbiter in matters concerning the interpretation and application of European law including the treaties establishing the EU.

The main types of action which may fall before the ECJ are:

- proceedings against member states for a failure to fulfil an obligation under EU law;
- proceedings to review the legality of acts or failures to act by certain Community institutions;
- references by national courts, which are in doubt as to the interpretation or validity of Community law (known as a preliminary ruling hearings).

EU Law

EU law is found in the EU Treaties, legislative acts of the EU institutions and the case law of the ECJ. The main legislative acts of the EU institutions are regulations, directives and decisions.

Directly effective EU law is supreme in member states in that national courts are required to apply it rather than national law where there is a conflict between the two. There is also a rule of interpretation that national legislation must be interpreted consistently with European law. In limited circumstances, EU law gives rise to directly applicable obligations on member states which may be enforced by individuals in their national courts.

Treaties

The EU Treaties set out the main powers of the EU institutions as well as procedures for law and decision making. They are of crucial importance in understanding the legal structure of the EU. The main treaty which established the European Community is the *Treaty of Rome 1957*.

Directives

Directives are the main type of legislative act used by the EU. They are addressed to member states and require them to implement their requirements within a specified time limit. As such, they usually require member states to amend domestic legislation or introduce new legislation. Some directives may be directly effective once the time limit for implementation has expired, provided they are sufficiently clear and precise on their face. This means that individuals may have enforceable rights under the directive even if the necessary national implementing legislation has not been passed. Directives are the principle type of EU legislation used for environment and health and safety matters.

Regulations

Regulations are generally directly applicable in and binding on member states and their citizens without the need for national implementing legislation. In this context, regulations are relatively limited in practice.

Decision, recommendations and opinions

Decisions are binding on the party to whom they are addressed. The European institutions may also issue recommendations and opinions which are designed to have a persuasive effect but are not legally binding.

Policy Making and Enforcement

Environmental law

Environmental law in England and Wales is regulated in a number of different ways.

Administrative action

These powers are exercised through the granting (or otherwise) of environmental permits and authorisations and the conditions contained within those permits. This type of regulation may also include formal action taken other than a prosecution such as the use of enforcement notices, the issue of warning letters etc.

Clean up

Regulatory authorities are provided with various powers to require the remediation of contamination if land or water is or has been polluted. They also have powers to take remediation action itself and recover the costs of so doing from the liable party (for example under *section 161* of the *Water Resources Act 1991* or under the contaminated land regime contained in *Part IIA* of the *EPA 1990*).

Criminal proceedings

Various environmental statutes create a number of criminal offences as a result of polluting activities or carrying out operations without the necessary permit (to name but a few). Many of these offences are *'either way'* offences and may be dealt with either in the Magistrates' Court or the Crown Court.

Civil proceedings

These type of proceedings will usually be taken by third parties which have suffered damage as a result of the actions of the defendant and/or the pollution caused by it.

Department of the Environment, Transport and the Regions

The government department with responsibility for environmental policy in England (and, to some extent, Wales) is the Department of Environment, Transport and the Regions ('DETR'). This department is the result of the consolidation on 16 June 1997 of the previous departments of Environment and Transport.

The DETR is the department which formulates and develops domestic environment policy, legislative proposals, guidance etc. It also has responsibility for co-ordinating environmental policy across other government departments. Due to the number of environmental issues which arise within other departments jurisdictions, this role should not be underestimated.

The DETR also has direct operational powers which are largely delegated to others. It deals with the conduct of appeals on a range of planning matters, discharge consents and local authority air pollution control authorisations. These matters are delegated to the Planning Inspectorate (an executive agency of the DETR).

Since the devolution of policy making powers to the Scottish and Welsh Assemblies in 1999, the role of the DETR in guiding the implementation of national environmental policies in these areas has clearly diminished. The Welsh and Scottish offices exercise responsibility in their areas on the direction of environment policy. The Northern Ireland office continues to exercise responsibility for environment policy within its geographical area.

Enforcing authorities

For historical reasons, there are a number of public authorities and bodies with powers to regulate and enforce environmental law. This regulatory framework was revised with the creation of the Environment Agency (and the Scottish Environment Protection Agency in Scotland) on 1 April 1996. This resulted from a merger of the National Rivers Authority ('NRA'), Her Majesty's Inspectorate of Pollution ('HMIP') and Waste Regulations Authorities. Despite this change, there remains overlap between separate enforcing authorities.

Environment Agency

On 1 April 1996, the Environment Agency ('EA') (and the Scottish Environment Protection Agency ('SEPA')) were created. The intention behind the merger was to create a unified regulatory body to achieve consistency of enforcement and to provide a 'one-stop shop' for regulated businesses.

The Environment Act 1995 (the *'EA 1995'*) created the EA and SEPA as independent corporate bodies. They operate within a matrix of powers, functions and objectives, many of which are contained in separate legislation and which were transferred to the agencies at the time of their creation.

The main regulatory areas of the EA include:

(1) waste management, including dealing with the issue and enforcement of waste management licences, the registration of waste brokers and waste carriers and the enforcement of the duty of care as regards waste (contained in *section 34* of the *EPA 1990*);

(2) water management, including the control of water pollution and development of water quality objectives, abstraction licensing, flood defence, fisheries and navigation and conservation;

(3) industrial process regulation under *Part I* of the *EPA 1990* and the issue and enforcement of integrated pollution

control (IPC) authorisations (being replaced by the new IPPC system);

(4) regulation of activities falling under the *Radioactive Substances Act 1993*;

(5) once in force, responsibility for 'special sites' under the contaminated land regime in *Part IIA* of the *EPA 1990*; and

(6) miscellaneous activities such as overseeing the producer responsibility obligations and compliance scheme under the *Producer Responsibility Obligations (Packaging Waste) Regulations 1997* (*SI 1997 No 648*) (as amended).

The principal aims and objectives of the EA are set out in *section 4* of the *EA 1995*. The EA is required by *section 39* of the *EA 1995* to have regard to the likely costs and benefits of the exercise (or otherwise) of its powers. However, certain strict legal requirements imposed on the EA remain unaffected by this duty.

The EA performs various roles. It exercises administrative powers relating to the issue of licences whilst also performing a role as regulator to determine whether environmental legislation is being complied with and taking enforcement action where this is not the case. In practice, this may give rise to conflicts between inspectors and regulated businesses seeking to build co-operative working relationships which can often be damaged by enforcement action.

As a regulator, the EA has considerable powers of entry and inspection contained in *section 108* of the *EA 1995*. Its officers are also authorised to carry out interviews under caution pursuant to the *Police and Criminal Evidence Act 1984*.

The functions, objectives and powers of SEPA are largely identical to those of the EA subject to minor differences.

Local authorities

Despite the restructuring brought about by the *EA 1995*, local authorities have retained regulatory powers under several statutory regimes, in particular:

(1) under the statutory nuisance provisions of the *EPA 1990*;

(2) under the contaminated land regime contained in *Part IIA* of the *EPA 1990*;

(3) for the control of smoke, dust, grit and fumes under the *Clean Air Acts* and associated legislation;

(4) the regulation of processes governed by the air pollution control regime in *Part I* of the *EPA 1990* (and they will retain responsibilities under the new IPPC system);

(5) as local planning authorities for the purposes of planning legislation. As such, they hold responsibility for the consideration, and issue, of planning consents, the development of local plans and the control of development within their areas;

(6) for associated matters such as the control of conservation areas, tree preservation orders, listed building consents and the control of derelict buildings.

Sewerage undertakers

Sewerage undertakers regulate discharges to sewers pursuant to powers in the *Water Industry Act 1991* (the *'WIA' 1991*). Discharges are normally regulated through the issue of trade effluent consents. Sewerage undertakers are, in practice, privatised water companies for the relevant area exercising public functions set out in the *WIA 1991*. Appeals relating to effluent consents or agreements are made to the Director-General of Water Services ('OFWAT').

Other bodies

There are a range of other bodies with responsibilities for regulating the impact of activities within their designated areas. For instance, the Nature Conservancy Council for England (known as English Nature) and the Countryside Commission have specific responsibilities for nature conservation within their areas. Others such as the National Park Authorities also exercise certain planning powers within their areas. These bodies may also be influential at a policy making level.

There are also a range of non-governmental advisory bodies which are used by the government to develop policies in particular areas. The UK Round Table on Sustainable Development is an example of one such organisation.

Health and safety

The *Health and Safety at Work etc. Act 1974* (the *'HSWA' 1974*) created a new system for the administration and enforcement of health and safety law comprising of the Health and Safety Commission ('HSC') and the Health and Safety Executive ('HSE').

The HSC is primarily concerned with policy making and administering health and safety matters. It is directly responsible to the Secretary of State for the Environment. The HSC submits proposals to the secretary of state for legislation, codes of practice etc.

The HSE is responsible to the HSC and the secretary of state, and is largely concerned with the direct enforcement of health and safety law. Both the HSC and HSE are bodies corporate created pursuant to *section 10* of the *HSWA 1974*.

Functions of the HSE

The main function of the HSE is to enforce health and safety law (including associated regulations). To exercise these powers the HSE has the ability to appoint inspectors, the powers for which are set out in *section 20* of the *HSWA 1974*.

The HSE also publishes a variety of guidance notes and advisory publications for organisations.

Functions of the HSC

The general functions of the HSC are set out in *section 11* of the *HSWA 1974* namely:

(1) to assist and encourage persons connected with health and safety matters relevant to *Part I* of the *HSWA 1974* to further those purposes;

(2) to make such arrangements as it considers appropriate to carry out research, training and information in connection with the purposes in *Part I* of the *HSWA 1974* and to encourage research in the provision of training and information of others.

(3) to make such arrangements as it considers appropriate for ensuring that government departments, employees, employers (and others) are provided with information and are kept informed of, and adequately advised on, matters relating to *Part I* of the *HSWA 1974*; and

(4) to submit from time to time to the secretary of state proposals for amending or adding to existing legislation and/or codes of practice.

The HSC does not have the power to actually make regulations itself although it is able to approve and issue codes of practice for the purposes of providing practical guidance on health and safety matters.

Access to Workplace

Gitsham v C H Pearce & Sons Ltd (31 January 1991) Court of Appeal (Times Law Reports, 11 February 1991)

[A1.1]

employee; damages; injuries; safe access; statutory duty

Background: An employee was injured when he slipped on a road covered with ice and snow outside his workplace. The accident took place at 8.45 a.m. His employer operated a system to clear snow and ice from roads but it appeared that the area where the accident took place had not yet been treated. Further, it was considered that at the time there were severe weather conditions. Mr Gitsham's action claiming damages for his injuries was unsuccessful and he appealed.

Decision: The Court of Appeal held that an established and proper system for ensuring safe access for employees existed at the premises of C H Pearce & Sons. The company had not breached its statutory duty under *section 29(1)* of the *Factories Act 1961* by failing to ensure that every area had been gritted by the start of the working day. C H Pearce & Sons Ltd was not liable for the plaintiff's injuries and his appeal was dismissed.

Comment: The satisfaction of the duty under *section 29(1)* of the *Factories Act 1961* should not have imposed a duty on the employer to do any more than was already being done – which was having an extensive procedure for clearing snow and ice from the access roads. The words 'reasonably practicable' have to be borne in mind in all cases of this nature and it remains a question of fact in the circumstances as to whether this requirement has been met.

Dorman, Long & Co Ltd v Hillier (18 January 1951) High Court, King's Bench Division ([1951] 1 All ER 357)

[A1.2]

workman; safe means of access; factories inspectorate

Background: A workman employed to strip corrugated roofing sheets from a factory was killed when he fell. Access to the roof was via a ladder and purlin bars. The workman safely reached the part of the roof to be worked on but stepped back onto an unsafe roofing sheet and fell though it. The Factories Inspectorate alleged that the occupier of the factory, Dorman, Long & Co Ltd, had contravened *section 26(1)* of the *Factories Act 1937* by failing to provide safe means of access to a place of work. The company was convicted and appealed.

Decision: The High Court held that Dorman, Long & Co Ltd had not failed in its duty under *section 26(1)* of the *Factories Act 1937*. The workman had been engaged to strip the roof as a whole and at the time of his accident had arrived at his place of work. The unsafe roofing sheet was not part of the means of access to that workplace. The appeal was allowed.

Comment: One interesting aspect of this case is that it considered the issue of whether a means of access can also be a place of work. The answer will depend on the particular facts of relevance to the case at hand. On the facts of *Dorman* the employer had used reasonably practicable means to provide a safe means of access to where the employee was working.

Cox v H C B Angus Ltd (3 April 1981) High Court, Queen's Bench Division ([1981] ICR 683)

[A1.3]

Factories Act 1961; breach of statutory duty; vicarious liability; employees' negligence

Background: Mr Cox worked for H C B Angus Ltd as an electrician involved in the fitting of fire engines. He was injured when he fell from the cab of an engine after turning his foot on a piece of piping. The piping was part of the engine's braking system and had been left on the floor of the cab by a fitter. Mr Cox claimed damages for his injuries, alleging negligence and breach of statutory duty under *section 29(1)* of the *Factories Act 1961*. Damages were agreed between Mr Cox and his employer; the court was left to determine liability.

Test: *Section 29(1)* of the 1961 Act requires that: 'There shall, so far as is reasonably practicable, be provided and maintained safe means of access to every place at which any person has at any time to work, and every such place shall, so far as is reasonably practicable, be made and kept safe for any person working there'.

Decision: The High Court held that the cab of the fire engine was a place of work for the purposes of this section and that the duty imposed by the second half of *section 29(1)* to make and keep the workplace safe should not be interpreted in the same way as the duty to provide and maintain a safe means of access in the first half (*Levesley v Thomas Firth & John Brown Ltd [1953]* see paragraph A1.4). It was therefore possible for there to have been a breach of the statutory duty to make and keep the workplace safe where the danger was only temporary. H C B Angus Ltd had breached its statutory duty under this section because it would have been reasonably practicable to keep the cab safe if the fitter had placed the piping where it would not have been trodden on. The company was vicariously liable for the negligence of the fitter, although this liability was reduced to fifty per cent because of the plaintiff's negligence in not seeing the pipe.

Comment: Whilst this case demonstrated that even a temporarily unsafe situation can amount to a breach of the relevant obligation to keep a work place safe, it is really a question of considering the particular facts of the case as to whether the circumstances are such (e.g. not exceptional) that a breach has occurred: *see Latimer v A.E.C.* [1953] AC 643.

Levesley v Thomas Firth & John Brown Ltd (20 July 1953) Court of Appeal ([1953] 2 All ER 866)

[A1.4]

safe access; maintain; obstruction; negligence; breach of statutory duty

Background: Within the factory of Thomas Firth & John Brown Ltd, a marked area fifteen feet and three inches wide had been provided as a safe means of access through which employees could walk on their way to various parts of the shop floor. Shortly before Mr Levesley's accident, a lorry parked in the safe access area to load up. This was normal practice. On finding his way partially blocked, Mr Levesley passed by the vehicle and tripped over a piece of metal packing about two inches high that was being used during the loading operation. The obstruction projected three to four inches into the safe access area. Mr Levesley fell and broke his leg. He claimed damages for negligence and breach of statutory duty of his employers under *section 26(1)* of the *Factories Act 1937*. The court held that the company was not guilty of negligence at common law but was in breach of its duty under the 1937 Act. Thomas Firth & John Brown Ltd appealed.

Test: *Section 26(1)* of the *Factories Act 1937* requires employers, so far as is reasonably practicable, to provide and maintain a safe means of access to the workplace. 'Maintain' is defined by *section 152(1)* of the 1937 Act as 'maintained in an efficient state, in efficient working order and in good repair'. The House of Lords decision in *Latimer v AEC Ltd [1953] AC 643* provides authority on the interpretation of 'maintain' in this context: the employer does not have an absolute obligation to maintain the safety of the access, but rather a relative obligation to maintain the safe access provided in an efficient state, efficient working order and good repair. The employer is not therefore responsible for every temporary obstruction that may occur by accident in the safe access area.

Decision: The Court of Appeal ruled that, given the temporary nature of the obstruction, the company had not breached its statutory duty under *section 26(1)* to maintain the safe access. The appeal was allowed.

Smith v British Aerospace (29 October 1981) Court of Appeal ([1982] ICR 98)

[A1.5]

safe access; personal injury; negligence; breach of statutory duty

Background: Mr Smith, an aircraft inspector, cut his head whilst climbing a set of portable step ladders to reach an inspection staging. The normal access route to the staging provided by British Aerospace was a fixed flight of stairs. The step ladders had only recently been delivered to the factory. Mr Smith brought an action in the County Court against his employer for damages for personal injuries caused by the company's negligence and breach of statutory duty under *section 29(1)* of the *Factories Act 1961* which requires the provision and maintenance of a safe means of access to an employee's place of work. The court ruled that the step ladders were a means of access within the meaning of *section 29(1)* and gave judgement for Mr Smith. However, the damages were reduced by half because he had been guilty of contributory negligence. British Aerospace appealed.

Decision: Where several means of access are provided by an employer, he has a statutory duty under *section 29(1)* of the 1961 Act to provide so far as is reasonably practicable that all the access routes are safe. In this case, the test was whether the portable step ladders had been 'provided' by Mr Smith's employer. The Court of Appeal found that there was no evidence that the ladders had been adopted by the company as a means of access to the staging and therefore they could not be said to have been 'provided'. There was no breach of duty under *section 29(1)*. The company's appeal was allowed.

Accidents Abroad

Johnson v Coventry Churchill International Ltd (30 July 1991) High Court, Queen's Bench Division ([1992] 3 All ER 14)

[A2.1]

injury sustained abroad; English law; foreign jurisdiction

Background: Mr Johnson, a joiner/carpenter, was injured when a rotten plank placed over a trench collapsed. At the time of his accident, he was working on a building site in Germany after being hired by the defendant, an English employment agency. He had signed a sub-contract and a letter of appointment with that company. Mr Johnson claimed damages for personal injury from the company alleging negligence.

Test: In general, an act done in a foreign country may only be pursued in England if that act is actionable both under English law and in the other country. However, a particular issue between the parties may be governed by the law of the country which has the most significant relationship to the occurrence and to the parties involved (*Chaplin v Boys [1969] 2 All ER 1085*).

Decision: The High Court held that Mr Johnson was employed by Coventry Churchill International Ltd under a contract of employment and that the company had a duty of care to him to provide a safe system of work. The court found that the company had failed to fulfil this duty. Under German law, however, it was not possible to pursue an action because employers are not liable for workplace injuries unless there has been wilful breach of duty. Although Mr Johnson's action failed the dual actionability test, it was decided that the exception recognised in *Chaplin v Boys [1969]* applied. The country with the most significant relationship to the occurrence and to the parties was England: both parties were English, Mr Johnson's contract was subject to English law, he had been recruited in England and was only to be abroad for a short time, and the omission which had led to the accident could be traced back to decisions made in England. The court ruled that English law should therefore apply and Mr Johnson's action should succeed.

Comment: This case makes clear that in interpreting a contract and attempting to establish whether the relationship of employer-employee is in existence, the actual intention of the parties, although relevant, is not conclusive, and a label put on the relationship by the parties will therefore not be taken as conclusive. The employer will not be able to avoid liability unless he proves that the temporary employer has assumed the right to control the mode of working. There must be an actual assumption, not merely proof that the employer did not have the right to control the method himself.

All Due Diligence

J H Dewhurst Ltd v Coventry Corporation (21 April 1969) High Court, Queen's Bench Division ([1969] 3 All ER 1225)

[A3.1]

section 18(1) of Offices, Shops and Railway Premises Act 1963; all due diligence; compliance

Background: A young man of sixteen years employed in J H Dewhurst Ltd butchers shop, cut off a finger whilst cleaning a cutting blade from a meat slicing machine. Under *section 18(1)* of the *Offices, Shops and Railway Premises Act 1963*, persons under the age of eighteen years should not clean any machinery forming part of the equipment of the premises if doing so could expose them to a risk of injury from a moving part. The company had taken action, through notices, written instructions and inspection visits to ensure that employees were aware of this prohibition. The young man had not followed his manager's instructions on how to clean the blade by leaving it in the machine and cleaning it whilst it was stationary. Instead he had removed the blade from the cutting machine when his manager was absent. J H Dewhurst Ltd appealed against its conviction under *section 18(1)* of the 1963 Act. It was argued that the young man had been asked to clean a machine of which no part was moving and that the company had used all due diligence to secure compliance with *section 18(1)* (a defence provided by *section 67* of the 1963 Act).

Decision: The High Court found that the cutting blade was a moving part for the purposes of *section 18(1)* of the 1963 Act, regardless of the fact that the young man should have used a cleaning method in which movement of the blade was not intended. *Section 18(1)* imposed an absolute prohibition, subject to the all due diligence defence provided by *section 67* of the Act. In this case, the prohibition imposed a special obligation of supervision which had not been discharged by the employer and the company could not argue that the accident was something which reasonable care could not have prevented or which it could not reasonably foresee. J H Dewhurst Ltd had failed to prove that it had used all due diligence to secure compliance with the prohibition of *section 18(1)*. The appeal was dismissed.

Comment: The special obligation of supervision in this case should have entailed the employer making every effort to determine the age of anyone likely to be using the relevant machinery, and if discovering any persons under the age of eighteen, making every effort to prevent such a person from coming into contact with the machine.

Asbestos

Barclays Bank plc v Fairclough Building Ltd (No. 2) (26 January 1995) Court of Appeal (Times Law Reports, 15 February 1995)

[A4.1]

asbestos; breach of contract; remedial action; contractor; reasonable care and skill

Background: Barclays engaged Fairclough as contractors to carry out maintenance work on its warehouses. The work involved cleaning asbestos sheeted roofs and was sub-contracted by Fairclough to Carne (Structural Repair) Company Ltd which in turn sub-contracted the work to Trendle Way Ltd. Trendle Way Ltd used high pressure hoses to clean the old asbestos sheeting. The water jet dissolved asbestos dust and fibres, creating a slurry which entered the warehouses and dried out causing dangerous levels of asbestos contamination. An environmental health officer served a prohibition notice following the incident and remedial action of approximately £4 million was required. At first instance the court had held that Trendle Way Ltd was in breach of contract and liable for half of the costs of remedial action. Carne (Structural Repair) Company Ltd appealed to the Court of Appeal.

Decision: The Court of Appeal took the view that any contractor working on asbestos materials should have by 1988 at the latest have been aware of the risks of such work. Further, if they did not know of the risks they had a duty to find out about them given the publicity surrounding the introduction of the *Control of Asbestos at Work Regulations 1987 (SI 1987 No 2115)*. The Court of Appeal did not agree with the grounds on which the judge in the first instance based his decision that Trendle Way Ltd was not liable for a breach of the implied term to exercise reasonable skill and care i.e. that the company carried out heavy industrial cleaning and had not held itself out as being expert in relation to health hazards from cleaning asbestos. The Court of Appeal held that this approach was incorrect and that the action taken by Trendle Way Ltd was clearly capable of causing risks from the exposure to asbestos. Trendle Way Ltd had, therefore, failed to exercise reasonable skill and care in performing its contractual obligations.

Comment: This particular case primarily concerned contractual duties and the level of contribution for the £4 million cost of remediation rather than a breach of regulations. It was considered that the *Control of Asbestos at Work Regulations 1987* and the publicity surrounding their introduction were relevant in terms of the awareness that individuals were expected to have of the risks posed by working with asbestos. Once there is an awareness of the risk (and in this case it was an objective level of awareness), then action should be taken to find out more about the risks prior to undertaking the relevant work. This is a general principle which applies to areas other than asbestos.

Budds v Marples Ridgeway Developments Ltd (13 October 1998) High Court, Queen's Bench Division (NLD, 13 October 1998)

[A4.2]

asbestos; general damages; past and future loss of earnings

Background: Mr Budds was diagnosed with pleural thickening of one lung in 1994. This was the direct result of exposure to asbestos during the course of his employment nearly thirty years ago. Deterioration of his physical condition had left him suffering from shortness of breath and a continuous pain in his right shoulder meant he had been unable to carry out even light work. Since he became aware of his condition, his mental state had also worsened with the development of a mixed anxiety and depressive disorder. In addition, there existed a fifty per cent risk that his condition would deteriorate further and his life expectancy had been reduced by two years. This claim was therefore for an appropriate award of general damages for pain, suffering and loss of amenity.

Decision: It was held that such an appropriate award would be £40,000. In addition, awards were made in respect of past and future loss of earnings and medical expenses. The total award was approximately £197,000 with interest to be assessed.

Comment: In this case the factors which may be taken into account in making awards based on future earnings were discussed. It was made clear that the court could bear in mind, in addition to whether the applicant would have stayed in gainful employment for a number of years, the probability that he may have taken a university degree which would have increased his earning potential. The nature of the person is also a factor to be taken into account – in this case the man was described as 'resourceful' which indicated that he would be in gainful employment until normal retirement age.

Bryce v Swan Hunter Group plc and Others (13 February 1987) High Court, Queen's Bench Division ([1987] 2 Lloyd's Report 426)

[A4.3]

mesothelioma; asbestos; damages; breach of duty by employer; causation

Background: This action was brought by Mrs Bryce, whose husband, a shipyard painter, died from malignant mesothelioma of the pleura, a rare form of cancer usually caused by exposure to asbestos. The fact that asbestos exposure had caused his death was not disputed. Mr Bryce had been exposed to the material during his employment by the three defendant companies. Mrs Bryce brought the action, claiming damages under the *Law Reform (Miscellaneous Provisions) Act 1934* and the *Fatal Accidents Act 1976*. She alleged that her husband's exposure to the asbestos was due, at least in part, to breaches of duty by his employers and that the resultant additional exposure attributable to those breaches had caused the mesothelioma. The employers denied any liability and argued that the necessary causal *nexus* between the illness and any breaches of duty did not exist.

Decision: Following a review of knowledge on the health effects of asbestos, the High Court held that at all material times, Mr Bryce's employers should have known or ought to have known that exposure to high levels of asbestos could lead to asbestosis and, from 1947, to mesothelioma. Applying the standards of knowledge at the time, the defendants were not under a common law duty of care to prevent Mr Bryce from all exposure to dangerous quantities of asbestos dust. However, they were obliged to take all steps reasonably practicable to reduce the amount of dust to which he was exposed. They had a statutory duty to take all practicable measures to protect their employees from the inhalation of asbestos dust. The court found that the additional exposure to asbestos dust attributable to breaches of duty on the part of each of the defendants was significant, although less in degree than the exposure Mr Bryce would have in any event experienced during his working life. On the question of causation, it was neither possible to prove on the balance of probabilities that the additional asbestos inhaled due to the breaches of duty was the cause of the mesothelioma nor that the breaches of duty were not at least a contributing cause of the disease. Following the principle established in *McGhee v National Coal Board [1973] 1 WLR 1* and identified in *Wilsher v Essex Area Health Authority [1986] 3 All ER 801*, the court held that the defendants' breaches of duty had increased the risk of Mr Bryce developing mesothelioma and accordingly, they must be taken to have caused the disease through those breaches of duty. Damages were awarded to Mrs Bryce under the 1934 Act and the 1976 Act.

Comment: A systematic approach was taken in this case to determine liability and the finding essentially turned on the issue of causation. It was not possible for the plaintiffs to prove that the additional fibres inhaled by Bryce were a cause of his mesethelioma. However, it was equally impossible for the defendants to prove on the balance of probabilities that their breach of duty was not a contributory cause of Mr Bryce contracting the disease. Given the reliance that *Bryce* placed on the earlier cases of *Wilsher* and *McGhee*, the decision should be reviewed in the light of the later decision in *Wilsher v Essex Area Health Authority [1988] 1 All ER 871*. In the later *Wilsher* case it had not been proven that excess oxygen caused or contributed to the disease suffered by the plaintiff, nor was it proven that excess oxygen would increase the risk that any other innocent agents would trigger the disease. It was considered that a 'robust and pragmatic approach' should be used to the primary facts of the case. The cases in this area reinforce the difficulties associated with causation and issues of contribution in occupational health cases. The questions of where, how, why and when a disease or condition arose, and who has the burden of proving certain facts may make it difficult for the plaintiff to establish that there has been a breach of duty (both in negligence and/or under statute).

Gunn v Wallsend Slipway and Engineering Co Ltd (7 November 1988) High Court, Queen's Bench Division (Times Law Reports, 23 January 1989)

[A4.4]

mesothelioma; asbestos fibres; inhalation of dust; prudent employer; foreseeable risk of injury; duty of care

Background: Mr Gunn, an employee of Wallsend Slipway and Engineering Co Ltd, was exposed to asbestos during his work. His working clothes were frequently impregnated with asbestos fibres. They were cleaned at home by his wife who would shake them and launder them in a wash tub. Mrs Gunn died from mesothelioma, a form of lung cancer caused by exposure to asbestos. Mr Gunn claimed damages for loss and damage sustained as a result of his wife's death from the company under the *Fatal Accidents Act 1976* and the *Law Reform (Miscellaneous Provisions) Act 1983*.

Decision: The High Court found that Mrs Gunn's mesothelioma was asbestos related and that the washing of her husband's asbestos contaminated work clothes was the source of that asbestos. Wallsend Slipway and Engineering Company Ltd's liability for her death depended on whether it owed a duty at common law. A pre-condition of demonstrating the existence of such a duty of care would be acceptable evidence that during the period of his exposure to asbestos, Mr Gunn's employers ought reasonably to have foreseen that there was some risk to Mrs Gunn as a result of the exposure. On the evidence presented, before 1965 when Mr Gunn's exposure to asbestos ended, no industrial company considered the risk of injury from domestic exposure to asbestos. The only exception was in 'asbestos neighbourhood' cases. The exposure of other people to asbestos arising from asbestos contaminated working clothes was not considered. There had been no relevant medical or safety warnings, or approved practice for washing and storing clothing. The court could not hold that any prudent employer would have foreseen some risk of injury to Mrs Gunn and therefore the company owed no duty of care to Mrs Gunn in relation to asbestos dust. Mr Gunn's action was dismissed.

Comment: This case highlights that where there is a lack of awareness in an industry of the potential risks associated with certain substances, employers cannot be expected to direct their employees' minds to the risk or take precautions in relation to them. Awareness could be acquired by distributing publications to the industry, medical warnings, bulletins or approved practices. For instance, in *Barclays Bank v Fairclough Building Ltd (No. 2) (1995)* (see paragraph A4.1) the publicity surrounding the introduction of the *Control of Asbestos at Work Regulations 1987 (SI 1987 No 2115)* was considered evidence as to the level of knowledge in the industry at the relevant time.

Edgson v Vickers plc and Another (1 March 1994) High Court, Queen's Bench Division (Times Law Reports, 8 April 1994)

[A4.5]

mesothelioma; damages; negligence; Asbestos Regulations 1969

Background: Mrs Edgson, the widow of a former Vickers plc employee, sought damages for negligence following the death of her husband from mesothelioma. The disease was the result of exposure to asbestos dust during his employment.

Decision: The *Asbestos Regulations 1969 (SI 1969 No 690)* impose a number of duties on employers when employees are exposed to asbestos at work. Under *Regulation 15(1)(a)*, all employers have a duty to comply with the Regulations, whilst *Regulation 3(2)* applies to every process involving asbestos or any article composed wholly or party of asbestos. The High Court ruled that dry sweeping of asbestos dust, although not a manufacturing process, was a process to which these requirements applied. Further, dry sweeping of dust containing asbestos in excess of the threshold limit value was a breach of *Regulation 10*. Damages were awarded to Mrs Edgson.

Comment: This case illustrates that the attitude of the court in extending the ambit of the *Asbestos Regulations 1969*, for example, to bring activities such as dry sweeping within the ambit of a 'process'. It is also of interest to note that the HSE is reviewing the existing regulatory position to strengthen the existing protection for employees and others who may be affected by asbestos in the work place.

Central Asbestos Co Ltd v Dodd (28 June 1972) House of Lords ([1973] AC 518)

[A4.6]

asbestos factory worker; asbestosis; disability benefit; damages; statute barred; negligence; breach of statutory duty; Limitation Act 1963

Background: Mr Dodd worked for Central Asbestos Co Ltd between 1952 and 1965. The company operated a number of processes involving asbestos and had consistently breached the *Asbestos Industry Regulations 1931 (SI 1931 No 1140)*. During Mr Dodd's work he was exposed to asbestos dust. In January 1964 he was found to be suffering from asbestosis for which he was awarded disability benefit based on ten per cent disablement. After that point he had knowledge that his condition had been caused by the inhalation of asbestos dust. He left the company in September 1965 on medical advice. He had been told by his works manager that he could not claim damages from his employer's because he was receiving disability benefit, advice that was corrected in April 1967 when he visited a solicitor. From that date he had actual or constructive knowledge that his disease was attributable in law to his employer's negligence or breach of statutory duty and that he had a cause of action to recover damages. In October 1967, Mr Dodd brought an action for damages against the company. He was successful in the High Court and was awarded damages for negligence and breach of statutory duty. Central Asbestos Co Ltd's appeal was dismissed by the Court of Appeal and the company then appealed again.

Decision: Central Asbestos Co Ltd argued that Mr Dodd's claim was statute barred. The House of Lords held that this was not the case. The *Limitation Act 1963* extends the three year time limit for bringing an action in cases where a 'material' and 'decisive' fact was outside the knowledge of the plaintiff for a time after the damage was suffered. Before a person can bring an action he must know or at least believe that he can establish: that he has suffered certain injuries; that the defendant has done or failed to do certain acts; that his injuries were caused by those acts or omissions; and that those acts or omissions involved negligence or breach of duty. In Mr Dodd's case, the first three facts were all known more than twelve months before the action was brought but the fourth was not. The test was whether the fact that that the company's acts amounted to negligence or breach of duty was or could be a 'material fact' of a 'decisive character'. The House of Lords ruled that as Mr Dodd had been ignorant that the disease was attributable in law to the negligence and/or breach of statutory duty of his employers until April 1967, this was a 'material fact' of a 'decisive character' within the meaning of the 1963 Act. He was therefore entitled to rely on the provisions of the Act so that his action was not statute barred.

Comment: Questions concerning the limitation period of actions were raised in *Dodd*. However, it was noted by Lord Reid that the *Limitation Act 1963* had the distinction of 'being the worst drafted Act on the statute book'. The basic position is that the requirements of the relevant provision in the Act must be met. There is no defence to an action providing that the plaintiff brings an action within three years of knowing that he had a worthwhile cause of action. The *Limitation Act 1963* which was discussed in *Dodd* was replaced by the *Limitation Act 1975* and the provisions of this now form part of the *Limitation Act 1980.* The present approach in personal injury cases is that the limitation period remains at three years. Time runs from the date when the cause of action accrues or from when the plaintiff has knowledge of the relevant circumstances, whichever is the later. Nevertheless, it also remains open to a court to exercise its discretion with respect to the time limit to allow an action to proceed.

Construction

Evans v Sant (1 November 1974) High Court, Queen's Bench Division ([1975] 1 All ER 294)

[A5.1]

construction workers; water main; safe place of work; Construction (Working Places) Regulations 1966.

Background: Three employees of Thomas Evans, a civil engineering contractor, were engaged in laying a water main beside a road. After the main was laid, it was tested to ensure that it could contain the pressure of water that it would have to carry. During the testing, the test head was blown out of the main and to avoid being hit, one of the employees ran into the road. He was knocked down and killed. It was alleged that Thomas Evans was an employer of workmen undertaking operations or works to which *section 127* of the *Factories Act 1961* and the *Construction (Working Places) Regulations 1966 (SI 1966 No 94)* applied. Further, the place of work at which the deceased employee worked was not so far as reasonably practicable made safe as required by *Regulation 6(2)* of the 1966 Regulations. Thomas Evans was convicted. He then appealed against this conviction.

Test: *Regulation 6(2)* of the 1966 Regulations requires that: 'Without prejudice to the other provisions of these Regulations, every place at which any person at any time works shall, so far as is reasonably practicable, be made and kept safe for any person working there.'

Decision: The High Court ruled that if a place was safe in every degree and the only thing which rendered it unsafe was the fact that a piece of equipment brought onto it temporarily for a particular purpose produced an element of danger, this did not mean that the place itself had not been made safe for the purposes of *Regulation 6(2)*. The appeal was allowed.

Comment: This case confirmed that equipment brought onto premises, which temporarily causes an obstruction does not in itself render the place unsafe under the *Construction (Working Places) Regulations 1966*. The obligation to make a place of work safe does not mean that a place of work is rendered unsafe by the position of a temporary piece of equipment.

Curran v William Neill & Son (St Helens) Ltd (6 June 1961) Court of Appeal ([1961] 3 All ER 108)

[A5.2]

construction worker; personal injury; damages; negligence; breach of statutory duty; statement of claim

Background: William Neill & Son (St Helens) Ltd, a company of steel erectors, employed Mr Curran to construct a gutter on a factory roof, consisting of lengths of guttering that were to be bolted together. A trade demarcation dispute between workmen at the factory meant that instead of being bolted together, the lengths of guttering were placed in position and secured by hook bolts. Mr Curran was walking along the gutter to lay the next piece when a hook bolt broke and he fell twenty three feet to the ground and was badly injured. He claimed damages for negligence and breach of statutory duty under the *Building (Safety, Health and Welfare) Regulations 1948 (SI 1948 No 1145)*. The High Court found that the hook bolt was defective but that its breaking could not have been foreseen. William Neill & Son (St Helens) Ltd was not found negligent at common law. Although there had been a breach of *Regulation 24(1)* of the 1948 Regulations, which requires a guard rail to be provided around a working place from which a person may fall more than six feet and six inches, this breach did not cause the accident since a guard rail would not have prevented it. Mr Curran's claim was dismissed and he then appealed on the grounds of breach of statutory duty, asking for leave to amend the statement of claim to enable him to rely on *Regulations 7(1), (4),*

8(1) and *12(2)* of the 1948 Regulations. In relying on these Regulations, it was contended that the gutter on which he was working was a scaffold.

Decision: The Court of Appeal held that there had been no breach of statutory duty under the 1948 Regulations that would allow Mr Curran to recover damages. He had alleged breaches of *Regulations 5, 7(1), 7(4), 8(1), 12(1)* and *24(1)* of those Regulations. *Regulation 5* requires that a scaffold should be provided for 'all work that cannot safely be done on or from the ground or from part of the building, or from part of a permanent structure or from a ladder or other available means of support'. The court held that whether work could be 'safely done' depended on whether, on the facts, the doing of that work involved foreseeable risk. In this case, this was not so and there had been no breach of *Regulation 5*. Mr Curran's amended statement of claim alleged that the guttering was a gangway and constituted a scaffold. *Regulations 7, 8* and *12* of the 1948 Regulations concern the construction, quality and condition of scaffolds and it was argued that use of the defective hook bolt was contrary to these Regulations. The court found that the employer's duty under these Regulations was absolute. The issue was whether the guttering came within the definition of 'scaffold' or 'gangway'. The court held that it did not. The court agreed with the High Court's ruling on the alleged breach of *Regulation 24*. The Court of Appeal concluded therefore that Mr Curran would not succeed under the proposed amendment. The amendment was refused and the appeal dismissed.

Comment: This case was applied in *Woods v Power Gas Corporation [1969] 8 KIR 834* which considered the *Construction Regulations 1961 (SIs 1961 Nos 1580, 1581), Regulations 7(2)* and *54*. Woods, a steel erector, sat astride a crossbeam twenty feet above the ground. Whilst inserting bolts, he fell and was injured. It was held that the beam was part of the permanent structure within *Regulation 7(2)* of the *Construction Regulations 1961* and work being done could safely be done from it. Further, *Curran* was considered in *Jennings v Norman Collison (Contractors)[1970] 1 All ER 1121* in which case the defendants were engaged to build a building. There was a ladder leading to the concrete roof, which rested against a concrete passageway, and to the left was a door of glass. The plaintiff fell and was injured. It was held that the passageway was not a gangway within *Regulation 27(2)* of the 1948 Regulations and consequently, the defendants were not in breach of failing to provide a safe means of access to the roof.

Quinn v J W Green (Painters) Ltd (15 October 1965) Court of Appeal ([1965] 3 All ER 785)

[A5.3]

painter; personal injury; negligence; breach of statutory duty; damages

Background: Mr Quinn, a foreman painter with the firm J W Green (Painters) Ltd, was engaged in painting the Victoria and Albert Museum. He borrowed two high trestles and some planks from other contractors working there which he inspected and found to be completely sound and suitable for the task to be undertaken. His employer approved the borrowing of the equipment. When Mr Quinn climbed onto one of the trestles it collapsed because of a latent defect. He fell and was blinded in his left eye. Although healthy, this eye had already been damaged by a previous accident and lacked a lens. Mr Quinn was awarded damages after successfully claiming that his employer was negligent and in breach of its statutory duty under *Regulations 5* and *7(1)* of the *Building (Safety, Health and Welfare) Regulations 1948 (SI 1948 No 1145).* The company appealed. They argued that if there had been a breach of statutory duty, Mr Quinn was also guilty of a breach of duty and was therefore not entitled to recover damages in respect of the breach. It was also argued that the company had not been negligent and that the damages awarded were excessive.

Decision: J W Green (Painters) Ltd alleged that Mr Quinn had breached *Regulations 5* and *7(1)* of the 1948 Regulations. The Court of Appeal held that there had been no breach by the employee. *Regulation 5* imposes a duty on the employer to provide scaffolding but no duty on the employee. An employee does have an absolute duty to construct a scaffold properly under *Regulation 7* (*Davison v Apex Scaffolds Ltd [1956] 1 All ER 473*), but in this case, the collapse of the trestle was due to it not being of sound material or adequate strength and not something that Mr Quinn had done or failed to do. The court found that the company had not been negligent although it had breached its statutory duty. The appeal was dismissed and it was also held that the award of damages was not excessive as it took account of the fact that if Mr Quinn were to lose the sight of his right eye, he would be completely blind.

Comment: With respect to damages, in *Quinn*, Salmon LJ considered that it was not advisable to decide the potential gravity of loss to a plaintiff such as this one, who had a defective eye, along mathematical principles. He relied on an assessment of the risk that the man may lose his eyesight permanently. (See also *Paris v Stepney Borough Council [1957] AC 367.*)

Vineer v C Doidge & Sons Ltd (P G W Holdings Ltd, third parties) (27 March 1972) Court of Appeal ([1972] 2 All ER 794)

[A5.4]

scaffolding; building operation; damages

Background: P G W Holdings Ltd, a glazing company, employed Mr Vineer and sent him to measure up for some house windows at a building site operated by C Doidge & Sons Ltd. The glazing of the windows had been sub-contracted to Mr Vineer's employer. The house visited by Mr Vineer was only partially built and it was necessary for him to use some scaffolding erected by C Doidge & Sons Ltd. Before stepping onto the scaffolding, Mr Vineer casually inspected it and checked with the construction company that it was all right for him to use. He fell from the scaffolding when a plank trapped. His subsequent action for damages against C Doidge & Sons Ltd was settled but in third party proceedings in that action, the judge ruled that C Doidge & Sons Ltd was not entitled to an indemnity or a contribution in respect of the liability from P G W Holdings Ltd. Mr Vineer's employer conceded that the settlement of the claim had been reasonably and properly made but argued that it was not liable because, *inter alia*, at the time of the injury, its employee was not engaged in a 'building operation' within the meaning of *section 176* of the *Factories Act 1961* and it could not therefore be in breach of *Regulation 23* of the *Construction (Working Places) Regulations 1966 (SI 1966 No 94)*. Further, the company had complied with that Regulation since Mr Vineer had inspected the scaffolding and was a competent agent. C Doidge & Sons Ltd appealed.

Decision: The Court of Appeal held that Mr Vineer had been engaged in a 'building operation' as defined by *section 176* of the 1961 Act (*Elms v Foster Wheeler Ltd [1954] 2 All ER 714*) at the time of his accident. Until the windows had been glazed, the houses would not be complete or constructed. *Regulation 23* of the 1966 Regulations applied therefore to the work at the time of the injury. It was found that P G W Holdings Ltd was in breach of that Regulation because the employer had not taken 'express steps, either personally or by a competent agent, to satisfy himself that the scaffold is stable'. The company had done nothing to meet the requirements of *Regulation 23*. As he had only been sent to measure up the windows, the duty of inspecting the scaffolding had not been specifically delegated to Mr Vineer as a competent agent (*Clarke v E R Wright & Son [1957] 3 All ER 486*). His employer had also failed to show that the accident would have happened even if *Regulation 23* had been complied with. Accordingly, P G W Holdings Ltd was liable to its employee and was apportioned twenty per cent of the blame for the accident.

Comment: The definition of 'building operation' in the *Factories Act 1961* was substituted by the *Construction (Health Safety and Welfare) Regulations 1996 (SI 1996 No 1592)*. This particular case considered the repealed definition but it may still be relevant to interpretation of the new definition. In the *Vineer case*, Roskill LJ stated that, although each case turns on its own facts, and it is impossible to say where the dividing line is in each case, 'in general, if a workman is at the time of the accident doing an act which can fairly be said to form part of or to be contributing to the operation of the construction of a building, he is engaged in a building operation.'

Hosking v De Havilland Aircraft Co Ltd and Others (11 February 1949) High Court, King's Bench Division ([1949] 1 All ER 540)

[A5.5]

contractor; occupiers' employees; personal injury; damages; negligence; Factories Act 1937; safe means of access; contract

Background: De Havilland Aircraft Co Ltd engaged contractors to carry out building work on land adjacent to its factory. As part of that work, a trench was excavated and a plank placed across it for the use of De Havilland Aircraft Co Ltd staff and the contractor's employees. Mr Hosking, a De Havilland Aircraft Co Ltd employee, was crossing the plank when it broke and he was injured. In his action for damages against his employer, Mr Hosking contended that the plank was a gangway within the meaning of *section 25* of the *Factories Act 1937* and that his employer had an absolute duty to ensure that it was of sound construction and properly maintained. It was also alleged that the company was liable under *section 26* of the 1937 Act which requires that the employer should provide, so far as is reasonably practicable, safe means of access. De Havilland Aircraft Co Ltd denied liability, contending that the contractor was liable for the accident because it had made the trench and owned the plank. The contractor was joined as a third party to the action and issued with a third party notice for indemnity on the basis that a clause in the contract between the parties provided that De Havilland Aircraft Co Ltd would be indemnified for any accident occurring because of the contractor's negligence.

Decision: The High Court found that the plank was a gangway within the meaning of *section 25(1)* of the 1937 Act. As the plank had been placed there partly for the use of its employees, De Havilland Aircraft Co Ltd had breached that section by failing to ensure that the gangway was of sound construction and properly maintained. Mr Hosking's employer was also liable to him for breach of its statutory duty under *section 26* of the 1937 Act (*Callaghan v Fred Kidd & Son (Engineers) Ltd [1944)]1 All ER 525*). Further, the contractor, as the person with responsibility for putting down the plank, was liable to Mr Hosking at common law for having caused the accident. The court gave judgement against both defendants and directed that De Havilland Aircraft Co Ltd should be indemnified by the contractor for the damages and costs.

Comment: The observations of Denning J on his interpretation of *section 26* of the *Factories Act 1937* in *Whitby v Burt, Boulton and Hayward [1947] KB 918* were relied on in this case (note that *section 26* has now been repealed). Denning J stated 'it is impossible to extricate building operations within a factory from other operations within a factory. Section 26, in my judgement, applies to this case and the occupiers were responsible for seeing that there was provided and maintained safe means of access.' The case also demonstrates the important principle that where a statute imposes a duty on a particular person, then that duty cannot be delegated and, it is no defence to say that the fault lay on the other person not meeting the duty on your behalf.

Boyle v Kodak Ltd (29 April 1969) House of Lords ([1969] 2 All ER 439)

[A5.6]

statutory duty; employer's liability; fault of employee

Background: Mr Boyle was a painter of sixteen years experience employed by Kodak Ltd. He was injured when a ladder that he was climbing slipped causing him to fall. He was engaged in painting an oil storage tank and, to reach the top of it, it was necessary to use a ladder, resting against the rail around the roof of the tank. When the accident occurred, Mr Boyle was climbing the ladder in order to lash it to the rail. In fact, there happened to be a staircase running around the outside of the tank and it would have been possible to lash the ladder from the staircase rather than from the ladder itself.

Regulation 29(4) of the *Building (Safety Health and Welfare) Regulations 1948 (SI 1948 No 1145)* required that: 'Every ladder shall so far as reasonably practicable be securely fixed so that it can move neither from its top nor from its bottom points of rest. If it cannot be so securely fixed it shall where practicable be securely fixed at the base or if such fixing is impracticable a person shall be stationed at the base of the ladder to prevent slipping.'

The trial judge found that there had been no negligence. However, Mr Boyle argued that, since it had been practicable to use the stairs to lash the ladder, Kodak Ltd was in breach of its statutory duty. Kodak Ltd admitted that the method was a breach, for which it was vicariously liable, but the question was whether it was liable to Mr Boyle when he himself was also in breach of the Regulation.

Test: Although in general an employer is under an absolute liability in respect of a breach of statutory duty, he may have a defence to an action by an employee where the employee is also in breach. According to Lord Diplock, the plaintiff establishes a *prima facie* cause of action by proving that there has been non-compliance with a regulation, which resulted in his injury. However, 'if the employer can prove that the only act or default of anyone which caused or contributed to the non-compliance was the act or default of the plaintiff himself, he establishes a good defence'. If, on the other hand, the employer proves that the breach was only in part the fault of the employee, this will not amount to a defence, but may serve to reduce the damages payable.

Decision: The House of Lords held unanimously that, even where the employee was a skilled worker, the employer still had a duty to take reasonable steps to ensure that the employee was aware of the Regulations and did not breach them. In particular, the Regulations may relate to things which the skilled worker might not know simply from his practical experience. There was no evidence that Kodak Ltd had given instructions or training on the impact of the Regulations. It was found that Mr Boyle and his mate were not aware of the Regulation and it was not reasonable of Kodak Ltd to have assumed that they were. It was held that although both parties were in breach, that Mr Boyle was not solely to blame for his injury and therefore, Kodak Ltd was liable for half the damages.

Comment: This case was distinguished from that of *Manwaring v Billington [1952] All ER 747*, also concerning the breach of *Regulation 29(4)*. In that case, the employee had been instructed not to climb a ladder without putting sacking under it and lashing it at the top. However the employee disobeyed these instructions and the employer had been held not liable. *Boyle v Kodak Ltd* touches on a number of issues of importance in health and safety law but it is of particular relevance to the nature of an employer's liability for the acts of employees and the principle that although there is no negligence there can still be a breach of statutory duty. Whilst there are conflicting rationales as to why and in what situations an employer should be liable for the actions of an employee, it seems that an employer will be liable for the wrongful acts of its employee.

McGovern v British Steel Corporation (21 March 1986) Court of Appeal ([1986] IRLR 411)

[A5.7]

back injury; breach of statutory duty; causal link

Background: Scaffolding on a British Steel Corporation site was fitted with toe boards, as required by the *Construction (Working Places) Regulations 1966 (SI 1966 No 94)*. Mr McGovern tripped over a toe board that had become displaced and was lying in the scaffold walkway. Although he was not injured by his fall, he suffered a severe back injury when he tried to move the toe board to prevent any other person from repeating his accident. He was forced to give up work and claimed damages from his employer for negligence and breach of statutory duty. The High Court held that British Steel Corporation was not liable in negligence but that it had breached *Regulation 30(2)* of the 1966 Regulations in failing to keep the scaffold walkway free from unnecessary obstruction. The company's breach was in law a cause of Mr McGovern's injury. British Steel Corporation appealed, arguing that the accident had not been caused by its breach of statutory duty and that the accident did not fall within the ambit of *Regulation 30(2)* of the 1966 Regulations.

Test: Where a statute creates a duty with the objective of preventing a mischief of a particular kind, a person who suffers loss of a different kind is not able to recover in respect of his loss, despite the fact that that loss was caused by the breach of statutory duty (*Gorris v Scott [1874] LR 9 Ex 125*). *Regulation 30(2)* of the 1966 Regulations imposes an absolute obligation on the employer: 'Every platform, gangway, run or stair shall be kept free from any unnecessary obstruction and material and free from rubbish and any projecting nails'. British Steel Corporation argued that this Regulation did not guard against injuries of the type suffered by Mr McGovern and that it was not therefore liable to him.

Decision: The Court of Appeal held that the company had not complied with the obligation under *Regulation 30(2)* and that, once the breach of the Regulation had taken place, the precise manner of Mr McGovern's injury was not important, provided that the injury had been caused by the breach. There was a causal link between the obstruction of the walkway and the injury that could lead to the conclusion that the injury was caused by the breach. Mr McGovern's action in attempting to lift the toe board did not break the chain of causation; it was a natural and probable consequence of the breach of statutory duty. The breach was in law a cause of the injury and British Steel Corporation was therefore liable to Mr McGovern. The company's appeal was dismissed and leave to appeal to the House of Lords refused.

This judgement sets out the approach to be taken to the issue of causation where breach of statutory duty has been established: (i) identify the relevant breach of statutory duty and the injury which it is alleged was caused by that breach; (ii) trace the events that form the link between the breach and the injury; and (iii) where human intervention is involved (either by the plaintiff or a third party), assess whether the intervention was a natural and probable consequence of the breach and if so, whether that conduct was nevertheless such to break the chain of causation (e.g. if the person acted foolishly or otherwise so that his act rather than the breach was the cause of the injury). The onus of proving the causal link rests with the plaintiff; it is not enough to merely prove that the breach of duty may have caused his injury. The question of causation should be decided by applying common sense to the facts of the case and not by applying some logical or scientific theory of causation (*Stapley v Gypsum Mines Ltd [1953] AC 663*).

Comment: The interrelationship between causation and mischief issues was explored in this case. It was stated by Lord Justice Neill that the two issues are closely linked and to some extent overlap. Nevertheless, there may cases where the breach of statutory duty can be shown to have caused the plaintiff's injury or loss but he will nevertheless fail to recover because the injury or loss was of a kind quite different from that against which the statutory provision was intended to guard. The critical point however is to consider the scope, wording and intention of the statute to determine whether any particular remedy is available.

Contractors

M J Ferguson v John Dawson & Partners (Contractors) Ltd (27 July 1976) Court of Appeal ([1976] IRLR 346)

[A6.1]

contractor; contract of service; working place; breach of statutory duty

Background: Whilst working on a flat roof with no guard rail, Mr Ferguson fell and was seriously injured. He was awarded damages in the Crown Court when it was found that John Dawson & Partners (Contractors) Ltd was in breach of its statutory duty under *Regulation 28(1)* of the *Construction (Working Places) Regulations 1966 (SI 1966 No 94)*. The company appealed, arguing that Mr Ferguson was a labour only sub-contractor working under a contract for services and was not an employee. Further, the roof was not a 'working place' within the meaning of the Regulations because it was not going to be used for an 'appreciable time', a necessary characteristic of a working place (*Gill v Humberstone [1963] 1 WLR 929*; *Kelly v Pierhead Ltd [1967] 1 WLR 65*; *Boynton v Willment [1971] 1 WLR 1625*).

Decision: The Court of Appeal held that whilst the expression of the parties intentions may be a relevant factor, this is not the conclusive factor in determining the true nature of a contract. Applying the established tests, the court found that in this case although Mr Ferguson was regarded as self employed by both himself and the defendant, he was employed under a contract of service. John Dawson & Partners (Contractors) Ltd therefore owed him the statutory duty of providing a guard rail in compliance with the 1966 Regulations and was liable for the damages awarded for the breach of that duty. Regarding the issue of whether the roof was a 'working place', it was held that even though Mr Ferguson was only working there for a short time (ten to fifteen minutes), on the authorities, this was an 'appreciable time'.

Comment: This case demonstrates that whatever name an employer and person working on his site and under his control have given to their relationship, if on the facts of the matter, the relationship is that of employer and employee, then the relevant obligations owed by an employer to an employee will apply.

R v Swan Hunter Shipbuilders Ltd and Telemeter Installations Ltd (30 June 1981) Court of Appeal ([1981] IRLR 403)

[A6.2]

sub-subcontractor; ship; fire risk; safe system of work

Background: An oxygen valve in a ship under construction at Swan Hunter Shipbuilders Ltd's yard was left open by an employee of Telemeter Installations Ltd, a sub-subcontractor. The result of this was that an oxygen enriched atmosphere was produced in a poorly ventilated area. A subsequent fire started by welding equipment was particularly intense because of the high oxygen levels and eight men were killed. Swan Hunter Shipbuilders Ltd's safety officer was aware of the fire risks associated with the use of oxygen in such circumstances and there had been two earlier fatal fires caused by oxygen enrichment. The safety officer had therefore prepared a 'blue book' instructing Swan Hunter Shipbuilders Ltd employees on the safe use of such equipment but these instructions were not given to Telemeter Installations Ltd employees or the employees of other contractors at the site who were working alongside Swan Hunter Shipbuilders Ltd employees. Both Swan Hunter Shipbuilders Ltd and Telemeter Installations Ltd were convicted in the Crown Court of offences under the *HSWA 1974*. Telemeter Installations Ltd appealed against the size of the fine. Swan Hunter Shipbuilders Ltd appealed against its conviction of breaching *sections 2* and *3* of the 1974 Act.

Decision: The principal question of law raised by the appeal was whether the duties imposed on Swan Hunter Shipbuilders Ltd by *sections 2* and *3* of the 1974 Act included the duty to provide the employees of Telemeter Installations Ltd with information on the danger of an oxygen enriched environment and with instructions to ensure the safety of workers. The Court of Appeal held that Swan Hunter Shipbuilders Ltd's failure to do so was in breach of its general duty to its own employees under *section 2(1)* of the 1974 Act. They were also in breach of the more specific duties under *section 2(2)* as in this case the provision of a safe system of work for its employees required that information and instruction be given to persons other than employees. Swan Hunter Shipbuilders Ltd's argued that the requirement to provide information and instruction to non-employees would place an intolerable burden on employers in situations where contractors and sub-contractors work alongside. This argument was not accepted. Neither could it be accepted that the company did not have the right to instruct another firm's employees. The court also found that the company had breached *sections 3(1)* and *3(3)* of the 1974 Act concerning the safety of and provision of information to persons not in its employment. The appeal was dismissed. Telemeter Installations Ltd's appeal was also dismissed.

Comment: This is a well known case which usefully sets out a number of relevant and applicable principles concerning contractors. This case confirmed that an employer is under a duty to instruct his own employees as well as non-employees who are working in the same place as to the dangers and risks posed by the place of work. The risks related to special conditions in the particular work place (on a ship). It was held that if the provision of a safe system of work depended on giving information and instruction as to potential dangers, then such information should be passed on to persons other than the employer's own where the employer was aware that such persons would be exposed to risk.

R v British Steel plc (20 December 1994) Court of Appeal (Times Law Reports, 31 December 1994)

[A6.3]

defence of reasonable practicability; proper delegation; directing mind of the company

Background: In 1990 British Steel decided to move a steel platform by crane through a new location. Two workers were provided by sub-contractors to do the repositioning work. All equipment was provided by British Steel and a British Steel engineer, Mr Crabb was made responsible for supervision. The platform was cut free from nearly all its ports but not suspended from the crane. While one of the workers was underneath the platform, another worker stepped onto it causing it to collapse. The man underneath suffered from fatal injuries as a result. At Sheffield Crown Court, British Steel accepted that the incident constituted on the face of it a breach of *section 3(1)* of the *HSWA 1974*. British Steel stated, however, that the defence of reasonable practicability enabled it to submit a defence on the basis that the 'directing minds' at senior management level had taken all reasonable care to delegate supervision to Mr Crabb. In making this submission, British Steel relied on the case *Tesco Supermarkets v Nattress [1972] AC 153*. The judge ruled that the defence of proper delegation did not arise in this case and British Steel was convicted. British Steel appealed to the Court of Appeal.

Decision: Again relying heavily on *Tesco Supermarkets v Nattress [1972]*, British Steel sought to rely in the Court of Appeal on a defence of proper delegation. Effectively, British Steel asked the court to read the words of *section 3(1)* 'it shall be the duty of every employer to conduct his undertaking in such a way as to ensure' as if the words 'through senior management' appeared after the word 'employer'. The Court of Appeal examined *Tesco Supermarkets v Nattress [1972]* which was a case under the *Trade Descriptions Act 1968* and distinguished it from the present case on the grounds that the wording of that Act differed and the intention behind it was not the same. The Court of Appeal held that *section 3(1)* imposes absolute liability subject to 'reasonably practicable' measures to avert the risk. The court held that it was not the intention of parliament that corporate employers should be able to avoid criminal liability because the Act in question was committed by someone who was not the directing mind of the company. The Court of Appeal, therefore, dismissed the appeal.

Comment: This case reinforces the concept that corporations cannot avoid liability simply because the act causing the breach was carried out by someone who was not the directing mind of the company. Nor can they avoid responsibility simply by taking reasonable care to delegate supervision. In cases such as this, it may be that the proposed legislation relating to corporate manslaughter will provide the HSE with greater powers to take action where fatalities occur.

R v Associated Octel Company Ltd (14 November 1996) House of Lords (Times Law Reports, 15 November 1996)

[A6.4]

contractor's employee; risk to health and safety; employer's undertaking

Background: Associated Octel operated a large chemical plant in Ellesmere Port. In June 1990 the plant was shut down for annual maintenance. A firm of specialist contractors was instructed to repair the lining of the tank. An employee of the contractor was working in the tank using acetone under light from an electric light bulb. While the contractor's employee was applying acetone with a brush, the light bulb broke causing a flash fire which injured him. Associated Octel was prosecuted for breaching *section 3(1)* of the *HSWA 1974*. The court held that Associated Octel had failed to control the works so as to ensure that persons not in its employment were not exposed to risks to their health and safety. The court took into account that the contractor was operating under a system whereby authorisation had to be given by Associated Octel's engineers before it could proceed. Associated Octel had, however, failed to provide the contractor's employee with appropriate equipment. Associated Octel appealed to the Court of Appeal but its appeal was dismissed. Associated Octel appealed again to the House of Lords.

Decision: *Section 3(1)* of the *HSWA 1974* requires employers to conduct their undertakings in such a way as to ensure so far as reasonably practicable that persons not in their employment who may be affected thereby are not thereby exposed to risks to their health and safety. Associated Octel argued that because it had employed a contractor, it did not have control over the works and therefore the maintenance operation was not part of the conduct of its undertaking. The House of Lords held that it was a question of facts in each case whether an activity constitutes conduct of an employer's undertaking. It held that Associated Octel's undertaking was the operation of a chemical plant which includes having the plant cleaned. Associated Octel, therefore, had to take reasonably practicable steps to avoid risk to the contractor's employees arising from the arrangements made between Associated Octel and the contractor. The court took into account the following evidence: the tanks formed part of Associated Octel's plant; the work was part of its maintenance programme; the contractor's employees were effectively integrated into Associated Octel's operations; and, Associated Octel provided the safety equipment and lighting. On these grounds the House of Lords confirmed the conviction and dismissed the appeal.

Comment: This case makes it clear that obligations under *section 3* of the *HSWA 1974* relating to the conduct of an employer's undertaking may extend as far as to activities which have been delegated to a contractor. It is a question of fact in each case as to whether an activity amounts to part of an employer's conduct of his undertaking. Issues such as whose equipment is being used, what work is being done and how integrated the employees are into the employer's work will be taken into account. The case illustrates the point that it is not permissible to simply delegate work to contractors without being cognisant of the risks potentially faced by the contractor's employees. In this case Octel had a permit to work system whereby a form was to be completed for every job specifying the work to be done. One of Octel's engineers would then indicate the safety precautions required. In this case, Octel was held to have failed to take reasonably practicable steps to address the risks completely in not providing a special air lamp. The interesting question for companies in controlling the risks faced by others from their undertaking is whether, by actively being involved in the management of risks, one increases the level of control expected with respect to others. The answer to this probably lies in the particular circumstances of each case. Although there are no hard nor fast rules, the simple point is that it is prudent to take steps to be aware of and control the risks faced others who may be affected by the conduct of one's undertaking.

RMC Roadstone Products Ltd v Jester (28 January 1994) Queen's Bench Divisional Court (Times Law Reports, 8 February 1994)

[A6.5]

independent contractor; employer's conduct of undertaking

Background: Two independent contractors were engaged by RMC Roadstone Products Ltd to carry out some repair work at its premises. During the work, one contractor fell from a roof and was fatally injured. It was established that although RMC Roadstone Products Ltd had been in a position to give specific directions to the contractors on how the work should be done, they were in fact left to do the work as they chose. The company had no duty to lay down a safe system of work for the contractors and did not do so. The company was convicted of failing to discharge its duty under *section 3(1)* of the *HSWA 1974* to conduct its undertaking in such a way as to ensure, so far as is reasonably practicable, that persons not in its employment were not exposed to risks to their health or safety. RMC Roadstone Products Ltd appealed against the conviction.

Decision: In order to be liable under *section 3(1)* of the 1974 Act, the work carried out by the independent contractors had to come within RMC Roadstone Products Ltd's conduct of its undertaking. The High Court held that although a defendant's conduct of its undertaking is not limited to activities over which it has complete control (*Carmichael v Rosehall Engineering Works Ltd [1984] SLT 40*), mere capacity or opportunity to exercise control over the activity of an independent contractor does not suffice to bring that activity within the ambit of the employer's conduct of his undertaking for the purposes of *section 3(1)* of the 1974 Act. There has to be the actual exercise of or the common law duty to exercise control over the activity. Thus, as the company was not under a statutory duty to set up a safe system of work for the contractors and it did not exercise control over their work, their activities did not fall within RMC Roadstone Products Ltd's conduct of its undertaking for the purposes of criminal liability. The appeal was allowed.

Comment: This case was consistent with the conclusion accepted by the Court of Appeal in *R v Swan Hunter Shipbuilders Ltd and Telemeter Unstallations Ltd [1981]* (see paragraph A6.2) and as far as *section 2* of the *HSWA 1974* was concerned, the provision was not intended to impose a duty which went beyond the common law.

Mailer v Austin Rover Group plc (27 July 1989) House of Lords ([1989] 2 All ER 1087)

[A6.6]

vehicle assembly plant; independent contractor's employees; control over premises

Background: Austin Rover Group plc engaged independent contractors to clean a spray painting booth. The contractors established a system of work imposing a series of safety measures. These safety rules were ignored and as a result, a flash fire occurred which killed one of the contractor's employees. The contractor was convicted of failing to provide a safe system of work for its employees and Austin Rover Group plc was also convicted for failing to take such measures as were reasonable for the company to take to ensure so far as is reasonably practicable that a sump and piped solvent supplies were safe, contrary to *section 4(2)* of the *HSWA 1974*. After a successful appeal by the company, the inspector of factories appealed to the House of Lords.

Decision: *Section 4(2)* of the 1974 Act imposes general health and safety duties on persons with some control over premises where non-employees are working. The House of Lords held that for a successful prosecution under this section on the present circumstances, it was necessary to prove that (i) the premises were unsafe and constituted a risk to health; (ii) Austin Rover Group plc had a degree of control over those premises and; (iii) it was reasonable, given the extent of control and knowledge of the likely use of the premises, for the company to take measures which would ensure that they were safe and without risk to health. If these three issues were proved, the onus would then be on the defendant to show, weighing the risk to health against the means of eliminating that risk, that it was not reasonably practicable to take the measures in question. If the premises were not a reasonably foreseeable cause of danger to persons using them in a manner or circumstances which might reasonably be expected to occur, it was not reasonable to expect measures to be taken against unknown and unexpected events. In this case, it could not be said that it was reasonable for Austin Rover Group plc to have taken measures to make the premises safe against the unanticipated misuse of the premises by the contractor's employees. The appeal was refused.

Comment: The central words relating to the level of control over premises where non-employees were working, were 'such measures as it is reasonable for a person in his position to take'. The test espoused by Hutchinson J was that: 'it seems to me inescapable that while the justices made findings which plainly involved that there were steps which the (respondents) could have taken, which would have in fact averted the fire and the unhappy consequences that flowed from it, they made no findings which justified the conclusion that it had been proved that those steps were steps it would have been reasonable for a person in the (respondents) position to take'.

Costs

Haiselden v P&O Properties Ltd (5 May 1998) Court of Appeal (NLD, 6 May 1998)

[A7.1]

health and safety; costs; litigants in person

Background: In February 1996, Mr Haiselden suffered an injury whilst at work. As a litigant in person, he sued his employer, P&O Properties Ltd for damages expressly limited to a sum not exceeding £1,000. The case ought to have been transferred automatically to the small claims procedure for arbitration. However, because of a court clerical error, the case was instead listed for trial at Lambeth County Court. Unaware of the mistake, Mr Haiselden accordingly provided the necessary paperwork and the £100 fee for setting the case down for trial. P&O, although aware of the mistake made by the court, requested further and better particulars, believing that the court's error was to its advantage as it would recover greater costs in the county court should it succeed.

Test: The court considered whether P&O had an obligation to draw Mr Haiselden's and the court's attention to the error that had been made.

Decision: The action was dismissed and Mr Haiselden was ordered to pay P&O costs on County Court Scale 1. Mr Haiselden appealed on the basis that the only costs that could have been awarded against him were those specified by *Order 19* of the *County Court Rules*. In allowing the appeal, the Court of Appeal held that a litigant in person, intending to invoke arbitration procedures in the County Court specifically to avoid the cost of incurring liability for a defendant's costs, should not be deprived of that protection.

P&O had an obligation to draw the mistake to the attention of Mr Haiselden and the court. The justice of the case demanded that Mr Haiselden's liability to P&O should be limited to such costs as would have been recovered in arbitration.

Comment: This case is of interest where litigation involves a litigant in person (as is often the case in environment law).

Burrows v Vauxhall Motors Ltd; Mongiardi v IBC Vehicles Ltd (19 November 1997) Court of Appeal (Times Law Reports, 17 December 1997)

[A7.2]

costs; health and safety; settlement

Background: In both cases, the employees, Burrows and Mongiardi, were injured in the course of their employment with Vauxhall Motors Ltd and IBC Vehicles Ltd respectively. The companies' insurers wished to explore the possibility of a settlement before the costs of litigation were incurred. In both cases, after having had sight of the medical reports served with the summons commencing proceedings, the companies made payments into court which were accepted by Burrows and Mongiardi. Through the companies, the insurers claimed that Burrows and Mongiardi had acted unreasonably in commencing proceedings before the insurers had had an opportunity to make an offer of settlement based on the medical reports which Burrows and Mongiardi had obtained.

Decision: The court held that where any act had been done or any omission made 'unreasonably or improperly', the county court had the power to disallow the costs 'in respect of' that act or omission or to order the party at fault to pay the other party's costs occasioned by the act or omission. Therefore, if it was found that the employees had acted unreasonably or improperly in commencing proceedings then, notwithstanding the fact that they had secured a settlement, they might be deprived of costs or ordered to pay the companies' costs after the issue of proceedings.

Comment: This case makes it clear that the question of whether an employee has acted unreasonably or improperly in commencing proceedings may turn on things done or not done before proceedings were in fact commenced.

Damages

Jameson and Another v Central Electricity Generating Board (16 December 1998) House of Lords (Times Law Reports, 17 December 1998)

[A8.1]

executors; damages; asbestos; mesothelioma; concurrent tortfeasor

Background: This case involved a claim by the executors of David Allen Jameson against Central Electricity Generating Board. Their claim for damages was based on the grounds that during the period that Mr Jameson was working at Central Electricity Generating Board's premises whilst employed by Babcock Energy Ltd, he was exposed to asbestos. This had lead to malignant mesothelioma. Before his death, Mr Jameson had brought an action against Babcock Energy Ltd for damages for personal injury due to exposure to asbestos at various places where he had worked during his employment, including the Central Electricity Generating Board's premises. 'In full and final settlement and satisfaction of all the causes of action in respect of which he claimed in the statement of claim', Mr Jameson had accepted £80,000 from Babcock Energy Ltd. Mr Jameson died before the performance of the settlement had been completed by payment of the full sum. It was assumed that during the period when Mr Jameson worked at the Central Electricity Generating Board premises, he had been exposed to asbestos as a result of the breach of duty on the part of both Babcock Energy Ltd and the Central Electricity Generating Board. The trial of the preliminary issues had proceeded on the basis that they were concurrent tortfeasors.

Test: The issue in this case was whether under *section 1(1)* of the *Fatal Accidents Act 1976*, as substituted by *section 3(1)* of the *Administration of Justice Act 1982*, the Central Electricity Generating

Board would have also been liable to Mr Jameson's action in damages if death had not ensued.

Decision: The court found that an agreement reached between an injured person and one concurrent tortfeasor could not extinguish his claim for damages against the other concurrent tortfeasor if his claim for damages had still not been satisfied. The critical question was therefore whether the claim had been satisfied. This would involve the court examining the terms of the agreement in light of the claim. The agreement would be considered to have the effect which the parties intended it to have. The fact that the agreement had been entered into by way of a compromise in order to conclude a settlement formed part of the background. However, the extent of the element of compromise varied from case to case. The effect of a compromise was to fix the amount of a person's claim in just the same way as if the case had gone to trial and the person had obtained judgement. Once this agreed sum had been paid, the person's claim against the tortfeasor would have been satisfied. This would therefore discharge the tort and create a bar to a future action in respect of it. On this premise, if the person's claim had been for the full amount of the loss for which the payer of the settlement, as the first concurrent tortfeasors, was liable to the aggrieved person in damages, satisfaction of the claim by him would have the effect of extinguishing the claim against the other concurrent tortfeasors. If the aggrieved person did attempt to bring a subsequent claim, the court in examining this claim is limited as to the inquiries it could make. It could not allow the question as to whether the agreed amount which was accepted in settlement from the first tortfeasor represented the full value of the claim. The pertinent question was whether the sum the aggrieved person had received in settlement was intended to be in full satisfaction of the claim or not. In the present case, the House of Lords held by a majority allowing the appeal by Central Electricity Generating Board, that the sum accepted by Mr Jameson was expressly accepted in full and final settlement and satisfaction of all his causes of action in the statement of claim. This therefore extinguished his claim against the other concurrent tortfeasor, notwithstanding that the settlement was for less than the full value of the claim. The court further held that the fact Mr Jameson had died prior to the settlement being executed in full was to have no effect. The date from which the claim of damages was to be treated as having been satisfied by reason of the settlement with the first concurrent tortfeasor was the date when the settlement had been entered into. Thus the claim of damages against the other concurrent tortfeasor was discharged from the date of the settlement. The executors could not therefore satisfy the requirements of *section 1(1)* of the *Fatal Accidents Act 1976* because the Central Electricity Generating Board would not have been liable, if death had not ensued, for an action in damages brought by the deceased in respect of the same tort.

Comment: This case was applied in *Heaton v Axa Equity and Law Life Assurance Society (Times Law Reports, 19 July 1999)*. The case was relied on for the principle that having settled claims with one defendant it was contrary to public policy to raise the same claims against another unless there was a clear reservation of rights.

Thomas v Bunn; Wilson v Graham; Lea v British Aerospace plc (13 December 1990) House of Lords (Independent, 14 December 1990)

[A8.2]

damages; personal injury; interlocutory judgement; interest

Background: This case concerned three appeals from separate decisions of the High Court that were heard together and went directly to the House of Lords. Each case concerned a claim of damages for personal injury arising out of a workplace or road accident. In all three cases, an interlocutory judgement in favour of the plaintiff had been given and the judge had ordered damages to be assessed. Interest on the judgement debt under *section 17* of the *Judgements Act 1838* was ordered to run from the date when the damages were ordered to be assessed and not the date when the damages were actually assessed.

Decision: The House of Lords held that the term 'judgement' in the context of *section 17* of the 1838 Act means the final judgement for a quantified sum, not an interlocutory judgement which establishes liability. Therefore, interest payable on an award of damages under that section should only run from the date of the judgement when the damages are finally agreed or assessed and judgement entered for that sum; not from the earlier date when, liability having been agreed or determined, an order is made for damages to be assessed.

Comment: The House of Lords held that the term 'judgement' in the context of the *Judgements Act 1838* means the final judgement for a quantified sum not an interlocutory judgement which establishes liability. This decision was applied in *Kuwait Airways Corporation v Iraqi Airways Co [1995] 1 WLR 1147* in which it was held that an order for costs, which is reversed on appeal, may only be backdated to a date that is not unfair to one of the parties. It was held that under *RSC Order 42 Rule 3(2)(a)* a costs order may be backdated to some date other than the date of judgement. Where on a successful appeal, a costs order is reversed and it is shown that the party should have won in the court below, generally it will be just for the court to backdate that part of the costs award regarding the costs of the action so that interest runs from the date that the court considers just.

Champion v London Fire and Civil Defence Authority (27 June 1990) High Court (Times Law Reports, 5 July 1990)

[A8.3]

negligence; damages; evidence; admissibility

Background: Mr Champion, a fireman, slipped on some eggs spilt by a colleague in the fire station kitchen and broke his wrist. His colleague admitted responsibility for the accident. Following his discharge from the fire service, Mr Champion sued the London Fire and Civil Defence Authority for damages on the basis that his injury was due to an accident at work due to the negligence of a fellow employee. Damages for pain and suffering were settled between the parties. Mr Champion also sought damages for loss of congenial employment. The issue was whether his colleague's statement was admissible as evidence imposing liability on the London Fire and Civil Defence Authority.

Decision: The High Court ruled that Mr Champion was entitled to a separate award of damages for loss of congenial employment. He had suffered significant loss of job satisfaction because of his discharge from the fire service. The statement by the other fireman admitting responsibility for his injuries was not admissible in evidence against the London Fire and Civil Defence Authority as an admission by an agent of the employer. However, such a statement could still be presented as evidence under the *RSC Order 38 rule 29(2)*.

Comment: The basic premise of the case was that admissions by servants will not usually be admissible when the plaintiff was the fellow servant suing the employer. There are statutory exceptions to this principle.

Dews v National Coal Board (4 June 1987) House of Lords ([1987] IRLR 330)

[A8.4]

miner; assessment of damages; pension scheme

Background: Mr Dews was injured as a result of his work as a miner. He was awarded damages from his employer. When these damages were assessed there was disagreement about how contributions to his occupational pension scheme should be treated. Mr Dews' membership of the Mineworkers' Pension Scheme was a condition of his employment with the National Coal Board. A prescribed percentage of his wages was paid directly into the scheme and an equal amount was contributed by his employer. No contributions needed to be made if he was off work and received no wages. The scheme also allowed that a break in contributions by both parties in times of illness would not result in a loss in terms of the ultimate benefit under the scheme, as long as the break was no longer than eighteen months. During his time away from work therefore, no contributions were made into the pension scheme. In his subsequent damages claim, Mr Dews attempted to claim both the amount that would have been paid in by himself and his employer, totalling £110. There would be no reduction in his final pension entitlement as he had been off work for less than eighteen months. The High Court held that he was entitled to recover the £55 he would have paid into the scheme, but not his employer's contribution. The National Coal Board's appeal against this decision was allowed by the Court of Appeal and Mr Dews appealed.

Test: Damages for personal injury are compensatory and should put the plaintiff in the same financial position as if an accident had not happened. They should be based on an assessment of what the plaintiff has actually lost. It is however also a fundamental principle governing the law of damages for personal injury that it is of no concern to the tortfeasor how the plaintiff might have chosen to spend his earnings had he not been injured.

Decision: In this case, it was necessary to consider separately that part of the employee's earnings intended for the pension scheme and that part intended for immediate expenditure. The tortfeasor would have no concern with how the latter was spent. However this could not apply to the sum of money paid into the pension scheme on his behalf as it was not intended to provide any immediate benefit. The House of Lords ruled that Mr Dews should not be entitled to recover his contribution as he would not have ever received the money as it would have been paid directly into the scheme and furthermore, he would not suffer any loss of future pension. The appeal was dismissed.

Comment: This case considered the principle that compulsory pension contributions, which would have been paid from the earnings, should be deducted from loss of earnings to avoid over-compensating the plaintiff. In the same way, income tax and national insurance contributions should also be deducted, according to respectively *British Transport Commissioner v Gourley [1956] AC 185* and *Cooper v Firth Brown [1963] 1 WLR 418.* It was suggested by Lord Griffiths that this approach should not be confined to cases involving compulsory pension schemes. Where evidence showed that a plaintiff had regularly been making contributions to a voluntary scheme in order to secure a pension so that, but for the accident, the probability pointed to a continuation of those contributions, the same principles should apply.

Willson v Ministry of Defence (6 July 1990) High Court ([1991] 1 All ER 638)

[A8.5]

personal injury; damages; provisional damages; serious deterioration; Supreme Court Act 1981

Background: Mr Willson was a fitter at a naval dockyard. He injured his ankle by slipping on a polished floor at work, an injury which left him with continuing disability and pain. Although he returned to work to carry out light duties, he later took voluntary redundancy and purchased a shop. Medical opinion was that the ankle might degenerate further and be prone to injury and possibly arthritis in the future. Mr Willson brought an action against the Ministry of Defence claiming damages for personal injury and also an award of provisional damages on the basis that if he fell due to the ankle injury and suffered another injury, or developed arthritis and required surgery or was forced to change his employment.

Test: Provisional damages may be awarded pursuant to *section 32A* of the *Supreme Court Act 1981* where it is proved that there is a probability in the future that the plaintiff will suffer some serious deterioration in physical condition as a result of the defendant's negligence. In this context, the 'chance' of an event occurring must be measurable rather than fanciful.

Decision: In Mr Willson's case, although the chance of him suffering further injury or developing arthritis was small, it was measurable. It could not be said however that such events would be a 'serious deterioration in physical condition' as required by *section 32A* of the 1981 Act: this must be a clear and severable risk rather than continuing deterioration, and the deterioration must also be beyond ordinary deterioration. On the facts presented, the High Court held that the events for which Mr Willson wished to claim provisional damages would not constitute serious deterioration; rather, they would merely be an aspect of the progression of his condition or be entirely speculative. His claim for an award of provisional damages was turned down and damages were awarded as a lump sum.

Comment: This case falls within the body of case law concerning situations where there is uncertainty as to the future. Where it cannot be ascertained as to how the uncertainties are to be taken into account or factored in, it is difficult to calculate a once-and-for-all assessment of damages. Consequently, a claim for provisional damages should be refused in such instances.

Smith v Manchester City Council (10 June 1974) Court of Appeal ([1974] 118 SJ 597)

[A8.6]

cleaner; future employment; damages; future earnings

Background: The plaintiff, a part-time cleaner in an old people's home, fell and broke her elbow when she slipped on the floor. She developed a frozen shoulder and was unable to work for fourteen months. In an action for damages for personal injuries, her employer admitted liability but disputed the amount of damages claimed. In the High Court, the plaintiff was awarded £2,300 general damages: £2,000 for pain and suffering and loss of amenity; and £300 for possible loss of future earnings. She appealed on the ground that the award was too low.

Decision: The Court of Appeal held that the damages for pain and suffering and loss of amenity were not far from the proper bracket and no alteration should be made to that sum. The damages for possible loss of future earnings were increased however to £1,000, as the plaintiff's injury meant that her position in the labour market had been weakened. The judge had been wrong in awarding the notional figure of £300. When assessing general damages, it was necessary to consider damages for these two heads separately. Thus, as the judge's award under one head had been wrong, the damages awarded should be altered, even though the overall increase was not very large. The appeal was allowed.

Comment: The dictum of Edmund Davies LJ was applied in *Moeliker v A Reyrolle & Co [1977] 1 WLR 132* where it was held that the Court of Appeal may interfere with a damages award if it considers that the damages under one head are substantially wrong; even though there is no resultant substantial variation in the total award. Where the plaintiff has some risk of losing his employment and if he would be at a disadvantage in obtaining alternative employment, the award of damages should take this into account.

Directors' Liability

Richardson v Pitt, Stanley and Others (29 July 1994) Court of Appeal (Times Law Reports, 11 August 1994)

[A9.1]

insurance; employer's liability; directors' liability; civil and criminal liability

Background: The plaintiff, an employee of a company, sustained damages, liability for which the company had failed to insure against pursuant to the *Employers' Liability (Compulsory Insurance) Act 1969*. Under *section 5* of the 1969 Act, an employer who fails to obtain proper insurance, is guilty of an offence. The 1969 Act also provides that where an offence is committed by a corporation but which is also committed with the consent or connivance, or facilitated by any neglect on the part of any director, manager, secretary or other officer of the corporation, he as well as the corporation shall be deemed to be guilty of the offence.

Test: The issue before the court was whether, bearing in mind that directors and officers can be criminally liable for the above corporate offence, that failure could also give rise to civil liability on the part of directors to pay damages to injured employees under the 1969 Act.

Decision: There was no such liability. There was no express provision in the 1969 Act creating civil liability on the part of either employers, directors or officers. In the absence of any such express provision, liability on the part of directors was restricted to criminal liability.

Comment: This case reiterated the principle that where a criminal statute has been breached, the affected party only has a right to take a civil action in tort where the relevant statute expressly provides for that right. In determining the intent of parliament, Hansard was used as evidence to determine that that it was not intended that a new civil liability offence be created. This case has been heavily criticised for running contrary to the policy underlying the introduction of the 1969 Act and in *Quinn v McGinty [1998] Rep LR 107* (Sheriff Court) the case was not followed. The decision in *Richardson* was largely based on the fact that the plaintiff could have relied on other remedies at common law e.g. negligence or breach of statutory duty. Thus, plaintiffs should give careful consideration to the basis of any action taken. Further, whilst this is an employment law decision, the principle may have general application in the context of criminal offences under environmental law. Environmental legislation contains numerous similar provisions regarding the criminal liability of directors and senior officers. Individuals who suffer as a result of environmental offences should consider other avenues by which they can take issue.

Duties to Employees

Canterbury City Council v Howletts and Port Lympne Estates Ltd (27 November 1996) High Court (Times Law Reports, 13 December 1996)

[A10.1]

prohibition notice; zoo keeper; breach of statutory duty; safe system of work

Background: Canterbury City Council served a prohibition notice after a zoo keeper who had entered a tiger enclosure was killed. The council stated that the zoo was in breach of *section 2(1)* and *2(2)(a)* of the *HSWA 1974* by failing to ensure a safe system of work by allowing keepers to enter enclosures whilst animals were freely roaming. The notice required that such activities should cease immediately. Howletts and Port Lympne Estates Ltd appealed successfully and the council then appealed against the industrial tribunal's decision. The council contended that *section 2* amounted to an absolute duty on the employer with regard to the safety of employees and that this could not be fulfilled if the method of accessing enclosures continued.

Decision: The High Court ruled that *section 2* of the 1974 Act (employer to ensure so far as is reasonably practicable the health, safety and welfare at work of all employees) is not intended to legislate as to what work can or cannot be performed. Instead it is concerned with the action that should be taken to ensure that employees are safe in the work which is the employer's business to carry out. Certain activities should not be outlawed just because they are inherently dangerous (*Coltness Iron Co v Sharp [1938] AC 90*). The appeal was dismissed.

Comment: This case illustrates that the essential nature of the undertaking and the operating practice of a business should be taken into account in determining whether the duty under *section*

2 of the *HSWA 1974* has been discharged. The words 'so far as reasonably practicable' import a duty to consider the application of the statute to the particular business that the employer is carrying out and any special limitations or considerations that may be required given the very nature of the business.

Bolton Metropolitan Borough Council v Malrod Insulations Ltd (13 November 1992) Queen's Bench Divisional Court (Times Law Reports, 26 November 1992)

[A10.2]

unsafe plant; breach of statutory duty; unsafe equipment

Background: An asbestos decontamination plant to be used by the employees of Malrod Insulations Ltd was found to be unsafe by a council inspector. The plant was not being used and had not been used by employees. Bolton Metropolitan Borough Council successfully prosecuted the company for breach of its duty under *sections 2(1)* and *(2)(a)* of the *HSWA 1974*. However, this conviction was overturned by the Crown Court on the basis that there was no case to answer because the duty to employees under *section 2* of the 1974 Act only applies when employees are 'at work'. As no work involving the unsafe plant was being undertaken, there was no breach. The council appealed.

Test: *Section 2* of the 1974 Act provides that: '(1) It shall be the duty of every employer to ensure, so far as is reasonably practicable, the health, safety and welfare at work of all his employees. (2) Without prejudice to the generality of an employer's duty under the preceding subsection, the matters to which that duty extends include in particular (a) the provision and maintenance of plant and systems of work that are, so far as is reasonably practicable, safe and without risks to health'.

Decision: The High Court held that this duty applies to all employees at work, not just those engaged in work involving the unsafe equipment. There was a statutory requirement to provide a safe plant. As the plant made available was not safe, there was a breach of that duty even though the plant had not been and was not being used. The appeal was allowed and the case remitted to be heard by the Crown Court.

Comment: This case determined that the duty under *section 2(1)* and *(2)* of the *HSWA 1974* is for employers to provide and maintain a safe and risk free plant and systems of work for all their employees 'at work'. The duty owed is not just limited to those employees engaged in the specific process for which the plant was made available. If an employer makes available an unsafe plant, there is a breach of the duty even if the plant had not been and was not being used at the time and in fact even if no actual injury occurs. There are numerous decisions relating to the meaning of 'maintain' and what constitutes the place of 'work' in other statutes which are of relevance in interpreting this provision.

R v Gateway Foodmarkets Ltd (19 December 1996) Court of Appeal (Times Law Reports, 2 January 1997)

[B10.3]

section 2(1) of Health and Safety at Work etc. Act 1974; head office; 'directing mind' of company; reasonable precautions

Background: The duty manager of a Gateway supermarket died when he fell though a trap door in a lift control room which had been left open by contractors. The purpose of the manager's visit was to free the lift which had jammed. This was a recurring problem and the lift maintenance contractors that had been engaged to solve any problems at the store had shown the staff how to free the lift. This practice had not been authorised by Gateway Foodmarkets Ltd's head office and no one there knew of it. The company was convicted of failing to discharge its duty under *section 2(1)* of the *HSWA 1974* to ensure so far as is reasonably practicable the health, safety and welfare at work of all employees. Gateway Foodmarkets Ltd appealed, arguing that as the supermarket was separate from the head office, the company's 'directing mind' (i.e. head office personnel and senior management) was not responsible.

Decision: The Court of Appeal ruled that the company was liable for a failure to ensure safety at store level, contrary to *section 2(1)* of the 1974 Act. An employer will be liable under this section (as under *section 3(1)* of the 1974 Act (liability towards non-employees) (*R v Associated Octel Co Ltd [1996]*, see paragraph A6.4) in the event that there is a failure to ensure the safety of an employee unless it can prove that all reasonable precautions have been taken by the company itself or on its behalf. The breach of duty and liability do not depend on any failure by the company, meaning those persons who embody the company, to take all reasonable precautions. The failure at store management level was attributable to the employer and Gateway Foodmarkets Ltd's appeal was dismissed.

Comment: The obligations arising under the *HSWA 1974* import a strict duty which must be discharged – there is no need to establish that those who embody the company by virtue of their position of control and management actually knew of the defect. It is sufficient that the company via its 'directing mind' failed to 'take all reasonable precautions'.

Duties to Non-Employees

R v Mersey Docks and Harbour Company (1995) Court of Appeal ([1995] 16 CR APP R (S) 806)

[A11.1]

petrol cargo; explosion; risk to health and safety; fines

Background: A ship that had previously carried a cargo of petroleum visited the port for which Mersey Docks and Harbour Company was responsible. Part of the petrol cargo had remained inside the ship; this found its way into a hold and created an explosive atmosphere. The company had failed to determine whether the ship had any dangerous spaces containing flammable gases so when a workman used cutting equipment to open the hold hatch covers there was an explosion and fire. Two people were killed and others were injured. Mersey Docks and Harbour Company was convicted of failing to discharge its duty under *section 3(1)* of the *HSWA 1974* (employer to conduct its undertaking in such a way to ensure so far as is reasonably practicable that persons not in its employment are not exposed to risks to their health or safety) and was fined £250,000. The company appealed, claiming that its responsibility for the accident was relatively minor and a lower fine was more appropriate. It was contended that the company was entitled to rely on the master of the vessel who was primarily responsible for safety.

Decision: The Court of Appeal held that the duty imposed on an employer by *section 3(1)* of the 1974 Act cannot be transferred or delegated. It was not a mitigating factor for the company to say that it had left its duty to be discharged by others. It was important for the courts to impose fines to emphasise the requirement to discharge that duty. In this case, the company had wholly disregarded the risk posed by the ship and had taken only superficial and inadequate action to fulfil its duty. The appeal was dismissed and the fine upheld.

Comment: The level of fines in this case should be considered in the light of the sentencing guidelines set out in *R v F Howe & Son (Engineers) Ltd [1999]* (see paragraph A14.1). The main issue of relevance is that this case reiterates the position that the obligations imposed under *section 3* of the *HSWA 1974* are non-delegable duties.

R v Board of Trustees of the Science Museum (9 March 1993) Court of Appeal (Times Law Reports, 15 March 1993)

[A11.2]

legionella; cooling tower; Health and Safety at Work etc. Act 1974; risk to public health and safety

Background: The Board of Trustees of the Science Museum ('BTSM') was convicted of failing to discharge its duty under *section 3(1)* of the *HSWA 1974* to ensure, so far as is reasonably practicable, that persons not in its employment are not exposed to risks to their health or safety. The prosecution alleged that an inadequate maintenance system allowed legionella bacteria to develop in a cooling tower, thereby exposing members of the public outside the museum building to a risk to their health. At the trial, the BTSM argued that there was no case to answer because no actual risk to the public's health had been proved and a possible or potential danger could not damage the health or safety of the public. This submission was rejected by the judge who held that it was only necessary for the prosecution to prove that there had been a risk of bacteria from the cooling tower being present in the air in the vicinity of the building. The BTSM appealed.

Decision: The Court of Appeal held that where an employer was charged under *section 3(1)* of the 1974 Act, it was sufficient to prove that members of the public were exposed to the possibility of danger, i.e. that there was a risk of the bacteria being in the air. The prosecution did not need to show either that members of the public had actually inhaled legionella or that bacteria had been in the air to be inhaled. *Section 3(1)* was intended to be an absolute prohibition on exposing non-employees to risks to their health or safety, subject only to the defence of reasonable practicability. In this case, the BTSM had not taken all reasonable steps to minimise the risks and its appeal was dismissed.

Comment: The question in this case was whether there had to be actual exposure of employees to particular risks in order for an employer to incur liability pursuant to the *HSWA 1974* or whether merely the risk of an employee being exposed is sufficient for an employer to incur liability. It was contended that the word 'risk' and the manner in which it was used in the 1972 Act, implied the idea of a possibility of danger. The interpretation that rendered the statute effective in protecting public health and safety was preferred – thus, the Act was interpreted so that it encompassed the risk of danger as well as actual danger.

R v Mara (5 November 1986) Court of Appeal ([1987] 1 WLR 87)

[A11.3]

cleaning machines; store workers; risk to health and safety; breach of statutory duty

Background: Mr Mara was a director of CMS Cleaning and Maintenance Services Ltd. This company had a contract to clean a store each weekday between 7.30 a.m. and 9 a.m. By agreement with the store, the company's cleaning machines were left there and could be used by store workers at other times if necessary. One of the cleaning machines had a damaged cable and a store worker received a fatal electric shock. The accident occurred on a Saturday afternoon. Mr Mara was charged and convicted of conniving and consenting to a breach by the company of its duty as an employer under *section 3(1)* of the *HSWA 1974* to conduct its undertaking in such as way as to ensure that persons not in its employment were not exposed to risks to their health or safety. He appealed, arguing, *inter alia*, that the company did not conduct its undertaking at the store on Saturdays.

Decision: *Section 3(1)* of the 1974 Act reads: 'It shall be the duty of every employer to conduct his undertaking in such a way as to ensure, so far as is reasonably practicable, that persons not in his employment who may be affected thereby are not thereby exposed to risks to their health or safety.' The Court of Appeal held that for the purposes of *section 3(1)* of the 1974 Act, the conduct of the company's undertaking was not limited to the hours when its employees were engaged in cleaning the store but also included the manner in which the cleaning machines were left at the store and their use by store workers. *Section 3(1)* had been breached and Mr Mara had been properly convicted of colluding or conniving to that breach. His appeal was dismissed.

Comment: This case raised a number of issues concerning the interpretation and construction of *section 3(1)* of the *HSWA 1974*, which had not previously arisen. Mr Mara's submission was that the subsection had no application to 'undertakings' whose prime function was the provision of services. The Court of Appeal had no hesitation in rejecting this. According to Parker LJ there was no indication that 'undertakings' were intended to or should be restricted in any way.

Electricity

R v Sanyo Electrical Manufacturing (UK) Ltd (24 February 1992) Court of Appeal (Times Law Reports, 6 March 1992)

[A12.1]

electric shock; reasonably foreseeable; statutory requirements

Background: An employee of Sanyo Electrical Manufacturing (UK) Ltd touched the wrong button on a microwave oven during a quality inspection. As a result, she received an electric shock but no serious injury. The company pleaded guilty to two offences of failing to prevent danger from electrical conductors, contrary to the *Electricity (Factories Act) Special Regulations 1908 (SR & O 1908 No 1312)* and *1944 (SR & O 1944 No 739)* and the *HSWA 1974*. The company appealed against the sentence on the ground, *inter alia*, that the accident had only occurred because of a number of coincidences which could not have been foreseen.

Decision: The Court of Appeal held that the purpose of the 1908 and 1944 Regulations was to protect employees against the consequences of doing things through inattention or inadvertence which they would not normally do. The sentence was not excessive and the company's appeal was dismissed.

Comment: This case demonstrates that under the relevant Regulations there is in fact a duty on employers to guard against employees who may act in such a way that is not reasonably foreseeable by the employers. Generally speaking, the Regulations relating to electricity and other extremely hazardous work situations e.g. confined spaces, tend to be strict duties, e.g. not qualified by the words 'reasonably practicable'.

Fencing of Machinery

John Summers & Sons Ltd v Frost (24 March 1955) House of Lords ([1955] 1 All ER 870)

[A13.1]

grindstone; workman's thumb; breach of statutory duty; Factories Act 1937

Background: A maintenance fitter employed by John Summers & Sons Ltd injured his thumb whilst grinding a piece of metal. The grindstone was partially fenced by a hood; only an area about seven inches long was exposed at the front of the machinery. Mr Frost alleged breach of statutory duty under *section 14(1)* of the *Factories Act 1937* which requires that every dangerous part of any machinery shall be securely fenced. His action was unsuccessful and the judge held that the real cause of the accident was his own negligence. This decision was reversed by the Court of Appeal and John Summers & Sons Ltd then appealed to the House of Lords.

Test: *Section 14(1)* of the 1937 Act imposes an absolute obligation on the employer. A dangerous part of machinery is securely fenced only if the presence of that fencing means it is not dangerous in that a reasonably foreseeable risk of injury to the user of the machinery no longer exists, even if he is careless or inattentive (*Mitchell v North British Rubber Co Ltd [1945] SC (J) 69*).

Decision: In this case, the House of Lords found that the grinding wheel was a dangerous part of machinery within *section 14(1)* and that it was not securely fenced. John Summers & Sons Ltd had breached its duty under that section, notwithstanding that securely fencing the machine to meet this statutory requirement would render the grindstone commercially unusable. Further, Mr Frost had not been guilty of contributory negligence.

Comment: The meaning of the term 'securely fenced' was considered in this case. The issue turned on construction of the particular statute in terms of the nature of the obligation imposed. Many statutory duties have a mechanism for dealing with the situation where strict compliance would be impractical and this prevents strict liability from arising in certain situations. For instance, certain statutes and obligations are qualified by the words 'so far as is reasonably practicable'.

Uddin v Associated Portland Cement Manufacturers Ltd (23 March 1965) Court of Appeal ([1965] 2 All ER 213)

[A13.2]

employee; unfenced machinery; personal injury; damages; breach of statutory duty

Background: Associated Portland Cement Manufacturers Ltd operated a cement grading and packing factory. On the second and third floors of the factory, the plant for packing the cement and collecting the dust produced by this activity was adjacent. However no direct access was provided between these areas. Mr Uddin, a machinery attendant who worked on these floors, descended to the first floor and climbed a ladder to a platform where the dust extraction machinery was located. He was not authorised to be in that location. The dust extraction machinery was fitted with a horizontal revolving shaft which was a dangerous part of machinery for the purposes of *section 14(1)* of the *Factories Act 1937*. The shaft was not fenced off and when Mr Uddin leaned over in an attempt to catch a pigeon, his clothing caught in the shaft and he was injured. Mr Uddin brought an action for damages against his employer. The High Court ruled that Associated Portland Cement Manufacturers Ltd had breached its statutory duty under *section 14(1)* of the 1937 Act by failing to fence the dangerous machinery. However, responsibility for the accident was apportioned as four fifths to Mr Uddin because his act of extreme folly was outside what could reasonably be anticipated. Accordingly, the damages were reduced by eighty per cent. The company appealed, arguing that: it had not breached *section 14* of the 1937 Act; that even if there had been a breach, the company owned no duty to Mr Uddin; and that, in any event, Mr Uddin's negligence meant that he should not be able to recover damages or that he should only be awarded a nominal percentage of those damages.

Test: The Court of Appeal considered two issues: did Mr Uddin have any cause of action under the *Factories Act 1937*; and, if so, should he be awarded as high a proportion of damages as twenty per cent in view of his own negligence and folly. *Section 14(1)* of the *Factories Act 1937* requires that: 'Every dangerous part of any machinery, other than prime movers and transmission machinery, shall be securely fenced unless it is in such a position or of such construction as to be as safe to every person employed or working on the premises as it would be if securely fenced.'

Decision: The Court of Appeal held that an employee was entitled to this protection even though he had left his allotted work for a private purpose and was not working or acting within the scope of his employment when the accident occurred. Associated Portland Cement Manufacturers Ltd was liable to Mr Uddin for breach of statutory duty. The company's appeal was dismissed. On the question of the apportionment of damages, the court held that this was peculiarly within the province of the trial judge. Although less blame might have been placed on the employers, in the absence of any error of principle, there was no justification for substituting another proportion for that already awarded.

Comment: The case considered the expression 'every person employed on the premises'. It was held that if a building as a whole constitutes office premises, the protection applies to all parts of it and protects employees even when acting outside the scope of their employment. This case was approved in *Westwood v Post Office (1974) AC 1*. The case illustrates the principle that in relation to breach of statutory duty, it is generally unnecessary to show that an employee was injured in the course of employment. *Uddin* was applied in *Allen v Aeroplane and Motor Aluminium Castings [1965] 1 WLR 1244*. Although it was held that where an accident happens which would not have occurred but for the breach and the relevant act is in the course of the injured man's employment, the factory owner can be held liable in damages even if the precise way in which the accident happened is unexplained.

Fines and Penalties

R v F Howe & Son (Engineers) Ltd (6 November 1998) Court of Appeal) ([1999] IRLR 434)

[A14.1]

sentencing guidelines; level of fines

Background: The case involved the appeal by F Howe & Son (Engineers) Ltd against a fine of £48,000 for four separate breaches of the *HSWA 1974* and related legislation.

Decision: The Court of Appeal allowed the appeal and substituted a fine of £15,000. The court also took the opportunity to detail some of the factors which should be taken into account by judges and magistrates when deciding the level of fine to impose for such health and safety offences. The judge stated it was necessary to look at how far below the appropriate standard the employer had fallen in failing to satisfy the test of what was reasonably practicable. The judge pointed out that the size of the company or its financial strength were irrelevant when looking at the standard of care which should be reached. The same standard applied across the board. Relevant factors regarding the level of fine included the degree of risk, the extent of the breach and the company's ability to pay the fine and the effect on its business. If the company was attempting to claim that it did not have the financial resources to pay the fine, it should produce before the court supporting accounts and other financial information. Failure to do so would result in the court fairly concluding that the company had the requisite resources to satisfy the penalty imposed. If the accounts were produced late, an adjournment for sentencing might be appropriate. The judge highlighted certain features, which if present, would be aggravating features of the offence and might increase the penalty imposed. Examples given of such features were: death of the employee; a deliberate breach with a view to profit from failure to take necessary steps; the running of a risk in order to save money and failure to take note of previous warnings. In addition, the judge pointed out various mitigating factors which the court would acknowledge such as a good health and safety record, a guilty plea and prompt steps taken to alleviate any breach. In relation to costs, it was noted by the judge that if the defendant appeared able to meet the whole of the prosecution's costs, there was no reason why the court should not make such an award.

Comment: This case sets down particularly useful guidelines concerning the imposition of fines. The case is also significant in its attempt to deal with the increasing criticism faced by courts for imposing inadequate fines for health and safety offences and their failure to reduce the uncertainty surrounding the basis on which fines are assessed. Similar criticism has been made of the courts in relation to fine levels for offences relating to the environment.

R v Rollco Screw & Rivet Co Ltd (26 March 1999) Court of Appeal ([1999] IRLR 439)

[A14.2]

asbestos offences; penalties; length of period for payment; fines

Background: Heavy penalties were imposed on Rollco Screw & Rivet Co Ltd and its two directors who pleaded guilty to two offences under the *HSWA 1974*. This followed an incident in which an asbestos roof had been removed from the company's factory. The directors had contracted the removal work to another company which in turn had engaged a sub-contractor. Neither of the contractors had the necessary asbestos licence required for such work; inadequate safety precautions were taken and asbestos was spread over the factory, endangering employees and the public. Waste asbestos was also dumped in unmarked bags in a number of locations around Birmingham. In the Crown Court, the company was fined £40,000 and ordered to pay costs of £30,000. £5,000 had to be paid within the first year and £1,000 each month thereafter, making a total period of six years and five months. The directors were fined a total of £10,000, plus £4,000 costs. They appealed, claiming that the penalty was grossly excessive and beyond the company's means, and that the period over which the sum was to be payable was also excessive.

Decision: *R v F Howe & Son (Engineers) Ltd [1999]* sets out the principles that should be applied when determining fines in health and safety cases. In this case, the proper approach was to pose two questions: first, what financial penalty does the offence merit; and secondly, what financial penalty can the defendant reasonably be ordered to meet (and over what time period should it be payable)? Fines should be imposed that emphasise the personal responsibilities of directors. However, in small companies, where directors are likely to be the shareholders, the effect of this may be a double punishment. A longer payment period may be acceptable for companies, as this may give a greater opportunity to control cash flow and survive difficult trading conditions. The Court of Appeal held that although the level of fine imposed was fully justified, the length of period for payment was excessive. This was reduced from six years and five months to five years and seven months by reducing the costs order by £10,000 to £20,000. Otherwise the sentence remained the same.

Comment: This case clearly illustrates the point that in terms of discharging health and safety obligations, the size of the employer is not a relevant consideration when determining whether the particular obligations have been adequately discharged. If this was not the case, the employee of a small to medium sized enterprise would find himself at greater risk than an employee of a large one. The size of the company is only of relevance in terms of how a company discharges its health and safety obligations. A large company with a department managing health and safety matters will approach the area differently to a smaller company, with perhaps only one safety officer or none at all. Those organisations, which do not have their own expertise in house, could contact the HSE to obtain a level of assistance e.g. in order to obtain relevant codes of practice, guidance or information in certain areas.

Hearing Damage

Mulcahy v Ministry of Defence (21 February 1996) Court of Appeal (Times Law Reports, 27 February 1996)

[A15.1]

soldier; hearing damage

Background: A soldier's hearing was damaged when a shell was fired from a howitzer by a colleague during the Gulf War. Mr Mulcahy sought damages for personal injuries from the Ministry of Defence, claiming that it was vicariously liable for the other soldier's negligence. The Ministry of Defence appealed against the refusal to strike out the claim as having no reasonable cause of action.

Decision: Although the elements of proximity and foreseeability of damage were present in this case (*Marc Rich & Co v Bishop Rock Marine Co Ltd [1995] 3 WLR 227*), it was also necessary to consider whether it was fair, just or reasonable to impose a duty of care on a soldier in his conduct to another when engaging the enemy. The same issue also applied when considering the Ministry of Defence's duty to maintain a safe system of work. The Court of Appeal held that one soldier did not owe a duty of care in tort to another when on active service. Neither was there a duty on the Ministry of Defence to maintain a safe system of work under battle conditions. Mr Mulcahy did not therefore have a cause of action in negligence against the Ministry of Defence. The appeal was allowed and the action dismissed.

Comment: This case demonstrated the special treatment given to battle conditions when considering the duties of employers and the duties of care that may be owed by one soldier to another.

The position of the police in battle conditions could be treated analogously to this.

Berry v Stone Manganese & Marine Ltd (6 December 1971) High Court, Queen's Bench Division ([1972] 1 Lloyd's Report 182)

[A15.2]

noise; protective equipment; employer's liability; limitation; damages

Background: Mr Berry was employed by Stone Manganese & Marine Ltd, in work involving the use of a pneumatic hammer on metal. As a result of the noise he became deaf and, in 1970, issued proceedings against the company on the grounds that his deafness was caused by its breach of duty.

When he started work in 1957, he was given protective ear plugs but, contrary to the manufacturer's instructions, the company failed to ensure that they were fitted properly. It was admitted that ear muffs would have given appropriate protection, but Mr Berry was only provided with ear muffs in 1966. He found them uncomfortable and so only wore them for one day. He was provided with a new, more comfortable, design in 1970, but still did not wear them.

The company argued that it had no duty to supply ear muffs until 1963. They claimed that even if it had done so before then, Mr Berry would not have worn them, and that his claim was statute barred except for negligence occurring since 1967.

Decision: On the question of the company's negligence, the judge found that it was in breach of its duty to take reasonable care in respect of the ear plugs; that ear muffs were available; that the company was or should have been aware by 1957 that men working in the pneumatic hammer area were going deaf; and that if the company had taken advice at that point, ear muffs would have been recommended. Consequently, it was in breach of its duty by failing to provide ear muffs from 1957.

On the point about the use of the ear muffs, the judge recognised that in certain cases it could be argued that the employer was not the cause of an injury where the employee would have refused to use protective equipment, even if it had been provided. However, he ruled that the employer had a duty to use some form of propaganda to persuade the employees to use the equipment. In this case, the company had not done this, and the judge considered that, had it done so, Mr Berry would have complied.

On the limitation point (based on the *Limitation Act 1963*), the judge held that Mr Berry could only claim damages back to 1967 i.e. three years back from 1970 when he started proceedings. He had been aware by 1960 that he was going deaf and that protection was needed and that other workers were going deaf because of their work. He also had appreciated that the ear muffs supplied in 1966 kept out far more sound than the ear plugs. Consequently, he could reasonably have been expected to have sought advice. Thus he did have constructive knowledge of his cause of action before 1967. On the issue of damages, however, the judge considered that £2,500 would have been appropriate for the whole eleven years of damage, but rejected the idea that, to arrive at a sum for the four years since 1967, four-elevenths of that sum should be calculated. He ruled that this did not give sufficient weight to the fact that to make a deaf person more deaf increased their handicap considerably, and awarded £1,250.

Comment: The obligation on employers to safeguard the health and safety of their employees implies a duty to go further than merely provide employees with protective equipment. Factors which dissuaded the employees from wearing the protective equipment were factors which should have been overcome by the use of persuasion and propaganda by the employers in order to adequately discharge their duty.

Thompson and Others v Smiths Shiprepairers (North Shields) Ltd and other actions (14 November 1983) High Court, Queen's Bench Division ([1984] 1 All ER 881)

[A15.3]

shipyard employees; hearing loss; ear protection; information; advice and protective equipment

Background: The hearing of a number of men who had been employed in shipyards was impaired by the high levels of noise at their workplaces. During the period of their employment (1940s or earlier to the 1970s), the employers knew that the noise levels experienced by their employees exposed them to a risk of hearing loss. However, no protective equipment was provided until the 1970s and there was a general feeling throughout the shipbuilding sector that high noise exposure was an unavoidable feature of that industry. No official guidance or expert advice on the problem was available until 1963. Actions were brought in 1980 and 1981, claiming that the employer's negligence in failing to provide ear protection or to assess and take advice on noise levels had caused the damage to the plaintiffs' hearing. Although it was impossible to determine how much hearing damage had been caused before 1963, on the facts, it was established that a substantial part of the damage had already occurred and that exposure to noise after this date had only aggravated an existing problem and accelerated the progress to hearing disability and handicap. It was admitted by the employer's that their employees' hearing had been damaged by noise exposure at work. They also argued that their failure to provide protection was only an actionable nuisance from 1963 and they were only liable for the damage caused after that date.

Decision: The High Court held that the appropriate test to be used to determine the date from which the employer's failure to provide ear protection devices amounted to actionable negligence was what would have been done by a reasonable and prudent employer, with proper but not extraordinary solicitude for his employees' welfare in the light of what he knew or ought to have known at the time. There would be no negligence if an employer was following a recognised practice common to an industry sector for a substantial time, even if that practice was not without mishap and the consequences of high noise exposure were considered an unavoidable feature of that industry. Also, whether an employer was negligent in not taking the initiative to seek out knowledge about facts which were not obvious was to be judged according to practice at the time in the industry (*Stokes v GKN (Bolts and Nuts) Ltd [1968] 1 WLR 1776*; *Morris v West Hartlepool Steam Navigation Co Ltd [1956] 1 All ER 385*). Using this test, the court found that the employer's failure was only actionable negligence from 1963. The plaintiffs could only recover damages for the additional impairment of their hearing that occurred in the period when the failure to provide ear protection became a breach of the employers' duty of care (i.e. from 1963). It was not possible therefore for the plaintiffs to recover all their loss although allowances in their favour should be made by the court to take account of the uncertainties involved in making such an apportionment.

Comment: The issue under consideration in this case was how the state of knowledge in an industry can affect duties owed by employers to their employees. The defendant employer was only allowed to rely on the defence of general inaction in the industry up until the time when knowledge and protection became available. The employer is obliged to keep up to date with developing knowledge in the field of areas of risk to employees.

McCafferty v Metropolitan Police District Receiver (1 February 1977) Court of Appeal ([1977] 2 All ER 756)

[A15.4]

ballistics expert; damaged hearing; noise

Background: Mr McCafferty, a ballistics expert, suffered from tinnitus. This condition arose because his workplace had not been properly sound proofed and he had not been provided with suitable ear protection. No investigations had been carried out by his employer to assess whether there was any risk of damage to his hearing. After complaining about ringing in his ears, Mr McCafferty used cotton wool on the advice of scientists at his work until he was told in 1967 that this offered insufficient protection. He then asked for ear muffs which were provided by his employer. Later that year, he consulted an ear specialist who diagnosed a hearing defect caused by acoustic trauma. He was advised that no further damage would result if he continued to wear the ear muffs. Mr McCafferty did not inform his employer about the hearing problem. A further check in 1969 indicated that there was no significant change in his hearing. In 1973, however, a routine audiogram conducted by his employer showed severe damage to his hearing and his employment was terminated on medical grounds. A subsequent hearing test showed that there had been no substantial change in his hearing since 1967 and the serious trauma identified in 1973 was temporary. Mr McCafferty claimed damages from the Metropolitan Police Receiver for negligence on the grounds that his hearing had been severely damaged by 1967 and his career prematurely terminated in 1973. He alleged that his employer had failed to take reasonable measures to protect his hearing and knew or ought to have known of the danger to which he was exposed. The High Court found that the Metropolitan Police Receiver had been negligent and that Mr McCafferty was not guilty of any contributory negligence in not finding out about safety requirements and protective equipment. The Metropolitan Police Receiver appealed.

Decision: The Court of Appeal held that the Metropolitan Police Receiver had been negligent in failing in its duty as a careful employer to take reasonable care to protect Mr McCafferty from the foreseeable risk of danger to his health. It should have been apparent that there was a risk of hearing damage associated with the firing of guns in the plaintiff's working place and competent advice on suitable precautions should have been taken. If such action had been taken, Mr McCafferty's hearing would probably not have been damaged to the extent that he would need to retire early. There was no evidence that Mr McCafferty had been clearly instructed to investigate the potential risks of his workplace and he was not a suitable person to do so as he did not have the relevant expertise. It was also held that Mr McCafferty was not guilty of contributory negligence because he was entitled to take the advice of scientists that cotton wool provided adequate protection and was also told that ear muffs would be sufficient. The appeal was dismissed.

Comment: This case confirmed that an employer cannot escape liability for injury to an employee by delegating responsibility for safety precautions to the employee. The employer in this case, and other similar cases, should, in the absence of having the necessary expertise or material available, look elsewhere for guidance.

Insurance

Morris v Ford Motor Co Ltd, Cameron Industrial Services Ltd (Third Party), Roberts (Fourth Party) (27 March 1973) Court of Appeal ([1973] 2 All ER 1084)

[A16.1]

idemnity clause; vicarious liability; doctrine of subrogation; insurance

Background: Cameron Industrial Services Ltd was contracted to provide cleaning services for Ford Motor Co Ltd. The contract contained a clause under which Ford Motor Co Ltd would be indemnified for all losses or claims for injury or damage arising out of or in connection with the cleaning operations. There was also a statement advising Cameron Industrial Services Ltd to obtain insurance to cover liability under the indemnity clause. Mr Morris, the plaintiff and an employee of Cameron Industrial Services Ltd, was injured as a result of the negligence of a Ford Motor Co Ltd employee. He brought an action against that company alleging that it was vicariously liable for the negligence of its employee and the claim was settled. Ford Motor Co Ltd brought Cameron Industrial Services Ltd into the action as a third party, claiming an indemnity in respect of its liability to Mr Morris. In turn, Cameron Industrial Services Ltd made the negligent Ford Motor Co Ltd employee a fourth party to the action on the ground that it was entitled to be subrogated to Ford Motor Co Ltd's right to recover damages and costs from the negligent employee. In practice, however, Ford Motor Co Ltd would not have sought to enforce that right because of the likelihood of industrial action. Similarly, the company's insurer would not have brought a claim against the negligent employee because of a gentleman's agreement made by members of the British Insurers Association. Cameron Industrial Services Ltd was not aware of such facts. Its claim was upheld and the fourth party, Mr Roberts, appealed.

Decision: Cameron Industrial Services Ltd's claim was dismissed by the Court of Appeal and Mr Robert's appeal allowed. Under the contract with Ford Motor Co Ltd, Cameron Industrial Services Ltd was entitled to be subrogated to the defendant's right of action against its employee. The exception to this was where it could be shown that the contract of indemnity by implication excluded that right or alternatively that it was not just or equitable to compel the defendant to lend its name to an action by the third party against the employee. In this case, the contract of indemnity was operative in an industrial setting in which it was unacceptable and unrealistic for the third party to be subrogated to the rights of the defendant. There should have been an implied term in the contract whereby the right of subrogation was excluded. Alternatively, it was neither just nor equitable to compel the defendant to lend its name to an action against its employee when it was likely to lead to industrial action. Further, it was unjust to make the fourth party personally liable because his employer was insured against the risk of his negligence and Cameron Industrial Services Ltd had been advised in the contract of indemnity to insure against its liability under the indemnity.

Comment: Although the case involved a detailed examination of the doctrine of subrogation and where, in particular instances the doctrine should not apply, the case is also of interest in terms of the issue of obtaining insurance to cover liabilities arising under an indemnity given by one party to another. In this particular case, this was especially so when the contract between the parties expressly indicated that insurance cover should be extended to specifically respond to particular risks. The case is a salient reminder that when granting indemnities, consideration should be given as to whether any existing insurance held would respond to the increased risks. One further point to consider, although not discussed in the case, is that even if an existing policy would respond to the 'new' risk, the question arises as to whether the notification clause in the policy requires that the insurance company be informed of the 'new' risk.

Bradley v Eagle Star Insurance Co Ltd (2 March 1989) House of Lords ([1989] 1 All ER 961)

[A16.2]

byssinosis; cotton mill; third party liability insurance; discovery; employer wound up

Background: In 1970, Mrs Bradley was certified as suffering from byssinosis, a respiratory condition caused by the inhalation of cotton dust. It was alleged that she contracted the disease as a result of her employment with Dart Mill Ltd during the period 1933–1970. That company was voluntarily wound up in 1975 and dissolved in 1976. Dart Mill Ltd had third party liability insurance with Eagle Star Insurance Co Ltd during her period of employment. In 1984, Mrs Bradley decided to bring an action against the insurer under *section 1(1)* of the *Third Parties (Rights against Insurers) Act 1930*, which transfers the tortfeasor's rights against insurers to the plaintiff. An application was made in 1986 for pre-action discovery of the insurance policies issued to Dart Mill Ltd. Although an order was made for disclosure, this was set aside on appeal, a decision upheld by the Court of Appeal. Mrs Bradley then appealed to the House of Lords.

Decision: To succeed in her action for discovery, Mrs Bradley had to show that there was a reasonable prospect of success against Eagle Star Insurance Co Ltd under the 1930 Act. Under an insurance policy against liability to third parties, the insured person cannot sue for an indemnity from the insurer unless and until the existence and amount of liability has been determined. Where such liability cannot be established because the insured has been wound up, no right of indemnity can be transferred to a third party pursuant to *section 1(1)* of the 1930 Act. Any action by Mrs Bradley would be bound to fail so an order for discovery would serve no purpose. The appeal was dismissed.

Comment: The position that under an indemnity policy an insured has no right of action against his insurer until his own liability to the injured person has been established was accepted as 'unassailably correct' by this case.

Bradburn v The Great Western Railway Company (6 November 1874) Court of Exchequer ([1874] LR Exch 1)

[A16.3]

accident insurance policy; damages; negligence

Background: Mr Bradburn was injured due to the negligence of the Great Western Railway Company whilst he was travelling as a passenger on a train. In the subsequent action for damages for personal injury, the defendant argued that Mr Bradburn's compensation should be reduced to take account of an amount he had received under an accident insurance policy.

Decision: The Court of Exchequer held that in an action for personal injury caused by negligence, any sum received by the plaintiff under an accident insurance policy should not be deducted from the damages award. This followed the principle laid down in *Dalby v India and London Life Assurance Company (15 CB 365)* that a plaintiff is entitled to retain the benefit he has paid for in addition to the damages which he recovers on account of the defendant's negligence. The plaintiff did not receive the money because of the accident but because he had made a contract providing for the contingency; the contract was the cause of his receiving the money, not the accident.

Comment: This case concerned the position relating to the receipt of other benefits after injury caused by another's wrongful act. The long standing principle is basically that where an injured individual benefits because they have planned for a contingency e.g. personal accident insurance, then that person should be no worse off in a claim for damages against the tortfeasor. The wrong doer should not obtain the benefit of the injured person's sagacious act and foresight.

Lead

Hewett v Alf Brown's Transport Ltd and Others (29 January 1992) Court of Appeal (Times Law Reports, 4 February 1992)

[A17.1]

employee's wife; lead poisoning; employee; duty of care to wife

Background: Mrs Hewett was diagnosed as suffering from lead poisoning. She alleged that her exposure to lead was due to the cleaning of her husband's work clothes. Mr Hewett was employed by Alf Brown's Transport Ltd to drive lorries loaded with waste, including lead oxide. An action was brought against the company for personal injury caused by negligence and breach of statutory duty under the *Control of Lead at Work Regulations 1980 (SI 1980 No 1248)*. The High Court dismissed the claim. It found that Mr Hewett had not been exposed to a significant risk of lead poisoning so his employer had not been negligent or breached its statutory duty of care to him. The company therefore owed no duty to Mrs Hewett and could not be liable for the injury she suffered. The plaintiff appealed.

Decision: The Court of Appeal held that the High Court's finding that Mr Hewett's exposure to lead was insignificant was correct. Although the employer owed a duty of care to members of an employee's family in respect of foreseeable risk, in the absence of significant exposure to lead dust, there was no duty to take precautions to ensure Mr Hewett's safety. His wife could not establish negligence or breach of statutory duty with regard to her condition. The appeal was dismissed.

Comment: The plaintiff suffered lead poisoning as a result of washing the clothes of her husband who worked for the defendants. The plaintiff's husband was not in fact closely involved in the demolition process, which had given rise to lead poisoning among other employees. The relevant regulation was *Regulation 8* of the *Control of Lead at Work Regulations 1980*, which provides 'every employer shall provide each employee who is liable to be exposed to lead with adequate protective clothing unless the exposure to lead is not significant.' Therefore, the central issue was to determine whether the lead to which the plaintiff's husband was exposed was significant. As the exposure was deemed to be insignificant then the possible claim of the wife was not allowed. See also exposure of a wife to asbestos in *Bryce v Swan Hunter Group plc and Others [1987]* (see paragraph A4.3).

Lifting Equipment

Beadsley and Others v United Steel Companies Ltd (12 October 1950) Court of Appeal ([1950] 2 All ER 872)

[A18.1]

lifting equipment; breach of statutory duty

Background: Mr Beadsley was injured and died after a heavy mould which was being lifted became unfastened and fell. United Steel Companies Ltd had provided the proper equipment for moving moulds but on the day of the accident, a colleague of Mr Beadsley had used other lifting equipment in which the mould was not securely fastened. A successful action was brought against the company by Mr Beadsley's widow and children, alleging breach of statutory duty under *section 23(1)* of the *Factories Act 1937* which requires that no chain, rope or lifting tackle will be used unless it is of good construction, sound material, adequate strength and free from patent defect. United Steel Companies Ltd appealed.

Decision: The Court of Appeal held that the company had not breached *section 23(1)* of the 1937 Act. That section only required that equipment which is of good construction, sound material, adequate strength and free from patent defect should be provided; this requirement had been fulfilled by the company. United Steel Companies Ltd should not be liable under that section for an accident caused by a workman using the wrong tackle. The appeal was allowed.

Comment: This case should be considered bearing in mind the obligations arising under the *Provision and Use of Work Equipment Regulations 1998 (SI 1998 No 2306)* and the relevant Code of

Practice (the Regulations and Code are of relevance to mobile plant and lifting equipment).

Gledhill v Liverpool Abattoir Utility Co Ltd and Another (21 February 1957) Court of Appeal ([1957] 3 All ER 117)

[A18.2]

lifting tackle; abbattoir; knowledge; danger

Background: Lifting tackle was used to transport pigs in an abattoir, consisting of chains which were placed around the animals legs. New chains had been provided by the owner of the abattoir, Liverpool Corporation, which were strong and without fault but which were unsuitable for the work as they were heavier than the old chains and less able to hold the animals. There had been several occasions when pigs had fallen due to the unsuitability of the new chains. Complaints had been made by employees to their employer, Liverpool Abattoir Utility Co Ltd, but these had not been relayed to Liverpool Corporation. One employee, Mr Gledhill, was injured when a pig slipped from the chains and fell on him. He brought an action against his employer, alleging negligence and failure to maintain a safe system of work. Liverpool Abattoir Utility Co Ltd denied liability and pleaded that the accident was the fault of Liverpool Corporation as it had breached *sections 23* and *24* of the *Factories Act 1937*. The plaintiff then also joined Liverpool Corporation as defendants. In the High Court, the employer and owner of the abattoir were both found to be liable to Mr Gledhill with each contributing fifty per cent of the damages. Liverpool Corporation appealed.

Decision: In the Court of Appeal, it was held that Liverpool Corporation had not breached its statutory duty under either *section 23* or *24* of the 1937 Act. Under *section 23*,the requirement that chains should be of good construction and adequate strength, 'good construction' did not require that a chain should be suitable for the particular task to be performed (*Beadsley and Others v United Steel Companies Ltd [1950]*) and using a stronger chain than necessary was not a breach of the obligation to use only chains of adequate strength. Neither had Liverpool Corporation breached *section 24*, requiring that the chain should be properly maintained. Further, as the plaintiff had full and complete knowledge of the problems associated with the use of the chains, this defeated his claim against the Liverpool Corporation at common law. The Corporation had no duty to the plaintiff at common law. Liability to the plaintiff rested solely with his employer and the appeal was allowed.

Comment: The importance of knowledge as far as unusual dangers are concerned was explored in this case. The knowledge in question must be full knowledge of the nature and extent of the danger. If a claimant discovers a defect he then 'cannot complain in respect of whatever mischief follows because it follows from his conscious volition in choosing to incur the risk or certainty of mischance' per Lord Wright in *Grant v Australian Knitting Mills [1936] AC 85*. This can be contrasted with situations involving urgency, as a plaintiff who acts reasonably in the circumstances, when there is a situation of urgency, will not be barred merely because he was aware of the risk he was running.

Ball v Richard Thomas and Baldwins Ltd (28 November 1967) Court of Appeal ([1968] 1 All ER 389)

[A18.3]

crane; breach of statutory duty; contributory negligence

Background: A workman was injured when the hook of a crane lost its purchase on a load and hit him in the face. The load was a 'scab' of molten metal which had been spilt onto the floor in a steel works. The crane was being used to raise one edge of the scab and it would then be completely loosened using welding equipment and lifted away by the crane. The workman was very experienced in this task and was fully aware of the potential dangers. At the time of the accident, however, he was standing within nine feet of the hook which he knew to be less than the safe distance. In the High Court, the employer was found to be in breach of its statutory duty under *section 26(1)* of the *Factories Act 1961*.

Decision: *Section 26(1)* of the 1961 Act requires that only lifting tackle which is of adequate strength may be used for the purpose of raising materials. The Court of Appeal held that the operation undertaken at the time of the accident did involve raising materials within the meaning of this section, despite the fact that the scab was not a calculable load and it was not therefore possible to determine what strength would be adequate strength. On the facts, it was held that the hook was not of adequate strength for its intended use (*Milne v C F Wilson & Co (1932) Ltd [1960] SLT 162*) and that there had therefore been a breach of duty under *section 26(1)*. As this breach had causally contributed to the accident, the company was liable to pay damages to the plaintiff. The appeal was allowed. The decision that the plaintiff's responsibility for the accident was twenty five per cent was upheld.

Comment: This case considers the issue of contributory negligence and highlights the fact that there is a very significant difference between (1) a plaintiff who stands in a dangerous place through mere inadvertence, done in the furtherance of his job and his employer's interests and (2) a plaintiff, who knows there is a risk, and that it is dangerous to stand within range, and could avoid standing in the dangerous place, in which instance the plaintiff will be guilty of negligence.

Galashiels Gas Co Ltd v O'Donnell (or Millar) (20 January 1949) House of Lords ([1949] 1 All ER 319)

[A18.4]

lift shaft; damages; duty to maintain; breach of statutory duty

Background: A failure in the braking mechanism of a lift at the defendant's gas works meant that the lift continued to move upwards in its shaft after an employee had exited the lift cage to empty a load. When he returned, having left the lift cage gates open, he fell down the shaft and was killed. The lift was examined but no problem could be found to account for the failure. The victim's widow brought a successful action for damages against Galashiels Gas Co Ltd and the company appealed to the House of Lords, claiming that in the absence of proof as to the defect that had caused the accident, there was no case and it was only under a duty to take such action as would ensure that the lift was in efficient working order.

Test: *Section 22(1)* of the *Factories Act 1937* requires that: 'Every hoist or lift shall be of good mechanical construction, sound material and adequate strength, and be properly maintained'. In this context, 'maintained' means maintained in an efficient state, in efficient working order and in good repair (*section 152(1)* of the 1937 Act).

Decision: Although it had been found by a lower court that the company had taken every practical step to ensure that the lift mechanism was working properly and was safe to use, the House of Lords held that the wording 'shall be ... properly maintained' in *section 22(1)*, taken together with the definition of 'maintained' in *section 152(1)*, imposes an absolute and continuing obligation on the employer. Nothing in the Act suggested that there should be any qualification of that obligation. It was only necessary to prove that the mechanism of the lift had failed to work efficiently and that that failure had caused the accident. The victim's widow had done so and the appeal was dismissed.

Comment: This case centred on statutory interpretation and the meaning of the word 'maintained' in the context of the relevant Act. This was held to import a duty on the employer to take such active steps as are necessary to ensure that the equipment is in proper working order. Despite the fact that this places a somewhat onerous burden on employers, the duty to maintain is a strict or absolute duty and neither intention nor lack of care need be shown in order to prove a breach of it. The ordinary use of language was relied on, and it was made clear that one cannot be said to maintain a piece of machinery in working order over a given period, if, on occasion within that period, the machinery, for whatever reason, is not in efficient working order. The statute specifies the result to be achieved rather than the means of achieving it. The defendants were thus found liable in breach of statutory duty albeit that they had no reason to believe that their lift, which crashed and killed a workman, was in anything other than perfect working order.

Blakeley v C & H Clothing Co and Another (17 December 1957) Crown Court ([1958] 1 All ER 297)

[A18.5]

lift; personal injury; damages; breach of statutory duty

Background: An employee of C & H Clothing Co had used a lift at his place of work. On exiting the lift, he shut the gates but put his hand through the outer gate to check that the inner gate was properly closed. At that moment, the lift began to move and his hand was injured. An action for damages was brought against both the employer and the owner of the premises who had control of the lift.

Decision: The Crown Court held that the employer had not been negligent. The court found that the owner of the premises had breached its duty under *section 22(3)* of the *Factories Act 1937*, requiring that a liftway should be efficiently protected by an enclosure to prevent any person coming into contact with any moving part of the lift when the gates are shut. This duty was absolute and the fact that a person could put a hand though the gate meant that the section had been breached.

Comment: This case concerned the statutory duties resting on employers, and the fact that obligations which were imposed by statute, such as the duty to adequately enclose a lift, are absolute obligations. The words were given their ordinary meaning and it was held that they did indeed impose an absolute duty on the employer.

Holmes v Hadfields Ltd (19 January 1944) Court of Appeal ([1944] 1 All ER 235)

[B18.6]

crane; personal injury; damages; breach of statutory duty; contributory negligence

Background: Mr Holmes' work was to use a ratchet drill on a platform. The wheel track of an overhead travelling crane was close by and it was possible for the crane to pass within twenty feet of the platform. Just prior to his accident, Mr Holmes left the platform because of the approach of the crane and climbed down to a girder eight feet below. However, the crane knocked the drill from the platform and he was injured. In the subsequent action for damages for breach of statutory duty under *section 24(7)* of the *Factories Act 1937*, the court found against Mr Holmes because he was guilty of contributory negligence in having signalled that it was safe for the crane to continue. The plaintiff appealed.

Decision: *Section 24(7)* of the 1937 Act requires that where a person is employed on or near to the wheel track of an overhead travelling crane in a place where he is liable to be struck, effective measures shall be taken by warning the crane driver or otherwise to ensure that the crane does not approach within twenty feet of that place. Hadfields Ltd contended that at the time of the accident Mr Holmes was not standing in a place where he was liable to be struck and that he was injured by the drill and not the crane. The Court of Appeal held however that as the duty under *section 24(7)* is absolute (*Lotinga v North Eastern Marine Engineering Co [1941] 3 All ER 1*), the company had breached that section in allowing the crane to come within twenty feet of the platform. Further, on the true construction of the section, it was immaterial whether the plaintiff was in a place where he was not liable to be struck or that the object which injured him was not part of the crane. On the facts, there was no contributory negligence by Mr Holmes. The appeal was allowed.

Comment: This case demonstrated that an employer can be held to have breached its statutory duty where it fails to conform to the statutory obligation relating to safety and allows the system to be replaced by a private safety system of its own. Further, where the system is one where the men are expected to look out for their own safety, and that system depends on the accurate giving and receiving of signals which are liable to be misunderstood, then the appellant cannot be guilty of contributory negligence. Principles of statutory interpretation were examined. In particular, a defendant should not be held liable merely because, by reason of his failure to perform that duty, some injury was suffered by the plaintiff. It must also be shown that the injury suffered by the plaintiff was an injury of a kind contemplated by the statute. A reasonable person's contemplation of injuries, which may be envisaged by the statute, should be adopted. The interrelationship between statutory obligations and common law were also considered, and it was held that in this case, having succeeded on breach of statutory duty, the appellant had no need to argue breach of employers' common law duties.

Oldfield v Reed & Smith Ltd (24 November 1971) High Court, Exeter Assizes ([1972] 2 All ER 104)

[B18.7]

falling load; duty to properly maintain; section 22 of Factories Act 1961; fork lift truck; hoist or lift

Background: A fork lift truck used in the factory of Reed & Smith Ltd appeared to have a faulty fork. Mr Oldfield, a chargehand fitter with responsibility for maintaining the fork lift trucks, was examining the equipment when a reel of paper used to test the equipment fell off and crushed his foot. He brought proceedings against Reed & Smith Ltd, alleging that his injury was caused by its negligence and/or breach of statutory duty under *section 22(1)* of the *Factories Act 1961* in that his employer had failed to properly maintain a hoist or lift.

Decision: As an employer's duty under *section 22(1)* of the 1961 Act is absolute (*Galashiels Gas Co Ltd v O'Donnell [1949],* see paragraph A18.4), if the forklift truck came within the definition of 'hoist or lift', there would be a breach. The High Court found that this was not the case and Reed & Smith Ltd had not breached its statutory duty under that section. Further, even if a breach had been proved it was necessary to show that the breach had caused the accident for the plaintiff to be entitled to damages. The court found that the cause of the accident was the plaintiff's own negligence in that he had been standing too close to the truck and had not secured the load properly. His claim was dismissed on all grounds.

Comment: The question to be determined in this case was whether the materials in question were properly maintained in accordance with the relevant statute (*section 22* of the *Factories Act 1961*). The issue of statutory construction also arose, in relation to whether a forklift truck would come within the definition of hoist or lift. It was decided that it would in fact be a straining of the English language to determine that the forks at the bottom of a fork lift truck could be called a platform, and would be attributing to the words a meaning that was not intended by the statute.

Lotinga v North Eastern Marine Engineering Co Ltd (23 July 1941) High Court, King's Bench Division ([1941] 3 All ER 1)

[A18.8]

crane; absolute duty

Background: An overhead travelling crane driven by a North Eastern Marine Engineering Co Ltd employee killed a colleague who was working close to the wheel track of the crane. A system of work whereby a notice was displayed forbidding cranes to approach within twenty feet of workmen and requiring workmen to notify crane drivers of their presence in the area had been operated by the company for thirty seven years without any incident occurring. In the Magistrates' Court it was found that the accident had been caused by the workman who, although aware of the danger, had not warned the crane drivers of his presence. It was also impractical for the crane driver to look out for workmen in the vicinity. On these findings, the company was acquitted of failing to comply with *section 24(7)* of the *Factories Act 1937* which requires that effective measures must be taken to keep overhead travelling cranes away from areas where workmen are employed.

Decision: The High Court found that *section 24(7)* of the 1937 Act imposes an absolute duty to take effective measures to warn crane drivers or otherwise ensure that cranes do not approach areas where workmen are liable to be struck by cranes. The company had failed in this duty and should have been convicted. The appeal by the Factories Inspector, Mr Lotinga, was allowed.

Comment: The absolute nature of the statutory duty in this case was confirmed and it was noted that a failure to impose an absolute obligation would water down the provisions of the relevant Act, which clearly intended to impose such an obligation on the employer.

Carrington v John Summers & Sons Ltd (9 November 1956) Crown Court ([1957] 1 All ER 457)

[A18.9]

crane; negligence

Background: Mr Carrington, a crane attendant, was injured when his foot became caught between the ground and the underside of a crane. Although the crane worked overhead, it moved by running along rails at ground level. The plaintiff claimed damages for personal injury from John Summers & Sons Ltd alleging negligence and breach of statutory duty under *section 24* of the *Factories Act 1937* which requires that effective measures shall be taken to warn drivers of overhead travelling cranes or otherwise ensure that cranes do not approach areas where workmen are liable to be struck by cranes.

Decision: The Crown Court held that *section 24(7)* of the 1937 Act did not apply to the crane involved in the accident because it ran on rails and was not therefore an overhead travelling crane. It was also held that the existence of *section 24* of the Act does not prevent *section 14* of that Act (fencing of dangerous machinery) applying in appropriate circumstances although the company was not in breach of *section 14*. John Summers & Sons Ltd was found to be negligent on the basis that the ground had been built up below the crane so that it was possible for a foot to be trapped there.

Comment: The interrelationship between statutory provisions was explored in this case. Despite the fact that a section of the relevant statute dealt specifically with cranes and lifting machinery, this could not be said to prevent the application of a more general provision.

Local Knowledge

Norbrook Laboratories (GB) Ltd v Health & Safety Executive (3 February 1998), High Court, Queen's Bench Division (Times Law Reports, 23 February 1998)

[A19.1]

health and safety; local knowledge

Background: Norbrook appealed against the decision of Carlisle Magistrates' Court which had included aspects of the magistrates own personal local knowledge.

Test: The extent to which magistrates could factor local knowledge into a decision.

Decision: The court accepted that magistrates were permitted to factor local knowledge into their decisions but held that the parties must be notified of this if it is the magistrates' intention to do so. Notification gives the parties the opportunity to comment. The appeal was upheld.

Comment: Local knowledge is likely to be of significance in many environment and health and safety cases. Many are dealt with in the magistrates' courts. As such, it is important for both parties to be clear as to the relevant facts on which a magistrates's decision is based.

Manual Handling

Colclough v Staffordshire County Council (30 June 1994) County Court (Current Law, October 1994)

[A20.1]

social worker; back injury; lifting, reasonably foreseeable

Background: The plaintiff, a social worker, was employed by Staffordshire County Council to assess the needs of elderly clients. She injured her back when it was necessary to lift a distressed elderly man in emergency circumstances. She had not been given any training or instruction in lifting techniques and it was on this ground that she brought an action against her employer alleging that the council had been negligent. The council denied liability, claiming that lifting tasks were not a normal part of a social worker's job and that in the circumstances she should have sought assistance from the emergency services.

Decision: The County Court held that it was reasonably foreseeable that a social worker with responsibilities for elderly people would encounter emergency situations. The council had a duty to warn social workers that they should not lift in such circumstances. It was not necessary to provide a long training course but the risks of lifting should be brought to their employees' attention. The claim was successful.

Comment: This case suggests that duties imposed on employers may be extended to cover the obligation to warn employees in similar positions to social workers about the risks of emergency situations which they anticipate may arise in the course of the employee's work.

Negligence

Robinson v The Post Office and Another (25 October 1973) Court of Appeal ([1974] 2 All ER 737)

[A21.1]

post office; doctor; anti-tetanus; negligence; damages

Background: Mr Robinson, a Post Office employee, cut his leg when he slipped on a ladder which was oily because of leakage from a pump. He visited his doctor for an anti-tetanus injection and because he had previously had an injection of this type, it was necessary to give a test dose before administering the full amount. The recognised test procedure was to wait for thirty minutes before giving the full dose. However, Mr Robinson's doctor followed his own practice whereby he only waited for an adverse reaction for a minute. Nine days later, Mr Robinson started to react to the injection and this culminated in him suffering brain damage due to encephalitis, a condition known to be a rare consequence of anti-tetanus injections. He brought an action for damages against his employer and his doctor. In the High Court, the doctor was not found to be liable, because although he had been negligent in administering the test dose improperly, no reaction would have occurred within the normal thirty minute period. The Post Office was found wholly liable for Mr Robinson's injury because it had been negligent in permitting the oil to leak onto the ladder. The Post Office appealed, contending that an essential link between the negligent act and the injury was missing as it could not have been foreseen that the anti-tetanus injection would give rise to serious illness.

Decision: The Court of Appeal confirmed that the doctor's negligence did not cause or materially contribute to Mr Robinson's injury as it was very unlikely that even if the proper test procedure had been followed a reaction to the injection would have been detected. Further, the giving of the injection was not a *novus actus interveniens* because the doctor had not been negligent or inefficient in deciding to administer the treatment and the failure to administer it properly had no causative effect. The court held that the employer had to take the employee as it found him, i.e. with an allergy to the anti-tetanus injection. As it was foreseeable that if oil were present on a ladder, he might slip and injure himself to the extent that medical treatment would be required, in the absence of a *novus actus interveniens*, the Post Office was liable for the outcome of that treatment even if it could not have foreseen the serious consequences.

Comment: This case illustrates the operation of the 'but for test'. If it cannot be shown that but for the defendant's conduct, the harm would not have been caused to the plaintiff, then the defendant cannot be held liable for this. This can be readily seen in cases involving the provision of safety equipment by employers. If it can be shown that the employee in question would not in fact have used the equipment or worn the protective clothing then the employer cannot be held liable for the plaintiff's suffering (*McWillians v Sir William Arrol & Co [1962] 1 WLR 295*).

Stapley v Gypsum Mines Ltd (25 June 1953) House of Lords ([1953] 2 All ER 478)

[A21.2]

mineworkers; breach of statutory duty; vicarious liability; contributory negligence

Background: Two mineworkers were instructed by their foreman to bring down the roof of part of the mine which was unsafe and likely to fall. They did not succeed in doing so and jointly decided to continue with other work, an action that was in breach of their duty under the *Metalliferous Mines General Regulations 1938 (SR & O 1938 No 360)*. One of the workers, Mr Stapley, went to work in the area of the mine where the roof should have been brought down and was killed by a roof fall. His widow was awarded damages after bringing an action against Gypsum Mines Ltd under the *Fatal Accidents Act 1846*. However, this decision was reversed by the Court of Appeal which held that the deceased's own negligence and breach of statutory duty were the substantial cause of his death. Mrs Stapley appealed.

Decision: The House of Lords found that the two workmen were equally negligent and in breach of their statutory duty when they ignored the instructions of the foreman. The negligence of the two men was so 'mixed up' that Mr Stapley's negligence could not be considered to be an independent act so as to make it the sole real or effective cause of the accident (*Admiralty Comsrs v SS Volute [1922] 1 AC 144*). The other workman's fault had contributed to the accident and Gypsum Mines Ltd was vicariously liable to Mr Stapley's widow and the appeal was allowed. With regard to the apportionment of liability, the deceased's action in entering and working in that particular area of the mine, whilst was unsafe, contributed more immediately to the accident than any act or omission by the other worker. Mr Stapley's share in the responsibility for the damage was therefore assessed at eighty per cent.

Comment: The importance of relying on a common sense approach to causation rather than a scientific and philosophical formula was stressed in this case. *Stapley* suggested that where a number of factors combined to lead to a situation where a claimant incurred loss, it might become appropriate to select the 'predominant' or 'real' or 'effective' cause of the claimant's loss.

Ward v T E Hopkins & Son Ltd (24 July 1959) Court of Appeal ([1959] 3 All ER 225)

[A21.3]

employer's liability; safe system of work; fault of employee; liability to rescuer

Background: Mr Ward was employed by a building company and was working to empty a well of water. He and another workman and a director of the company built a platform down inside the well and were using a petrol-driven pump to remove the water. After an hour and a half, the engine stopped and a haze of fumes was visible. Carbon monoxide had also built up, invisibly. That evening, the director returned to the well and noticed the haze and the smell of fumes. The next morning he told the two workmen to go to the well, but told Mr Ward that they weren't to go down it until he arrived. The workmen did not wait and went down the well and were overcome by fumes. A doctor was called who went down with a rope tied round him to rescue the men, although he had been warned not to. He was also overcome by fumes and the rope around him caught on a pipe and he could not be pulled up. The doctor, Mr Ward and the other workman all died.

Decision: In relation to the death of Mr Ward, it was held that the company had been negligent and had adopted a dangerous system of work. Although the director had warned Mr Ward not to go down the well, he had not been sufficiently clear about the danger involved and so this did not discharge the company's duty. However, due to the warning, it was found that there was contributory negligence on the part of Mr Ward (ten per cent).

The court rejected the arguments that the doctor's intervention had been an unforeseeable break in the chain of causation or that the company was not liable since the doctor had willingly exposed himself to the danger or had acted recklessly. It was a natural and proper consequence of the company's negligence towards its employees that someone would attempt to rescue them.

Comment: This case explored the defence of *volenti non fit injuria*. Morris LJ referred to the judgment of Wills J in *Osborne v London and North Western Rly Co [1888] 21 QBD* 220, namely the proposition that 'if the defendants desire to succeed on the ground that the maxim *volenti non fit injuria* is applicable, they must obtain a finding of fact that the plaintiff freely and voluntarily, with full knowledge of the nature and extent of the risk he ran, impliedly agreed to incur it'. The special position of rescuers in this context was examined and it was made clear that conduct on the part of a brave and human doctor could not be said to be unforeseeable as this would constitute an insult to the doctor's profession.

Stokes v Guest, Keen and Nettlefold (Bolts and Nuts) Ltd (4 October 1968) High Court, Birmingham Assizes ([1968] 1 WLR 1776)

[A21.4]

scrotal cancer; mineral oils; periodic medical examinations; reasonable and prudent employer

Background: Mrs Stokes' husband died from scrotal cancer. It was established on the balance of probabilities that this was induced by contact with mineral oils during the course of his employment as a toolsetter with Guest, Keen and Nettlefold (Bolts and Nuts) Ltd and that this work played a part in the development of his cancer. In the action against her husband's employer, Mrs Stokes alleged negligence and breach of duty to provide a safe system of work. She contended that the company knew or ought to have known that contact with mineral oils could lead to a risk of cancer and should have warned her husband of the dangers of the material, instructed him on safe working practices, provided protective measures and conducted periodic medical examinations. Although the company had employed a medical officer from 1941, no warnings or information were provided about the potential risks of mineral oils. Also no medical examinations were conducted, despite expert recommendations to the contrary since that date and a Factory Inspectorate leaflet on the dangers of scrotal cancer in 1960. The medical officer believed that periodic medical examinations were unnecessary because of the low incidence of the disease.

Decision: The High Court held that an employer will meet the standard of a reasonable and prudent employer taking positive thought for the safety of its workers where that employer follows a recognised and general practice . The practice must have been followed for a substantial period in similar circumstances without mishap unless in the light of common sense or newer knowledge it is clearly bad. Where there is developing knowledge concerning the safety of workers, however, a reasonable and prudent employer should keep reasonably abreast of it and not be too slow to apply it. If the employer has a more than average knowledge of the risks, more than the average precautions should be taken. When determining what action to take, the risk of injury occurring and its consequences should be weighed against the effectiveness, expense and inconvenience of that action. Where the employer falls below the standard to be expected of a reasonable and prudent employer, it has been negligent. In situations where a task requiring a special skill is delegated to a servant such as a medical officer, the servant's performance should be judged by the standards pertaining to that skill so far as he is possessed of and exercising it. However, more general principles should be used to judge the non-medical aspects of the medical officer's work, such as advice concerning economic and administrative considerations. Applying these tests, the High Court held that the company's medical officer was negligent in failing to conduct medical examinations of employees at risk of developing scrotal cancer and failing to issue a notice drawing attention to that risk. Guest, Keen and Nettlefold (Bolts and Nuts) Ltd was vicariously liable for that negligence.

Comment: The idea was developed that employers who are responsible for the health and safety of their employees, should keep up to date with developing knowledge in the various fields of potential illnesses that their employees may be exposed to as a result of their work. A subjective element was imported into the test to be applied to employers, in that when determining the liability of the employer, it is necessary to take into account the amount of knowledge and awareness of developments in the law which the employer actually has. Where an employer has a greater than average knowledge of the risks, he should put into place precautions which reflect this greater level of knowledge. This will affect employers, for example, who employ specialists with health and safety expertise in particular fields as the employers will be expected to institute protective and precautionary measures to reflect this greater degree of knowledge.

Caswell v Powell Duffryn Associated Collieries Ltd (25 July 1939) House of Lords ([1940] AC 152)

[A21.5]

mineworker; breach of statutory duty; contributory negligence; degree of care; factory or mine workers

Background: The mother of a mineworker who was killed at work brought an action against her son's former employer. The mineworker was responsible for cleaning a coal conveyor line and his dead body was found with his arm caught in the machinery of that line. A moveable plate which he should have been replaced after cleaning was not in place. Although Mr Caswell had been instructed that the machinery should not be cleaned whilst it was in motion, no system to inform the cleaner that the line was about to move existed. Powell Duffryn Associated Collieries Ltd argued that Mr Caswell was partly to blame for his own death. The High Court ruled that the plaintiff had failed to prove negligence or breach of statutory duty and this decision was upheld by the Court of Appeal. Mrs Caswell appealed to the House of Lords.

Decision: *Section 55* of the *Coal Mines Act 1911* requires that employers should ensure that exposed and dangerous parts of machinery used in mines are kept securely fenced. The House of Lords held that Powell Duffryn Associated Collieries Ltd had failed to comply with this duty because the moveable plate had not been replaced and that the system in place regarding the movement of the line was defective. The company had failed to show that it was not reasonably practicable to avoid or prevent the breach and it was therefore liable in damages. When contributory negligence is raised as a defence in a case of breach of statutory duty, an employee should not be debarred from recovering damages because of carelessness or inadvertence which throws him into the danger caused by the breach. It is the breach, not the act of carelessness or inadvertence which is the dominant or effective cause of the injury. Further, the circumstances of the employee (such as hours of work, fatigue etc.) must be taken into account and a lower standard of care might be expected from a factory or mineworker than from an ordinary person. In this case, there was no evidence of negligence on the part of Mr Caswell. Mrs Caswell's appeal was allowed.

Comment: This case made clear that negligence, and what will be held to constitute negligence, varies according to the circumstances. It is not a matter of uniform degree. It was suggested that it may even vary when the same person is responsible. Lord Wright suggested that 'a surgeon doing an emergency operation on a cottage table with the light of a candle might not be properly held guilty of negligence in respect of an act or omission which would be negligence if he were performing the same operation with all the advantages of the serene atmosphere of his operating theatre; the same holds good of the workman. The jury have to draw the line where mere thoughtlessness or inadvertence or forgetfulness cease and where negligence begins'.

Watt v Hertfordshire County Council (7 May 1954) Court of Appeal ([1954] 2 All ER 368)

[A21.6]

fireman; negligence

Background: A fireman was injured when a heavy jack moved inside a vehicle on the way to an emergency in which a woman was trapped beneath a heavy vehicle a short distance from the fire station. The jack had been lent to the fire service and only one vehicle was specially fitted to carry it. That vehicle was away on another call so the jack was loaded onto a lorry, the only suitable remaining vehicle. There was no means of securing the jack within the lorry. The injured fireman's subsequent action, alleging that his employer had been negligent, was dismissed and he appealed.

Decision: The Court of Appeal held that Hertfordshire County Council had no duty to ensure that a specially fitted vehicle was available at all times. The risk taken was such as would normally be undertaken by a fireman and was not unduly great in relation to the end to be achieved. The county council had not been negligent.

Comment: It was held that the purpose to be served in this case was the saving of life and the firemen were prepared to take that risk. They were not called on to take any risk other than that which might normally be encountered in the fire service and the employers had not been guilty of any failure of duty which they owed to the firemen. This case was approved in *Bittner v Tait Gibson Optometrists (1964) 44 DLR*. It was held that a finding of contributory negligence against a police officer who slipped on a patch of ice on the defendant's property while hurrying to investigate a suspected crime on the property should be reversed on the ground that the end to be achieved outweighed the consideration of the risk. This could be applied similarly for other services where the taking of risks is routine.

Paris v Stepney Borough Council (13 December 1950) House of Lords ([1951] 1 All ER 42)

[A21.7]

special duty of care; goggles; eye protection

Background: A one-eyed garage worker became completely blind after a chip of metal entered his good eye. It was not usual practice for Stepney Borough Council to provide protective goggles to its employees working in garages on the maintenance and repair of vehicles. No protective equipment had been given to Mr Paris. After his accident he claimed damages from his employer, alleging negligence. He was successful in the High Court but that decision was reversed by the Court of Appeal. Mr Paris then appealed to the House of Lords.

Decision: The House of Lords held that where an employer is aware that an employee has a disability which although does not increase the risk of an accident occurring but does increase the risk of serious injury, special precautions should be taken if the employer is to fulfil its duty to take reasonable care for the safety of that employee. The condition of Mr Paris' eyes, the employer's knowledge of his condition, the likelihood of an accident occurring and the gravity of the consequences should an accident occur were all to be considered in determining whether the employer took reasonable steps to protect its employee's safety. In these circumstances, Stepney Borough Council owed a special duty of care to Mr Paris and had been negligent in failing to supply goggles to him, even though such equipment was not given to other employees.

Comment: The application and development of the principles expounded in this case can be seen in *Parkes v Smethwick Corporation (1957) 121 JP 415*. The plaintiff, who was employed as an ambulance driver by the defendants, suffered a hernia when lifting a patient into an ambulance. The plaintiff had suffered a hernia prior to his employment with the defendants but had not informed them of it. From time to time, ambulance drivers had complained to the defendants that their work was heavy and awkward and suggested the refitting of retractable stretcher gear to the ambulance, but it had not been so equipped. It was held that the defendants were not under a duty to examine the plaintiff as to his capacity for work or fit all their ambulances with retractable gear, or lay down an exact system of working for their ambulance men. Consequently, the defendants had not failed in their duty as employers.

Occupational Disease

Gardiner v Motherwell Machinery and Scrap Co Ltd (6 July 1961) House of Lords ([1961] 3 All ER 831)

[A22.1]

dermatitis; course of employment; prima facie presumption; evidence

Background: Mr Gardiner was employed by the defendant to assist in the demolition of buildings, work which was liable to lead to dermatitis. He subsequently contracted the disease which started on his hand and spread all over his body. A successful action was brought against his employer on the ground that the nature of his work was liable to cause dermatitis and proper washing facilities to guard against the disease should have been provided. Motherwell Machinery and Scrap Co Ltd appealed on the grounds that the dermatitis was not caused by Mr Gardiner's work. Their appeal was successful and Mr Gardiner challenged it.

Decision: The House of Lords held that where a man who has not previously suffered from a disease contracts that disease after being subjected to conditions likely to cause it, and when he shows that it started in a way typical of disease caused by such conditions, he establishes a *prima facie* presumption that his disease was caused by those conditions. It is incumbent on the employer to rebut that presumption if it can. In Mr Gardiner's case, the facts did establish such a presumption and his employer was not able to establish that his disease was due to another cause. The appeal was allowed.

Comment: This case reinforced the importance of presumptions raised during the course of evidence in that the employer failed to rebut the presumption that the employee had sustained the dermatitis in the course of his employment. The presumption arose given that he worked in conditions which were likely to result in dermatitis, and he had not been exposed to any other potential causes. Evidence that the relevant statute was enacted to protect employees from precisely the type of injury, which was suffered in a particular case, was held to be relevant in determining the liability of the employer. (See also the discussion of the *Wilshire case* under *Bryce v Swan Hunter Group plc and Other [1987]*, paragraph A4.3 in terms of causation *Group plc and others [1987]*.)

Bonnington Castings Ltd v Wardlaw (1 March 1956) House of Lords ([1956] 1 All ER 615)

[A22.2]

pneumoconiosis; silica dust; breach of regulations; statutory duty; evidence; damages

Background: Mr Wardlaw suffered from pneumoconiosis, caused by the inhalation of silica dust at his workplace, the dressing shop of a steel foundry. There were several sources of the dust. The main source was the pneumatic hammers, one of which Mr Wardlaw operated. Silica dust was also produced by the floor grinders and swing grinders. During the material period, there was no known protection against silica dust produced from pneumatic hammers but *Regulation 1* of the *Grinding of Metals (Miscellaneous Industries) Regulations 1925 (SR & O 1925 No 904)* required that the ducts of the dust extractors of the swing grinders were kept free from obstruction. Bonnington Castings Ltd admitted that it had been in breach of this statutory duty and that dust from the grinders had escaped into the workshop. The company argued however that as there was no evidence to show how much dust came from the different sources in the workshop, Mr Wardlaw could not show that the dust from the swing grinders contributed materially to the dust he inhaled. Mr Wardlaw brought a successful claim for damages for breach of statutory duty against Bonnington Castings Ltd. The company's first appeal was dismissed and it appealed again to the House of Lords.

Decision: A plaintiff must prove not only negligence or breach of duty at common law but also that such fault caused or materially contributed to his injury (*Wakelin v London & South Western Ry Co (1886) 12 App Cas 41*; *Caswell v Powell Duffryn Associated Collieries Ltd [1939] 3 All ER 722*). There is no reason why this should alter where there is breach of statutory duty (unless the statute or regulation provides otherwise). The plaintiff must be able to prove on a balance of probabilities that the breach of duty caused or materially contributed to his injury. In this case, the question to be answered was whether the dust from the swing grinders materially contributed to the pneumoconiosis. It was found that the proportion of dust produced by the swing grinders and inhaled by Mr Wardlaw was not negligible and it had contributed materially to his contracting the disease. The House of Lords considered that Mr Wardlaw had discharged the onus of showing that his employer's fault was a material contributing cause of his illness. Bonnington Castings Ltd was therefore liable to him in damages for breach of statutory duty and the company's appeal was dismissed.

Comment: In this case the House of Lords dismissed the notion that the burden of establishing a causal link should be any less onerous in breach of statutory duty than in negligence. The idea of material contribution raised in this case has been applied in several cases. For instance, in *McGhee v National Coal Board [1973] 1 WLR 1*, it was held that it is actionable to materially increase the risk of another's injury even if it cannot be proved that the injury was definitely caused. The basic position has been that the onus of proof in civil actions concerning a defendant's wrongdoing rests with the plaintiff. However, it is important to note that the issue is not straightforward and consideration should be given to the *Wilshire case* (discussed in *Bryce v Swan Hunter Group plc and others [1987]*, paragraph A4.3).

Occupiers' Liability

Addie (R) & Sons (Collieries) Ltd v Dumbreck (25 February 1929) House of Lords ([1929] AC 358)

[A23.1]

occupiers' liability; common law duty; trespassers; trespassers negligence

Background: Dumbreck, a four year old boy, died after being crushed in the terminal wheel of a haulage system belonging to the colliery company. The field in which the wheel stood was surrounded by a hedge which was inadequate to keep out the general public. It was common knowledge that the field was used as a shortcut by local residents and as a playground by local children. The colliery officials had, on numerous occasions, warned both adults and children out of the field. The wheel was dangerous and attractive to children and at the time of the accident inadequately protected. The boy's father brought an action for damages against the company.

Test: The judge stated that the only question that arose was in what capacity the deceased child was in the field: by the invitation, express or implied, of the occupier; with the leave and licence of the occupier; or as a trespasser. The duty which rests upon the occupier of the premises would differ according to the category into which the visitor falls. In the case of a trespasser, the occupier would have no duty to take reasonable care for his protection or even to protect him from concealed danger. An occupier would only be liable where there was a deliberate act done to harm the trespasser, or at least some act done with reckless disregard of the presence of the trespasser.

Decision: The House of Lords held that the boy was a trespasser and went on to the colliery premises at his own risk. As such, the company owed him no duty to protect him from injury. The judge defined a trespasser as a person who 'goes on the land without invitation of any sort and whose presence is either unknown to the proprietor or, if known, is practically objected to'.

Comment: There were two main reasons why the trespasser could not recover against the occupier. First, it was felt that to make the occupier potentially liable to trespassers might 'seriously impede the conduct of his lawful activities'. Secondly, it was felt that a trespasser should not be allowed to take advantage of his own wrong. This rather stringent reasoning was subsequently side-stepped by a number of devices including the doctrine of 'allurement' and the occupier's knowledge of a regular trespass amounting to an implied license. This all led in 1972 to the House of Lords in *British Railways Board v Herrington [1972] AC 877* reversing its own decision in *Addie v Dumbreck* and holding that a trespasser was, after all, owed a limited duty of care. In many respects this case is now largely of academic interest since *section 1* of the *Occupiers' Liability Act 1984* imposes a statutory duty on occupiers with respect to trespassers.

Perry v Butlins Holiday World (t/a Butlins Ltd) (28 November 1997) Court of Appeal ([1997] PLSCS 315)

[A23.2]

occupiers' liability; duty of care; reasonable care; visitor; negligence

Background: Perry was a four year old child staying at Butlins Holiday World. He suffered severe laceration to his right ear when he fell onto a low brick wall surrounding a restaurant which formed part of the Butlins Holiday World site. The wall was near an open area on which shows for children were performed. Perry brought an action based on breach of the common law duty of care under the *Occupiers' Liability Act 1957*. He claimed that the use of sharp grade A blue engineering bricks with ninety degree edges used in the construction of the wall was unsuitable and potentially dangerous where young children were expected to be present. Expert evidence was given referring to British Standard BS 5692 [1982] effecting outdoor play equipment and providing that regular inspections should be made for 'protrusions, sharp points or edges'. It was said that materials with rounded edges other than engineering bricks could have been used, and that in designing the wall it would have been sensible to take into account that the area was likely to be frequented by large numbers of children.

Test: The duty of care in *section 2(2)* of the *Occupiers' Liability Act 1957* 'to take such care as in all the circumstances of the case is reasonable to see that the visitor will be reasonably safe in using the premises for the purposes for which he is invited or permitted by the occupier to be there' was further elaborated in *section 2(3)(a)* of the 1957 Act in relation to children which requires that 'the occupier must be prepared for children to be less careful than adults'.

Decision: The court ruled in favour of Perry because the wall was low and therefore of greater danger to children. The edge was highly sharp and could have been made of rubber or given rounded edges. The presence of children in the area of a wall of such low height with sharp edges was a dangerous combination and Butlins Holiday World had therefore failed to take reasonable care.

Comment: This case made it clear that the standard of care under the occupiers' liability legislation will be higher where children are involved. Occupiers will be expected to take greater care given that children are less likely to be as careful as adults. The case supports the view that a higher standard of care is required for those who are at special risk. Occupiers should consider the nature of risks posed by their premises bearing in mind the type of individuals permitted or invited to be on the premises.

Ratcliff v McConnell and Others (13 November 1998) Court of Appeal (Times Law Reports, 3 December 1998)

[A23.3]

occupiers' liability; aware of risk; accepted risk; duty of care; locked premises; trespassers; negligence

Background: This case was an appeal by the owners and occupiers of a college open-air swimming pool. Mr G R McConnell and Mr E W Jones, on their own behalf and as representative governors of Harpur Adams Agricultural College, appealed against a finding that they were liable in damages to Mr Ratcliff for breach of the duty owed to him under the *Occupiers' Liability Act 1984*. Mr Ratcliff, a student at the college, had climbed over a locked gate at night which had prevented normal access to the occupiers' premises and had dived headfirst into the swimming pool located on the premises. Mr Ratcliff hit his head on the bottom of the swimming pool, as a result of which he suffered tetraplegia.

Test: *Section 1* of the *Occupiers' Liability Act 1984* imposes a duty on the occupier to trespassers in respect of any risk of their suffering injury on the premises by reason of any danger due to the state of the premises or to things done or omitted to be done on them. Such duty, if found to be in existence, requires the occupier to take such care as is reasonable in all the circumstances of the case, and varies greatly depending on whether the trespasser was very old or very young and so might not appreciate the danger which may be or ought to be apparent to an adult. *Section 1(6)* of the *Occupiers' Liability Act 1984* does, however, provide that no duty is owed by the occupier to any person (including a trespasser) who willingly accepts the risk as his own. Mr Ratcliff had admitted that he had been fully aware that the pool was closed for the winter, that the water level was low and that it was dangerous to dive headfirst into shallow water. As such, he had been aware of the risk and had willingly accepted it. The court allowed the appeal.

Decision: The court held, allowing the appeal, that Mr Ratcliff had been aware of the risk and had willingly accepted it. Accordingly Mr McConnell and Mr Jones, in their relevant capacities, owed no duty towards Mr Ratcliff.

Comment: This case makes it clear that although the owner or occupier of premises may owe a statutory duty of care to trespassers, this duty is not without limitation. As such, it will not extend to such a trespasser who whilst aware of the risk willingly accepts and exposes themselves to the risk in question. It is sufficient if an occupier takes reasonable steps in the circumstances to prevent trespassers from entering the premises.

Adams v Southern Electricity Board (23 September 1993) Court of Appeal (Times Law Reports, 21 October 1993)

[A23.4]

occupiers' liability; statutory duty; trespassers; contributory negligence

Background: Southern Electricity Board appealed against the decision that they owed a duty of care to Adams, an intelligent fifteen year old, who had been electrocuted after climbing a high voltage electrical installation. At the time of the accident, the anti-climbing device was in defective condition.

Test: If there is a clear statutory duty, a failure to satisfy such a statutory duty will still give rise to a cause of action even where there is substantial contributory negligence on the part of the plaintiff.

Decision: The appeal was dismissed. Southern Electricity Board had a statutory duty to maintain effective anti-climbing devices and was, therefore, liable in part for Adams' injuries. The amount of damages was reduced by two thirds to take account of the substantial contributory negligence by Adams.

Comment: Where there is a statutory duty even 'crass stupidity' by the plaintiff will not negate the liability of the person on whom the duty is imposed. However, the foolishness of the individual will be a factor in determining the level of contributory negligence.

Hartley v Mayoh and Co and Another (15 January 1954) Court of Appeal ([1954] 1 All ER 375)

[A23.5]

occupiers' liability; statutory duty; class of persons; cause of action; fireman; rescuer; invitee; trespassers; negligence; emergency services; visitor

Background: Hartley was killed whilst attending a fire at the factory occupied by Mayoh and Co. In order that he could cut the mains supply of electricity, Hartley had been directed by the factory manager to electricity switches on the ground floor. They all thought that the entire supply of electricity to the premises was then cut off. However, unknown to both the firemen and the manager, the lighting circuit was controlled by two unconnected tumbler switches. Notwithstanding that the tumbler switches themselves were not switched off, there should have been no current flowing through the lighting circuit on the upper floor where the fire was blazing, as the master switch which controlled the lighting circuit on the upper floor was turned off. Due to a wiring fault the circuit was still live and as a result Hartley was electrocuted. The second defendants were the authority responsible for the supply of electricity to the factory. In January 1950, they had fitted a new meter to the premises but had failed to test the circuits. If they had done so they should have detected the wiring fault. An action for damages was brought by Hartley's widow against the first and second defendants, the claim against the second defendant being based mainly on their failure to test the circuits in January 1950. By their defence the second defendants pleaded that the accident was caused, either whole or in part, by the negligence of the deceased or of some other officer of the fire brigade.

Test: (1) Although a fireman should understand the usual and normal methods of cutting off the electricity supply in premises in which a fire had taken place, he was not required to possess a detailed knowledge of obsolete mechanisms. As such, neither he nor any other member of the fire brigade was to blame for the accident. (2) Firemen attending a fire on an occupiers' premises attained the status of a invitee, whether or not they are summoned to that fire by the occupier themselves or by a third party. (3) The first defendant, as occupiers, should have been aware of the way in which the mains supply to the lighting and power circuits could be switched off. They had failed in their duty to the deceased, as an invitee, to give him due warning of an unusual danger of which they ought to have been aware, and they were liable in damages for negligence. (4) On the facts, the first defendant had failed to comply with the requirements of the *Electricity (Factories Act) Special Regulations (SR & O 1908 No 1312 as amended by SR & O 1944 No 739)* in force at the time. The judge decided that their liability to persons injured by a breach of the regulations was not confined to persons in their own employment, notwithstanding that 'danger' was defined in the Regulations as meaning danger 'to persons employed'. It would extend to all other employed persons on the premises. (5) The failure of the second defendant to test the circuits in January 1950 was a negligent omission on their part and constituted a breach of their legal duty which they owed to the deceased. They should have been aware that their omission to make a proper test would be likely to cause damage to any persons lawfully on the premises who had occasion to come into contact with any part of the wiring or the lighting system. In addition, they were also in breach of their duty under the *Electricity Supply Regulations 1937*.

Decision: The court held that both the first and second defendants were liable in negligence. Because the fault of the first defendant was comparatively venial, the liability for damages should be borne ten per cent by the first defendant and ninety per cent by the second defendant.

Comment: The decision was appealed to the Court of Appeal. The original decision was upheld except as to the liability of the occupier under The *Electricity (Factories Act) Special Regulations* (point 4 above). The Court of Appeal held that the fireman was not a person for whose benefit the electricity regulations were made, not being of the class of 'persons employed', and the first defendants were, therefore, not liable for their breach of their statutory duty in respect of his death. This reflects the position today. Non-compliance with a statutory duty cannot be actionable unless the injury was of the type which the statute was passed to prevent. As such, where statutes are aimed at protecting a particular group of individuals e.g. employees, then only that category of individual will be protected and have a potential cause of action.

Salmon v Seafarer Restaurants (British Gas Corporation, Third Party) (29 June 1982) High Court, Queen's Bench Division ([1983] 1 WLR 1264)

[A23.6]

occupiers' liability; rescuer; duty of care; foreseeability; negligence; fireman; emergency services; visitor

Background: Salmon was a fireman who attended a fire at the Seafarer fish and chip shop. The fire had been caused by an employee of the owner failing to put out a light under the chip fryer before closing the shop for the night. Salmon had been ordered by a senior officer to gain access to the second floor via a flat roof. Whilst on the roof, an explosion occurred, caused by the heat melting the seals on gas meters on the premises and allowing gas to escape. Salmon sustained injuries in the explosion and as a result brought an action for damages for personal injuries alleging that the fire had been started by the defendants' negligence and that he had been injured as a result of that negligence. The defendants denied that they owed a duty of care to Salmon.

Test: An occupier's duty of care will extend to a fireman attending at his premises to put out a fire. Such a duty would cover ordinary risks and dangers inherent in a fireman's occupation. The occupier would be taken to have breached that duty of care where it was foreseeable that the fireman, in carrying out his job of putting out a fire, would be injured as a result of the negligence of the occupier in causing the initial fire.

Decision: On the question of whether an occupier owes a duty of care to a fireman attending at his premises to put out a fire, the court decided that a duty of care did exist. Such a duty would extend to the ordinary risks and dangers inherent in a fireman's occupation and was not limited to a requirement to protect the fireman only against special, exceptional or additional risks. The fireman's special skills and training were relevant in determining liability. However, where it was foreseeable that a fireman exercising those skills would be injured through the negligence of the occupier, the occupier was in breach of his duty of care. In this case the fire had been caused by the defendants' negligence. As it was foreseeable that the plaintiff would be required to attend the fire and would be at risk of the type of injuries he received from the explosion which was caused by the negligence, the defendants were liable for those injuries and damages were recoverable by Salmon.

Comment: The effect of *section 2(3)(b)* of the *Occupiers' Liability Act 1957* is that an occupier is not liable to a fireman merely because the state of his premises makes fire fighting more hazardous. However, an occupier who negligently starts a fire in his own premises may be liable under the general law of negligence to a fireman who is foreseeably injured while trying to put it out, even though fire-fighting is part of his job.

Hartley v British Railways Board (28 January 1981) Court of Appeal (Times Law Reports, 2 February 1981)

[A23.7]

occupiers' liability; negligence; visitor; duty of care; unnecessary risk; fireman; emergency services; reasonable care

Background: In this case a railway servant had left the railway station unmanned without giving his superiors the required notice.

A fire occurred at the railway station and was attended by firemen. The firemen suspected that the employee was still in the railway station and went on to an upper floor. As a result of this, one of the firemen was injured. The judge in the first instance rejected the fireman's claim for damages on a number of grounds. First, he rejected the argument that the fire had been caused by the negligence of the employee for whose acts the British Railways Board were responsible. Secondly, that there was no duty owed by the British Railways Board to Hartley. Hartley appealed the decision to the Court of Appeal.

Test: Under *Donoghue v Stephenson [1932] AC 562*, the duty of the occupier is to take reasonable care not to expose any visitor to unnecessary risk. A breach of this duty will occur where the occupier places a firemen at a greater degree of hazard than normal.

Decision: The Court of Appeal rejected the first finding. This was a case where the initial fire could be shown to have been caused by negligence. With regard to the second ground, the court stated that the fireman had gone on to a part of the premises, namely the upper floor, which was more hazardous, specifically to look for the missing person. The duty of the occupier is to take reasonable care not to expose the visitor (in this case the fireman) to unnecessary risk. It was irrelevant that it was a risk which the fireman, in other circumstances, may have had to face from time to time. It was a risk which put the firemen at a greater degree of hazard than normal and accordingly, there was a breach of the duty. As such the fireman was entitled to recover.

Comment: The court, when considering the question of liability, primarily examined the responsibilities of occupiers to firemen irrespective of whether they were the initiators of the fire by negligence. The remarks which seem to indicate that the liability be limited to unnecessary risks must be viewed in that context. Compare this to *Salmon v Seafarers Restaurants [1983]* (see paragraph A23.6) where the occupier's employee negligently started the initial fire.

Personal Protective Equipment

Bux v Slough Metals Ltd (6 July 1973) Court of Appeal ([1974] 1 All ER 262)

[A24.1]

damages; personal injury; protective equipment; breach of statutory duty; negligence; contributory negligence; safe system of work

Background: The plaintiff brought an action for damages for personal injury against his employer, Slough Metals Ltd, after an accident in which molten metal splashed into his eye. Mr Bux was not wearing protective goggles at the time of the incident. When he was originally trained by the company, no eye protection had been provided and he had not been instructed to wear such equipment. Goggles were subsequently provided to all employees and Mr Bux used these for a few days until he discarded them because they hindered his work by steaming up. He told the superintendent of works they were useless and asked if any better goggles could be provided but received no response. Mr Bux alleged that the company had breached its statutory duty under *Regulation 13(1)* of the *Non-Ferrous Metals (Melting and Founding) Regulations 1962 (SI 1962 No 1667)* by failing to provide goggles and had been negligent. In the High Court, it was held that there had been no breach of statutory duty but that the company had been negligent. The court also found that Mr Bux had breached *Regulation 13(4)* of the 1962 Regulations. As a consequence due to contributory negligence on the part of Mr Bux, the damages awarded were reduced by twenty per cent. Both parties appealed.

Decision: In the Court of Appeal, Slough Metals Ltd argued that if it had fulfilled its statutory duty, it was absolved of any breach of common law duty. The court found however that each case depends on its facts as to whether statutory duty is co-extensive with, or more or less extensive than the common law duty. In this case, the company's common law duty was not superseded by its statutory duty under *Regulation 13(1)* of the 1962 Regulations. This was because the Regulations did not specify the legal position in a situation where an employer knew that the protective goggles provided were not being worn by employees in work which posed a danger to their eyesight. The legal position was the same as it had been before the coming into effect of the Regulations. In determining whether instruction, persuasion or insistence should be used to ensure the use of protective equipment, the facts of each case should again be considered, including the nature and degree of the risk of serious harm liable to occur if the equipment was not used. In Mr Bux's case, the evidence presented to the court indicated that if he had been instructed to wear the goggles and supervised in that respect, he would have worn them. The court found the company to have breached its common law duty to maintain a reasonably safe system of work by giving instructions and enforcing these with supervision. Slough Metals Ltd's appeal was dismissed. With regard to the plaintiff's contributory negligence, it was found that a substantial degree of the blame rested with Mr Bux because of his own breach of statutory duty. The reduction in the damages award was increased to forty per cent.

Comment: This case reinforced the distinction between the common law duty of care and breach of statutory duty. Compliance with the statutory duty may provide evidence that the duty at common law has been complied with but that conclusion does not always follow. Health and safety regulations can be considered, in some instances, to set minimum requirements or standards. Thus the common law duty, which imposes a requirement to take reasonable care with respect to the health, safety and welfare of employees, is not restricted to compliance with the statutory requirements. In order for the employer to satisfy its obligations relating to the provision of personal protective equipment under the legislation/or at common law, the employer was under a further duty to instruct employees to wear the protective equipment and to supervise that this occurs. Whilst this case related to 1962 Regulations, the principle remains the same under the existing legislation. Employers' liability may be reduced where the employee fails to meet the statutory duty owed to the employer, in this instance, to wear the protective equipment provided. More importantly however, consideration should be given as to whether the plaintiff would have behaved differently had the employer stressed that he should wear the protective equipment at all times. The nature of the plaintiff's wrong-doing should be considered *vis a vis* the obligations imposed on the defendant.

Crouch v British Rail Engineering Ltd (25 February 1988) Court of Appeal ([1988] IRLR 404)

[A24.2]

employer's liability; safe system of work; protective equipment; fault of employee

Background: Mr Crouch worked for British Rail Engineering Ltd as a skilled mechanical fitter doing general maintenance around the site. While using a hammer and chisel to unscrew a bolt, and not wearing goggles, his eye was damaged by a fragment of chisel. The system for the provision of goggles was that if a skilled worker felt they were necessary, it was up to them to get a pair from the foreman or the stores.

Test: 'The extent of the duty of care owed by an employer to an employee depends upon the particular circumstances of each case. Those circumstances include the risk of injury; the gravity of any injury which might result; the difficulty of providing equipment or clothing as a means of protection; the availability of that protective equipment or clothing and the distance to which the individual workman might have to go to fetch it; the frequency of the occasions on which the employee was likely to need the protective equipment or clothing; and the experience and degree of skill to be expected of the employee'. (Lord Justice Neill)

Decision: The court overturned the trial judge's finding that British Rail Engineering Ltd had operated a reasonable system for the provision of goggles. The court accepted that Mr Crouch was an experienced workman who knew that he should have been wearing goggles for the task, and that they were available.

However, the court found that in the circumstances of the present case, the duty on the employer extended to the actual provision of goggles into the hand of the employee. Lord Justice Stocker considered that the distance which Mr Crouch would have had to go to get goggles (about five minutes walk from where he was working) was an incentive for him to take a chance, which would probably have been removed by the actual provision of goggles. However, Mr Crouch had been in breach of the duty of care to himself by failing to wear goggles when he knew of the risk. His damages were therefore reduced by fifty per cent to take account of his contributory negligence.

Comment: This case reinforced the principle that the gravity of the potential outcome of employees' failure to wear protective equipment must be taken into account. If the nature of the hazard is great, then the obligations on the defendants will extend to more than merely having the equipment available.

Pape v Cumbria County Council (23 May 1991) High Court ([1991] IRLR 463)

[A24.3]

employer's liability; protective equipment

Background: Mrs Pape was employed as a cleaner by Cumbria County Council, using chemical cleaning materials and detergents as part of her work. The cleaners were issued with rubber gloves but rarely used them. They were not instructed to wear the gloves by the council, nor warned of the risk of irritant contact dermatitis from the chemicals, which could be prevented by using gloves.

After some years, Mrs Pape started to suffer from eczema on her hands and wrists. A primary irritant dermatitis was diagnosed and the dermatologist advised her to wear cotton gloves under rubber gloves at work. Mrs Pape did this, but the eczema remained and then spread to her face. Further conditions developed, affecting her entire skin, and she gave up her job on the advice of the dermatologist.

Test: The judge applied the test set out by the House of Lords in *General Cleaning Contractors v Christmas [1953] AC 180*, namely: 'Whether it is the duty of the [defendants] to instruct their servants what precautions they ought to take and reasonable steps to see that those instructions are carried out'.

Decision: Mrs Pape was awarded damages. It was not enough for the council simply to provide the cleaners with gloves. To discharge its duty as an employer to provide a safe system of work, the council should have warned the cleaners about the dangers of handling the cleaning chemicals without protection, and instructed them to wear gloves at all times.

'The dangers of dermatitis or acute eczema from the sustained exposure of unprotected skin to chemical cleansing agents is well known, well enough known to make it the duty of a reasonable employer to appreciate the risks it presents to members of his cleaning staff but at the same time not so well known as to make it obvious to his staff without any necessity for warning or instruction'. (Mr Justice Waite).

Comment: This case reinforced the position taken in *General Cleaning Contractors v Christmas [1953]* that it is the duty of the employer, both to provide employees with necessary protective equipment, and in addition, to warn them of the difficulties of not using the equipment effectively. The duty applies when the dangers of not using the equipment or following the appropriate procedures are not obvious to the staff without any warning or instruction. This signals that a proactive approach is required from employers rather than the mere fact of supplying the necessary equipment. The defendant employer will not avoid liability unless it can be shown that even if all reasonable steps had been taken to ensure the plaintiff used the protective equipment, he still would have refused to do so or evaded these precautions.

Prohibition Notice

Nico Manufacturing Co Ltd v Hendry (HM Inspector of Factories) (18 April 1974) Industrial Tribunal ([1975] IRLR 225)

[A25.1]

power press; prohibition notice

Background: A power press at Nico Manufacturing Co Ltd's premises was examined by the company's appointed 'competent person' and found to be faulty. He considered that the machinery should be taken out of service until mended and reported the defect to the company and to the HM Inspectorate of Factories. Before the defect had been remedied however, the technical director of the company operated the machine, a contravention of the *Power Press Regulations 1965 (SI 1965 No 1441)*. The HM Inspectorate of Factories issued a prohibition notice prohibiting further use of the press until it had been mended. Nico Manufacturing Co Ltd appealed, contending that the worn state of the press was not dangerous to employees and that depriving the company of the use of the press would cause serious loss of production and endanger the jobs of several employees.

Decision: On the evidence, the Industrial Tribunal preferred the opinion of the Engineering Inspector of Factories as to the state of the press. Although the chances of the press actually breaking up and causing danger to employees were small, there was nevertheless a very real danger that there could be a fracture of the crankshaft or falling off of the flywheel that would cause serious danger. The prohibition notice was therefore rightly issued and the press should not be used until the defect had been remedied. The company's argument concerning the financial impact of taking the press out of service was dismissed, as was the appeal against the notice.

Comment: The fact that the odds of damage resulting from the press breaking up in this case were small, it was unimportant in the light of the fact that there was a real danger. Situations which may result in real danger were pinpointed, and for this reason the prohibition notice had clearly been rightly issued.

Psychiatric Damage

Walker v Northumberland County Council (16 November 1994) High Court (Times Law Reports, 24 November 1994)

[A26.1]

psychiatric damage; employers' duty of care; foreseeability of risk; safe workplace

Background: Mr Walker, an area social services officer employed by Northumberland County Council, suffered a mental breakdown in late 1986. He had no history of mental disorder and it was common ground that his heavy workload was the reason for his illness. On medical advice, he remained off work until March 1987. He then resumed his work but little practical assistance was provided and he suffered a second nervous breakdown and was eventually dismissed on the basis of permanent ill-health. Mr Walker brought an action against his employer alleging that the local authority had breached its duty of care in failing to take reasonable steps to avoid exposing him to a health endangering workload.

Decision: The High Court held that there was no logical reason why psychiatric damage should be excluded from the scope of an employer's duty of care. Evidence regarding forseeability and causation could be problematic however, particularly in professional environments. In this case, although it was not reasonably foreseeable to his employer that the workload to which Mr Walker was exposed would give rise to a material risk of mental illness in 1986 or that he was subject to a greater than ordinary risk of this occurring, after the first nervous breakdown his employer should have foreseen that if he were again exposed to the same workload there was a risk that another breakdown would occur. The plaintiff was more vulnerable to psychiatric damage than he had been in 1986. The High Court held that Northumberland County Council had breached its duty of care to provide a safe workplace for Mr Walker because it had failed to relieve the pressure of work on him so that he suffered a second nervous breakdown.

Comment: Prior to this case there was little judicial authority on the extent to which employers owe employees a duty not to cause them psychiatric injury by the amount of work they expect of them. Following this case, guidelines were produced by the HSE, aimed at small to medium sized companies, which told employers to take more account of their employees' feelings in order to prevent stress-related ailments. This was the first official commentary regarding occupational stress. Despite this, it is safe to say that this area is not settled and that more cases are likely to follow especially in the light of the increasing pressure faced by employees and the difficulties and stresses associated with trying to balance work with other aspects of life.

Young v Charles Church (Southern) Ltd (24 April 1997) Court of Appeal (Times Law Reports, 1 May 1997)

[A26.2]

dangers from electric equipment; severe psychiatric illness; negligence; breach of statutory duty

Background: Mr Young claimed damages in respect of a severe psychiatric illness he had suffered since an accident at work in which a colleague had been electrocuted. In the High Court Mr Young's claim in negligence and for breach of statutory duty was dismissed. He appealed to the Court of Appeal.

Decision: The Court of Appeal held that Mr Young's employer Charles Church (Southern) Ltd was liable in negligence at common law. On the claim for breach of statutory duty, Charles Church (Southern) Ltd admitted that it was in breach of *Regulation 44(2)* of the *Construction (General Provisions) Regulations 1961 (SI*

1961 No 1580) in respect of the deceased worker. However, it denied it was in breach of that provision with regard to Mr Young. The company based this argument on the fact that Mr Young was not injured or affected by electrocution i.e. the transmission to him of an electric current. The company, therefore, argued that Mr Young's injury was not of the nature or caused in the manner which the Regulations in question were intended to prevent. The court held that *Regulation 44(2)* was not limited to actual electrocution. It was intended to protect employees from all injuries likely to occur where electrical cable or apparatus is used so as to become a source of danger to employees. The court held that this definitely included psychiatric illness caused by the sight of a colleague electrocuted close to Mr Young who was lucky to escape himself.

Comment: This case concerned the ambit of protection of employees from dangers from electric equipment. *Regulation 44(2)* addressed electrically charged cables which might be a source of danger to persons employed during any relevant operations or work. The defendant argued that the ambit of protection under the Regulation was targeted at dangers arising from direct contact with the equipment. However it was held that the legislation was not limited to physical contact and psychiatric injury resulting from witnessing a colleague being electrocuted in close proximity was reasonably foreseeable and came within the Regulations.

Alcock and Others v Chief Constable of South Yorkshire (28 November 1991) House of Lords (Times Law Reports, 29 November 1991)

[A26.3]

nervous shock; proximity

Background: This case arose out of the Hillsborough Stadium disaster in 1989 when ninety five people were crushed to death and more than 400 injured. The Chief Constable for South Yorkshire Police admitted liability in negligence in respect of the deaths and physical injuries. This case, however, was an amalgamation of actions brought by people who had suffered nervous shock resulting in psychiatric illness as a result of the disaster. They had not been in the area of the disaster themselves, but were connected to people who were.

Mr Alcock and Mr Harrison had been in the West Stand and from there witnessed the scenes in pens 3 and 4, during which Mr Alcock's brother in law and two brothers of Mr Harrison died. Other claimants had not been present at the grounds at all: Mr and Mrs Copoc, whose son died, and Alexandra Perk, whose fiance died, watched the scenes on live television.

Test: Following *McLoughlin v O'Brian [1983] 1 AC 410*, in the case of 'nervous shock' caused by physical injury or peril to another, public policy issues mean that foreseeability does not of itself give rise to a duty of care. In addition to the reasonable foreseeability of psychiatric injury, to establish liability there must be a relationship of proximity between the claimant and the defendant.

The class of persons to whom a duty of care is owed is limited to those with a relationship involving close ties of love and affection to the victim, since it is reasonably foreseeable that if anything happens to that person, they may be at real risk of psychiatric illness. In addition, the shock must be suffered through the sight or hearing of the event or of its immediate aftermath.

Decision: The House of Lords dismissed the claims. They ruled that the mere fact of a particular relationship was not enough to place someone within the class of people to which a duty of care was owed, and that close ties of love and affection must be proved by the claimant. In the cases of Mr Alcock and Mr Harrison, there was no evidence of particular close ties of love and affection.

In the cases of the Copocs and Alexandra Perk, the Lords held that the closest ties of love and affection fell to be presumed from the fact of the particular relationships, and there was no suggestion of anything which might tend to rebut that presumption. However, those three had only watched the disaster on television, and the suffering of recognisable individuals was not shown since this was against the broadcasting code of ethics. This could not amount to them being within sight or hearing of the event or its immediate aftermath; it did not create the necessary degree of proximity. Anxiety for the safety of the relative was not the same as seeing their fate during or shortly after the event. Nor could the television scenes reasonably be regarded as giving rise to shock, in the sense of a sudden assault on the nervous system.

Comment: The position of the relatives contrasts with that of employees and rescuers suffering psychiatric illness in *Frost and Others v Chief Constable of South Yorkshire Police and Others [1997]* (below) which also arose out of the Hillsborough disaster.

Frost and Others v Chief Constable of South Yorkshire Police and Others (31 October 1996) Court of Appeal ([1997] 1 All ER 540, Times Law Reports, 6 November 1996)

[A26.4]

employers' liability; post-traumatic stress disorder; rescuers

Background: The claimants were police officers who had been involved in the Hillsborough Stadium disaster in 1989 and who subsequently suffered post-traumatic stress disorder. One of the officers had helped to free people from the pens, two had attended make-shift morgues, two were brought to the stadium in the immediate aftermath, and the sixth had not been at the ground but had dealt with relatives and liaised between the hospital staff and casualty bureau, and later went to the temporary morgue.

The chief constable admitted that the disaster had been caused by police negligence but contended that he owed no duty of care to these claimants since they were secondary victims, having not been exposed to the physical danger themselves. Secondary victims could only claim if they had ties of love and affection with the primary victims. In addition, it was argued that the officers could not establish a duty of care as rescuers as they were all professional rescuers and it was therefore not foreseeable that they would be affected by nervous shock.

Test: (Judge LJ dissenting) Where there is an employer/employee relationship, a duty of care exists regardless of whether the employee is a primary or secondary victim, and the limiting conditions in respect of secondary victims do not apply.

Equally, in so far as the distinction between primary and secondary victims is relevant to rescuers, the rescuer is in a primary relationship with the person whose negligence allows the dangerous situation to arise, and it makes no difference if the rescuer is a professional rescuer.

According to Lord Justice Rose, whether a particular person is a rescuer is a question of fact. Among the factors to be considered are: 'the character and extent of the original incident caused by the tortfeasor; whether that incident was finished or was continuing; whether there was any danger, continuing or otherwise, to the victim or the plaintiff; the character of the plaintiff's conduct, in itself and in relation to the victim; and how proximate, in time and place, the plaintiff's conduct was to the incident'.

Decision: The five officers who were at the stadium were owed a duty of care, variously by virtue of the employer/employee relationship or as rescuers.

The sixth officer admitted she was a not a rescuer and it was held that, since she was not at the stadium when the negligent loss of control occurred, she was not owed a duty of care by virtue of the employer/employee relationship. According to Rose LJ: 'What she subsequently did was no more than could properly be asked of any police officer in the ordinary carrying out of her duties following a serious incident'.

Comment: This case should be compared with *Alcock v Chief Constable of the South Yorkshire Police (1991)* (see paragraph A26.3) which also dealt with psychiatric injury arising out of the Hillsborough disaster. In *Frost*, the court was keen to try to emphasise that no favouritism was being shown to the police officers, who recovered damages, as opposed to the relatives in Alcock, who did not.

Hale v London Underground Ltd (4 November 1992) High Court, Queen's Bench Division) ((1992) 11 BMLR 81)

[A26.5]

post-traumatic stress disorder; quantum

Background: Mr Hale was a fireman who assisted in the rescue of victims of the King's Cross Underground Station fire in 1987. He was not physically injured, but some time later it became apparent that he was suffering from post-traumatic stress disorder, which was having a damaging effect on his work and family life. London Underground admitted liability for negligence, so the only issue in the case was quantum.

Decision: The judge accepted medical evidence that Mr Hale would continue to suffer from a deep rooted depression, even after the stress of the litigation had ended, and that he was unlikely to return to work as a fully operational fireman. He awarded general damages of £27,500. He also awarded sums under various specific heads of damages. This included £5,000 for the loss of congenial employment. The judge accepted that Mr Hale had derived great satisfaction from his former employment, which he did not get from his present non-operational job as fire prevention officer, and was unlikely to get from any other job he might be able to obtain. He also awarded damages totalling £77,500 for future loss of earnings. Mr Hale was still employable, his condition would put him at a considerable disadvantage in the job market, and he was likely to have periods of great difficulty in obtaining employment. Total damages came to £144,389.95, plus interest.

Comment: Quantification of damages for psychological distress and resultant future loss of earnings was developed in this case. It demonstrates that even someone in the position of a trained rescuer, such as a fireman, who faces danger and risks as a matter of routine, may be able to recover damages for psychological damage brought on by the performance of his professional duties.

McFarlane v EE Caledonia (29 July 1993) Court of Appeal ([1994] 2 All ER 1)

[A26.6]

bystander; witness; proximity

Background: Mr McFarlane was a witness to the Piper Alpha disaster. He was off duty on a nearby support vessel when a series of explosions destroyed the oil rig. Although he suffered no physical injury, he claimed damages from EE Caledonia for psychiatric illness suffered as a result of his experience. On the trial of a preliminary issue, the judge held that his employer owed him a duty to exercise reasonable care to avoid causing him psychiatric injury. EE Caledonia appealed.

Decision: Two categories of people suffering nervous shock though fear of injury were identified in *Alcock v Chief Constable of the South Yorkshire Police [1991]*: those involved immediately as a participant in the event who feared injury to themselves; and passive and unwilling witnesses of injury to others. In this case, Mr McFarlane could not be said to be a participant for the purposes of recovering damages for nervous shock and the Court of Appeal held that it is not possible for a plaintiff who was a mere bystander or witness to recover damages for psychiatric harm. The exception to this was where there was a sufficient degree of proximity, requiring both nearness in time and place and a close relationship of love and affection between plaintiff and victim. It could not have been reasonably foreseen that Mr McFarlane would suffer psychiatric harm. Further, it had not been shown that it was reasonably foreseeable that a man of ordinary fortitude in the plaintiff's position would be so affected that he would suffer injury. The plaintiff was not entitled to succeed and the appeal was allowed.

Comment: This case illustrates that, in order to succeed in a claim for nervous shock, it is necessary to demonstrate, both that the sufferer viewed the accident from sufficient proximity but also that there were ties of love and affection between the plaintiff and the defendant. The question of whether a duty could ever be owed to mere bystanders was considered in *Alcock*. Lord Ackner and Oliver refused to exclude the possibility of a duty being owed 'given circumstances of such horror as would be likely to traumatise even the most phlegmatic spectator'. Lord Ackner gave the illustration of a petrol tanker crashing into a school and bursting into flames. However, this duty was not extended to the plaintiff in McFarlane because Stuart Smith LJ said that this would run counter to the whole basis of the decision in *Alcock* which established that the test is not merely reasonable foreseeability. He also suggested that to allow the plaintiff to succeed in these circumstances would be to import an element of subjectivity as peoples reactions to horrific events are very varied.

Reasonably Practicable

Readmans Ltd and Another v Leeds City Council (10 March 1992) High Court, Queen's Bench Division ([1992] COD 419)

[A27.1]

prohibition notice; burden and standard of proof

Background: Readmans were a cash and carry store using shopping trolleys which had a seat for babies or toddlers. There were a number of incidents in which it was alleged that trolleys had tipped forward due to the weight of children being carried in them. As a result, Leeds City Council Environmental Health Inspector served a prohibition notice stating that the use of the trolleys to carry children involved 'a risk of serious personal injury' and contravened *section 3(1)* of the *HSWA 1974*. Readmans appealed to an industrial tribunal, which held that Readmans had not put forward any convincing evidence as to why the prohibition notice should be lifted.

Decision: The judge considered the correct burden and standard of proof. He held that the tribunal had misdirected itself and that it was for the inspector to establish, on the balance of probabilities, that there was a risk of serious personal injury and to make out a *prima facie* case that there had been a breach of the 1974 Act. If this was established, the burden then shifted to Readmans to show, again on a balance of probabilities, that they had ensured, so far as was reasonably practicable, that visitors to Readmans' cash and carry were not exposed to those risks. In this regard, the judge stated that Readmans 'do not have to guarantee absolute safety, if such a thing is achievable, nor do they have to show that they have done what is practicable, that is to say, all that is physically possible. What they would have to establish is that they have done what is reasonably practicable to ensure that such risks as exist are avoided'.

Comment: The burden of proof rests on the defendant to establish that all reasonably practicable steps have been taken in the circumstances. In this case, evidence was presented concerning the fact that no other local authorities had moved to impose prohibition notices on the relevant trolleys – although the trolleys were in wide use. Whilst such evidence may assist the defendant in certain limited circumstances, it is unlikely that a failure of one local authority to enforce relevant laws would demonstrate that no risk exists or that all reasonably practicable steps have been taken.

Edwards v National Coal Board (21 March 1949) Court of Appeal ([1949] 1 All ER 743)

[A27.2]

coal miner; reasonably practicable; breach of statutory duty

Background: Mr Edwards, a coal miner, was killed when material fell from the side of a travelling road in a mine. The area where the fall occurred had no form of artificial support, although some propping and lining had been carried out elsewhere where weaknesses were apparent. Under *section 49* of the *Coal Mines Act 1911*, the National Coal Board was required to make the roof and sides of every travelling road secure. Mrs Edwards brought an action for damages against her husband's employer alleging breach of duty at common law and breach of statutory duty. The National Coal Board claimed protection under *section 102(8)* of the 1911 Act which provides that: 'The owner of a mine shall not be liable to an action as for damages for breach of statutory duty in respect of any contravention of or non-compliance with any of the provisions of this Act if it is shown that it was not reasonably practicable to avoid or prevent the breach'. It was contended that it was not reasonably practicable to have avoided or prevented the insecurity of the road at that point because there was nothing to indicate that a latent defect existed. It would be an impossible burden for the company to support all roads in the mine. The

High Court gave judgement for the defendant and Mrs Edwards appealed.

Decision: The Court of Appeal upheld the High Court's ruling that Mr Edward's employer had not been negligent. On the issue of the breach of statutory duty, 'reasonably practicable' was a narrower term than 'physically possible' (*Coltness Iron Co Ltd v Sharp [1937] 3 All ER 593*). In order to determine whether it was 'reasonably practicable' to avoid or prevent a breach of statutory requirements, the employer should weigh the quantum of risk against the sacrifice made (whether in terms of money, time or trouble) in carrying out the measures necessary to avert that risk. Where there was a gross disproportion between the two – the risk being insignificant in relation to the sacrifice – the onus placed on the employer under *section 102(8)* of the 1911 Act was discharged. This computation must be made before the accident. In this case, however, there had been a clear breach of statutory duty and the National Coal Board had failed to establish that it was not reasonably practicable for it to have avoided or prevented that breach. The appeal was allowed.

Comment: This case illustrates the principle that 'reasonably practicable' is a narrower term than 'physically possible'. Further, certain considerations may be balanced in determining whether the duty has been breached. Bearing in mind that in some instances it is sufficient to breach the statute if a mere risk arises, it is necessary to balance the level of the risk and the costs associated with the action required. Where the words 'reasonably practicable' are used cost considerations may be taken into account. *Edwards* was applied in *Sanderson v NCB [1961] 2 All ER 796* where it was stated that the onus of proving that the precautions required by the relevant Act were impracticable are on the employer. It is not sufficient to show that the employer took reasonable care. *Edwards* was distinguished in *Jackson v NCB [1955] 1 All ER 145* where the plaintiff claimed damages against the defendants who employed the deceased as a shot-firer. The deceased was killed by being buried under a roof which collapsed caused by an explosion of an abnormal character. It was held that (1) the conduct of the deceased caused the roof to fall which the defendants could not reasonably be expected to provide for, and (2) it was not reasonably practicable within the meaning of the relevant section.

Even if there had been a breach of the defendants' duty it was not reasonably practicable to avoid or prevent it. Consequently, judgement was in favour of the defendants.

Belhaven Brewery Co Ltd v A McLean (HM Inspector of Factories) (13 August 1975) Industrial Tribunal ([1975] IRLR 370)

[A27.3]

appeal improvement notice; 'reasonably practicable'

Background: Belhaven Brewery Co Ltd was served with an improvement notice requiring that a safety screen with an interlocking device be fitted around a kegging plant. The interlocking device would cut off the power and compressed air supply to the plant when a screen door was opened. The company appealed against the notice, arguing that a far cheaper safety screen could be fitted which would still meet statutory requirements. Further, company staff were sufficiently intelligent to ensure that the screen was kept in place whilst the machinery was operating and there would be a high level of management supervision. The HM Inspectorate of Factories disagreed and maintained that irrespective of the staff's level of intelligence and the degree of supervision, only a system with an interlocking device could be secure and comply with the relevant legislation.

Decision: The Industrial Tribunal considered that failure to fit a system with an interlocking device would be a contravention of *sections 13(1)* and *14(1)* of the *Factories Act 1961* (provision of secure fencing) and *section 2(1)* of the *HSWA 1974* (employers to ensure so far as is reasonably practicable the health, safety and welfare at work of all employees). Applying the test in *Edwards v NCB* [1949] as to what is reasonably practicable (i.e. weighing the risk against the sacrifice involved in averting that risk in terms of money, time or trouble), it was considered reasonably practicable for the company to fit the interlocking device. This was because the risk associated with not fitting the device was not insignificant in relation to the sacrifice involved in fitting it. The improvement notice was affirmed without modification.

Comment: The defendants contended that there were no alternative, less onerous ways of satisfying their duties. However, it was held by the tribunal that a failure to fit a system with the requisite device amounted to a breach. The risk associated with not fitting the device was not insignificant when measured against the sacrifice involved in fitting it. If the employers failed to fit the system they would be failing to satisfy their duty under *section 2(1)* of the *HSWA 1974* to ensure the health, safety and welfare at work of their employees.

Repetitive Strain Injury

Pickford v Imperial Chemical Industries plc (25 June 1998) House of Lords (Times Law Reports, 30 June 1998)

[A28.1]

repetitive strain injury; medical evidence; burden of proof

Background: The plaintiff worked for ICI plc as a secretary. She was employed to carry out a range of tasks, including typing which took up at least fifty per cent of her time. In 1988, she first experienced pain in her hands when typing and this culminated in her employment being terminated in 1990. She brought an action against her employer, alleging that its negligence had caused her to suffer from PDA4. This prescribed disease was recognised by the DHSS for the purposes of industrial injury benefit, which is defined as cramp of the forearm due to repetitive movements. The plaintiff claimed that the disease was organic in origin (rather than psychogenic) and that she had contracted it because her work involved large volumes of typing which she carried out for long periods without any rest breaks. The plaintiff's claim was dismissed in the High Court where it was held that: (i) the plaintiff had failed to prove that the PDA4 was organic in origin; (ii) the plaintiff had failed to prove that the condition was due to typing; (iii) it was not reasonably foreseeable that a secretary carrying out the plaintiff's duties would suffer from PDA4; and (iv) it was not incumbent on the company to specify that rest periods should be taken or to warn of the risk of PDA4. This decision was reversed by the Court of Appeal and ICI plc appealed.

Decision: The House of Lords considered that the trial judge's findings should not have been disturbed. The judge had been unable to decide from the conflicting medical evidence alone what the cause of the plaintiff's condition was. The judge was therefore entitled to consider all the other evidence and conclude that she had failed to prove her case that the condition was organic in origin and caused by excessive typing, rather than merely being associated with that activity. Further, the conclusion that the defendant was not negligent and her PDA4 was not reasonably foreseeable was based soundly on the evidence. The appeal was allowed.

Comment: This case held that the burden of proof in establishing the particular condition complained of rested on the plaintiff. Further, the employer was not considered negligent in failing to warn the secretary who was employed to perform a range of services that the typing tasks should be broken up with the other duties she was employed to do thereby introducing natural breaks by the rotation of work. The case also discussed the principle that caution should be exercised with respect to illnesses and conditions that were not well understood.

Ladds v Coloroll (In Liquidation) (14 August 1995) High Court (Current Law, October 1995)

[A28.2]

carpal tunnel syndrome; causation

Background: The plaintiff suffered from carpal tunnel syndrome. In an action against her employers, it was argued that although her work as a quilt manufacturer had not caused the carpal tunnel syndrome, it had caused tenosynovitis which then led to the other medical condition.

Decision: On the evidence presented, the High Court found that the plaintiff did not initially have tenosynovitis but had suffered from carpal tunnel syndrome from the start. This condition had not been caused by her employment but had been highlighted by the work she carried out which was repetitive. The plaintiff had failed to establish either foreseeability or medical causation. Further, the employer had not been negligent; the employee's tasks were not of the type and frequency to lead to a repetitive strain injury and after she had revealed the problem, she had been moved to different work.

Comment: This case illustrates the necessity of proving, in order to establish the requisite causation, that the type of work being undertaken by the employee is of a nature which is likely to result in the loss allegedly suffered.

Mughal v Reuters Ltd (28 October 1993) High Court (Times Law Reports, 10 November 1993)

[A28.3]

journalist; repetitive strain injury

Background: A Reuters journalist alleged that the pain felt in his fingers, hands, arms and shoulders was caused by his working for long periods at a desk and the position he had to sit in as he worked at his computer. He claimed that his employer had failed to provide him with adequate advice and equipment to enable him to work safely and as a result he experienced permanent disability from repetitive strain injury (RSI).

Decision: Conflicting medical evidence was presented concerning the existence of RSI and the plaintiff's condition. The defendant's evidence was preferred and the High Court ruled that repetitive strain injury was not a condition known to medical science and did not represent a condition promoted by repetitive work. It did not have either an identifiable pathology or an existence as a clinical condition and could not therefore form the basis of an action against an employer alleging negligent working methods. An employer could not provide and maintain a safe system of work if there was no consensus as to what this would be in particular circumstances. There had been no breach of duty by Reuters and the claim for damages was dismissed.

Comment: This case centres around the recognition of RSI as a condition. Information and awareness of RSI has progressed significantly since this case as has the importance of posture in the workplace.

McSherry v British Telecommunications plc; Lodge v British Telecommunications plc (16 December 1991) Mayor's and City of London Court ([1992] 3 Med LR 129)

[A28.4]

repetitive strain injury; employer's liability

Background: Mrs McSherry and Mrs Lodge were employed by BT as data processing officers, involving long hours of high speed repetitive keyboard work. The system of work included incentives to work faster, and the chairs and desks were not chosen with ergonomic considerations in mind. Nor were the workers given any guidance as to working posture. After a few years of this, both developed painful and ongoing RSI symptoms which prevented them from being able to continue their work.

Test: Since RSI was a developing area of occupational medicine, the question was what BT knew or ought to have known about it around the time when Mrs McSherry and Mrs Lodge's symptoms were developing in the early 1980s.

Decision: BT was held liable for the full extent of the injury suffered by both Mrs McSherry and Mrs Lodge. On the facts, the judge held found that both women suffered RSI as a result of their work. The strain of the repetitive unsupported movement of hands and arms was added to by the strains arising from the working systems in place and poor posture due to the poor ergonomics of the workstation, unsuitable chairs and, in Mrs Lodge's case, the uncorrected bad habits of the operator. On the question of BT's knowledge of the risk of RSI, the judge held that the company had not known enough about it to take steps to prevent the injuries. However, the risk of serious musculoskeletal damage as a result of bad posture was well known, and BT ought to have taken steps to correct its workers' postures – whether those postures were a result of unsuitable chairs, bad table design or the sitting position chosen by the operator. Posture was not the sole cause of Mrs McSherry and Mrs Lodge's RSI, but it contributed substantially to it, and so was sufficient to establish liability.

In addition, the judge stated: 'it is sufficient in law if the tortfeasor should reasonably have foreseen that his breach of duty was likely to cause injury within the broad category of injury which was in fact caused: *Hughs v Lord Advocate [1963] 1 All ER 705*. As I have found, I am satisfied that the defendants should have been aware that bad posture would cause musculoskeletal problems. The fact that the injuries sustained were more extensive than those that they might have envisaged is of no consequence in law'.

The judge also ruled that BT was in breach of its statutory duty, under *section 14* of the *Offices Shops and Railway Premises Act 1963*, to provide suitable chairs, and that this breach substantially contributed to the women's injuries.

Comment: This case stresses the importance of posture and ergonomics in the workplace. This came to be recognised throughout the 1980s and there were a number of publications compiled on the subject, which stressed that office furniture, as well as being necessary for comfort, is clearly a matter of health and safety as well.

Reporting of Injuries, Diseases and Dangerous Occurrences

Woking Borough Council v BHS plc (18 October 1994) Magistrates' Court (Times Law Reports, 4 November 1994)

[A29.1]

Background: BHS plc was prosecuted by Woking Borough Council for failing to report an accident involving a customer under the *Reporting of Injuries, Diseases and Dangerous Occurrences Regulations 1985 (RIDDOR) (SI 1985 No 2023)*. The Magistrates' Court held that it was not necessary for accidents to members of the public to be reported in this way and the case was dismissed. Woking Borough Council appealed.

Decision: The court ruled that as *Regulation 3* of the 1985 Regulations refers to 'any person', the duty to report within seven days of an accident extends to visitors, customers and other invitees to the premises, in addition to employees, the self-employed and those undergoing training for employment. The case was remitted to the justices.

Comment: This makes clear that RIDDOR cannot be confined, in its application, to those who are employed, but that the reference to 'any person' must be interpreted literally.

Safe System of Work

Nilsson v Redditch BC (31 October 1994) Court of Appeal ([1995] PIQR 199)

[A30.1]

dustman; safe system of work; alternative system of work

Background: Mr Nilsson worked as a dustman, employed by Redditch Borough Council. Black plastic bags were used for rubbish collection. The accident happened when Mr Nilsson was swinging a bag up into the collection van and was nicked on the leg by a piece of glass which had worked its way through the bag. The surprise caused him to slip and fall, injuring his shoulder. He argued that the council was negligent for failing to provide a safe system of work. During the first instance hearing, Mr Nillson raised the issue of the use of wheelie bins as an alternative.

Test: Have the employers taken reasonable steps to provide a system which will be reasonably safe, having regard to the dangers necessarily inherent in its operation? In answering this question, the court must consider the extent to which the system is widespread or of long-standing; if it is both, the claimant will have a heavy burden to establish a breach of duty of care. Where the claimant claims that an alternative system of work should have been adopted, that alternative must be judged comparatively, taking into account issues of practicability and commercial viability as well as safety.

Decision: The Court of Appeal overturned the first instance decision, and held that Mr Nilsson had not been able to show that the bin bag system was unsafe. It was widespread consensus across the country, and could be taken as evidence that the system was reasonably safe. Waite LJ considered that there had not been enough evidence adduced to enable a proper comparison of the competing bin bag and wheelie bin systems according to practicability, commercial viability, safety and extent of use elsewhere.

Comment: This case shows the importance of a system being commonplace and generally accepted as a system which is safe. The case of *Ward v Hertfordshire CC [1970] 1 WLR 356* was considered in this case where Ward, a young boy, injured himself on a flint wall in the playground at school. The wall was held not to be dangerous on the grounds that it was an ordinary wall, and a large number of walls in the village and indeed the country were the same. Applying this rationale to the case at hand, the rubbish system was used throughout the country and it would have cost a great deal of money to replace the present system.

General Cleaning Contractors Ltd v Christmas (10 December 1952) House of Lords ([1952] 2 All ER 1110)

[A30.2]

window cleaner; provision of safe system of work

Background: A window cleaner employed by General Cleaning Contractors Ltd was cleaning the outside of the windows of a club. There were no fittings to which he could attach a safety belt so he stood on the sill of the window, a method commonly used by his colleagues. A defective sash fell on his hand, causing him to let go and fall. He was awarded damages against both his employer and the occupier of the premises. However the decision against the occupier was reversed on appeal (because the defective window was not an 'unusual danger' of which the occupier was bound to warn the window cleaner). The employer appealed to the House of Lords.

Decision: The House of Lords ruled that where the practice of ignoring an obvious danger had developed, it was not reasonable to expect the individual employee to take the initiative in devising and taking precautions against that danger. Regardless of the fact that other systems of work were not practical. General Cleaning Contractors Ltd was still obliged to consider the situation, to take reasonable steps to provide a system that would be reasonably safe having regard to the dangers inherent in the operation and to ensure that its employees were instructed on how to prevent accidents in their work, including providing implements. The employer had not done so and had not discharged its duty to the employee. The company's appeal was dismissed.

Comment: This case provided an explanation as to the relationship between the duty of care owed by employers and the obligations on workmen to take reasonable care for their own safety. Workmen are not in the position of employers when taking decisions and it was stated that 'workmen do not perform their duties in the calm atmosphere of a board room with the advice of experts. They have to make their decisions on narrow window sills and other places of danger and in circumstances where the dangers are obscured by repetition'. It is the responsibility of the employer to take the initiative in devising and using precautions and the workman is not expected to do so himself. The basic position is that if a man is doing work as specified and expected by his employer and there has been a failure to take adequate precautions, then the blame should not rest on the man for the want of additional precautions that are over and above those the employer was prepared to take on his behalf. The main issue is whether the employer himself has taken responsibility and reasonable care to provide a safe system of work for the employees. Where a practice of ignoring an obvious danger has developed then it is not the workman's responsibility to devise a system to tackle it. In deciding what is reasonable, the employer's conduct and the long established practice in the trade is relevant.

Scope of Employment

Aldred v Nacanco (27 March 1987) Court of Appeal ([1987] IRLR 292)

[A31.1]

personal injury; practical joke; reasonably foreseeable; employer's responsibility; vicarious liability

Background: The plaintiff was injured as the result of a practical joke played by a colleague. The other employee pushed an unsteady wash basin against Miss Aldred and, in turning quickly, she hurt her back. The wash basin was known to be unsteady. Miss Aldred brought an action against her employer, Nacanco, claiming that the wash basin was not as reasonably safe as a reasonable employer should have made it and further, that her employer was vicariously liable for the other employee's act which had caused her injury. Her claim was dismissed and she appealed.

Decision: The Court of Appeal upheld the judgement of the High Court concerning the employer's responsibility as a reasonable employer: Nacanco was not directly liable for Miss Aldred's injury because the wash basin was as reasonably safe as a reasonable employer should have made it. The use of the wash basin in a practical joke was not reasonably foreseeable. The court also held that Nacanco was not vicariously liable for its employee's action. An employer will not be vicariously liable where an employee carries out an unauthorised and wrongful act which is not so connected with an act authorised by the employer to do, but is instead an independent act. In such a case, the employee is not acting in the course of their employment but has gone outside of it (*Salmond on Torts*, 18th Edition, page 437). In Miss Aldred's circumstances, her colleague's action was a deliberate act which was unconnected with anything she was employed to do and was something completely outside of her employment. The appeal was dismissed.

Vandyke v Fender and Another, Sun Insurance Office Ltd (Third Party) (5 March 1970) Court of Appeal ([1970] 2 QB 292)

[A31.2]

damages; negligence; employer's insurers; indemnity; contract of service; course of employment

Background: Two men who worked thirty miles away from their homes were provided with a car by their employer who also paid for the petrol. On one journey, Mr Vandyke was seriously injured through the negligent driving of Mr Fender. He brought an action for damages for negligence against Mr Fender and their employer. The employer's insurers were joined as a third party as an insurance policy provided an indemnity for liability if any person under a contract of service sustained injury arising out of and in the course of their employment. In the High Court, it was held that Mr Vandyke had been injured in the course of his employment and that the insurance company must indemnify the employer under the policy in respect of a judgement given against Mr Fender and the employer. The insurer appealed.

Decision: The Court of Appeal held that the phrase 'arising out of and in the course of his employment' in the Road Traffic Acts and in employers liability policies, must be interpreted as meaning that a person travelling to or from work in transport provided by an employer on a public road or outside work premises is not in the course of his employment unless he is obliged to travel in that way. In this case, Mr Vandyke was not obliged to travel in the car provided by his employer and his injury did not arise out of and in the course of his employment. The insurers were not therefore liable to indemnify the employer.

Harvey v R G O'Dell Ltd and Another (Galway Third Party) (18 February 1958) High Court ([1958] 1 All ER 657)

[A31.3]

damages; negligence; vicarious liability; third party notice; contract of service; scope of employment

Background: Two workmen had been sent to work at a location away from their employer's premises. In such circumstances, the employer, R G O'Dell Ltd, either provided transport or employees made their own travelling arrangements and were reimbursed by the company. Travelling time was treated as working time and if it was necessary to travel to obtain a meal, the cost of the journey to the meal place would also be reimbursed. In this case, Mr Galway, a storekeeper, drove himself and the other employee. It was necessary to travel to a nearby town to obtain a meal and more materials. On the return journey there was an accident in which Mr Galway was killed and the second employee, Mr Harvey, was injured. Mr Harvey brought an action for damages against his employer, claiming that the company was vicariously liable for its employee's negligent driving. R G O'Dell Ltd served a third party notice claiming contribution from Mr Galway's estate under *section 6(1)* of the *Law Reform (Married Women and Tortfeasors) Act 1935* or claiming damages for breach of an implied term in Mr Galway's contract of service that he would indemnify the company for any liability due to his negligence.

Decision: On the facts, it was found by the High Court that the journey to the meal place should be regarded as fairly incidental to the work that that Mr Galway was employed to do and within the scope of his employment (*Canadian Pacific Ry. Co v Lockhart [1942] 2 All ER 464*; *McKean v Raynor Brothers Ltd (Nottingham) [1942] 2 All ER 650*). R G O'Dell Ltd was therefore vicariously liable for his negligence. As regards the third party proceedings, the court held that as Mr Galway had been employed as a storekeeper and not a driver, there was no implied term in his contract that he would indemnify the company if he failed to drive with care while on business. However, R G O'Dell Ltd was entitled to a 100 per cent contribution from Mr Galway's estate under the other provisions.

Comment: This case can be compared with *Vandyke v Fender and Another [1970]* (see paragraph A31.2).

Rose v Plenty and Another (7 July 1975) Court of Appeal ([1976] 1 All ER 97)

[A31.4]

children; milkman; personal injury; damages; negligence; scope of employment; vicarious liability

Background: Contrary to his employer's clear instructions, which were that no children should be employed or transported on milk floats, a milkman paid a thirteen year old boy to assist him on his milk round. The boy was injured in an accident when the milkman drove the milk float negligently and an action for damages for personal injuries resulting from the milkman's negligence was brought against the milkman and his employer. In the High Court, the claim against the milkman's employer was dismissed because the milkman had been acting outside the scope of his employment when he employed the plaintiff and transported him on the milk float against his employer's instructions. The plaintiff appealed.

Decision: The Court of Appeal held that the employer's instructions regarding the involvement of children concerned the conduct of the milkman within the scope of his employment; they did not define the scope of that employment. Thus, even though the milkman's actions were prohibited by his employer, they had been performed for the purpose of the company's business and the employer was vicariously liable for its employee's negligence. The appeal was allowed.

Faulkner v Chief Adjudication Officer (18 March 1994) Court of Appeal (Times Law Reports, 8 April 1994)

[A31.5]

policeman; personal injury; disablement benefit; course of employment

Background: Mr Faulkner applied for disablement benefit after he was injured whilst playing for the Staffordshire police football club. A social security appeal tribunal decided that he had sustained an industrial accident and was eligible for the benefit under *sections 50(1)* and *107(5)* of the *Social Security Act 1975*. This decision was set aside by a social security commissioner who referred to the judgement in a similar case, *R v National Insurance Commissioner, ex parte Michael [1977]* (see paragraph A31.6). Mr Faulkner appealed.

Decision: In *R v National Insurance Commissioner, ex parte Michael [1977]*, the issue was not whether the claimant was on duty at the time of the injury, but rather whether he was injured in the actual course of his work. Mr Faulkner argued that since that judgement, the whole ethos of policing had changed and in view of the importance of community policing, it was no longer possible to consider football as only recreational. The police should therefore be protected by industrial injuries benefit. The Court of Appeal found that in deciding whether, when playing football, he had been in the course of his employment, the main issue to be considered was the extent of Mr Faulkner's employment: when doing so. The implication of a contractual term must be based on ordinary legal principles (as in *Liverpool City Council v Irwin [1977] AC 239, 254*), and not on the basis that it seems reasonable or sensible that a term should be implied or because community policing is considered important by the police. In this case, there was no evidence upon which it could have been properly held that the policeman had been injured in the course of his employment. The appeal was dismissed.

R v National Insurance Commissioner, ex parte Michael (26 November 1976) Court of Appeal ([1977] 2 All ER 420)

[A31.6]

industrial injury benefit; police football match; course of employment; whether injury occurred in actual course of work

Background: After injuring his leg in a police inter-force football match, Mr Michael claimed industrial injury benefit under *section 5(1)* of the *National Insurance (Industrial Injuries) Act 1965* because his injury had been caused by an accident 'arising out of and in the course of his employment'. Despite the policeman's arguments that he was expected by his superiors to play for the team and the importance attached to this activity by the force, a national insurance commissioner dismissed his claim. It was held that football was a recreation and not something done in the course of a policeman's employment; it was not 'reasonably incidental' to that employment. An application for judicial review of this decision was dismissed by the High Court and Mr Michael appealed.

Decision: The Court of Appeal held that the issue of whether the policeman had been injured 'in the course of his employment' within the meaning of *section 5(1)* of the 1965 Act was an important question of law as to the interpretation of that section. For this reason and also because there was disagreement between different commissioners, the decision was considered by the court (rather than referring it back to the commissioner). The test was whether the injury was suffered in the actual course of the work that the policeman was employed to do or by reason of some event incidental to that work. It was not whether Mr Michael had been injured whilst engaged in an activity 'reasonably incidental' to his employment. This phrase does not appear in *section 5(1)* and although it had been applied in other cases to assist in the interpretation of the legislation, those cases involved injuries which occurred at the workplace during an interruption in work. 'Reasonably incidental' should only be used in that context. Authority on the meaning of 'in the course of his employment' is provided by many cases, *inter alia, Charles R Davidson & Co v M'Robb [1918] AC 304* and *Armstrong, Whitworth & Co v Redford [1920] All ER Rep 316*. The court found that playing in the football team was not part of Mr Michael's work as a policeman and was not incidental to that work, even though he was expected by his superiors to participate. It did not follow however that playing football could never form part of an activity in the course of a policeman's work because a recreational activity of this type could form part of police training. The appeal was dismissed.

R v D'Albuquerque, ex parte Bresnahan (11 November 1965) High Court ([1966] 1 Lloyd's Report 69)

[A31.7]

industrial injuries benefit; certiorari; course of employment; error in law

Background: Mrs Bresnahan applied for industrial injuries benefit after her husband, a dock worker, was drowned. His death occurred when he used a fork lift truck to move some pallets and fell into the water. He was not authorised to use the truck for his work. Mrs Bresnahan's claim was finally rejected by the Deputy Commissioner for the National Insurance (Industrial Injuries) Acts because her husband's driving of the fork lift truck was not within the scope of his employment and therefore his death was not caused by an accident arising out of and in the course of his employment. Mrs Bresnahan applied for an order of certiorari to quash that decision.

Decision: *Section 8* of the *National Insurance (Industrial Injuries) Act 1946* provides that an accident shall be deemed to arise out of and in the course of a person's employment, notwithstanding that the person suffering the accident is acting in contravention of the orders of his employer, if the accident would have been deemed so to have arisen had the act not been done in contravention and the act is done for the purposes of and in connection with the employer's trade or business. The High Court held that Mr Bresnahan's driving of the truck, regardless of whether this was unauthorised, was different from the work for which he was employed to do. *Section 8* of the 1946 Act could not therefore bring his act within the scope of his employment. The decision of the Deputy Commissioner was correct in law and the application for an order of certiorari was dismissed.

Comment: There is a distinction to be drawn in situations where an employee acts beyond or outside the course of his duties as compared to those situations where an employee performs his duties improperly. In *R v D' Albuquerque* the deceased had no authority whatsoever to drive a fork lift truck as he was neither the driver nor the relief driver and no one had given him permission. The findings of this case were doubted and must be viewed in the light of *Kay v ITW [1968]* (see paragraph A31.9) where an employee moved a truck which was causing an obstruction and caused injury to another. Thus, a master can be liable for acts done by his servant in the course of his employment even though such acts are not authorised. However, the relevant unauthorised act causing the damage must be so connected with acts which have been authorised that it may be regarded as a mode, albeit an improper one, of doing them.

Davidson v Handley Page Ltd (20 December 1944) Court of Appeal ([1945] 1 All ER 235)

[A31.8]

accident; personal injury; damages; course of employment; common law duty of employer; safe system of work; reasonably incidental

Background: An employee slipped on a wet duckboard whilst washing her tea cup. The floor in the workshop in which she worked was prone to become wet and a system was in place to clean the floor or put sawdust down. At the time of her accident, neither operation had been carried out on the slippery surface. Her claim for damages for personal injury against her employer was dismissed because although it was found that Handley Page Ltd had failed to provide a safe system of work, she was not engaged in an activity directly connected with her work at the time of the accident. The employee appealed.

Decision: In the Court of Appeal it was held that an employer's common law duty to provide safe appliances extends to cover all acts normally and reasonably incidental to an employee's daily work. This duty therefore covered the activity of the employee at the time of her accident. The appeal was allowed.

Comment: This case concerned the scope of an employer's duty to employees under common law and it was made clear that the duty of an employer extends to matters that are reasonably incidental to the employment. The system provided by the employer, with workmen arbitrarily putting down sawdust, was not considered adequate. The only proper system would have been one under which continuous attention was given to control the risks associated with acts and work being undertaken.

Kay v I T W Ltd (24 April 1967) Court of Appeal ([1967] 3 All ER 22)

[A31.9]

employee; negligence; authorised act carried out in unauthorised way; scope of employment

Background: Mr Kay, chief storekeeper at I T W Ltd's warehouse, was injured when he was hit by a lorry driven by another employee. This employee, Mr Ord, was a general assistant in the warehouse with authority to drive small fork lift trucks and vans. He was returning to the warehouse in a fork lift truck and found the only entrance blocked by a lorry that was being loaded. Despite the fact that the lorry belonged to another company and he had no right to interfere, Mr Ord attempted to move the vehicle. He did not give any warning of this action. When started, the lorry moved backwards because it had been left in reverse gear: Mr Kay was standing behind the vehicle assisting with the loading operation and was injured. He successfully brought an action against his employer for damages for personal injuries caused by Mr Ord's negligence. I. T W Ltd appealed.

Decision: An employer is responsible for a wrongful act done by his employee if it is done in the course of that person's employment. This includes an unauthorised act, provided that the act is so connected with an authorised act that it might be regarded as a way of doing it (*Salmond on Torts*). The facts of each case must be viewed in the light of this principle. In this case, the Court of Appeal held that Mr Ord was acting within the scope of his employment with I T W Ltd when he started the lorry because he was attempting to return the fork lift truck to the warehouse, something he did as part of his work. His conduct was not so gross and extreme as to take his act outside the scope of his employment. I T W Ltd was therefore liable for his negligence. The appeal was dismissed.

Comment: As noted in the commentary in the case of *R v D'Albuquerque ex parte Bresnahan [1966]* (see paragraph A31.7), often there is a difficulty of determining what conduct is 'within the course of employment'. In *Kay v I T W*, Sachs LJ considered that there are instances when the dividing line can be very fine when comparing acts which constitute a 'very stupid mode of doing an authorised act' and 'acts which involve doing something which the employee has no business at all to be doing'. Sachs LJ contended that 'the line should be drawn fairly high in favour of the innocent sufferer injured by the act of somebody who was employed by the defendant employer and who was seeking to further that employer's interests.'

Smith v Stages & Darlington Insulation Co Ltd (1 December 1987) House of Lords ([1988] IRLR 107)

[A31.10]

temporary workplace; travelling time; personal injury; negligence; vicarious liability; course of employment

Background: This action was brought by the widow (Mrs Smith) of Mr George Machin who worked as an insulation lagger for Darlington Insulation Co Ltd. He was working on one job when he was sent, together with the first defendant, to carry out some urgent work on a power station in Wales. His travel expenses were paid by the company and he also received wages for the time that he was travelling. During the return journey, the car driven by the first defendant crashed and Mr Machin was injured (his subsequent death was unconnected to these injuries). He brought an action against both the first defendant and his employer on the ground that the company was vicariously liable for his colleague's negligence. The High Court found that Mr Machin's colleague was negligent but that he had not been acting in the course of his employment when driving home. This decision was reversed by the Court of Appeal and Darlington Insulation Co Ltd appealed to the House of Lords on the ground that it was not vicariously liable for its employee's negligence.

Decision: An employee is acting in the course of his employment when he is doing what he is employed to do (*Canadian Pacific Ry Co v Lockhart [1942] 2 All ER 464*, *St Helens Colliery Co Ltd v Hewitson [1924] AC 59*). In this case, the House of Lords held that the paramount rule was that an employee travelling on the highway is acting in the course of his employment if he is at the material time going about his employer's business. This duty to travel to work must not be confused with the duty to turn up for work. Where an employee is required to work some distance away from his usual workplace for a short time, he is acting in the course of his employment when travelling home at the completion of that work, if the journey is taken in the employer's time. As the employee was paid wages for the journey time (not just a travelling allowance), he was travelling in his employer's time. Darlington Insulation Co Ltd was therefore vicariously liable for the employee's negligence. The appeal was dismissed.

Comment: Consequently, this case clarified the principles in this previously troubled area of law concerning employees travelling to work, and whether this would be deemed to be in the course of employment. Whilst in this case the employer was held vicariously liable, this should be compared to the case of *Highbid v Hammett [1932] 49 TLR 104*. In that case, an employer was not considered to be liable for its employee's negligence and subsequent injury when the employee was cycling home to lunch even though he had permission to use the bicycle for that purpose. Further, in considering whether something is within the course of employment, see also *R v National Insurance Commissioner, ex parte Michael [1977]* (paragraph A31.6).

Duffy v Thanet Council (13 December 1983) High Court (1984, 134 NLJ 680)

[A31.11]

apprentice; personal injury; course of employment; vicarious liability

Background: Two apprentices (1 and 2) were making a wooden arch. When a third apprentice (3) began to damage the arch with a chisel, there was a struggle between persons 2 and 3 with the result that the chisel was released and hit apprentice 1 in the eye. He brought an action for personal injury against the employer of apprentices 2 and 3.

Decision: The High Court held that despite the fact that his action had been stupid and unauthorised, apprentice 2 had acted on behalf of his employer in seeking to protect the arch as this was done in the course of his employer's business. It followed therefore that the employer was vicariously liable for his act. The action by apprentice 3 was also unauthorised but had no connection with his employer who was not liable for his act.

Comment: An employer will remain responsible for an employee's conduct provided it is reasonably incidental to his employment – this remains so in terms of practical jokes and horseplay. Further as noted in *Hudson v Ridge Manufacturing Co [1957] 2 QB 348*, where there is consistent horseplay, the employer should take action. This position should be compared to the circumstances in *Aldred v Nananco [1997]* (discussed in paragraph A31.1) where the act under consideration was considered deliberate and not within the employee's scope of employment.

Sex Discrimination

Page v Freight Hire (Tank Haulage) Ltd (3 November 1980) Employment Appeal Tribunal ([1981] 1 All ER 394)

[A32.1]

potentially harmful chemical; transportation; sex discrimination; section 51 of Sex Discrimination Act 1975; section 2 of Health and Safety at Work etc. Act 1974

Background: A young woman lorry driver complained to an industrial tribunal that her employer had breached *section 1* of the *Sex Discrimination Act 1975* by refusing to allow her to drive a vehicle containing a chemical that was potentially harmful to women of child bearing age. It was held that although Freight Hire (Tank Haulage) Ltd had discriminated against her, there was no breach of *section 1* of the 1975 Act because this had been done in the interests of her safety. Mrs Page appealed.

Test: Acting in the interests of an employee's safety is not in itself a defence against a claim of unlawful discrimination under the 1975 Act. *Section 51(1)* of the 1975 Act however provides that an employer's action will not be unlawful if it is necessary to comply under an obligation under an earlier statute.

Decision: In this case, Freight Hire (Tank Haulage) Ltd had a duty under *section 2* of the *HSWA 1974* to ensure so far as is reasonably practicable the health, safety and welfare of its employees, including in particular, ensuring safety and absence of risks to health in the use, handling, storage and transport of articles and substances (*section 2(2)(b)*). The Employment Appeal Tribunal ruled that the company was entitled to argue that the only way that *section 2* could be complied with was to refuse to allow Mrs Page to drive a vehicle containing the chemical. Freight Hire

(Tank Haulage) Ltd was protected by *section 51* of the *Sex Discrimination Act 1975*. The appeal was dismissed.

Comment: When considering whether the action taken by the employer was reasonable, it was necessary to consider the measures that could have been employed to eliminate the risk. The Equal Opportunities Commission's arguments that the duty on the employer was to show that this was the only course of action open to the employer were rejected as being too high a standard. The only duty placed on the employer is to ensure the reasonable health and safety of employees.

Transport of Dangerous Goods

West Cumberland By Products Ltd v Director of Public Prosecutions (26 October 1987) High Court ([1988] RTR 391)

[A33.1]

transport of dangerous goods; section 36 of Health and Safety at Work etc. Act 1974; pleadings

Background: An information was issued against West Cumberland By Products Ltd for an offence under *section 33(1)* of the *HSWA 1974* for failing to comply with *Regulation 10(2)* of the *Dangerous Substances (Conveyance by Road in Road Tankers and Tank Containers) Regulations 1981 (SI 1981 No 1059)*. It was alleged that information concerning a tanker containing a dangerous substance was not readily accessible and that information for other substances not being carried was not destroyed or removed from the vehicle. Under *Regulation 10* of the 1981 Regulations, both the operator (*Regulation 10(1)*) and the driver (*Regulation 10(2)*) of the vehicle have duties: the operator must provide the written information to the driver and the driver must make this accessible and destroy or remove any irrelevant information. At the court hearing, it was found that the driver was in breach of his duty under *Regulation 10(2)* and that the operator had not failed in its duty under *Regulation 10(1)*. The company was convicted however under *section 36* of the 1974 Act which provides that where a person commits an offence due to the act or default of another person, that other person is also guilty of the offence and may be charged and convicted, regardless of whether proceedings are taken against the first person. This was inspite of the fact that there had been no suggestion that West Cumberland By Products Ltd was being charged under that section because the driver's offence under *section 33* of the 1974 Act was due to the company's act or default. The company appealed.

Decision: The issue here was whether it was appropriate to convict in reliance on *section 36* of the 1974 Act when the prosecution had not presented its case on that basis. The information laid against the company indicated that an offence under *Regulation 10(2)* of the 1981 Regulations was being charged. The High Court held that *Regulation 10(2)* applied to the driver and not the operator. The operator had no duty under *Regulation 10(1)* which went beyond the ambit of what that the Regulation provides. The offence under *section 36* was not a separate offence: the offence under which the company could be convicted was that under *section 33* of the 1974 Act and it was not appropriate to convict of an offence under *Regulation 10(2)* by virtue of *section 36*. The information in the summons must make it clear what case the defendant has to meet. The conviction was quashed.

Comment: This case stresses the importance of adequate pleadings being raised against a defendant in order that the defendants know all of the case they have to answer.

Vibration Induced Conditions

White v Holbrook Precision Castings Ltd (10 August 1984) Court of Appeal ([1985] IRLR 215)

[A34.1]

vibration induced condition; Raynaud's Phenomenon; health and safety risks; employer's duty

Background: Mr White, a labourer employed by Holbrook Precision Castings Ltd, was offered a position as a grinder in the company's factory. After about three years, he developed the vibration-induced condition Raynaud's Phenomenon in a finger joint. He was removed from grinding work and given a less well paid position with the company. In an action against his employer, Mr White claimed that the company should have warned him of the risk of developing the condition and that he should have undergone periodic examination for the condition. This claim was dismissed and he appealed.

Test: An employer has a duty to warn an employee of the health and safety risks of a specific type of work where such risks are not commonly known but are ones which are or should be known by the employer . This includes risks which the employer cannot guard against by taking precautions, and where knowledge of those risks would be likely to affect the decision of the employee to undertake that work.

Decision: The Court of Appeal held that the company knew that Raynaud's Phenomenon caused minor discomfort which did not affect capacity for work in most cases and only minor and trivial inconvenience in other activities. It would inevitably have concluded that Mr White would have regarded the condition as of no consequence when deciding whether to take up the position. Further, as the association of Raynaud's Phenomenon with grinding work was common knowledge among employees, Mr White was aware of the potential problem of his developing the condition when he was offered the position. Holbrook Precision Castings Ltd did not have a duty therefore to warn Mr White. His appeal was dismissed.

Comment: This case concerned the duty placed on employers to warn potential employees of risks associated with the job they are applying for. As noted, the case formulated the principle that there was a duty to warn employees of the risks associated with the particular work involved where those risks are not common knowledge and are ones which the employer does or should know of. This duty does not extend to situations where if the employee had been informed of the risks then he would not have acted on that information. The relevant information is that which is likely to affect the decision of a sensible and level headed employee.

Vicarious Liability

Century Insurance Co Ltd v Northern Ireland Road Transport Board (4 February 1942) Court of Appeal ([1942] 1 All ER 491)

[A35.1]

petrol tanker; explosion; negligence; master and servant; course of employment

Background: A fire and explosion were caused at a petrol station when the driver of a lorry delivering petrol lit a cigarette and threw away the lighted match. The driver was employed by Northern Ireland Road Transport Board ('NIRTB'), the owner of the lorry, and there was a contract between this company and Holmes & Co, the owner of the depot supplying the petrol. The contract contained a clause requiring that employees of NIRTB engaged in petrol deliveries should accept and obey the orders of Holmes & Co but that this did not mean or imply that they were employees of Holmes & Co. NIRTB was insured with Century Insurance Co Ltd ('CIC') against liabilities to third parties. CIC resisted a claim under the relevant policy and appealed against the judgement of the Court of Appeal, contending that at the time of the accident, the driver was the servant of Holmes & Co, not the insured. It was also claimed that the driver's negligent act was not in the course of his employment as a servant and therefore his master was not responsible for the consequences.

Test: When determining liability for a servant's actions, the tests to be applied are which party has the right to control the doing of the relevant act (*Donovan v Laing, Wharton & Down Construction Syndicate [1893] 1 QB 629*) and whether the servant himself has been transferred between the parties or only the use and benefit of his work (*Moore v Palmer [1886] 2 TLR 781*).

Decision: The House of Lords held that the driver was employed by NIRTB and the company was an independent contractor using its own vehicles and servants. The driver was only subject to the orders of Holmes & Co so far as was necessary to allow the petrol delivery contract to be fulfilled and that contract did not involve the transfer of the driver to the service of Holmes & Co. Further, the driver's negligence arose in the course of his employment with NIRTB. The company was therefore liable for that negligence and was entitled to claim under the insurance policy. Century Insurance Co Ltd's appeal was dismissed.

Comment: The above case was distinguished in *Kirby v National Coal Board [1958] SLT 47* where an individual was injured by an explosion of fire damp in the waste near the junction of two stints in a mine. Evidence indicated that smoking had taken place near this place. The Court of Session held that the fact that striking a match was illegal would not necessarily mean that the defendants were not liable for the consequences of the act. However, as no miner was employed to be at the relevant place, going there for an illicit smoke was outside the scope of any miner's employment and the defendants were not liable. This case was again distinguished in *A G v Hartley [1964] NZLR 785.* In this case, the principles by which 'course of employment' are to be defined were considered. It was held that it is not enough to decide whether what was done was a prohibited act since prohibition may either limit the scope of the employment or merely regulate the conduct of the employee within its sphere.

Mersey Docks and Harbour Board v Coggins & Griffiths (Liverpool) Ltd and McFarlane (26 July 1946) House of Lords ([1946] 2 All ER 345)

[A35.2]

crane driver; negligence; personal injury; damages; servant; contract of service

Background: Coggins & Griffiths (Liverpool) Ltd hired the use of a crane and a crane driver from Mersey Docks and Harbour Board to assist in the loading of a ship. The driver operated the crane negligently and Mr McFarlane, an employee of the forwarding agents who had engaged Coggins & Griffiths (Liverpool) Ltd, was injured. The contract concerning the hire of the crane referred to the Board's regulations which stated that crane drivers provided in such circumstances were the servants of the hirer during the hire period. In this case, the crane driver was an experienced man who was paid by the Board and who only the Board had the power to dismiss. Although Coggins & Griffiths (Liverpool) Ltd was able to tell the driver what should be lifted, it was not authorised to specify how the crane should be operated. Following his accident, Mr McFarlane brought a successful action for damages for negligence against Mersey Docks and Harbour Board. The Board appealed to the House of Lords, seeking to have that judgement substituted by one against Coggins & Griffiths (Liverpool) Ltd.

Decision: The question to be answered was whether the crane driver's employer or the hirer of the crane was liable for his negligence. The Board argued that under the terms of the contract, Coggins & Griffiths (Liverpool) Ltd should be the liable party. In the House of Lords, it was held that this question should be determined by considering the facts of the case and who had the authority to control the execution of the relevant acts of the driver, rather than by any contract between the parties. It was found that Mersey Docks and Harbour Board had failed to prove that the hirer of the crane had sufficient control over the actions of the driver to be liable as an employer for his negligence. This was because the hirer was not authorised to instruct the driver how to operate the crane. The appeal was dismissed.

Comment: The position of an employee relative to an employer was considered in this case. It was stated that a contract of service is made between master and man, and an arrangement is made for the transfer of his services from one master to another. Such transfer can only be effected with the employee's consent, express or implied. This is partly a contractual matter and partly a case of taking into account a number of factors to determine whom the employee was working for at the relevant time. Relevant factors may be (1) who is responsible for paying the employee, (2) who can dismiss the employee, (3) how long the alternative service lasts for, (4) what machinery is employed. It was acknowledged that there is no universal and conclusive test, which may be laid down. The most important issue was considered to be who has the right to control the employee's method of working. The task to be performed and the method of performing it must be under the control of someone else for the employer of the defendant to be discharged from liability.

McDermid v Nash Dredging & Reclamation Co Ltd (16 April 1986) High Court ([1986] 3 WLR 45)

[A35.3]

personal injury; damages; breach of contract; negligence; reasonable care; safe system of work; vicarious liability

Background: Nash Dredging & Reclamation Co Ltd was engaged in a joint enterprise with a Dutch company, Stevin, to dredge a fjord. Mr McDermid, an employee of Nash Dredging & Reclamation Co Ltd, was instructed to work on a tug captained alternately by a captain also employed by Nash Dredging & Reclamation Co Ltd and a captain who was an employee of the Dutch company. During his work, Mr McDermid was seriously injured and he was later forced to leave his job. He claimed damages from his employer for personal injury, loss and expense caused by the company's breach of a contract of employment and/or by the company's negligence in failing to take reasonable care of the safety of its employee. In the High Court, it was held that Mr McDermid's injuries were caused by the Dutch captain's negligence and that the captain was deemed to have been acting as the defendant's employee. Nash Dredging & Reclamation Co Ltd was therefore vicariously liable for that negligence. The company appealed.

Decision: Under the common law of vicarious liability, an employer's safety duties are owed to each employee individually, having regard to the employee's experience and skill. If that duty is delegated to another person, regardless of whether that person is an employee, the employer is still responsible for the performance of that duty and will be liable for injury to the employee through the delegate's negligence. In this case, Nash Dredging & Reclamation Co Ltd had placed the plaintiff, who was young and inexperienced, under the control and care of the Dutch captain who was the defendant's delegate to perform its duty towards the plaintiff, i.e. to take reasonable care to devise and carry out a safe system of work on board the tug. The defendant was liable for the captain's negligence because its duty had been entrusted to him, not because he was deemed to be its employee. The appeal was dismissed.

Comment: In addition to cases where the employer remains responsible for the negligence of his delegate, there are cases where the employer is under a duty to see for himself that his employees, whilst working on other premises and/or under the control of a third party, are not subjected to an unsafe system of work. The basic duty of an employer is to conduct his operations so as not to subject those employed by him to unnecessary risk – thus, whether liability arises where an individual is working on a site away from the employer's main premises, will depend on the circumstances at hand. The relevant circumstances include: (a) the skill and expertise of the injured employee, (b) the nature of the task on which the employee was working, (c) the place where the injured employee was working and the degree of control which the employer exercised at that place, (d) the relationship, if any, between the employer and the individual tortfeasor, (f) the interest, if any, of the employer in the task which the individual tortfeasor was performing when the accident occurred.

Imperial Chemical Industries Ltd v Shatwell (6 July 1964) House of Lords ([1964] 2 All ER 999)

[A35.4]

shotfirers; explosion; contributory negligence; breach of statutory duty; vicarious liability; volenti non fit injuria

Background: George and James Shatwell were employed by ICI Ltd as shotfirers. They both had the appropriate certificates and were experienced in this work. ICI Ltd prohibited the testing of electrical circuits for shotfiring unless all persons in the vicinity had withdrawn to shelter. This was also a requirement under *Regulation 27(4)* of the *Quarries (Explosives) Regulations 1959 (SI 1959 No 2259)* which placed a statutory duty on the Shatwell brothers, not their employer. They were fully aware of the prohibition and the reasons for this and also knew that a shotfirer who had disregarded the prohibition had had his certificate revoked. Despite this, they tested a shotfiring circuit in the open instead of waiting for a longer cable that would enable them to withdraw to a safer distance. James Shatwell gave his brother two short wires attached to a detonator and George Shatwell touched a galvanometer terminals with them. The explosion which followed injured them both. George Shatwell brought an action against ICI Ltd, claiming that the company was vicariously liable for James Shatwell's negligence and breach of statutory duty. George Shatwell's damages award was reduced by half to take account of his contributory negligence. The company's appeal was dismissed by the Court of Appeal and the company then appealed to the House of Lords.

Decision: The House of Lords held that although James Shatwell's action was a contributing cause of his brother's injury, ICI Ltd was not liable. The company had not breached any duty and therefore any liability would be vicarious liability for the fault of James Shatwell: the principle *volenti non fit injuria* afforded a defence as both Shatwell brothers knew and accepted the risk of testing the circuit in a way that breached the statutory requirements and their employer's rules. Secondly, each of the brothers was the author of his own injury and neither should be considered to have contributed a separate wrongful act injuring the other.

Comment: This case is important in that it permitted a limited departure from the general principle that *volenti* is not a defence to a breach of statutory duty. It was made clear that there is a considerable difference between two fellow servants collaborating carelessly so that the acts of both contribute to cause injury to one of them, and two fellow servants combining to disobey an order deliberately, though they knew of the risk involved. This case was applied in *Bolt v William Moss and Sons [1966] 110 SJ 385* where the plaintiff and fellow employee consistently disregarded their foreman's orders that a scaffold was not to be moved when anyone was standing on the platform. The plaintiff was on the platform when E grasped the scaffold and moved it; the scaffold fell over and the plaintiff claimed damages. It was held that E and P had combined to disobey orders and had known the risk involved. In that case, *volenti* was a complete defence and the employers were not at fault.

Access to Environmental Information

R v British Coal Corporation, ex parte Ibstock Buildings Products Ltd (21 October 1994) High Court, Queen's Bench Division ((1995) 247 ENDS 41)

[B1.1]

environmental information; confidentiality

Background: During the consideration of applications by Ibstock Building Products Ltd for planning permission, British Coal Corporation had disclosed to the local planning authority that it had been told by an informant that mine shafts under Ibstock's sites had been previously used for the dumping of munitions. The information surrounding the allegation was vague. Ibstock had argued that it was crucial for it to have the name of the informant so that enquiries could be made to determine the reliability of the comments.

Test: The issue before the court was whether the identity of the informant was 'information relating to the environment' within the meaning of the *Environmental Information Regulations 1992 (SI 1992 No 3240)* (the *'1992 Regulations'*) and, if so, whether there was any restriction in the *1992 Regulations* preventing the disclosure of the informant's identity.

Decision: The court held that the informant's identity was environmental information. It was necessary to know the source of the information in order to assess the credibility of the information. The court also concluded that the identity of the informant was confidential within the terms of *Regulation 4* of the *1992 Regulations*. Ibstock was awarded costs.

Comment: The purpose of the *1992 Regulations* was to provide for freedom of access to information on the environment. It would be strange if parliament had intended that only the bare information itself should be disclosed, without it being possible to ascertain whether it was right or wrong. This case was also one of the first to consider the judicial interpretation of the *1992 Regulations*.

Wilhelm Mecklenburg v Kreis Pinneberg-Der Landrat (17 June 1998) European Court of Justice (Case C-321/96 (17 June 1998) (ECJ), [1999] All ER (EC) 166)

[B1.2]

environmental information; exception to disclosure

Background: In March 1993, Mecklenburg requested that Pinneberg-Der Landrat send him a copy of a statement submitted by the local countryside protection authority in relation to a planning consent for the construction of a road. Pinneberg-Der Landrat rejected his request on the grounds that (1) the authority's statement was not 'information relating to the environment' within the meaning of *Article 2(a)* of *Directive 90/313/EEC on the freedom of access to information on the environment* because it was merely an assessment of information already available to Mecklenburg and; (2) the criteria for refusing a request for environmental information set out in *Article 3(2)* of *Directive 90/313/EEC* applied because a development consent procedure should be regarded as 'preliminary investigation proceedings'. An administrative appeal lodged by Mecklenburg was dismissed in September 1993. In October 1993 Mecklenburg brought an action in the Administrative Court in Schleswig-Holstein, claiming that the countryside authority's statement constituted an administrative measure, that the authority's evaluation of the information in its possession did not detract from its nature as 'information relating to the environment', and that development consent proceedings did not constitute 'preliminary investigation proceedings' within the meaning of *Article 3(2)*. This action was dismissed on the grounds that the information sought by Mecklenburg was covered by confidentiality provisions relating to the proceedings of public authorities set out in the legislation that had transposed *Directive 90/313/EEC* into German law.

Mecklenburg subsequently appealed. That court expressed a view that the countryside authority's statement constituted an 'administrative measure for the protection of the environment' within the meaning of *Article 2(a)*. However, the court decided to stay the proceedings and refer the following issues to the ECJ for a preliminary ruling: (1) whether a statement of views given in development consent proceedings by a countryside protection authority constitutes an administrative measure designed to protect the environment within the meaning of *Article 2(a)* of *Directive 90/313/EEC*; and (2) whether the proceedings of an administrative authority are 'preliminary investigation proceedings' within the meaning of *Directive 90/313/EEC*.

Test: The court noted that the legislation makes it clear that the concept of environmental information' is very broad. *Article 2(a)* of *Directive 90/313/EEC* applies to any information on the state of the environment as well as to activities or measures which may adversely affect or protect the environment including administrative measures. The use, in *Article 2*, of the term 'including' indicates that administrative measures are merely an example of the activities covered by the Directive. In order to constitute 'information relating to the environment' it is sufficient for an authority's statement of views to be an act capable of adversely affecting or protecting the environment. That will be the case where the statement is capable of influencing the outcome of development consent proceedings.

In relation to the second question, the court noted that, as far as the objective of *Directive 90/313/EEC* is concerned, the principle of freedom of access to information is laid down in *Article 1* of the Directive. The preamble to the Directive emphasises that a refusal to comply with a request for information relating to the environment may, however, be justified in 'certain specific and clearly defined cases'.

Decision: *Article 2(a)* is to be interpreted as covering a statement of views given by a countryside protection authority (or similar body) in development consent proceedings, if that statement is capable of influencing the outcome of those proceedings in relation to the protection of the environment.

It is clear that, by virtue of the third indent of *Article 3(2)*, the exception to the general principle of freedom of access to information includes proceedings of a judicial or quasi-judicial nature. As such, 'preliminary investigation proceedings' must refer to the stage immediately prior to judicial proceedings or an enquiry.

Accordingly, the term 'preliminary investigation proceedings' in the third indent of *Article 3(2)*, can be taken to include an administrative procedure which prepares the way for administrative measures if it immediately precedes a contentious or quasi-contentious procedure, and arises from the need to obtain proof or to investigate a matter prior to the start of the actual procedure.

Comment: This was the ECJ's first judgement concerning the interpretation of *Directive 90/313/EEC*. The court's liberal approach may have future implications for as and when further conflicts of interpretation arise.

R v Secretary of State for the Environment, Transport and the Regions and Another, ex parte Alliance Against The Birmingham Northern Relief Road and Others (29 July 1998) High Court, Queen's Bench Division (NLD, 29 July 1998)

[B1.3]

environmental information; exception to disclosure

Background: Pursuant to a concession agreement with the secretary of state, Midland Expressway Ltd (MEL) proposed to design, build, finance and operate the Birmingham Northern Relief Road. MEL would recover its costs by charging a toll for usage. The Alliance Against The Birmingham Northern Relief Road sought to obtain a copy of the concession agreement from the Department of Environment. This was refused in writing on 23 September 1998 for reasons of commercial confidentiality. The Alliance sought to challenge this decision by way of judicial review.

Test: The question was whether the concession agreement constituted information relating to the environment within the meaning of *Regulation 2(1,)(a)* of the *Environmental Information Regulations 1992 (SI 1992 No 3240)* and, if so, whether any of the exceptions in *Regulation 4* applied.

Decision: The court held that where issues arose as to whether information related to the environment, the question had to be decided by the court. This decision had to be based on the facts as found by the court itself, and not whether the secretary of state was himself satisfied that the concession agreement contained information which related to the environment and which could be treated as confidential. The fact that the concession agreement was defined as a commercial agreement in no way meant that it could not contain information relating to the environment. It simply meant that if such information was contained in the agreement, it is possible that it would fall within one of the exceptions in *Regulation 4*.

The court held that a concession agreement is not, in itself, intrinsically confidential. The fact that the parties wished to treat the agreement as confidential is a relevant factor for deciding whether any commercial or industrial confidentiality is to be attached. The information must have been both capable of being treated as confidential within *Regulation 4(2)(e)* and the parties must have agreed to treat it as such, so that any disclosure would constitute a breach of the agreement.

In this case, the agreement as a whole did not fall within the exception in *Regulation 4(2)(e)* and the applicants were entitled to be provided with those parts of the agreement which did not fall within this sub-section. The decision of 23 September 1998 was quashed but it was still up to the secretary of state to decide how to respond to the Alliance's request.

Comment: This is an important decision relating to the extent to which commercial agreements could become disclosed under the *Environmental Information Regulations 1992.*

Contaminated Land

Blue Circle Industries v The Ministry of Defence (10 June 1998) Court of Appeal (Times Law Reports, 16 June 1998)

[B2.1]

radioactive contamination; Nuclear Installations Act 1965; nuisance; negligence; damages; physical harm

Background: In this case, the Court of Appeal had to address the issue of compensation for the loss of a sale of land due to contamination. Blue Circle Industries was in the process of selling its property to Sun Microsystems when it and the prospective purchaser became aware of contamination on the site. The court of first instance found that this discovery led to the collapse of the sale and a fall in the market value of the property. There was little dispute that the Ministry of Defence was responsible for the contamination and that the remediation costs could be claimed by Blue Circle against the Ministry of Defence as a direct head of damages. However, this alone would not have compensated Blue Circle for its losses. Blue Circle therefore sought to recover damages for its losses resulting from the aborted sale and the fall in market value.

Blue Circle's property bordered the Atomic Weapons Establishment site at Aldermaston which was operated by AWE plc. A number of ponds on the site operated by AWE contained radioactive silts. Heavy storms in the late 1980s caused these ponds to flood and disperse the radioactive contaminated silts onto the Blue Circle property. Blue Circle only became aware of the contamination during the course of negotiations to sell the property.

During sale negotiations, the anticipated purchase price was £10.3 million. Sun Microsystems pulled out after learning of the radioactive contamination. In an attempt to recover its losses due to not being able to sell the property, Blue Circle originally brought an action under the *Nuclear Installations Act 1965*, nuisance, *Rylands v Fletcher*, negligence and trespass. The common law causes of actions were ultimately stayed and only the action under *section* 7 of the *Nuclear Installations Act 1965* was pursued. This section imposes strict liability on a licensee of a nuclear site for damage to property caused by nuclear matter. It was established that the level of radioactive contamination was in excess of the requirements under the *Radioactive Substances Act 1960*. Clean up was therefore required.

Test: Whilst the court had to consider whether the damage caused was within *section* 7 of the 1965 Act, the difficult question was assessing the level of damages to be awarded as a result of contamination, particularly when considering the loss of opportunity (i.e. the sale of the property).

Decision: The judge at first instance accepted that the loss of this sale was directly attributable to the physical damage to the property by the radioactive contamination. He accepted that the loss in property value was a consequence of that physical damage. He held that the loss of the bargain which had occurred after the date of contamination and before the date of remediation was foreseeable. As such, Blue Circle could obtain damages for its losses during this period. In order to calculate the damages for loss of sale, the court looked at the proposed purchase price. They also gave consideration to expert opinion on the value of the property following Sun Microsystems' withdrawal and deducted a sum to represent the chance that the sale to Sun Microsystems could have collapsed in any event for reasons unconnected with the contamination. Taking all that into account, Blue Circle was awarded in excess of £6 million for the loss of sale, remediation costs and interest. The Court of Appeal upheld this reasoning and dismissed the appeal.

Comment: Whilst this case will no doubt be highly relevant to common law claims relating to the contamination of third party property, there is a danger in drawing too many conclusions from the judgement. It is not an authority for the proposition that contamination linked to a fall in market value will always render the fall in market value actionable as a head of damages. It must also be noted that Blue Circle's land was intended for a particularly sensitive use and was contaminated with nuclear material which, even at the lowest levels, is likely to generate considerable concern.

Merlin v British Nuclear Fuels plc (2 April 1990) High Court, Queen's Bench Division ([1990] 3 All ER 711)

[B2.2]

Nuclear Installations Act 1965; physical harm; radioactive contamination; radioactive substances; damages; economic loss; Rylands v Fletcher; nuisance

Background: The plaintiff purchased a house six miles south of a nuclear reprocessing plant operated by the defendant. The plaintiff sampled dust from the house which was found to contain high levels of radioactive contamination. The plaintiff put the property on the market for £65,000 but it was eventually sold at auction in 1984 for £35,500. The plaintiff claimed compensation under *section 12(1)* of the *Nuclear Installations Act 1965* for the diminution in value of the house caused by the contamination. It was argued that the ingress of radiation into the house constituted damage to property within the meaning of *section* 7 of the 1965 Act. The defendant argued that an assessment of damages needed to be considered in accordance with *Article I(k)(i)* of the *Vienna Convention on Civil Liability for Nuclear Damage 1963* (as the 1965 Act was enacted to fulfil the UK's obligations under that convention). The 1963 Convention defined nuclear damage as loss of life, personal injury or loss of or damage to property arising from the radioactive properties of nuclear fuel, radioactive products or waste from nuclear installations. As such, it did not extend to compensation for an increased risk of such damage occurring or compensation for economic loss.

Test: The scope of *section* 7 of the 1965 Act and whether it extended to compensation for increased risks of damage and economic loss.

Decision: *Section* 7 of the 1965 Act did not extend liability for nuclear damage beyond that provided for in the *Vienna Convention*. As such, liability under the 1965 Act for nuclear damage did not extend to loss or damage other than proved physical or mental personal injury and physical damage to property caused by the radiation. The ingress of radiation into the house did not amount to injury to person or property within *section* 7. There was no reason why compensation under the 1965 Act should extend to pure economic loss which would not be recoverable at common law in any event. The plaintiff's action was dismissed.

Comment: Following the Court of Appeal's decision in *Blue Circle Industries v The Ministry of Defence (1998)*, it is likely that the courts will often find ways to distinguish subsequent cases from this case and thus award damages to plaintiffs in similar situations.

Environmental Impact Assessment

Twyford Parish Council v Secretary of State for the Environment and Secretary of State for Transport (26 October 1990) High Court, Queen's Bench Division ([1992] 1 Env. L.R. 37)

[B3.1]

pipeline projects; planning; Twyford Down

Background: The issue in this case was the effect on the so called 'pipeline' projects of *Directive 85/337/EEC on the assessment of the effects of certain public and private projects on the environment*. In this instance, the project was a section of the M3 motorway at Twyford Down. Part of the Directive had been implemented through the *Highways (Assessment of Environmental Effects) Regulations 1988 (SI 1988 No 1241)*. These Regulations include a provision exempting projects whose draft orders had been published before 21 July 1988 (when the Regulations were published). A question arose as to whether this exemption as it applied to 'pipeline' projects was a proper implementation of the Directive and, if not, whether the Directive had direct effect.

The Twyford Down scheme had been formerly proposed by the Secretary of State for Transport in 1987, and a public inquiry had been completed prior to July 1988. The inspector's report from the inquiry was not published until October 1988 and the decision of the secretaries of state to confirm the orders was made twenty months after the Directive came into force.

Decision: The judge concluded that, in the absence of transitional arrangements in the Directive, it (the Directive) was not held to apply to this project. Had it been the intention of the Commission to apply the Directive to pipeline cases, appropriate provisions would have been set out in the Directive to deal with the same.

Comment: This is one in a series of so called 'pipeline' cases. See also *Lewin & Rowley v Secretary of State for the Environment and Secretary of State for Transport (1991)* (see paragraph B3.4).

Kincardine and Deeside District Council v Forrestry Commissioners (8 March 1991) Court of Session ([1992] Env. L.R. 151)

[B3.2]

direct effect; planning; afforestation; judicial review

Background: The petitioners sought judicial review of a decision of the Forestry Commissioners who approved an application for a grant for the afforestation of more than 800 hectares of moorland in Scotland. The petitioners' argument was that the Commissioners should have carried out an environmental impact assessment (EIA) before making their decision and without which their decision was invalid. *Directive 85/337/EEC* came into force in July 1998 and was implemented in relation to afforestation in the UK by the *Environmental Assessment (Afforestation) Regulations 1988 (SI 1988 No 1207)*.

Test: The Scottish court had to consider whether the 1988 Regulations applied to the afforestation project.

Decision: The Court of Session held that *Directive 85/337/EEC* had conferred rights on the petitioners as it could affect the economy or amenity of their area. A close link between the payment of the grant and the afforestation meant that there was a 'reasonable connection between the decision and the matters in which the petitioners have an interest'. However, the application was received two days before the 1988 Regulations came into effect (13 July 1988).

Moreover, the court held that the Directive was not unconditional and sufficiently precise to have direct effect in the UK. *Article 4(2)* together with *Annex II* of the Directive combined to accord a high degree of discretion to member states to decide whether an EIA was necessary for *Annex II* projects. The discretion conferred by *Article 4(2)* was not a discretion as to the means of implementation but a discretion as to whether steps should be taken at all in a particular context.

Comment: In limited circumstances, European directives can be deemed to have 'direct effect'. This means that they will have a direct legal effect in member states even though they have not yet been implemented by domestic legislation. However, in this case, the project concerned fell within *Annex II* of *Directive 85/337/EEC* and, hence, it was left to the discretion of member states as to whether to require an EIA for the projects concerned.

R v Swale Borough Council and Medway Ports Authority, ex parte The Royal Society for the Protection of Birds (5 February 1990) High Court, Queen's Bench Division (JEL Volume 3 No. 1 1991)

[B3.3]

judicial review; delay in issue of proceedings; planning; consultation

Background: Swale Borough Council (SBC) granted planning permission to the Medway Ports Authority (MPA) to reclaim part of a mud flat near the Medway estuary. The RSPB applied for judicial review of that decision on the basis that (1) it had a legitimate expectation that it would be consulted before the planning consent was granted and (2) SBC had failed to conduct an EIA as required by the *Town and Country Planning (Assessment of Environmental Effects) Regulations 1988 (SI 1988 No 1199).*

Test: Whether the project required an EIA pursuant to the 1988 Regulations and whether the grounds for obtaining leave for judicial review had been satisfied.

Decision: On the first ground, the court held that the RSPB had sufficient interest to bring the proceedings. This was despite the application being made three months after the SBC decision was taken and, hence, arguably outside the time limit required to bring a judicial review application. The RSPB did have a legitimate expectation that it would be consulted. However, at the substantive judicial review hearing, the court held that the three month delay between the grant of the planning permission and the bringing of proceedings was unreasonable. The court refused to grant the relief sought by RSPB.

On the second ground, the court held that the project fell within *Schedule 2* of the 1988 Regulations and, hence, it was for the local authority to decide whether an EIA was required. SBC had considered this and concluded that no EIA was required. The court said that was not an unreasonable decision.

Comment: This case confirms the need for swift action when applying for judicial review.

Lewin and Rowley v Secretary of State for the Environment and Secretary of State for Transport (17 July 1991) High Court, Queen's Bench Division ((1992) JPL 342)

[B3.4]

planning; roads

Background: Representatives of the Society for the Preservation of the Field of the Battle of Naseby (Society) challenged a decision to extend the A1/M1 link road which would pass across the battle site. The Society argued that (1) at the public inquiry which looked at the side road orders, the inspector did not consider the Society's representations regarding the route of the link road and alternative routes; and (2) the respondents failed to obtain an EIA in breach of the *Highways (Assessment of Environmental Effects) Regulations 1988 (SI 1988 No 1241)*. The Society was of the view that an EIA was mandatory and that the limited environmental statement produced by the respondents was inadequate as it did not cover the whole scheme.

Test: The court considered whether the secretaries of state had erred in law in not accepting the Society's representations at the inquiry and whether the project required an EIA in accordance with the 1988 Regulations.

Decision: On the first issue, the court found that the route of the link road had been properly determined under *section 10* of the *Highways Act 1980* after a public inquiry. The secretaries of state did not err in law in deciding that the subsequent inquiry was not the correct forum to discuss the side road orders.

The 1988 Regulations had come into effect between the two public inquiries on the scheme. As such, the secretaries of state were required to consider whether an EIA was required in relation to the side road order. The secretaries of state had, in fact, ordered an EIA but had limited its scope to the proposed side road orders. It was not considered by the court that the project fell under *Annex 1* of *Directive 85/337/EEC* and, hence, an EIA was not mandatory. The side road orders fell under *Annex 2* of the Directive and, as such, it was up to the inspector to decide whether the EIA had fulfilled its statutory requirement. The inspector had held that the statutory requirements had been fulfilled and thus the Society's application was dismissed.

Comment: In effect, the Society was attempting to have the whole road scheme reconsidered. However, this had been settled some time before *Directive 85/337/EEC* was implemented.

Burgemeester en wethouders van Haarlemmerliede en Spaarnwoude and Others v Gedeputeerde Staten van Noord-Holland (18 June 1998) European Court of Justice (Case C-81/96 (18 June 1998) (ECJ), [1998] ECR I-3923)

[B3.5]

environmental impact assessment; planning; European Union

Background: In May 1993, authorities in northern Holland approved the 'Ruigoord 1992' land use plan for a port and industrial development. A number of people brought an action challenging the decision to approve the plan on the grounds that the plan had been authorised without an EIA having been carried out as required by *Directive 85/337/EEC on the assessment of the effects of certain public and private projects on the environment*. The Directive was transposed into Dutch law in May 1987 by the *Order on Environmental Impact Assessment*. This Order listed the projects (or 'activities') for which an EIA was required and the construction of a port for civil use (for inland waterway or maritime navigation) was a relevant 'activity' where the port permits the passage of vessels of 1,350 tonnes or more. As such, the adoption of a plan which provides for the possible construction of such a port is to be preceded by an EIA. However, an EIA report was not obligatory where an activity/ project had already been incorporated in a current structural, zoning or regional plan. The projects featured in the Ruigoord 1992 plan were contained in earlier development plans. Accordingly, the national court was of the opinion that there was no obligation under the Order to carry out an EIA before authorising the Ruigoord 1992 plan. However, the national court stayed the proceedings and referred the issue to the ECJ.

Test: Whether *Directive 85/337/EEC* was to be interpreted as allowing member states to waive the obligations concerning EIA's, where projects have already been the subject of a consent granted before the date when the Directive was transposed into national law, but where a fresh consent procedure was formally initiated after that date.

Decision: The ECJ held that where a consent procedure is formally initiated after the Directive has been transposed into national law, the consent procedure is subject to the obligations imposed by the Directive.

Comment: As the ECJ noted, any other solution to the circumstances of this case would detract from the objective of *Directive 85/337/EEC* that an EIA be carried out in relation to certain major projects.

Greenpeace International and Others v European Commission (2 April 1998) European Court of Justice (Case C-321/95P (2 April 1998) (ECJ), [1998] All ER (EC) 620)

[B3.6]

locus standi; judicial review; European Union

Background: The legality of the decision by the EC to grant structural funds to Spain for the construction of two power stations on the Canary Islands was challenged by local residents, local environmental pressure groups and Greenpeace. The decision was challenged on the grounds that the Spanish authorities had not complied with *Directive 85/337/EEC on the assessment of certain public and private projects on the environment*. Greenpeace contended that the distribution of EC funds to a project which does not comply with European law was illegal. This argument by Greenpeace was not fully considered as the case centred on whether Greenpeace (and the other applicants) had standing to bring the application before the ECJ.

Test: *Article 173* of the *Treaty of Rome 1957* provides that third parties may challenge either decisions addressed directly to them or decisions addressed to another party, if they can demonstrate that the decision is of direct and individual concern to them. Case law has established that to satisfy this latter test, an applicant must prove that the decision affects him due to certain attributes which distinguish him from other persons who may be affected by the decision. The ECJ had to consider whether these were satisfied in this instance.

Decision: The European Court of First Instance did not see how the interests of the local residents, environmental pressure groups or Greenpeace differed from those of any other members of the public affected by the decision. It also rejected Greenpeace's argument that case law in this area had principally been developed in the context of economic interests and a more liberal approach should be adopted in environmental cases. Greenpeace (and the other applicants) then appealed to the ECJ. Interestingly, in his written opinion, the Advocate General suggested that procedural requirements may be relaxed in environmental cases. The ECJ, however, did not explore this suggestion and confirmed the decision of the European Court of First Instance in ruling that Greenpeace and other environmental pressure groups did not have the standing to challenge a decision of the EC concerning structural funds.

Comment: The approach of the ECJ was confirmed in subsequent cases brought by Greenpeace (see, in particular, *Stichting Greenpeace Council and Others v Commission CFI ICH (April 1996, ECJ, TCR, 23 April 1996)*).

European Union

R v Secretary of State for the Environment, ex parte Friends of the Earth Ltd and Another (25 May 1995) Court of Appeal (ILR, 7 June 1995)

[B4.1]

water, water quality; judicial review; locus standi

Background: In 1992, the ECJ ruled that the UK was in breach of *Directive 80/778/EEC* relating to water quality. In order to rectify that breach, the Secretary of State for the Environment accepted undertakings from Thames Water Utilities Ltd and Anglian Water Services Ltd, that those water companies would take whatever steps appeared to him to be appropriate for those companies to secure or enforce compliance with their duties to supply wholesome drinking water, pursuant to *section 68(1)(a)* of the *WIA 1991*. The secretary of state accepted those undertakings pursuant to *section 19(1)(b)* of the *WIA 1991*. The applicants, Friends of the Earth Ltd and Christine Orengo, sought judicial review of the secretary of state's decision, arguing that an enforcement order ought to have been issued.

Test: The court had to consider whether the secretary of state had properly exercised his powers in accepting the undertakings and/ or whether an enforcement order should have been issued.

Decision: The applicants' case was rejected by the Court of Appeal.

Comment: It is to be noted, that the evidence did not show that the secretary of state, in accepting the undertakings, adopted too leisurely an approach. The court noted that the secretary of state's acceptance of the undertakings did not inhibit his powers to serve an enforcement order at any subsequent time if he thought such a step was appropriate.

Brasserie du Pêcheur SA v Federal Republic of Germany; R v Secretary of State for Transport, ex parte Factortame Ltd and Others (No. 4) (5 March 1996) European Court of Justice (Case C–46/93 (5 March 1996) (ECJ) Times Law Reports, 7 March 1996)

[B4.2]

damages; fisheries

Background: These were joined cases in which courts of the member states referred a number of questions concerning compensation to individuals for legislative breaches of Community law by member states.

Brasserie du Pêcheur, a French company, claimed that several years ago it was forced to discontinue exports of beer to Germany because the German authorities considered that the beer did not comply with the purity requirements laid down under German law. Subsequently, the ECJ held that the German law was incompatible with *Article 30* of the *Treaty of Rome 1957* (the *'1957 Treaty'*).

Separately, Factortame Ltd (and other applicants) challenged the compatibility of *Part II* of the *Merchant Shipping Act 1988* with Community law and, in particular, *Article 52* of the *1957 Treaty*. The ECJ held that the registration system under the 1988 Act was incompatible with Community law. The ECJ reiterated the principle that member state's liability for loss and damage caused to individuals as a result of breaches by member states of Community law was inherent in the system under the *1957 Treaty*. That principle held good whatever the organ of the state it was whose act or omission was responsible for the breach. In determining the conditions under which a member state's liability gave rise to a right on the part of an individual to reparation, it was pertinent to refer to the ECJ case law on non-contractual liability on the part of the Community and, in particular, to *Article 215* of the *1957 Treaty*. The ECJ would have regard to the wide discretion available to the institutions in implementing Community policies.

Test: The ECJ stated that Community law conferred a right on individuals to reparation where three conditions were met, namely (i) the rule of law infringed must be intended to confer rights on individuals; (ii) the breach must be sufficiently serious and (iii) there must be a direct causal link between the breach of the obligation resting on the member state and the damage sustained by the injured party. With regard to the second element, the court held that the decisive test for determining whether a breach of community law was sufficiently serious was whether the member state or the Community institution had manifestly and gravely disregarded the limits of its discretion. In that regard, the factors which could be taken into consideration included the clarity and precision of the rule breached; the measure of discretion left by the rule to national authorities; whether the infringement and damage caused were intentional or voluntary; whether any error of law was excusable; the fact that a position taken by a Community institution might have contributed towards the omission and the adoption or retention of national measures contrary to Community law.

Decision: The first condition was simple in the present cases as *Articles 30* and *52* of the *1957 Treaty* manifestly conferred rights upon individuals. As for the third condition, the ECJ stated that it was for the national courts to determine whether there was a direct causal link and thus referred the matters back to the domestic courts.

Comment: Neither of these two cases related directly to environment law. However, much of the UK's domestic environment law stems from EU law and thus the principles set out in these cases could very well prove highly relevant.

R v Ministry of Agriculture, Fisheries and Food, ex parte Hedley Lomas (Ireland) Ltd (23 May 1996) European Court of Justice (Case–5/94 (23 May 1996) (ECJ), Times Law Reports, 6 June 1996)

[B4.3]

animal welfare; damages; judicial review

Background: Despite the adoption in Spain of *Council Directive 74/577 on the stunning of animals before slaughter*, the Ministry of Agriculture, Fisheries and Food became convinced prior to April 1990 that a number of Spanish slaughter houses were not complying with the Directive. That conviction stemmed from information obtained from the Spanish Society for the Protection of Animals. The ministry accepted that it did not have sufficient evidence as to the overall position in Spanish slaughter houses. However, it did still form the view that the information in its possession indicated a degree of non-compliance, so that a substantial risk of treatment contrary to the Directive would be suffered by animals exported to Spain. As a result, the ministry systematically refused to issue licences for the export to Spain of live animals for slaughter during the period April 1990 to 1993. Hedley Lomas (Ireland) Ltd made an application for a licence in 1992. That application was refused. That refusal was maintained even though Hedley Lomas produced evidence that the slaughter house in question was complying with the Directive and the ministry did not have any evidence to the contrary. Hedley Lomas sought a declaration from the court that the refusal to grant the export licence was contrary to *Article 34* of the *1957 Treaty* and also claimed damages.

Test: The ministry accepted that the refusal to grant such licences placed a quantitative restriction on exports. Its defence was, however, that the export ban was justified under *Article 36* which provides that 'the provisions of *Articles 30–34* shall not preclude prohibitions or restrictions on ... exports ... justified on grounds of ... the protection of health and life of ... animals ... '. The court had to consider the scope of *Article 36*.

Decision: The ECJ ruled that Community law precluded one member state from invoking *Article 36* of the *1957 Treaty* to justify a limitation on exports of goods to another member state on the sole grounds that, according to the first member state, the second member state was not complying with the requirements of a Community harmonisation Directive. The ministry was therefore at fault in this regard. Further, a member state had an obligation to make reparation for the damage caused to an individual by refusal to issue an export licence where the Community law infringed was intended to confer rights on individuals, the breach of which was sufficiently serious and there was direct causal link between the breach and the damages sustained by the individuals.

R v Secretary of State for the Environment, ex parte Royal Society for the Protection of Birds; The Port Authority of Sheerness Ltd (11 July 1996) European Court of Justice (Case C–44/95 (11 July 1996) (ECJ), OJ, 9 November 1996, No. C336)

[B4.4]

wild birds; judicial review

Background: This was a reference to the ECJ by the House of Lords for a preliminary ruling on the interpretation of *Articles 2 and 4* of *Council Directive 79/409/EEC on the conservation of wild birds*.

Test: One of the questions considered by the ECJ was whether economic considerations are relevant to the decision whether to classify an area as a special protection area. No economic or non-ornithological considerations are referred to in *Article 4*.

Decision: The ECJ held that economic requirements are not to be taken into account by a member state when designating special protection areas under *Article 4* of the Directive.

Criminal Proceedings Against Luciano Arcaro (26 September 1996) European Court of Justice (Case C–168/95 (26 September 1996) (ECJ), (1996) 262 ENDS)

[B4.5]

non-implementation of EU directives

Background: The ECJ was asked by an Italian court to consider issues relating to discharges by Luciano Arcaro of cadmium without an authorisation where, under Italian law, those discharges may have constituted offences.

Test: The two issues referred to the ECJ were whether (i) Italian law properly implemented *Directive 76/464/EEC* and the *cadmium daughter Directive 83/513/EEC* and, if not, (ii) did those Directives have direct effect in any event.

Decision: On the first issue, the ECJ found that the 1976 and 1985 Directives were not properly implemented under Italian law. With regard to the second issue, the court following precedent, held that Directives were only binding upon member states and emanations of the state. Directives are not directly binding upon citizens of member states.

Criminal Proceedings against Censi (12 September 1996) European Court of Justice (Joined Cases–C58/95, C75/95, C112/95, C119/95, C123/95, C135/95, C140/95, C141/95, C154/95 and C157/95 (12 September 1996) (ECJ), [1997] (CMLR 32))

[B4.6]

waste; criminal law; implementation

Background: *Article 5* of the *1957 Treaty* obliges member states to guarantee by appropriate measures the application of EU law and

Article 189(3) allows member states to choose measures appropriate to ensure the effective implementation of Directives.

Decision: This case held that a member state is entitled to impose criminal sanctions for a breach of domestic legislation implementing *Directive 91/156/EEC* on waste. The elements of the offence, the procedure and sanctions must not differ greatly from analogous national laws and the criminal sanctions must be effective and proportionate. The Directive does not set any specific requirements in this regard.

Chemische Afvalstoffen Dusseldorp BV and Others v Minister van Volkshuisvesting, Ruimtelijke, Ordening en Millieubeheer (25 June 1998) European Court of Justice (Case C–203/96 (25 June 1998) ECJ, [1999] All ER (EC) 25)

[B4.7]

waste; self sufficiency principle; proximity principle; transfrontier shipments of waste

Background: In 1994 Chemische, a Dutch company, applied for the relevant authorisation to export 2,000 tonnes of oil filters and 60 tonnes of related waste for processing in Germany. The relevant minister rejected the application. He applied the principles established in the Dutch government's *Plan for waste disposal and recovery*. This required (1) the processing of oil filters to be performed in the Netherlands unless there was a superior process available abroad and (2) the incineration of related waste to be carried out in the Netherlands where emission controls are stricter. The requirements of domestic processing under the Plan were developed in accordance with the principles of self-sufficiency and proximity as outlined in the *Framework Directive on waste 75/442/EEC* (as amended). Whilst *Regulation 259/93 on the supervision and control of shipments of waste within, into and out of the European Community* applied the principles of self-sufficiency and proximity to shipments of waste for disposal, there was no such express mention of these principles in relation to shipments of waste for recovery. Chemische argued that these principles were thus not relevant to the shipment of waste for recovery and that the Dutch government's Plan was contrary to Community environmental policy.

Test: The Dutch court submitted four questions to the ECJ.

(1)(a) Do the principles as stated in *Directive 75/442/EEC* (as amended) of self-sufficiency and proximity apply to the shipment of waste for recovery under the scheme of *Regulation 259/93* on the supervision and control of shipments of waste within, into and out of the EC?

(b) If the principles do not apply, can the Dutch government justify the requirements of the Plan under *Article 130t* of the *1957 Treaty*?

(2) Does the pursuit of best quality disposal constitute the implementation of self-sufficiency and proximity?

(3)(a) If the requirements of the Plan are acceptable, do the measures fall within *Article 34* of the *1957 Treaty*, as having an equivalent effect to a quantitative restriction on exports?

(b) In that context does it matter whether the principles are applied at a state or Community level?

(4) The Dutch authorities have given one company the right to incinerate such waste. Is this compatible with *Articles 90(1), (2) and 86* of the *1957 Treaty*?

Decision: The ECJ found that the principles of self-sufficiency and proximity were not applicable to the shipment of waste for recovery (thus questions 2 and 3 became irrelevant). It held that there was a deliberate absence of express reference to these principles in *Regulation 259/93*. The court found that this is consistent with the general Community environment policy of encouraging recovery. To encourage Community wide recovery, waste must be able to move freely (provided there is no threat to the environment or to human health). Thus the court found that the requirements of the Plan were not justified under *Article 130s* of the *1957 Treaty*.

The court then had to consider (question 1(b)) whether *Article 130t* of the *1957 Treaty* provided a basis for the provisions. The court found that the more stringent provisions of the Plan were not compatible with the *1957 Treaty*. As the transport of the waste did not constitute a threat to human health, the requirements of domestic processing could not be justified. The Plan was equivalent to a quantitative restriction of trade and the Dutch government had failed to establish grounds for a derogation. Further, the ECJ found that a requirement to deliver waste for recovery to a national undertaking which has an exclusive right will be contrary to *Articles 90 and 86* of the *1957 Treaty* (a national undertaking will be favoured and its dominant position increased) unless the national court can be satisfied that there are objective general economic reasons for such a requirement.

Comments: This case raised interesting questions about the controls imposed on the transfrontier shipment of waste.

Beside BV and IM Besselsen v Minister van Volkshuisvesting, Ruimtelijke Ordening en Millieubeheer (25 June 1998) European Court of Justice (Case C–192/196 (25 June 1998) (ECJ), [1998] ECR I–4029)

[B4.8]

waste; transfrontier shipment of waste

Background: Beside BV, in Holland, obtained a quantity of waste from Germany (eight bales of plastic mixed waste including six live rounds of ammunition) which it was storing pending export. The shipment was received without notifying the Dutch authorities and Beside was ordered to return it to Germany. Beside and one of its directors contested this ruling.

Regulation 259/93 on the supervision and control of shipments of waste within, into and out of the European Community (as amended) defined three categories of waste for which the level of notification to competent authorities differs. The three categories are known as green, amber and red list wastes. For 'green waste' no notification is necessary. A shipment of either amber or red listed waste, made without the requisite notifications, is illegal waste and may be subject to an order that it be returned to source. The Dutch authorities contended that the waste was municipal/household waste (which is amber list waste) but that, in any event, even if the waste was green list waste, certain information had to be produced to confirm the green waste was destined for recovery.

Test: Three questions were put to the ECJ.

(1) Due to the mixed nature of the waste whether it was necessary to define 'municipal/household waste' as green list waste?

(2) To determine the level of information needed to ensure that green waste was destined for recovery processes:

(a) was 'storage of materials intended for a submission to any operations in this annex' extended to storage before a recovery process outside the community?; and

(b) what level of evidence is required to show that waste is destined for a recovery process where no notification of shipment is given?

(3) Whether a competent authority in the state which receives the waste is under the same obligations pursuant to *Regulation 259/93* as the competent authority in the state of despatch.

Decision: The ECJ found that the waste which is, for the most part green waste mixed with other categories of waste, would constitute municipal/household waste and was correctly categorised as amber waste. Further, storage prior to a recovery process would be a recovery operation and the location and ultimate destination (even if outside the EC) were immaterial. The ECJ also found that a competent authority may require the minimum information provided for in *Article 11* of *Regulation 259/93 on the supervision and control of shipments of waste within, into and out of the European Community* (as amended), to determine that green waste is destined for recovery. This information should relate to the recovery process even if outside the EC. The final issue for the ECJ was to determine the obligations as between the member states. The court found that, pursuant to *Regulation 259/93*, the member state of destination must notify the member state of despatch of the return of the waste and that the member state of despatch may not oppose such return if a 'duly motivated' request is received.

EC Commission v Germany (23 October 1998) European Court of Justice (NLD, 23 October 1998)

[B4.9]

failure to implement EU law; environmental impact assessment

Background: This case involved an action by the European Commission against Germany for failure to comply with obligations relating to the transposition of *Directive 85/337/EEC on the assessment of effects of certain public and private projects on the environment.*

Decision: The ECJ held that, notwithstanding the fact that the Commission had already obtained a preliminary ruling from the ECJ that Germany had breached *Article 12(1)* of the Directive, it was still appropriate to make a formal declaration under *Article 169* of the *1957 Treaty*. Thus the ECJ found that Germany, by not requiring an assessment for all projects on which environmental impact assessments had to be carried out in accordance with the Directive, had failed to fulfil its obligations under *Article 12(1)* of the Directive. In addition, the court held that *Article 2(4)* of the Directive did not empower a member state to exclude from possible assessment one or more of the classes in the *Annex* of the Directive as projects which might require assessment.

Commission of the European Communities v Kingdom of Spain (25 November 1998) European Court of Justice (Case C–214/96 (25 November 1998) (ECJ))

[B4.10]

water pollution; dangerous substances; non-implementation of EU law

Background: The European Commission brought an action against the Spanish government for its failure to fulfil its obligations under *Directive 76/464/EEC of 4 May 1976 on pollution caused by certain dangerous substances discharged into the aquatic environment of the European Community. Article 7(1)* of the Directive provides that member states must adopt and communicate a programme for reducing pollution of waters by substances set out in *List I* and *List II* as provided for in *Article 7(1).*

Decision: The Spanish government first claimed that, although it had been bound by the Directive since its accession to the Community, it had as a result had to deal with many far reaching changes in its administration. In addition, the state of the Spanish legislation relating to protection of the environment at the time of accession had not attained EC levels. The court rejected these arguments on the well established grounds that a member state may not plead provisions, practices or circumstances existing in its internal legal system in order to justify a failure to comply with the obligations and time limits laid down in Directives. Secondly, the Spanish government contended that the national law implemented in Spain on 2 August 1985 established two lists of polluting substances coinciding with *Lists I* and *II* in the Directive. However, it also acknowledged that the catchment basin plans laying down quality objectives were still to be approved and as such the plans did not fulfil the obligations to provide the programmes for reducing pollution waters. It went on to claim, however, that domestic legislation implemented on 7 April 1995, laying down additional measures for the regulation and monitoring of discharges did satisfy such obligations, even though the Act in question did not contain the words 'programme for reducing pollution' in the title. The court in rejecting the Spanish government's arguments, stated that it was settled case law that the question of whether a member state had failed to fulfil its obligations must be determined by reference to the situation prevailing in the state at the end of the deadline when such legislation was to be imposed. Subsequent changes could not be taken into account. In this case, the relevant legislation had been brought into force after the expiry of the two month deadline stated in the European Commission's reasoned opinion issued on 17 November 1994. Furthermore, only specific programmes including quality objectives with regard to water may be considered to be programmes within the meaning of *Article* 7 of the Directive. A series of ad hoc legislative measures which cannot amount to an organised and co-ordinated system of quality objectives relating to specific watercourses or bodies of standing water is not sufficient. Accordingly, so far as concerns surface waters, the Spanish government had failed to fulfil its obligations under *Article* 7 of the Directive. The same applied for discharges into the sea, for which no legislation had been implemented. The ECJ therefore upheld the European Commission's action and ordered the Spanish government to pay costs.

Commission of the European Communities v Portuguese Republic (21 January 1999) European Court of Justice (Case C–150/97 I(21 January 1999) (ECJ))

[B4.11]

environmental impact assessment; non-implementation of EU law

Background: The European Commission brought an action against Portugal for its failure to fulfil its obligations to fully transpose *Directive 85/337/EEC, on the assessment of the effects of certain public and private projects on the environment*, into national law. *Article 12(1)* of the Directive required that the member state comply with the Directive within three years of its notification. The European Commission contended that the provisions of the Directive had to apply from 3 July 1998 to all decisions concerning consent applications but national law transposing this

Directive was not implemented until 7 June 1990. The national law and hence the provisions of the Directive, therefore did not apply to projects in respect of which the approval procedure was already underway on the date on which the national law came into force. The Portuguese government argued that, in order to observe their principles of legal certainty, national law should not be given retrospective effect.

Test: Whether the member state should be permitted to waive provisions of a Directive, and whether failure to fulfil an obligation imposed by a rule of community law constitutes a breach of duty under the *1957 Treaty* even if the failure has no adverse effect.

Decision: The ECJ followed the decision in *Bund Naturschutz in Bayern and Others v Freirstaat Bayern [1994] ECR 1 – 3717*. It stated that member states should not be permitted to waive the provisions of the Directive and that they could not plead provisions, practices, or circumstances existing in internal legal systems in order to justify a failure to comply with obligations and time limits laid down in Directives. In addition, the court stated that failure by a member state to fulfil an obligation imposed by a rule of community law is sufficient to constitute a breach of obligations under the *1957 Treaty* and the fact that the failure had no adverse effect is irrelevant. The European Commission's action was therefore successful and the government of Portugal was ordered to pay costs.

European Parliament v Council of the European Union (25 February 1999) European Court of Justice (Cases C–164/97 and C–165/97 (25 February 1999) (ECJ))

[B4.12]

air pollution; environmental protection; procedure

Background: These two cases concerned the annulment of *Regulations EC 307/97* and *308/97*. The European Parliament submitted that the Regulations were adopted on the basis of an incorrect Treaty provision. The Regulations concerned the protection of forests against atmospheric pollution and against fire and both were adopted on the basis of *Article 43* of the *1957 Treaty*, entitled *'Agriculture'*. The European Parliament submitted that the Regulations should have been adopted on the basis of *Article 130* of the *1957 Treaty* which provides that the Council of Ministers shall decide what action is to be taken by the Community in order that Community policy on the environment be observed.

Test: Whether *Regulations EC 307/97* and *EC 308/97* should have been adopted on the basis of *Article 43* of the *1957 Treaty* entitled *'Agriculture'* or on the basis of *Article 130.*

Decision: The ECJ decided that the Regulations should have been adopted on the basis of *Article 130* of the *1957 Treaty*. The court stated that the aims and contents of the Regulations, read together with the Regulations that they were amending, clearly fell within the ambit of *Article 130*, and in particular within the policy on 'preserving, protecting and improving the quality of the environment'. The court therefore concluded that the Regulations should be annulled.

Comment: In its decision to annul the Regulations, the ECJ took into account the detrimental effect that such annulment may have to the progress of action undertaken in the member states for protection of the environment. As a result, it decided that the annulled Regulations should be fully maintained until the Council of Ministers had adopted, within a reasonable period, new Regulations having the same subject matter.

Commission of the European Communities v French Republic (18 March 1999) European Court of Justice (Case C–166/97 (18 March 1999) (ECJ))

[B4.13]

wild birds; special protection area

Background: The European Commission sought a declaration that the French Republic had, by 3 September 1995, failed to classify a sufficiently large special protection area ('SPA') in the Seine estuary for the purposes of *Directive 79/409/EEC on the conservation of wild birds*, that the protection regime adopted for the SPA was legally inadequate, and that the construction of a titanogypsum plant had led to deterioration of the SPA. The ECJ upheld the European Commission's application on the first two points. On the third point, regarding the construction of the titanogypsum plant, the European Commission contended that it had been built in wet prairies which are very important for the staging, feeding and breeding of numerous protected bird species and that it should, therefore, have been included within the Seine estuary SPA. In addition, that harm caused by the construction was incompatible with the conservation requirements set out in *Article 4* of the Directive namely that the French Republic should take all reasonable steps to avoid irreparable deterioration so that a site can later be classified as an SPA.

Decision: The court, rejecting the Commission's arguments, stated that the mere fact that the site in question was included in an inventory of important areas for bird conservation, did not prove that it ought to have been classified as an SPA. As the French government had indicated, the inventory is no more than an initial survey of the country's ornithological wealth. As to the argument that the site comprised of wet prairies, the court stated that the titanogypsum plant only covered a small part of the nesting and feeding area and that according to a study by the Museum of Natural History, none of the rarest species in the region would suffer directly from the plant. The Commission's complaint as to the construction of the titanogypsum plant was, therefore, rejected.

R v Ministry of Agriculture, Fisheries and Food, ex parte British Agrochemicals Association Ltd (11 March 1999) European Court of Justice (Case C–100/96 (11 March 1999) (ECJ), Times Law Reports, 13 April 1999)

[B4.14]

pesticides; European economic area

Background: Under the *Control of Pesticide Regulations 1986 (SI 1986 No. 1510)*, imported pesticide products must be identical to a master product already approved in the United Kingdom. 'Identical' means products in which the active ingredient was manufactured and the formulation was produced by the same company as manufactured the United Kingdom master product or by an associated undertaking or licensee. In this case, the applicants, representing thirty-nine members of the agrochemical manufacturing industry, were challenging the legality of the *Control of Pesticide Regulations 1986* on the grounds that the Regulations were contrary to *Council Directive 91/414/EEC concerning the placing of plant protection products on the market*. In particular, they argued that the Directive put in place a rigorous system for the issuing of marketing authorisations and that this system did not permit the grant of authorisations by a simplified procedure.

Decision: The court following its decision in *Medicines Control Agency, ex parte Smith and Nephew Pharmaceuticals Ltd (1996) ECR 1-5819*, decided that pesticides which had already been authorised in a European Economic Area (EEA) country for marketing in accordance with the procedures set out in the Directive, did not need fresh authorisation under that procedure when imported from an EEA country into a member state of the EC. This was as long as they had the same formulation, active ingredients and effect as a product already authorised in the importing state. An authorisation would, however, still be required when the importation was from a non-EEA country and no marketing authorisation had been granted in another member state, even if the competent authority of that country considered the product to be identical.

Commission of the European Community v United Kingdom of Great Britain and Northern Ireland (22 April 1999) European Court of Justice (Case C–340/96 (22 April 1999) (ECJ), Times Law Reports, 13 April 1999)

[B4.15]

drinking water; water quality; non-implementation of EU law

Background: The European Commission took an action against the UK for failure to fulfil its obligations under *Directive 80/778/ EEC relating to the quality of water intended for human consumption.* The Directive requires member states to take the necessary measures to ensure that water intended for specified requirements is of sufficient quality. The UK had implemented the Directive into its national law by means of the *WIA 1991*. Under *section 18* of this Act the secretary of state has the power to make an enforcement order where a water company supplies impure water. However, such an order is unnecessary if the secretary of state is satisfied that the company has given an undertaking to take appropriate steps to secure or facilitate compliance with the relevant rules. The Commission complained that due to the provision for and use of such undertakings in the *WIA 1991* there was no enforcement of the water company's compliance with the standards required in the Directive.

Decision: The ECJ therefore found that the UK's acceptance of undertakings from water companies for the purpose of ensuring that water complied with the requirements of *Directive 80/778/ EEC* and the absence of conditions governing the acceptance of such undertakings, meant that the UK had failed to fulfil its obligations under the *1957 Treaty* and the Directive.

R v Secretary of State for the Environment and Another, ex parte Standley and Others: National Farmers Union, Intervener (29 April 1999) European Court of Justice (Case C–293/97 (29 April 1999) (ECJ), Times Law Reports, 13 April 1999)

[B4.16]

water pollution; nitrates; judicial review

Background: Mr H A Standley and others and Mr D G D Metson and others owned or farmed land. With the support of the National Farmers' Union, they challenged decisions of the Secretary of State of the Environment and the Minister of Agriculture, Fisheries and Food. The challenge was based on the secretary of state's decision to identify certain rivers as waters which were affected or could be affected by pollution within the meaning of *Directive 91/676/EEC concerning the protection of waters against pollution caused by nitrates from agricultural sources* and designating the areas of land draining into those waters as vulnerable zone. *Article 2(j)* of that Directive defined pollution as 'the discharge, directly or indirectly, of nitrogen compounds from agricultural sources into the aquatic environment [with harmful effects]'. *Article 3(l)* provided that 'waters affected by pollution and waters which could be affected by pollution if action pursuant to *Article 5* is not taken shall be identified by the member states ... ' *Article 5* provided for the establishment of action programmes involving monitoring and a variety of mandatory measures. *Article 3(2)* states that member states 'shall designate as vulnerable zones all areas of land in their territories which drain into the waters identified in [Article 3(1)]'. The government's approach was based upon whether agricultural sources were making a significant contribution to the levels of pollution detected. Standley and Metson claimed that the action programmes restricting agricultural use which would apply following designation would be harmful as they would decrease land values and income from their farming businesses. Standley and Metson agreed that waters could only be designated waters which if they were affected by pollution where agricultural sources were the only nitrate source. The ECJ held that member states are not required to identify what proportion of pollution is attributable to nitrates. On the contrary, it would be incompatible with the Directive to restrict the identification of waters affected by pollution to just cases of pollution caused by agricultural sources. In particular, when establishing action programmes under *Article 5,* the Directive expressly requires other sources to be taken into account. The court stated further that this must logically be the case, given the power of member states to designate their whole territory nitrate vulnerable zone without individually identifying water affected by pollution.

Decision: The court therefore held that the Directive applies where nitrogen compounds from agriculture make a significant contribution to pollution. The ECJ therefore held that member states must identify waters as affected by pollution, and designate the land draining into those waters as vulnerable zones if agriculture is a significant source of pollution. It is unnecessary for agriculture to be the only source of pollution.

R v Secretary of State for Transport, ex parte Factortame Ltd and Others No. 5 (28 October 1999) House of Lords (Times Law Reports, 3 November 1999)

[B4.17]

fisheries; discrimination

Background: This case is one in a series of cases concerning the United Kingdom government's defence of British fishermen. In this case the question was whether the United Kingdom's breach of EC law was sufficiently serious to entitle Factortame Ltd to compensation. The Queen's Bench Divisional Court answered the question in the affirmative and the Court of Appeal upheld the decision. This case concerns the secretary of state's appeal to the House of Lords. He argued that the United Kingdom was adopting legislation to deal with this serious economic problem. He maintained that even where there is a breach of EC law there could be no liability to compensate where the breach was excusable.

Decision: The court found that the United Kingdom had acted in good faith and with the intention of protecting British fishing communities rather than with the deliberate intention of harming Spanish fishermen. It held, however, that there had been a deliberate adoption of legislation which was clearly discriminatory on the ground of nationality and was in manifest breach of fundamental EC Treaty obligations. It ruled that it was a grave breach both intrinsically and with regard to the consequences, it was bound or at least most likely to have an effect on Factortame Ltd. It was therefore held that the adoption of legislation which was discriminatory on the ground of nationality in respect of the registration of British fishing vessels and in breach of clear and unambiguous rules of EC law, was sufficiently serious to give rise to liability and damages to individuals who suffered loss as a consequence.

World Wildlife Fund and Others v Autonome Provinz Bozen and Others (16 September 1999) European Court of Justice (Case C–435/97 (16 September 1999) (ECJ), Times Law Reports, 12 October 1999)

[B4.18]

environmental impact assessment; locus standi

Background: The case concerned the interpretation of *Council Directive 85/337/EEC on the assessment of the effects of certain public and private projects on the environment*. The question arose out of a project in Bolzano, involving the transformation of an airfield which had been used for private flying and military purposes into an airport which could be used commercially with regular scheduled flights and charter and cargo flights. After carrying out an environmental impact study which was in accordance with Bolzano law but not with *Directive 85/337/EEC*, the project was approved by a decision of the Bolzano government. The World Wildlife Fund sought the setting aside of these decisions on the grounds that since the project was likely, by virtue of its nature, size and location to have significant effects on the environment, it fell within *Article 2(1)* of the Directive and should have been made subject to the assessment procedure under *Article 4(2)* in conjunction with *Annex II.*

Decision: The ECJ held that criteria and thresholds mentioned in *Article 4(2),* were designed to facilitate examination of the actual characteristics of any given project, in order to determine whether it is subject to the requirement to carry out an assessment and not to exempt in advance from that obligation certain whole classes of projects listed in *Annex II.* Therefore, the ECJ concluded that member states were not entitled when exercising the discretion given to them under the Directive, to exclude whole classes of projects from the environmental impact assessment procedure established by the Directive, that were likely to have significant effects on the environment.

IPC and Air Pollution

Brooks v Boots Co Ltd (23 October 1998) High Court, Queen's Bench Division (NLD, 23 October 1998)

[B5.1]

asbestos; limitation periods

Background: This was an action brought by the administrators of the estate of six persons who had all worked assembling gas masks at a Boots factory at different periods between 1939 and 1945. All of the deceased had been diagnosed with mesothelioma, the earliest diagnosis being made in 1967 and the latest in 1991. The administrators claimed that the disease and subsequent deaths were caused by exposure to asbestos during the course of their employment with Boots. Boots claimed that the actions could not proceed as they were time-barred under *section 11* of the *Limitation Act 1980*.

Test: *Section 11* of the 1980 Act provides for a special time limit for actions in respect of personal injuries and *section 33* allows for the discretionary exclusion of time limits for actions in respect of personal injuries or death.

Decision: The court held that, in five of the six cases, the actions were time-barred, with the balance of prejudice falling in favour of Boots. In exercising its discretion under *section 33* of the *Limitation Act 1980*, the court had to consider the relative strengths and weaknesses of the administrators' case against Boots.

The court concluded that a fair trial could not be conducted in relation to events which took place fifty years ago. Owing to the lapse of time, the evidence which would have to be relied upon by Boots in disproving causation and showing that it had discharged the relevant duty of care would have been weakened. The court did take into account the latent nature of the disease. However this still did not explain the substantial delay before the actions were brought. Another factor given consideration, was that all of the plaintiffs were legally aided, so the costs in the action would be largely irrecoverable by Boots. A desire on behalf of the families of the deceased to force the defendant to acknowledge responsibility was not a sufficient reason for bringing the action. In one action, however, the balance of prejudice fell on the other side. In this case, the latency period of the disease had been much longer, with diagnosis only occurring in 1991. This action was therefore allowed to proceed.

R v Chief Inspector (HMIP), ex parte Chapman (ELM, August 1995)

[B5.2]

judicial review; BATNEEC; orimulsion; air pollution

Background: Under *Part I* of the *EPA 1990*, the HMIP (now the EA), authorised the burning of orimulsion, a controversial bitumen based fuel, to power an electricity generating station owned by National Power. A resident near to the plant, with cystic fibrosis, applied for judicial review of the decision. The grounds for the challenge were that the use of orimulsion would lead to an increase in atmospheric pollution that would damage his health. As such, it was contended that HMIP should not have authorised the use of this land or National Power should have been required to use an allegedly superior pollution control technology.

Test: The court had to consider whether the grounds for granting leave to apply for judicial review were satisfied.

Decision: The court granted leave to apply.

Comment: This was the first third party challenge based on BATNEEC (best available techniques not entailing excessive costs) to the grant of an authorisation and a direct challenge to HMIP's determination. The challenge alleged that HMIP had misapplied its powers by accepting the use of an allegedly less than optimal means of pollution control.

West Yorkshire Waste Regulation Authority v MJN Ltd (September 1994) Magistrates' Court ((1994) 236 ENDS 40)

[B5.3]

waste; waste gas; HCFC; ozone depleting substances

Background: A service engineer from MJN Ltd lacked the equipment necessary to remove and contain hydrochloroflnorocarbons (HCFC) from an air conditioning unit which he was repairing on site. He tried to collect the HCFC in milk bottles but ten kilograms were released in that process.

Test: The prosecution was brought under *sections 33(1)(c)* and *34(1)(a)* of the *EPA 1990.*

Decision: The company pleaded guilty and was fined £2,500 and ordered to pay costs of £4,500.

Comment: *Section 33(1)(c)* of the *EPA 1990* requires that a person shall not treat, keep or dispose of controlled waste in a manner likely to cause pollution of the environment or harm to human health other than under and in accordance with a waste management licence.

Section 34(1)(a) of the *EPA 1990* imposes a duty on any person who imports, produces, keeps, treats or disposes of controlled waste or, as a broker, has control of such waste, to take all such measures applicable to him as are reasonable in the circumstances to prevent any contravention by any other person of *section 33* of the Act.

This case confirms that the waste provisions of *sections 33* and 34 of the *EPA 1990* can apply to the escape of waste gas as well as liquid and solid waste.

O'Fee v Copeland Borough Council (March 1995) High Court, Queen's Bench Division (Times Law Reports, 22 April 1995)

[B5.4]

clean air; Clean Air Act 1993; air pollution

Background: This was an appeal by O'Fee against a conviction of emitting dark smoke from industrial or trade premises contrary to *section 2(1)* of the *Clean Air Act 1993*. O'Fee argued that because the emissions did not escape from over the boundaries of his land, there was no emission from land for the purposes of the 1993 Act.

Test: The question at issue was whether it was necessary for the prosecution to show that dark smoke was emitted over and beyond the territorial boundary of the defendant's land, and/or whether it was sufficient that dark smoke had been emitted into the air for the purposes of the 1993 Act.

Decision: *Section 2(1)* of the 1993 Act applied to dark smoke emitted into the air within the boundaries of any industrial or trade premises and was not limited to emissions which went beyond particular boundaries.

Margereson v J W Roberts Ltd; Hancock v J W Roberts Ltd (2 April 1996) Court of Appeal (Times Law Reports, 17 April 1996)

[B5.5]

asbestos; children; mesothelioma; damages; reasonably foreseeable risk

Background: This case related to the death by mesothelioma of Jane Hancock and Mr Margereson as a result of their exposure to asbestos dust emanating from J W Roberts Ltd's asbestos processing site in Armley, Leeds. When they were children, Margereson and Hancock lived in close proximity to the processing site and would play with the dust which lined the streets. Margereson and Hancock both died from mesothelioma. The case focused solely on the issue of whether J W Roberts Ltd owed a duty of care to Margereson and Hancock. That issue revolved the question of whether the personal injury caused to them was reasonably foreseeable at the relevant time. If so, then J W Roberts Ltd would be liable.

At trial, J W Roberts Ltd conceded that the measures it had taken to combat asbestos dust emissions were 'woeful'. The company was aware of the health dangers of working with asbestos and even set up a fund to pay for anticipated compensation claims. It contended, however, that what had to be reasonably foreseeable was the mesothelioma itself and, secondly, that the mesothelioma could be caused by environmental exposure. Margereson and Hancock argued that what was required was an objective foresight of personal injury per se and that that foresight was there at all material times.

Test: The Court of Appeal had to consider the extent to which the damage was foreseeable and the scope of the company's duty of care to those outside the factory walls.

Decision: Despite findings of facts by the court of first instance that at no material times did anyone (including the medical witnesses) foresee that asbestosis was likely to be caused by environmental exposure outside the workroom, and that mesothelioma was an unknown concept to medicine at the time, J W Roberts Ltd was nonetheless held to be negligent. The company were found negligent because the emission of asbestos dust from the factory effectively replicated the situation within the factory, and at all material times it was known that asbestos dust could cause personal injury to employees. There was a close similarity between the asbestos exposure faced by the employer and the neighbouring public.

Comment: This case is very specific to its facts and should not be treated on a test case. It does, however, provide useful guidance on the issues of the duty of care and foreseeability.

R v Secretary of State for the Environment and R J C Compton & Sons, ex parte West Wiltshire DC (6 March 1996) High Court, Queen's Bench Division ([1996] Env. L.R. 312)

[B5.6]

air pollution control authorisation; judicial review

Background: R J C Compton & Sons applied for an air pollution control authorisation under *Part I* of the *EPA 1990* in respect of its animal rendering business. The council refused the application on the grounds that the company was not able to carry on the process so as to comply with the conditions in the authorisation. The company appealed. The planning inspector ruled in favour of the council, on the grounds that the company did not have the requisite management ability and was unable to carry on the process as required. The Secretary of State for the Environment rejected the inspector's recommendations and granted the authorisation subject to various conditions. The council sought a judicial review of the secretary of state's decision.

Test: Whether the secretary of state had correctly applied *section 6(4)* of *Part I* of the *EPA 1990.*

Decision: The court upheld the council's application and found that the secretary of state had not applied *section 6(4)* of the *EPA 1990* properly and, as such, was not entitled to overturn the inspector's decision.

Comment: *Section 6(4)* of the *EPA 1990* requires that an application should not be granted under *Part I* of the *EPA*, unless the authority is satisfied that the applicant will be able to carry on the process so as to comply with the conditions of the authorisation. The council successfully argued that enforcement action (to ensure compliance) merely gave short term protection and provided no guarantee of ensuring that the company would carry out the process to the required standard.

Tameside Metropolitan Borough Council v Smith Brothers (Hyde) Ltd (23 December 1996) Magistrates' Court ((1997) 264 ENDS 45)

[B5.7]

air pollution control authorisation; rendering

Background: Eleven charges were brought by Tameside MBC against Smith Brothers, a rendering business, under *section 23(1)* of the *EPA 1990* for breaches of its local authority air pollution control authorisation.

Decision: Smith Brothers was found guilty on all eleven charges. The magistrates commented that the company had shown a 'blatant disregard' of its legal obligations and a 'tardy attitude' towards remedying the pollution. The court imposed the statutory maximum fine of £20,000 for nine of the charges and £18,000 for the other two charges. In addition, Smith Brothers was ordered to pay £21,000 in costs.

Comment: The company was not unsuccessful in its argument that some of the charges should be struck out on the grounds that conditions of an authorisation can only be breached once.

Tameside Metropolitan Borough Council v Smith Brothers (Hyde) Ltd (4 October 1995) High Court, Queen's Bench Division ((1995) 250 ENDS 42, [1996] Env. L.R. D4)

[B5.8]

injunction; rendering; odour; air pollution control authorisation; judicial review; enforcement notice

Background: Smith Brothers, which operated a rendering business, was served by Tameside MBC with an enforcement notice. The notice alleged odour nuisance in breach of the conditions of the company's air pollution control authorisation issued under *Part I* of the *EPA 1990*. The company applied for judicial review of, amongst other things, the service of the enforcement notice and the notice itself. These proceedings were brought by the council for an interlocutory injunction against Smith Brothers pending the outcome of the judicial review proceedings. Under *section 24* of the *EPA 1990*, the council was entitled to take civil proceedings where it considers that a body has failed to comply with an enforcement notice and criminal proceedings would be ineffective.

Test: In determining whether to grant an injunction, the plaintiff must demonstrate to the court that there is a serious issue to be tried. The court must then decide whether the 'balance of convenience' lies in favour of granting the injunction or whether damages would be an adequate remedy.

Decision: It was held by the court that whilst the council had shown an arguable case that Smith Brothers had not complied with the enforcement notice, they had failed to show an arguable case that the enforcement notice was invalid. The court refused to grant the injunction for those reasons. The court also considered whether the 'balance of convenience' lay in favour of granting an injunction and decided that it did not. If the injunction was granted there was a possibility that Smith Brothers might be forced out of business.

Comments: Interestingly, the court noted that this was not a case where civil proceedings could be used to gain more onerous sanctions than those available in the criminal courts. Further, one important factor given weight by the court was that the council had refused to give an undertaking to pay damages in the event that they lost the proceedings. Such a refusal was looked upon gravely by the court.

R v London Borough of Greenwich, ex parte W (a minor) and Others (26 April 1996) Court of Appeal ([1997] Env. L.R. 190)

[B5.9]

air pollution; road traffic

Background: The applicants sought a declaration that the local authority's power under *section 14(2)* of the *Road Traffic Regulation Act 1994*, to close a road or restrict its use where there was a 'likelihood of danger to the public or serious damage to the road', is available where pollution levels are such that they constitute a danger to the public.

Decision: The Court of Appeal found that the power did not apply to risks to the public from air pollution and was intended only to cover direct danger from motor vehicles.

R v Environment Agency and Redland Aggregates Limited, ex parte Gibson; R v Environment Agency and Redland Aggregates, ex parte Ledim; R v Environment Agency, ex parte Sellars and Petty (8 May 1998) High Court, Queen's Bench Division ((1998) 280 ENDS 49)

[B5.10]

BATNEEC; BPEO; judicial review; waste

Background: In related actions, the court heard three applications by local residents regarding IPC authorisations issued pursuant to *Part I* of the *EPA 1990*. Mr Gibson, amongst other applicants, challenged the EA's decision to grant site operators of lime and cement works, a prescribed process variation under *section 11* of the *EPA 1990* to use substitute liquid fuels. Mr Gibson had three main arguments:

(1) *Section 7* of the *EPA 1990* requires the EA to consider the BATNEEC and to have regard to the 'best practicable environmental option' (BPEO) when reviewing authorisation applications. In two of the cases, the EA considered the BATNEEC/BPEO of the existing process authorisation and of the method proposed in the variation. Mr Gibson claimed that the EA had to conduct a full BPEO survey as *section 11* expressly referred to *section 7*.

(2) The EA had to consider all relevant objectives relating to the prevention of detriment to amenities. Under the *Waste Management Licensing Regulations 1994 (SI 1994 No 1056)*, issues such as noise, smell, visual impact and traffic movements must be considered where a prescribed process involves waste disposal or recovery. Redland Aggregates reserved its position to contest that its use of solvent fuel was a 'waste' product but accepted it was for the purpose of the present case.

(3) A separate BATNEEC assessment had to be carried out for the waste treatment element of the plant's works. This, he

contended, was required under the *1984 EC Framework Directive 84/360/EEC* on industrial air pollution. The court held that this was unnecessary.

Decision: In relation to Mr Gibson's first argument, the court held that the EA was required to ensure BATNEEC/BPEO standards were met but not to conduct a full enquiry in every circumstance. In the present case, the EA was entitled to have regard to the previous assessment of BATNEEC/BPEO. The variation was regarded by the EA as an environmental improvement in the context of existing BATNEEC/BPEO assessments. Thus, the court rejected this argument of Mr Gibson.

In relation to Mr Gibson's second argument, the court found that the EA could not equate its obligations under the *Waste Management Licensing Regulations 1994* with BATNEEC/BPEO analysis and was wrong to do so. The court found that the EA had inadvertently assessed the amenities considerations and thus Mr Gibson's argument failed.

In relation to Mr Gibson's final argument, the court found that two authorisations for the same process would not be required. The *Environmental Protection (Prescribed Processes and Substances) Regulations 1991 (SI 1991 No 472)*, state that only one application is necessary where waste treatment is ancillary to the works of a plant, as was the case here. In any event, the court doubted whether a further BATNEEC assessment would have had any effect on the authorisation.

Comment: The court did not consider whether, on the facts of the case, a change in fuel is a change in use requiring planning permission.

R v Petrus Oils (6 November 1998) Crown Court ((1998) 286 ENDS 17)

[B5.11]

odour; abuse of process; prohibition notice; abuse of process

Background: The oil recycling firm, Petrus Oils, commissioned a new refinery in Staffordshire in 1996. Within days of start-up, the EA received numerous complaints regarding unpleasant odours emitted from the site. A prohibition notice was served by the EA a few days after the refinery started operating. This led to a five day shut-down.

Further major incidents occurred in autumn 1996 leading to a second prohibition notice and a warning from the EA that is was considering a prosecution. The EA eventually brought eleven charges against the company. Six related to the incidents in autumn 1996. Five further charges, which at the time of this hearing were still pending before the courts and concerned alleged offences relating to incidents in April and July 1997.

On 18 June 1998, Petrus Oils applied for one of the charges to be stayed. This charge related to an alleged breach of an IPC authorisation, requiring the company to carry out the process using the techniques described in the application, to be stayed. The ground for the application was a claim by Petrus Oils that the EA had abused the legal process.

The process itself related to a flame failure device which the application said would be fitted to the refinery's flare stack to detect failure of the pilot flame. The device would reignite the flame or, if this was not possible, trigger an alarm. When the plant was initially commissioned, the pilot flame was fuelled with impure propane. The judge accepted that the device and alarm had been operational at this time. On 5 September 1997, an inspector from the EA, concerned that the impure propane was causing the odour, agreed to a switch to bottled propane. This meant that the flame failure device was detached. The judge had no doubt that the EA had motivated the change to bottled propane, which raised the issue as to whether the EA had expressly or implicitly approved the resulting breach of the authorisation. The court was informed that Petrus Oils had explained to the EA that a switch to bottled propane would result in disconnection of the flame failure device. The judge noted that the EA had neither notified the company of the breach nor sought to correct it by serving an enforcement or prohibition notice. The judge further stated that such a prosecution for this matter would be wholly contrary to what Petrus Oils had been led to expect by the EA. The judge dismissed the charge as an abuse of process. This prompted the EA to drop two more of the remaining ten charges, both relating to alleged reporting failures by the company.

The trial of the remaining charges began on 9 September 1998. Petrus Oils pleaded not guilty to all the charges. The first issue to be dealt with concerned the company's application to have the second charge struck out on the grounds of abuse of process. This charge concerned the allegation that the existence of a pipeline discharging vapour to the flare stack was not authorised under the company's IPC authorisation. Petrus Oils claimed that the charge should be struck out on two grounds. First, the pipework was implicitly required by the authorisation and in particular by the 'residual duty' to use BATNEEC imposed on all operators by *section 7(4)* of the *EPA 1990*. Petrus Oils' second claim of abuse of process related to the fact that the EA had effectively 'agreed by its conduct' or 'acquiesced' to the existence of the pipework.

Decision: In relation to the first ground put forward by Petrus Oils that the pipework had been implicitly required by the authorisation, the judge concluded that this issue was one for a jury to decide and so refused to strike out this charge.

As to Petrus Oils' second claim of abuse of process, the judge accepted that there had been an unreasonable delay between the EA's discovery of the pipework in issue and its decision to prosecute for the unauthorised installation of the line. The EA first notified a breach of the authorisation on 30 September 1997, but the prosecution was not formally initiated until the end of July 1998. The judge ruled that once the EA had taken exception to the pipework, it should have investigated the circumstances with due expedition. Its failure to do anything about it was conduct which amounted to tacit consent or acquiescence. Further, the judge said that it was almost impossible for the EA to prosecute for an offence which had already been the subject of less severe enforcement action. The EA had made decisions which could have involved consideration of the pipeline and then attempted to revoke those by bringing a prosecution. The judge held that the EA's decision to prosecute Petrus Oils over the pipework was manifestly unfair and oppressive and upheld the company's claim. This led to the eventual collapse of the remainder of the six charges relating to the autumn 1996 pollution incidents. In addition, the judge ordered that Petrus Oils' costs to be met by the EA rather than from the central funds.

Judicial Review

R v Secretary of State for Trade and Industry, ex parte Duddridge (3 October 1994) High Court, Queen's Bench Division ([1995] Env. L.R. 151)

[B6.1]

Treaty of Rome; judicial review; electro-magnetic radiation; electricity; precautionary principle; causation; Article 130; environment policy; European law

Background: This case concerned an application for judicial review of the decision of the Secretary of State for Trade and Industry, not to issue regulations under the *Electricity Act 1989*, to restrict emissions of electromagnetic radiation from underground high voltage electrical cables being laid in North London as part of the national grid. The application was made on behalf of three children living in South Woodford, one of the areas affected by the cable laying. It was claimed by the applicants that the electromagnetic fields might expose them to a risk of developing leukaemia. Under *section 29* of the *Electricity Act 1989*, the secretary of state may make regulations to protect the public from dangers arising from the generation, transmission or supply of electricity etc. In this case, he decided that measures to limit non-ionising radiation emissions were not necessary or appropriate. Judicial review of this decision was applied for on the grounds that either pursuant to the policy set out in the Government White Paper *'This Common Inheritance'*, or under *Article 130r* of the *1957 Treaty* (relating to environmental policy), the secretary of state is obliged to apply the 'precautionary principle' if the possibility of risk to the environment or human health exists. Expert advice did not suggest that a causal link between exposure to electromagnetic fields and cancer had been established, although the possibility of a connection was recognised.

Test: Whilst the precautionary principle is enshrined within *Article 130r(2)* of the *1957 Treaty*, as amended at Maastricht, it only lays down a general principle upon which EC policy on the environment should be based but does not impose a direct obligation on any member state.

Decision: The judge held that as the White Paper sets a threshold for action where a significant risk of damage arises, the secretary of state's conclusion was not unreasonable or perverse. Moreover, *Article 130r* did not oblige him to apply the precautionary principle to his duties under the *Electricity Act 1989*. As such, the application for judicial review was rejected.

Comment: On appeal, the Court of Appeal denied leave to appeal the decision of the Queen's Bench Divisional Court. The applicants had argued that the EU law issue should be referred for resolution to the ECJ. The court rejected that suggestion saying that it (the Court of Appeal) could resolve that issue.

R v Northumbrian Water Ltd, ex parte Newcastle and North Tyneside Health Authority (15 December 1998) High Court, Crown Office ([1999] Env. L.R. 715)

[B6.2]

water; artificial fluoridation

Background: This judicial review concerned the powers and duties of health authorities and water undertakers, relating to the artificial fluoridation of water supplies under the statutory scheme contained in *sections 87–91* of the *WIA 1991. Section 87* provides that 'Where a District Health Authority has applied in writing to a water undertaker for the water supplied within an area specified in the application to be fluoridated, that undertaker may . . . increase the fluoride content of the water supplied by the undertaker within that area.' *Section 89* provides for a publicity and consultation exercise that must be undertaken by a health authority before making such a request. *Section 90* gives the

Secretary of State for Health the power to grant an indemnity to the water undertaker in connection with a fluoridation scheme.

In March 1994, Newcastle and North Tyneside Health Authority made an application to Northumbrian Water Ltd requesting that it artificially fluoridate waters supplied to certain regions. In September 1997, the board of Northumbrian Water Ltd resolved not to accede to the request of the health authority. The health authority sought to challenge the legality of that decision by means of judicial review proceedings.

Northumbrian Water Ltd's reasons for its decision were twofold. First, few of its customers had shown any interest in the subject of artificial fluoridation, and those that had shown an interest clearly demonstrated that it was a very divisive issue on which strong views were held on both sides of the argument. As regards the merits of the public health benefits of artificial fluoridation, Northumbrian Water Ltd took a 'neutral stance'. Secondly, artificial fluoridation would expose Northumbrian Water Ltd to an increased possibility of criminal and civil liability, a substantial part of which would not be covered by the proposed indemnity that had been discussed with the Department of Health. The health authority attacked both aspects of the decision. It claimed that under the statutory scheme, as the health authority was the primary body concerned with public health matters, once it (the health authority) had made its application, it was not permissible for the water company to take a neutral stance on the issue of the public health benefits of fluoridation. As regards the second reason, the health authority argued that it would be against public policy (and therefore unlawful) to offer an indemnity in respect of criminal liabilities. It was therefore irrational for Northumbrian Water Ltd to refuse the request on the basis that the secretary of state would not offer such an indemnity.

Test: The judge held that whilst decisions of privatised water companies are amenable to judicial review, such companies are not to be regarded in the same way as public bodies which have an obligation to exercise their powers for the public good. As a commercial organisation, Northumbrian Water Ltd had to take into account its obligations to its shareholders. It was only required to exercise its powers for the public good to the extent required by statutory provisions laid down by parliament. The judge was shown passages from Hansard setting out the parliamentary debate relevant to the *Water (Fluoridation) Act 1985* which contained the predecessor to *section 87*. There were clear ministerial statements in the Houses of Commons and Lords, which supported Northumbrian Water Ltd's contention that the purpose of the Act was simply to provide the power to artificially fluoridate if both the health authority and the water undertaker wishes to do so. The discretion given to water companies under *section 87* was therefore very broad.

Decision: Northumbrian Water Ltd was within its rights to refuse the health authority's request for the reasons given.

Comment: The case ultimately turned on the scope of the discretion granted to water companies under *section 87* of the *WIA 1991* (which notably provides that the water company 'may' rather than 'shall' fluoridate). It is also a good example of a privatised utility being subject to the judicial review process in relation to its 'public' functions.

R v Secretary of State for Transport, ex parte Richmond Upon Thames London Borough Council and Others (December 1994) High Court, Queen's Bench Division (Times Law Reports, 29 December 1994)

[B6.3]

noise; airport

Background: This was a judicial review of the decision by the Secretary of State for Transport, concerning night time flying restrictions at Gatwick, Heathrow and Stansted airports. The London Borough of Richmond and other borough and district councils claimed that they were misled as to the basis upon which the secretary of state's proposals were put forward during the consultation process in 1993. In short, the proposals, if implemented, would have resulted in an increase in the noise levels, (exceeding the levels experienced in the summer of 1988), which was contrary to the policy of the secretary of state and was not apparent from the relevant consultation paper. The consultation paper was, therefore, materially misleading which in turn meant that there was not a full and fair consultation.

Decision: The judge held that the secretary of state's decision was unlawful.

Comment: The court noted that the secretary of state might, in taking into account the relevant considerations, move away from his previously expressed policy (i.e. that noise levels must remain below the summer 1998 levels). If he was to do so, he must include a recognition that he had done so.

R v Secretary of State for Foreign Affairs, ex parte World Development Movement Ltd (9 November 1994) High Court, Queen's Bench Division ([1995] 1 All ER 611)

[B6.4]

locus standi; environmental protestors

Background: This was a case of judicial review of the Foreign Secretary's actions in granting aid for the Pergau Dam project in Malaysia. That decision was made against the advice of officials of the Overseas Development Administration, who had concluded that the project was uneconomic. The World Development Movement Ltd (WDM) was a non-partisan pressure group which campaigned to increase the amount and quality of British aid to developing countries. One of the significant issues which arose was whether the WDM had sufficient right or interest ('locus standi'), to apply for judicial review of the Foreign Secretary's decision.

Test: On the issue of locus standi, the court had to consider (i) the merits of the challenge, (ii) the importance of vindicating the rule of law and of the issues raised, (iii) the likely absence of any other responsible challengers, (iv) the nature of the breach of duty against which relief was sought and (v) the prominent role of the WDM in giving advice, guidance and assistance with regard to aid.

Decision: The court held that the WDM did have locus standi to make the application.

Comment: This was an interesting and important decision for environmental pressure groups. The principles underlying this decision have been relevant to subsequent judicial review applications by such bodies where issues of standing have arisen.

R v Ministry of Defence, ex parte Smith and Others (7 June 1995) High Court, Queen's Bench Division (ILR, 8 June 1995)

[B6.5]

human rights

Background: This case was a judicial review of the Ministry of Defence's policy of discharging homosexual men and lesbian women from the armed forces. That policy is reviewed by parliament every five years. The policy reasoning for banning homosexuals from the armed forces was stated to be morale, unit effectiveness of the fighting forces, and the forces role of 'in loco parentis'. The applicants, three men and one woman, challenged that policy on the grounds that it was irrational, and that it was a breach of the *European Convention on Human Rights* and of the *Equal Treatment Directive 79/7 EEC.*

Test: In determining a purported restriction of fundamental human rights by the decision of a minister, the court needed to consider whether that minister could show an important competing public interest which he could reasonably judge sufficient to satisfy the restriction. Only if the minister's purported justification outrageously defied the logic or accepted moral standards, could the court strike down the minister's decision.

Decision: Whilst the court thought that admitting homosexuals to the fighting forces would not diminish its operational efficiency and effectiveness, it could not say that the opposing view was irrational in the sense that it was an outrageous defiance of logic. The court was particularly conscious of its constitutional bounds, namely that it was restricted to a secondary decision making role particularly as the matter was debated by parliament every five years.

Comment: Human rights and the *European Convention on Human Rights* are issues which increasingly arise in the environmental sphere. Whilst this case does not relate to an environmental issue, the principles could on occasion be applicable to judicial review of governmental policy relating to the environment. It is also worth noting that in several other countries, for example India, the use of human rights laws to protect the environment is considerable.

R v Secretary of State for Transport, ex parte Richmond upon Thames London Borough Council and Others (No. 4) (18, 19, 26 July 1996) Court of Appeal ([1996] 4 All ER 903)

[B6.6]

noise; airport noise

Background: This case related to aircraft noise restrictions at night and constitutes the appeal from the decision of the High Court covered earlier in paragraph B6.3. The Secretary of State for Transport had power to exercise control over night flying and, in August 1995, he made an order imposing new night flight restrictions at Heathrow, Gatwick and Stansted airports. The new Order was to apply for a period from October 1995 to 1998 and would replace the existing Order made in 1988. The new Order, which followed consultation papers in January 1993, March 1995 and June 1995, imposed aggregate night time noise levels which varied seasonally. The noise levels under the previous Order had never reached the maximum permitted levels, particularly in the summer when the actual noise was considerably lower than that which had been permitted. The new Order allowed more noise than had been actually experienced to date but less noise than had been permitted by the earlier Order. Richmond Council and other local authorities applied for judicial review of the secretary of state's decision.

The judge, at first instance, dismissed their application and the local authorities appealed to the Court of Appeal. They argued that the secretary of state's decision (1) infringed the local residents legitimate expectation that the Order would not be withdrawn without an opportunity to comment and without local authorities being given an opportunity to communicate rational grounds against the Order, (2) that the secretary of state had failed to adequately explain his reasons for his decision and (3) that the decision was irrational.

Decision: The Court of Appeal dismissed the appeal. On the first argument, it held that the secretary of state had set out the proposals fairly and rationally in the three consultation papers and had not, therefore, infringed the legitimate expectations of the local residents. Secondly, the secretary of state was under no legal duty to explain why he chose to make his particular Order. The reasons that he provided in the consultation papers were adequate because they explained his conclusions on the 'principal important controversial issues'. Thirdly, there were no grounds or evidence before the court to show that the secretary of state's decision was not rational.

R v Secretary of State for the Environment, ex parte Torridge District Council (25 April 1997) High Court, Queen's Bench Division ([1997] EGCS 61)

[B6.7]

air pollution control; odour; rendering

Background: Peninsular Proteins Ltd operated a blood processing and animal tissue rendering plant in Devon. The plant was situated on low ground 500 metres from the nearest dwellings. Despite modernisation and erection of a fifteen metre stack in 1992, the plant continued to give rise to numerous complaints of offensive odours. Both processes required air pollution control authorisations under *Part I* of the *EPA 1990*. Despite being prepared to make further improvements and accept the common condition imposed under *section 7(1)(c)* of the *EPA 1990* that 'all emissions to air shall be free from offensive odour outside the process boundary', an authorisation was refused on the grounds that the plant would not be able to comply with such a condition as it lay on ground considerably lower than the dwellings affected. The secretary of state, applying non-statutory guidance *AQ16(95)*, allowed Peninsular's appeal on the grounds that such a condition, couched solely in terms of its aims, should only be used in exceptional circumstances such as where the process was extremely close to residential areas. The council applied for judicial review of this decision.

Decision: In allowing the council's application for judicial review, the court held that the effect of the condition was to require achievement of its aim and not to restate the aim of the non-statutory guidance. The condition was not inherently unenforceable and, therefore, the decision was illogical. The secretary of state did not clarify why the distance from housing should be the decisive factor in the present case and should have allowed the council the chance to point to other material considerations.

R v Secretary of State for Trade and Industry, ex parte Greenpeace (14 October 1997) High Court, Queen's Bench Division ((1997) 273 ENDS 43)

[B6.8]

habitats directive; delay in issue of proceedings; oil exploration licences; locus standi

Background: This case arose out of the decision by Greenpeace to challenge by way of judicial review the secretary of state's decision in April 1997, to award oil exploration licences to over twenty companies for exploration in the North Atlantic (on the UK continental shelf). Greenpeace sought to argue that *Directive 92/43 EEC on habitats* should apply to the areas covered by the licences on the basis that they constituted 'reefs' under the Directive by reason of the deep water cold coral found there. The Directive would impose stricter environmental obligations than the exploration licences. The UK regulations implementing the Directive applied to land and territorial waters (i.e. up to the twelve mile limit). Greenpeace argued that the Directive should apply to the continental shelf. The government and oil companies opposed this argument and took the stance that the coral in question did not constitute a reef. Before the substantive issues could be heard, Greenpeace had to first apply for leave to apply for judicial review.

Test: In order to be eligible to apply for judicial review, the party making the application (in this case Greenpeace) must show to the court that it has raised a genuine legal argument, and has a sufficient interest in the matter and that the application had been brought in time. Applications for leave to apply for judicial review must be made promptly or in any event within three months of the date when the grounds for the application first arose.

Decision: The court accepted that Greenpeace had a sufficient interest and, therefore the necessary standing to apply for judicial review. The court said that in effect Greenpeace was acting in the public interest.

The court held that the time constraints on bringing an application for judicial review are of particular importance in cases involving public interest applicants. Greenpeace applied for leave just within the three months after the date on which the licences had been awarded (April 1997). The government and the oil companies put forward a number of other dates (dates prior to the date of the awarding of the licences). They argued that Greenpeace's cause for complaint arose from those dates and as Greenpeace's application had not been filed promptly after those dates (or at least within three months of those dates), the application should be rejected.

The court rejected the first two dates put forward by the government and the oil companies. The third date suggested was November 1995. This was when the government identified the areas to be offered for licences. In December 1996, a formal announcement of the deadline for making applications was published in the EC Official Journal. The government argued that it was then clear that none of the areas available for licences were to be within special areas of conservation. Greenpeace counter-argued that it could not assess the impact on particular habitats until it was clear which licences had been awarded. The judge rejected this argument stating that Greenpeace's contention was, in reality, that the government should have followed certain procedures under the Directive before granting licences.

The court held that Greenpeace had the necessary information after November 1995 and in any event after December 1996. Greenpeace was therefore too late in making its application. The judge went on to consider whether, if he was wrong and the correct reference date was April 1997, Greenpeace had nevertheless not taken prompt enough action despite being within the three month limit. The judge noted the lack of advanced warning of the proceedings given by Greenpeace to the oil companies and that Greenpeace had not sought counsel's opinion until late May 1997. The judge therefore held that Greenpeace had not acted sufficiently promptly, that it would not be correct to apply the court's residual discretion to permit late applications and that therefore the application was dismissed.

Comment: This case stresses the importance of prompt action where judicial review applications are contemplated.

R v Bolton Metropolitan Borough Council, ex parte Kirkman (19 December 1997) High Court, Queen's Bench Division (NLD, 22 December 1997)

[B6.9]

planning process; waste incineration; waste policy

Background: Bolton MBC granted a company planning permission for a waste incinerator. Mr Kirkman was a local resident and objected to the plan. Mr Kirkman applied for judicial review of the decision to grant planning permission on the grounds that: (1) Bolton MBC had failed to address or answer questions relating to hazards caused by air emissions but had left them to the EA, (2) Bolton MBC had misunderstood and failed to discharge its duties under *Article 4* of the *European Waste Framework Directive 75/442/EEC* (as amended) as implemented by the *Waste Management Licensing Regulations 1994 (SI 1994 No 1056)*, (3) its decision was procedurally flawed in that it failed to delay the decision until further information requested by an environmental health officer had been obtained and that new material lodged by Friends of the Earth had been considered, (4) in relation to the BPEO, Bolton MBC had failed to address or answer the question whether the proposal for the incineration of waste represented BPEO for the relevant wastes, and (5) Bolton MBC had misunderstood and failed to discharge its duties under *Article 3* of the *Waste Framework Directive*.

Decision: The court refused the application for judicial review and upheld the planning permission. *Gateshead MBC v Secretary of State [1994] Env. L.R. 37*, had established that the impact of air discharges was a material planning consideration but in considering this, the planning authority was entitled to take into account the system of controls available under the IPC regime. Unless it appeared on the face of the information before the planning authority that the discharges might be unacceptable to the EA, it was proper to leave the matter to be dealt with by the Agency under the IPC system. There was nothing in the wording of *Article 3* of the *Waste Framework Directive* which suggested that priority should be given to recycling or recovery of energy because they were treated as alternatives in this Directive. Therefore, the planning authority had not failed in its duty to consider and address to what extent the proposals represented BPEO. There was no statutory or policy requirement for the planning authority to carry out a BPEO exercise in every case and a statement in the planning authority's draft plan could not be taken as creating a binding legal commitment. BPEO was capable of being a material consideration in law and the planning authority's had recognised it as such and therefore its conclusion was reasonable and lawful.

The court ruled that it was crucial to distinguish between the 'correct question' and the 'material' needed to answer it. Failure to take account of a particular consideration will not invalidate a decision unless, first, it is required to be taken into account by the statute or the nature of the decision, and second there is a real possibility that taking it into account would have affected the decision. A distinction had to be drawn between formal policy statements which were material to the resolution of questions and informal policies which were guidance only.

Landfill Tax

Taylor Woodrow v Customs & Excise (12 November 1998) VAT and Duties Tribunal ((1998) 286 ENDS 17)

[B7.1]

contaminated land; exemption; waste

Background: The case concerned a dispute between Taylor Woodrow and Customs & Excise over a Taylor Woodrow project in Bury. The project involved reclamation of derelict land, including an unlicensed tip, as part of a new retail development. In order to avoid imposing costs on land reclamation projects, the government has granted an exemption from landfill tax for material excavated from contaminated sites. This project involved the removal of 10,800 tonnes of waste material and the consignment of this to a landfill. Customs & Excise refused to grant an exemption in respect of 2,800 tonnes of this waste. This decision was on the basis that the waste would have had to have been removed anyway because of its unsuitability due to the risk of settlement and such operation would be 'construction' to which the exemption does not apply. Taylor Woodrow requested a review of this decision by the Customs & Excise Appeals and Complaints Team. In May 1997, the team upheld the officer's decision. Taylor Woodrow then appealed to the VAT and Duties Tribunal.

Test: To qualify for the exemption from landfill tax for excavated contaminated materials the remediation must constitute or include cleaning the land of pollutants which are causing or may potentially cause harm.

Decision: In coming to its decision, the tribunal took issue with a number of points in an Information Note (May 1997) issued on the matter by Customs & Excise. First, the Information Note stated that, to qualify for an exemption, 'the reclamation [must] include clearing the land of pollutants which would unless cleared prevent the land being put to the intended us'. This is subject to proof by the developer that removal is necessary due to the potential for the pollutants to cause harm and that, if not removed, would prevent the intended use of the land. On this point, the tribunal stated that Customs & Excise was setting excessively restrictive rules. There is nothing in the relevant legislation requiring the reclamation to be necessary in order to develop the land or for the development to be the primary or only purpose of the works. Secondly, the Information Note also stated that Customs & Excise 'will not accept any claim that, although the pollutants fall below the limit generally recognised as safe for the intended use of the land, they have to be removed for other reasons' including unsuitable soil structure or a need to reduce the site level. On this point, the tribunal agreed with Taylor Woodrow that this was also imposing a primary motive test which was not in the legislation. The tribunal looked to *section 43B(8)(a)* of the *Finance Act 1996* which requires that, for an exemption to be permitted, the reclamation must constitute or include cleaning the land of pollutants which are causing or may potentially cause harm. The tribunal was satisfied that, in the present case, the waste removed had the potential to cause harm.

As such, Taylor Woodrow needed only to show that the removal of pollutants was necessary to 'facilitate development'. The condition is satisfied if 'best current practice' would require the pollutants to be removed. In the present case, removal of the waste was best practice as there was no safer alternative.

The tribunal upheld the appeal and awarded costs against Customs & Excise and the certificate of exemption from landfill tax was reinstated.

Comment: This case was one of the first relating to the scope of landfill tax exemptions. It addressed the concerns of industry over the precise nature of this particular exemption and the narrow interpretation being adopted by Customs & Excise.

Negligence

Tutton v A D Walter (12 October 1984) High Court, Queen's Bench Division ([1985] 3 WLR 797)

[B8.1]

negligence; duty of care; neighbours; lawful activity

Background: Mr Tutton kept bees on land adjacent to land owned by Mr Walter. Mr Walter grew oilseed rape on his land (which is particularly attractive to bees). He sprayed the crop with insecticide giving Mr Tutton only twenty four hours notice of the spraying. As a result the bees died. Mr Tutton brought an action in negligence.

Test: Whether Mr Walker owed a duty of care to his neighbours when spraying his crops.

Decision: The court found that Mr Walter owed a duty of care to neighbouring beekeepers and was, therefore, liable for damages.

Comment: The case confirmed that even when carrying out a lawful activity, a person may be liable for a failure to warn others who may be harmed by substances which originate from his property. A defence of carrying on a lawful or licensed activity is one often raised in relation to environment cases.

Graham and Graham v ReChem International (16 June 1995) High Court, Queen's Bench Division ((1995) 245 ENDS 18)

[B8.2]

nuisance; private nuisance; negligence; causation; balance of probabilities; evidential burden; incinerator; forseeability; duty of care; breach of duty; causal link

Background: The Grahams owned a piece of land two miles west of ReChem's hazardous waste incinerator which was in operation between 1974 and 1984. In 1980, the Grahams began using this piece of land as seasonal grazing for bullocks and dairy cattle. The health of the herd deteriorated and this led to the collapse of the plaintiff's business. The Grahams' central allegation was that the emission of polyhalogenated aromatic hydrocarbons (PHAHs), polychlorinated biphenyls (PCBs), dioxins and furans from the incinerator had contaminated the land and poisoned their herd. Damages of £1.5 million were claimed against ReChem. The basis of the claim was in nuisance and negligence.

Test: Whether the plaintiff sufficiently demonstrated the elements of negligence and nuisance and, in particular, causation.

Decision: The Grahams' case was dismissed.

On the claim of nuisance, the judge held that liability was strict and that any damage must be foreseeable. He accepted the Grahams' submission that the only real issues in nuisance were whether PHAHs had been emitted from the incinerator and, if so, whether such PHAHs had, on the balance of probabilities, made a material contribution to the alleged damage to the Grahams' animals. The plaintiffs contended that they had. On the claim for negligence, the judge decided that such a claim would only be upheld where the Grahams could demonstrate that ReChem both breached the duty of care that they owed to their neighbours, and that such breaches resulted in emissions of PHAHs which caused the alleged damage.

In the event, the judge did not accept that PHAH toxicosis was to blame for the ill-health of the cattle. The judge concluded that the deterioration in the herd had been the result of an illness known as 'fat cow syndrome', caused by the Grahams over feeding their animals. As such, the Grahams had failed to establish a causal link between ReChem's operations and the damage caused to their herd. The case was dismissed.

Comment: This case illustrates the difficulty in establishing causal links in such cases where scientific evidence in the form of the monitoring of releases and of the effect on the environment is so sparse. The case builds on the principles in the *Cambridge Water Co case [1994]* (see paragraph B10.10).

Gallon and Others v Swan Hunter Ship Builders Ltd (12 May 1995) Court of Appeal (Solicitors Journal, 7 July 1995)

[B8.3]

negligence; toxic tort; personal injury; causal link; noxious fumes; breach of statutory duty

Background: Gallon and others were employees of Swan Hunter and brought actions against the company alleging personal injuries, which arose from their exposure during their employment to noxious fumes. Swan Hunter requested further and better particulars of the plaintiffs' claims. In particular, they requested particulars identifying each noxious fume complained of and matters relied upon to support the allegation that Swan Hunter Ship Builders Ltd had knowledge of the health risks to which the employees had been exposed.

Test: The rules relating to further and better particulars were set out in the *Rules of the Supreme Court Order 18, Rule 12* and required 'that every pleading must obtain the necessary particulars of any claim'.

Decision: The Court of Appeal held that the rules of court require that necessary particulars of any claim be given to the defendant. However, in an action for damages for breach of statutory duty or negligence, it was not necessary to prove that the alleged breach was the whole or even the main cause of the damage. Evidence that it materially contributed to the damage was sufficient. The Court of Appeal held that to properly determine this litigation, it would be both impossible and unnecessary to determine in detail the nature of the employees exposure to fumes in terms of their concentration and composition. Further, as there were many actions proceeding against Swan Hunter and others in relation to very similar claims, there was no ground in this class of litigation for ordering particulars of the company's knowledge of the health risks.

Comment: The decision in this case may be extremely helpful for future toxic tort cases, where one of the most difficult issues in such cases is establishing the causal link between the contamination or toxic substance and the resulting damage.

Lidl Properties v Clarke Bond Partnership (13 June 1997) High Court, Queen's Bench Division ([1998] Env. L.R. 662)

[B8.4]

negligence; duty of care; professional negligence; environment consultants; Hedley Byrne Principle; reasonable skill and care

Background: This case concerned a site in Leicestershire which was purchased by Lidl in October 1993. The site had been occupied by a chemical works and was known to have been contaminated. The Clarke Bond Partnership, having made investigations into the site, was asked to advise at a meeting on 30 September 1993 on measures needed to remove contaminated groundwater from land drains. Lidl alleged that the advice was negligent as it did not (1) warn of the risk that the measures required to deal with the contamination would be more expensive than estimated, (2) make clear that there were differing opinions amongst other consultants and planners as to the measures required and (3) advise on the difficulties and consequences involved with the differing opinions held and the planning position at the time. Lidl claimed £3,722,478.64 for the cost of the site, professional fees, construction costs and the costs of remedying the contamination.

Clarke Bond had carried out its investigations (at first) on behalf of G Gallifords (UK) Ltd, a potential purchaser, on the basis of data collected by other consultants. However, they did not have access to the commentary and interpretation in the previous reports.

Clarke Bond was subsequently instructed by Morrison Developments Ltd to make further site investigations and these were carried out by the British Geotechnical Survey. Morrison intended to purchase the site and sell it to Lidl following remediation. High levels of phenols were found by the British Geotechnical Survey which exceeded the Dutch action levels.

In the meantime, a significant competitor of Lidl, Aldi, had put in an unconditional offer on the site. Clarke Bond attended the meeting on 30 September 1993 only knowing of the Lidl interest in the site. On 1 October 1993, Lidl purchased the site.

Clarke Bond was involved in discussions on the contaminated groundwater issue with the NRA, Severn Trent Water and the planning authority. Agreement in principle was reached on the Clarke Bond remediation scheme.

Lidl commenced works at the site without final planning permission and the works did not properly conform to the Clarke Bond scheme. During the works, strong smells of phenols were detected which were a cause of concern to the authorities. The planning authority required that work stop. Lidl had to proceed with an expensive scheme of further works to satisfy the planning authority's requirements. Hindsight, however, showed that the Clarke Bond scheme had been suitable for the levels of contamination at the site.

Test: Whether Clarke Bond owed Lidl a duty of care in relation to advice provided on contamination and remediation.

Decision: The judge held that Clarke Bond did owe a duty of care to Lidl under the principle in *Hedley Byrne & Co Ltd v Heller & Partners Ltd [1964] AC 465*. This duty was to exercise the reasonable skill and care expected of a consulting engineer with experience of contamination. However, Clarke Bond did not know and could not reasonably have known that Lidl would rely on what was said in deciding whether or not to purchase the property. Lidl did not place significant reliance on anything said by Clarke Bond in reaching its decision.

Comment: This case demonstrates the difficult position consultants find themselves in when advising on contamination and remediation in the context of a proposed sale of land. It reinforces the need to be clear as to which parties can place reliance on the advice and the basis on which such advice is given. In light of *Urban Regeneration Agency and English Partnerships (Medway) Ltd v Mott MacDonald (1998)*, (see paragraph B8.7) we await to see the extent of negligence actions arising from advice given in relatively new and innovative remediation schemes.

W Lamb Ltd v J Jarvis & Sons plc (21 July 1998) High Court, Queen's Bench Division ([1998] 60 Con LR 1)

[B8.5]

negligence; faulty work; joint and several liability; professional negligence

Background: J Jarvis & Sons plc subcontracted the installation of pipework for a petrol station to W Lamb Ltd. J Jarvis & Sons remained responsible for the concrete supporting and surrounding of the pipework. The pipework developed leaks and had to be replaced. The parties agreed that the pipework would be replaced yet reserved themselves as to cost as each sought to make the other liable for the cost. This case addressed liability only, the only issue being whether the failure of the pipework was due to the faulty work of the W Lamb Ltd or J Jarvis & Sons.

Test: The court had to consider whether both parties could be equally at fault for the negligence.

Decision: There was no rule of law which prevented both parties to the action being found equally at fault for the resulting negligence.

Comment: This case is of interest to those faced with potential litigation particularly where several defendants may be involved.

Kahl and Another v Holderness Borough Council and Another (27 November 1998) High Court, Queen's Bench Division (NLD, 23 November 1998)

[B8.6]

negligence; duty of care; local authority; purchaser

Background: This was a claim in negligence for compensation by Ms Kahl against Holderness Borough Council. The claim was for injuries suffered by her when, in 1990, a section of a cliff fell onto her. The council had owned and operated the caravan park located at the top of the cliff until three weeks before the action when it had been sold on to another person. Ms Kahl also brought an action against this person. The council was fully aware that the area had been particularly susceptible to coastal erosion in the last twenty years.

Test: Whether a duty of care was owed by the council to users of the beach despite it having sold the site.

Decision: The council did owe a duty of care to Ms Kahl. The construction of steps leading from the caravan park to the beach was a positive action, inviting persons to use the beach and so venture into the vicinity of a known danger. The failure to erect a warning notice was so irrational that no reasonable local authority would have erected the steps without an accompanying warning notice.

The duty of the local authority was a continuing one and it was not reasonable to impose such a duty of care on the new owner and occupier of the site after just three weeks of occupation and ownership.

Comment: Although not a case directly relating to the environment, it did raise an interesting point with general application namely the possibility of a continuing duty of care after sale of property.

Urban Regeneration Agency and English Partnerships (Medway) Ltd v Mott MacDonald (27 October 1998) High Court, Queen's Bench Division ((1999) 291 ENDS 25)

[B8.7]

negligence; professional negligence; environment consultants; negligent remediation; risk assessment; professional duty of care

Background: Mott MacDonald (MM) was engaged by the Urban Regeneration Agency (URA) to act as consultants, to investigate the extent of contamination on the former Royal Docklands site in Chatham. It was also responsible for advising on decontamination and the letting of contracts. The actual remediation work was carried out by a third party contractor between 1990 and 1993 with MM acting as consulting engineer. A subsidiary of the URA, English Partnerships (Medway), carried out the day-to-day running of the project.

URA contended that the project only made economic sense if the cost of the decontamination was not greater than the value of the site if restored. The cost of the project rose drastically when unforeseen contamination was encountered. URA claimed that MM had failed to provide proper advice and estimates of the degree of contamination and the clean up costs before the project was undertaken and further failed to provide corrective advice during the project. English Partnerships argued that, had URA been given proper advice at the outset of the project or had interim warnings been given, the scheme would have been aborted. English Partnerships claimed over £65 million in damages from MM.

Test: The court had to consider the standard of clean-up required by the contract and whether MM had exercised all reasonable skill and care in performing various aspects of the contract.

Decision: The court held that the contract required that the clean up should be carried out to a standard reasonably required to have the site redeveloped, even though this might be more onerous than the standard required solely by engineering standards. The court also concluded that MM had failed to exercise reasonable care and skill in various aspects of the contract. It had failed to provide adequate advice on different approaches of its strategy or guidance as to how a risk assessment must be carried out or linked to the URA's concerns about public perception. The court found that, on two occasions, URA would have abandoned the clean up had it received full and proper advice from MM.

On the question of damages, the court decided that the basis of assessing URA's loss was to calculate a percentage of the overall remediation costs to be paid by MM. This was on the grounds that they could not be recovered from the subsequent redevelopment and that the URA lost the opportunity of abandoning the project at an early stage. The court considered that there was a fifty per cent chance of recovering all expenditure and that the URA was entitled to recover fifty per cent of the costs in excess of the original estimate. This was roughly £18.5 million.

Comment: This case raised some interesting issues on the conduct of remediation programmes. It confirms the need to expressly address the issue of cost overruns, the importance of clear communication both before and during the project and the need to clearly define remediation standards. Of particular interest was the use by Mott McDonald of a risk based approach, at a time before this had become common or even accepted practice in circumstances where the client expected a higher level of remediation than would have been required by reference to published guideline values. In short, the judge found that the consultant failed to adequately communicate.

Connelly v RTZ Corporation plc and Others (24 July 1997) House of Lords ([1997] 3 WLR 373)

[B8.8]

forum; forum non-conveniens; competent jurisdiction; financial assistance; conditional fee; forum shopping

Background: Mr Connelly, a British Citizen, contracted cancer of the larynx following five and a half years employment with Rossing Uranium Ltd (RUL), a uranium mining company in Namibia. He brought an action against the England registered parent company of RUL, RTZ Corporation plc, claiming that his cancer was a result of inhaling silica uranium at the mine and that RTZ had failed to provide a safe system of work to protect him from the effects of such uranium or dust. The Court of Appeal initially upheld the High Court's decision to stay the proceedings on the grounds that Namibia was the appropriate forum for the hearing. During the hearing, they stated that it was not possible to take into account Connelly's eligibility for legal aid in the UK when determining the most appropriate forum. The Court of Appeal subsequently decided to lift the stay after Connelly undertook not to apply for legal aid and instead entered into a 'no win no fee' arrangement with his solicitor. RTZ appealed against this decision to the House of Lords.

Test: In order to stay proceedings on the grounds of *forum non-conveniens*, the court should be satisfied that there is some other tribunal, having competent jurisdiction, in which the case might be tried more suitably for the interests of all the parties and for the ends of justice.

If a more appropriate forum had been identified, the stay would not normally be refused simply because the plaintiff would not have financial assistance available to him overseas which would be available in the UK. However, the availability of financial assistance could be a relevant factor if the plaintiff could show that substantial justice would not be done if he had to proceed in a forum where no assistance was available.

Decision: The court allowed Connelly's appeal and dismissed RTZ's appeal. *Section 33 (1)(b)* of the *Legal Aid Act 1988* was never intended to apply to an application to stay proceedings brought by the plaintiff on the grounds of *forum non-conveniens*. The correct test was whether the court was satisfied that there was some other tribunal, having competent jurisdiction, in which the case might be tried more suitably for the interests of all the parties and for the ends of justice (*Sim v Robinow (1892) 19 R 665*, followed). Where the possibility of either legal aid or a conditional fee arrangement was an issue, the general principle was that if a more appropriate forum had been identified, the stay would not be refused simply because the plaintiff would not have financial assistance available to him overseas which would be available in the UK. However, exceptionally, the question of the availability of financial assistance could be a relevant factor if the plaintiff could show that substantial justice would not be done if he had to proceed in a forum where no assistance was available to him (*Spiliada Maritime Corporation v Cansulex Ltd [1987] AC 460*, applied).

Accordingly, because this case involved complex issues, and scientific and other expert witnesses were needed (thereby making for a costly trial), financial assistance and highly professional representatives would be required and, therefore, the appropriate forum would be England.

Comment: As a result of this decision, UK based multi-national companies may potentially be sued in Britain for alleged pollution damage caused by subsidiaries overseas. This case therefore makes the issue of forum shopping for legal remedies a serious concern for multi-national companies. In addition, where a claim involves complex issues and requires specialist representation and/or witness evidence, the local jurisdiction may be found to be an inappropriate forum for the trial.

Noise

Aitken v South Hams District Council (7 July 1994) House of Lords ([1994] 3 All ER 400)

[B9.1]

abatement notice; nuisance; enforcement; statutory nuisance

Background: On 25 November 1983, Marian Aitkin was served with a notice to abate noise pursuant to *section 58* of the *Control of Pollution Act 1974*. On 1 January 1991, *section 58* was repealed and replaced by new statutory provisions which came into force pursuant to the *EPA 1990*. Between 30 August and 15 October 1991, Marian Aitkin allowed noise to reoccur, which it was alleged was in contravention of the notice served on 25 November 1983, and consequently a criminal offence. Marian Aitkin argued that an effect of the repeal of *section 58* of the *Control of Pollution Act 1974* was the repeal of all notices served under that section. Therefore, she argued, contravention of such notices was not a criminal offence.

Test: A notice to abate noise served under the *Control of Pollution Act 1974* was not itself repealed by the repeal of the Act in the absence of a clear intention by Parliament to do so, and the obligations under such a notice served the repeal of the operative legislation.

Decision: The House of Lords rejected Marian Aitkin's argument. Even after the repeal of *section 58* of the *Control of Pollution Act 1974*, there existed the obligation to comply with a notice served prior to the repeal. The repealing legislation, the *EPA 1990*, did not contain anything contrary to the intention to preserve not only the effectiveness of the notice served under that section, but also the ability to enforce that obligation. Failure to comply was, therefore, a criminal offence.

Comment: The decision in this case is likely to help avoid unintentional gaps or failures in enforcement when there is a transition from one piece of legislation to another. Therefore, except where the subsequent Act clearly provides for the repeal of any notice served under the previous Act, such notices and proceedings shall survive.

Network Housing Association Ltd v Westminster Council (1 November 1994) Queen's Bench Divisional Court (Times Law Reports, 8 November 1994)

[B9.2]

noise; abatement notice; specified works; enforcement; statutory nuisance

Background: Following a complaint from a tenant, Westminster Council, served a noise abatement notice upon Network Housing Association Ltd, the landlord of the property in question. The notice required Network Housing Association Ltd to make alterations, so as to reduce noise levels in the complainant's flat. The offending noise emanated from the flat above the complainant's. The abatement notice, however, whilst specifying the required reduction in noise, did not indicate what work should be carried out.

Test: In this instance, it was not enough for the abatement notice simply to specify a particular result (i.e. the reduction in noise levels) without also stating what work was to be put in hand to achieve that result. An important factor considered by the judge in reaching his decision was that there are penal sanctions imposed for non compliance with an abatement notice. Therefore the recipients of such a notice should clearly understand what is expected of them.

Decision: The court held that the abatement notice was defective and unenforceable against Network Housing Association Ltd.

Comment: As nuisance cases are on the increase, the principle underlying this decision may become increasingly relevant whilst at the same time making enforcement of such provision a more complicated and technically demanding process.

Carr v Hackney London Borough Council (21 February 1995) Queen's Bench Divisional Court (Times Law Reports, 9 March 1995)

[B9.3]

defence; nuisance; statutory nuisance; enforcement; default or sufferance

Background: Mr Carr complained of a statutory nuisance consisting principally of condensation, dampness and mould in his flat which he rented from Hackney Borough Council. The council accepted that the nuisance had existed, but by completion of the hearing it had abated. The question then became whether the nuisance was likely to recur. Mr Carr had refused entry to the council when it had previously tried to install electric convector heaters in the flat to alleviate the nuisance. The council, therefore, argued that, under the true construction of *sections 79–82* of the *EPA 1990* (pursuant to which the nuisance proceedings had been brought), a person could avoid liability by showing that he was not a person by whose act, default or sufferance the nuisance arose or continued.

Test: In this instance, the council had attempted to alleviate the nuisance and, therefore, under the true construction of *sections 79–82* of the *EPA 1990*, it was not through their act, default or sufferance that the nuisance arose or continued.

Decision: The court agreed with the council.

Comment: This case highlights the need for those claiming nuisance to act responsibly when faced with suggested solutions.

Gillingham Borough Council v Medway (Chatham) Docks Co Ltd (31 July 1991) High Court, Queen's Bench Division (Times Law Reports, 10 October 1991)

[B9.4]

nuisance; public nuisance; planning; traffic noise

Background: Medway (Chatham) Docks Co Ltd acquired a lease of part of a disused naval dockyard and applied for planning permission to develop the land as a commercial port. Gillingham Borough Council granted planning permission in the knowledge that residents living in the vicinity would be affected by the noise of the heavy vehicles travelling to and from the port. The council felt that the presence of an operational commercial port would have a positive economic effect on the community. The level of traffic travelling to and from the port seriously affected the residents enjoyment of their properties. Therefore, the council acting under *section 222* of the *Local Government Act 1972*, applied for a declaration that the dock company and sub-lessees had created a public nuisance, and for injunctions to prevent heavy goods vehicles coming to and from the port between 7pm and 7am.

Decision: The action was dismissed. When granting a planning permission, it was assumed that the local planning authority would balance the interests of the community against those of individuals. The measure of disturbance to individuals had to be balanced against the improved character of the neighbourhood which was in the public interest. Accordingly, the two roads gave access to a commercial dock operating twenty four hours a day, the serious disturbance to individuals was not an actionable nuisance.

Comment: A planning authority has the power to alter the character of a neighbourhood and, where a planning permission had been granted, the question of nuisance had to be determined on the basis of the character of the neighbourhood after the permission had been granted. The test here referred to an area with planning permission for use as a commercial dock. The disturbance to the residents was not actionable (*Halsey v Esso*

Petroleum Co [1961] C.L.Y 6344, Allen v Gulf Oil Refining [1981] 1 All ER 353 followed).

Wheeler v J J Saunders Ltd and Others (19 December 1995) Court of Appeal (Times Law Reports, 9 January 1995)

[B9.5]

nuisance; statutory permission; character of neighbourhood; private rights; economic interests; statutory authority; public law right; planning permission

Background: J J Saunders Ltd and others built and operated pig rearing operations in compliance with planning permission on land near the house of Mr and Mrs Wheeler. In fact, these were intensified operations as pig rearing had been carried on previously on the same land. The Wheelers claimed that smells emanating from the pig farm constituted a nuisance and sought damages in that regard, together with an injunction to stop that nuisance continuing. The Wheelers were successful J J Saunders Ltd appealed. The simple question on appeal was whether the planning permission for intensified pig rearing provided a good defence for an action in nuisance as a result of the smells which naturally occurred from such operations.

Test: Planning permission does not automatically provide immunity from any claims in nuisance. However, the court recognised that in some circumstances where planning permission has been granted, it would not be in the public interest to grant an injunction following a nuisance action.

Decision: The Court of Appeal, in accepting that a grant of planning permission might change the character of the neighbourhood, and that any subsequent nuisance action had to be considered in that light, rejected the wider proposition that a planning decision automatically provided immunity from any claims in nuisance. The court could well see circumstances in which grant of an injunction following a nuisance action would not be in the public interest. However, the court said that it should be slow to acquiesce in the extinction of private rights without compensation, particularly if that were to result from administrative decisions which could not be appealed and were difficult to challenge.

Comment: The decision in *Wheeler* appears to have severely restricted an earlier and significant decision in *Gillingham Borough Council v Medway (Chatham) Docks Co. Ltd (1991)* (see paragraph B9.4), to the extent that only major strategic developments such as docks can change the nature of a locality sufficiently to exclude subsequent actions for nuisance. This case and the *Gillingham case*, illustrates an inevitable conflict between the exercise of a right conferred by public law powers which has been granted by reference to the public interest and private law rights which have been unreasonably interfered with.

Hunter and Others v Canary Wharf Ltd: Hunter and Others v London Docklands Development Corporation (24 April 1997) House of Lords (Times Law Reports, 2 May 1997)

[B9.6]

nuisance; property interest; exclusive possession; damage suffered; TV reception; public nuisance; planning permission

Background: The plaintiffs, all whom lived in the Isle of Dogs, London Docklands, claimed damages in both private and public nuisance for interference with their television reception during the period 1989–1992 following construction of the Canary Wharf Tower. This interference ceased when aerials were adjusted or replaced. Canary Wharf Ltd sought to defend the action on the grounds that the interference was an inevitable result of the statutory scheme for the development of the London Docklands and that a defence of statutory authority arose. At first instance the court rejected this argument and held that interference with television reception was capable of constituting both a private nuisance and a public nuisance.

The Court of Appeal held that the construction of a building in the path of television transmission which causes interference with television reception is not actionable in nuisance as an interference with the use and enjoyment of land. In its reasoning the court drew analogy with the loss of a view which is similarly non actionable.

Test: In order to bring an action in nuisance, the complainant must be in exclusive possession of the land. To allow a licensee to sue in private nuisance would make nuisance into a tort against the person rather than against land.

Decision: The House of Lords' ruling in these cases concentrated specifically on two issues in relation to the law of nuisance. The first issue was the question of whether interference with television signals by the Canary Wharf Tower gave rise to an action in private nuisance. The second issue involved the question of the plaintiffs' right to sue in nuisance in the absence of a clear legal interest in the affected properties. Some of the plaintiffs were householders with no exclusive rights to possession of the places where they lived.

On the first issue, the House of Lords decided that preventing television signals from reaching a person's land was insufficient to constitute a private nuisance. It is a general principle that subject to planning controls a person may build on his own land. This is not restricted by the fact that the building might interfere with a neighbour's enjoyment of his land. Normally an action in private nuisance arises from something emanating from the offending land and only rarely would activities on the land be sufficient to constitute a nuisance. With regard to the second issue, the House of Lords stated that it was settled law that a person who had no rights over land could not sue in private nuisance except where in exclusive possession of the land affected by the relevant nuisance. The House of Lords was not prepared to follow the Court of Appeal decision allowing those with a 'substantial link' with the land to sue, as in their opinion it would make nuisance into a tort against the person rather than against land. Therefore, it is not settled law that a mere licensee cannot sue in private nuisance. It should be noted, however, that Lord Cooke of Thornden, delivered a dissenting judgement advocating a more modern approach to liability which would recognise the status of the modern family unit.

Comment: Many commentators have used the House of Lords decision in this case as evidence to support arguments that there exists within the judiciary in England and Wales a general antipathy towards the development of the law of nuisance as an effective legal mechanism for environmental protection.

Holbeck Hall Hotel Ltd and Another v Scarborough Borough Council; Scarborough Borough Council v Geotechnical Engineering (Northern) Ltd (2 October 1997) Official Referee (Times Law Reports, 15 October 1997)

[B9.7]

nuisance; duty to neighbour; Leaky v National Trust; adopting a nuisance; landslip

Background: A hotel situated uphill from land owned by Scarborough Borough Council was destroyed when a landslip occurred on the council land. Geotechnical Engineering (Northern) Ltd had provided the council with professional advice on the prevention of a landslip at the site. Holbeck Hall Hotel Ltd contended that a downhill neighbour owes the same duty of care to an uphill neighbour as *Leakey and Others v National Trust for Places of Historic Interest or Natural Beauty [1980] 1 QB 485* established that an uphill owner owes to a downhill owner.

Decision: The court upheld Holbeck Hall Hotel Ltd's case. This duty of care could require positive steps to prevent damage to a neighbour, and failure to take such steps could give rise to a claim in damages. To make a distinction in duties owed between uphill and downhill neighbours was considered irrelevant, as was the relative value or importance of the land uses. As long as both occupiers were aware of the potential danger, both would need to be involved in steps to prevent that danger, and one or both would suffer in enjoyment of the land if the danger was not averted. It would be irrational to impose a duty on an uphill occupier and not a downhill occupier. Accordingly, the court held Scarborough Borough Council to be liable in nuisance for damages for breach of their duty to Holbeck Hall Hotel Ltd.

Hussain and Another v Lancaster City Council (14 May 1998) Court of Appeal (ILR, 19 May 1998)

[B9.8]

nuisance; negligence; landlord; statutory powers; tenant; occupier

Background: Mr and Mrs Hussain were joint owners of premises on a housing estate owned by Lancaster City Council. They commenced proceedings against the council, alleging that it had caused or permitted a nuisance and had acted negligently in failing to take appropriate action against other residents who had racially harassed them. Mr and Mrs Hussain relied on provisions in Lancaster City Council's standard tenancy agreement, its equal opportunities policy and the *Housing Act 1985* in arguing that the council ought to have taken appropriate action in the circumstances (e.g. possession proceedings).

Test: The court found that in the tort of nuisance, the person liable is the occupier of the property from which the nuisance emanated. Consequently, a landlord is not liable for a nuisance committed by his tenant unless he authorised the tenant to commit the nuisance. To succeed in a claim of negligence, Mr and Mrs Hussain would have to establish either (1) that the council had been irrational in not exercising its statutory powers or (2) that there were exceptional grounds for holding that the policy of the statute in question required compensation to be paid to persons suffering loss because a power had not been exercised. The court decided that the case did not fall within either category. Moreover, the court was reluctant to impose liability on a body who had been charged with protecting society from the wrong-doing of others.

Decision: The court allowed Lancaster City Council's appeal against an order dismissing the council's application to strike out Mr and Mrs Hussain's claim as disclosing no reasonable cause of action. The court decided that Mr and Mrs Hussain did not have a viable cause of action in nuisance or negligence. Accordingly, Lancaster City Council was not liable for its failure to prevent its tenants (or members of their households) from committing criminal acts of harassment against a nearby property owner.

Comment: Although the facts of this case do not relate directly to the environment, the case does deal with important principles relating to negligence and nuisance which are important causes of action in environmental law.

Nuisance

Rylands v Fletcher (1868) House of Lords ((1868) LR3 HL 330)

[B10.1]

nuisance; strict-liability; non-natural use; foreseeability; dangerous substances; escape

Background: This case arose from the construction of a reservoir on land belonging to Fletcher. The constructors of the reservoir had failed to block off old mine shafts which extended to join a colliery built by Rylands on neighbouring land. This resulted in the reservoir filling and the water flooding the mine belonging to Rylands.

Test: In making its decision, the House of Lords approved the judgement made in the lower court that ' ... the person who for his own purposes brings onto his land and collects and keeps there anything likely to do mischief if it escapes, must keep it in at his peril, and, if he does not do so, is prima facie answerable for all the damage which is the natural consequence of its escape.'

Decision: Although Fletcher had not himself been negligent, the House of Lords held that he was liable for the damage caused.

Comment: This decision has established the principle known as the 'rule in *Rylands v Fletcher*'. It imposes strict liability (but not absolute liability) for any damage caused by the escape of matters brought onto thc land which are likely to do harm if they so escape. No evidence of fault is required, although the responsible party must still be identified. In the past, the rule has been applied in relation to water, gases, explosions, fire, oil, chemicals vibrations, trees and electricity, to name but a few.

There are limitations imposed on the use of the rule. The most important restriction is that the keeping of matter on the land must be a 'non-natural use' of that land. Originally this may have meant, in the case of *Rylands v Fletcher*, that had the water been a natural lake rather than a man made reservoir then there would have been no liability. In *Rickards v Lothian [1913] AC 263*, Lord Moulton described non-natural use as 'some special use bringing with it increased danger to others and must not merely be the ordinary use of the land or such a use as is proper for the general benefit of the community', thereby effectively limiting the use of the rule to 'abnormal' uses of land. In addition to the non-natural user restriction, there must be an escape of the matter from the land on which it is kept. The rule will not apply for the benefit of a plaintiff with no interest in the land affected by the escape and whose only damage is financial loss. In addition, the principle applies specifically to protect landowners and their tenants and licensees and as such, no action for purely personal injuries in the absence of an interest in land which has been affected can be brought under the rule. In the more recent decision of *Cambridge Water Co v Eastern Counties Leather plc [1994]* (see paragraph B10.10), the House of Lords made it clear that foreseeability of the resultant damage was a prerequisite of liability under the rule. The court took the view that the rule should form a natural extension of the law of nuisance to cover isolated escapes from land and should not be developed any further. As a result of this decision, it could be argued that the effectiveness of the rule has been diluted to such an extent so as to make it less effective for purposes of environmental protection. However, the obiter comments in that case may have restricted the non-natural user exception so that any industrial use of land such as the storage of chemicals could be considered a non-national use of land and thereby caught by the rule in *Rylands v Fletcher*.

There are a number of defences available for an action brought under the rule:

(1) that the plaintiff has consented, either expressly or impliedly, to the accumulation of the matter or thing complained of on the defendant's land. An extension of this defence is where the defendant has benefited from the harmful activity, for example where the damage was caused

by gas, water or electricity supplies on the plaintiff's property;

(2) that the activity is authorised by statute;

(3) that the damage was caused by an Act of God, for example if the escape was the result of hurricanes, earthquakes and other freak acts of nature.

Rainham Chemical Works Ltd (in liquidation) v Belvedere Fish Guano Co Ltd (28 July 1921) House of Lords ([1921] 2 AC 465)

[B10.2]

munitions; Rylands v Fletcher; non-natural use; dangerous substances; escape; dangerous operations; damage to third parties; explosives; occupier

Background: Rainham Chemical Works Ltd operated a munitions factory during the First World War. Explosives were manufactured from dinitrophenol (DNP) which was delivered to the premises by the Minister of Munitions. The DNP was stored close to other flammable materials and when a fire broke out, there was a violent explosion that damaged neighbouring property. The Court of Appeal held both the company and the two directors (who were tenants on the land and had sold the benefit of that tenancy on to the company without the previous consent of the landlord) jointly liable. The defendants appealed to the House of Lords.

Test: Whether the company and/or directors were liable under the rule in *Rylands v Fletcher* by storing dangerous substances on land. Another issue was whether the storage of DNP was a non-natural use of land and therefore within the scope of the rule in *Rylands v Fletcher.* The court also had to consider whether the directors had effectively divested themselves of occupation.

Decision: The House of Lords affirmed the Court of Appeal's decision and the company was held to be liable under the rule in *Rylands v Fletcher* for (1) storing explosives and (2) carrying on the business of manufacturing explosives without preventing damage to third parties. The activities were held to be a non-natural use of land and the explosion amounted to an escape albeit that the escape was of fragments of building rather than the substance stored (i.e. the explosive itself).

Comment: This case confirms that any occupier of land who authorises, expressly or by implication, persons to enter on his land for the purposes of carrying on a dangerous operation which involves or may involve the accumulation of a dangerous substance which subsequently escapes from that land, will be liable for damage caused to third parties.

Read v J Lyons & Co Ltd (18 October 1946) House of Lords ([1947] AC 156)

[B10.3]

Rylands v Fletcher; escape; dangerous substance; munitions; explosives

Background: J Lyons and Co owned a munitions factory. Read was employed as a supervisor on the shop floor and was injured there by an exploding shell. No allegations of negligence were made against her employer.

Test: The basis of her claim was that the defendants carried on the manufacture of high explosive shells knowing that they were dangerous and, as such, the principle in *Rylands v Fletcher* should apply.

Decision: The House of Lords affirmed the Court of Appeal's decision that J Lyons and Co was not liable on the grounds that the rule in *Rylands v Fletcher* does not apply unless there has been an escape of something dangerous. In this case, however, they decided there had been no escape. As such, no damages were awarded. The correct course of action would most probably have been for Read to have brought an action in negligence against her employers.

St Helen's Smelting Co v Tipping (1865) House of Lords ((1865) HL 11)

[B10.4]

nuisance; private nuisance; locality; personal discomfort; physical damage; reasonable user

Background: Mr Tipping owned land in a highly industrialised area in St Helens which was the centre of the English alkali industry. The physical impact of the works had left most vegetation in the area dead. Mr Tipping claimed damages under the law of private nuisance from the company for damage caused to trees on his land.

Test: The House of Lords had to consider whether the judge had been correct to guide the jury that (1) every man must use his property so as not to injure his neighbour; (2) the law did not regard trifling inconveniences; (3) matters must be looked at from a reasonable point of view; (4) the injury, to be actionable, must be such as to visibly diminish the value of the property; and (5) the locality must be taken into consideration. The House of Lords drew a distinction between actual physical damage to property (and concluded liability should be strict regardless of locality) and a nuisance which would only cause 'personal discomfort'. In the case of personal discomfort, the locality of the nuisance would be a material factor.

Decision: Mr Tipping was awarded damages. The House of Lords upheld the trial judge's direction to the jury that every man must use his own property so as not to cause actual damage to his neighbour or his neighbours land.

Comment: This case clearly established one of the fundamental principles of private nuisance. In cases of actual physical damage, liability will be strict but in cases involving only loss of enjoyment or mere personal discomfort the courts would have to balance this against the reasonableness of the use of land which has given rise to the nuisance.

Sturges v Bridgman (1879) Court of Appeal ((1879) 11 ChD 852)

[B10.5]

noise; nuisance; injunction; existing nuisance; coming to a nuisance

Background: Bridgman, a confectioner, had used a noisy pestle and mortar in his premises for over twenty years without complaint. Dr Sturges, who resided at the back of the site, built a new consulting room at the back of his garden and close to Bridgman's operational area. Consequently, the noise and vibrations became a problem and Dr Sturges sought an injunction.

Test: (i) An activity will only give rise to a nuisance at the time when it first interferes with the use or enjoyment of someone else's interest in land; and (ii) as Thesiger LJ stated 'what would be a nuisance in Belgrave Square would not necessarily be so in Bermondsey'.

Decision: The Court of Appeal, in granting the injunction, stated that Bridgman had not acquired a right to pollute by prescription. The court was of the opinion that the nuisance had commenced only after the consulting room had been constructed, since previously the activities complained of did not give rise to any interference. The fact that the noise and vibration had been made for years without complaint, did not therefore mean that a right to make such noise and vibration had been established. The twenty year period did not therefore start until the construction of the consulting rooms.

Comment: This is an important consideration to be taken into account where new developments are built near long established industries. Occupants of the new buildings may have an action in nuisance arising from the nearby industry albeit that the process may have been carried on for many years and without any previous complaints ever having been made.

Bellew v Cement Company ((1948) IRR 61)

[B10.6]

noise; nuisance; injunction; proprietary rights

Background: The company were responsible for supplying eighty per cent of the cement used in Ireland. The cement was created using materials from a quarry near to Bellew's house. Bellew applied for an injunction restraining the noisy blasting at the quarry on the basis that it interfered with his occupation of the house.

Decision: The court granted the injunction. They did not accept the company's defence that such an injunction would stop cement production in Ireland at the expense of employment and construction.

Test: It is not a defence to claim that consideration of the public interest should be placed before consideration of the private rights of persons to whom a nuisance is being caused.

Comment: This case illustrates the proprietary nature of the law of nuisance which is that the protection provided is directed towards controlling proprietary interests rather than the control of an individuals conduct.

Halsey v Esso Petroleum Co Ltd (23 February 1961) High Court, Queen's Bench Division ([1961] 2 All ER 145, [1961] 1 WLR 683)

[B10.7]

nuisance; private nuisance; public nuisance; Rylands v Fletcher; injunction; odour; noise; emissions

Background: Halsey lived in a residential area which was adjacent to an industrial zone where Esso operated an oil distribution depot. Acid smuts containing sulphate released from the depot damaged Halsey's washing and also the paint work to his car. The depot also emitted a nauseating odour and noise levels which at times caused the windows and doors in the plaintiff's house to vibrate. Halsey brought an action for the damage caused to his washing and the paintwork of his car, the nauseating smell and also for noise pollution caused by both the boilers on the depot and by tankers supplying the depot throughout the night. In addition to damages, Halsey sought an injunction to stop the nuisance from continuing.

Test: The court had to determine the extent to which the rule in *Rylands v Fletcher* and public and private nuisance applied.

Decision: The court found the company liable in both public and private nuisance and under the rule in *Rylands v Fletcher* for the emission of acid smuts; private nuisance for the smells and noise and in public and private nuisance for the tankers. In addition, the court granted an injunction to stop the nuisance from continuing.

Comment: A public nuisance exists when a nuisance affects a wide class of the public in general. It is a criminal offence to cause a public nuisance. It becomes a private nuisance when an individual suffers particular damage as a result. The court only awarded £200 in damages but did grant an injunction to prevent the nuisance from recurring.

Lippiatt and Another v South Gloucestershire County Council (31 March 1999) Court of Appeal ([1999] 4 All ER 149, Times Law Reports, 22 October 1999)

[B10.8]

nuisance; travellers; owner; occupier

Background: Lippiatt claimed damages from South Gloucestershire County Council for acts of nuisance carried out by travellers while they were occupying the neighbouring land owned by the council. The travellers had trespassed, dumped rubbish and tethered goats on Lippiatt's land and had also prevented access to that land. The council was aware of the presence of the travellers and had even provided water and toilet facilities. The council contended, following the decision in *Hussain v Lancaster City Council (1998) 77 P&CR 89*, that the claim in nuisance had no prospect of success, and that the statement of claim should be struck out on the basis that it disclosed no cause of action. The judge accepted these submissions, struck out the statement of claim and entered judgement for the council. Lippiatt appealed.

Decision: The court said that there was no rule of law which prevented the owner or occupier of land from being held liable under the tort of nuisance, by reason of the activities of his licensees which took place off his land and on the land of the claimant. The court distinguished the present case from *Hussain v Lancaster City Council.* In that case shop owners had claimed in nuisance against the local housing authority whose tenants occupied the neighbouring housing estate. The court had held that the disturbance was a public nuisance, for which the individual perpetretors could be held liable, and that their conduct was not in any sense linked to, nor did it emanate from, the homes where they lived. In the present case, the allegation was that the travellers had been allowed to congregate on the council's land and that they had used it as a base for the unlawful activities on Lippiatt's land of which Lippiatt, as neighbour, complained. It was at least arguable that such unlawful activities could give rise to liability in nuisance on the part of the council and accordingly the court held that the claim should not have been struck out.

Baxter v Camden London Borough Council (No. 2) (21 October 1999) House of Lords (Times Law Reports, 22 October 1999)

[B10.9]

noise; nuisance; landlord; tenant

Background: These cases were both actions by tenants who complained that they were disturbed by the ordinary and reasonable activities of their neighbours in the council flats. The cases involved a block of flats which was not sound insulated when it was built in 1919. Although the noise was not unreasonable, the tenants were disturbed by the noise of televisions, babies crying, arguments and conversations.

Test: Interpretation of the meaning of quiet enjoyment of the premises which 'shall not be interfered with by the council'.

Decision: The court interpreted the meaning of 'shall not be interfered with by the council' to mean that the tenants' possession of the land should not be substantially interfered with by the landlord. However, the court held that this reasoning did not apply to things done before the grant of the tenancy, even though they may have unfortunate consequences for a disturbed tenant i.e. the lack of sound insulation. When the tenants rented the property, it was taken in its current physical condition and it was within their reasonable contemplation that there would be other occupants of the flats. The landlord council could not be held responsible for inherent structural defects and a covenant for the quiet enjoyment could not propose a positive obligation to insulate. In relation to the claim in nuisance, the court held that nuisance would, in these cases, involve doing something on adjoining or nearby land which constitutes an unreasonable interference with the tenancies of the land. The judge held that a noise from the neighbouring flats was reasonable and not a nuisance.

Cambridge Water Co Ltd v Eastern Counties Leather plc (9 December 1993) House of Lords ([1994] 1 All ER 53)

[B10.10]

Rylands v Fletcher; nuisance; foreseeability; water pollution; negligence; contamination

Background: Cambridge Water Co purchased a borehole at Sawston Mill in 1976 to extract water to supply to the public. In 1983 it tested the water to see if it complied with the minimum standards for the quality of water for human consumption required by new EC legislation and discovered that it was contaminated with an organochlorine solvent, Perchloroethane. On investigation, it emerged that the solvent came from the Eastern Counties Leather plc tannery, about 1.3 miles from the borehole. The tannery had existed since 1879 and, until 1976, had had the solvents it used in its business delivered in forty gallon drums, which were then transported on forklift trucks and tipped into a sump. From 1976, solvents were delivered in bulk and stored in tanks, and then piped to the tanning machinery. There was no evidence of any spill from the tanks or pipes, and it was concluded that the aquifer had been contaminated by frequent spills under the earlier system. Cambridge Water Co claimed damages against Eastern Counties Leather plc alternatively for negligence, nuisance and under the rule in *Rylands v Fletcher.*

At first instance, Mr Justice Ian Kennedy found that Eastern Counties plc could not have foreseen this type of damage and, therefore, disallowed the claims in nuisance and negligence. Further, he was of the view that the actions of Eastern Counties plc constituted a natural use of the land and consequently dismissed the claim based on the rule in *Rylands v Fletcher.* Cambridge Water Co appealed to the Court of Appeal relying solely on the rule in *Rylands v Fletcher*, and the Court of Appeal found Eastern Counties Leather plc to be strictly liable for the contamination of the water. Eastern Counties Leather plc appealed to the House of Lords.

Decision: The House of Lords unanimously found that Eastern Counties Leather was not liable for the water contamination.

The main issue was whether the foreseeability of the damage suffered by Cambridge Water Co was relevant to a claim under the rule in *Rylands v Fletcher.* The Lords accepted Kennedy J's finding that a reasonable supervisor employed by Eastern Counties Leather plc would not have foreseen that the solvent would leak from the tannery floors down into the water source, or that significant traces of the chemical would be detected in any nearby water source, and consequently could not have anticipated the risk of the pollution in or before 1976; it was thought at the time that any spilt solvent would evaporate and that the only foreseeable risk was that if large quantities were spilled someone might be overcome by the fumes.

The rule in *Rylands v Fletcher*, as opposed to in negligence, imposes strict liability, in that a defendant may be held liable despite having taken all due care to prevent the escape. However, it did not follow that foreseeability of the risk was irrelevant, and Lord Goff quoted Blackburn J in *Rylands v Fletcher* as referring to 'anything likely to do mischief if it escapes'. The Court of Appeal had based its decision on *Ballard v Tomlinson [1885] 29 ChD 115*, but Lord Goff found that that case had not considered whether a person could be liable for unforeseen damage. Referring to the *Wagon Mound (No 2) 1967*, he considered that it was logical to make foreseeability a requirement for liability for damages under the rule in *Rylands v Fletcher*, in line with the test for recovering damages in private nuisance.

He considered that the rule in *Rylands v Fletcher* was, essentially, an extension of the law of nuisance to cases of isolated escapes from land - although it was not limited to isolated escapes. Since, in this case, the escape of the solvent from Eastern Counties Leather plc was a continuing escape, it would classically be regarded as a case of nuisance, and it would seem strange if, by characterising the case as one falling under the rule in *Rylands v Fletcher*, Eastern Counties Leather plc's liability should be stricter.

Since it appeared that pools of the solvent were still at the base of the chalk aquifer, and therefore still dissolving into the water and contaminating the borehole, it was argued for Cambridge Water Co that Eastern Counties Leather plc should be liable for damage caused from the time when such damage had become foreseeable. Lord Goff rejected this, on the basis that the solvent had passed beyond the control of Eastern Counties Leather plc.

Lord Goff went on to consider whether the rule in *Rylands v Fletcher* should be developed in such a way as to impose stricter liability for injury to others on people who conduct ultra-hazardous operations on their land. His Lordship felt that this was not desirable for two reasons. Firstly, because of the decision of the House of Lords in *Read v J Lyons & Co Ltd (1947)* (see paragraph B10.3), which established that there would be no liability under the rule in *Rylands v Fletcher* except where injury had been caused by an escape from land under the control of the defendant, such a development could not apply to all injuries caused by the ultra-hazardous operations. Secondly, he referred to the Report of the Law Commission on '*Civil Liability for Dangerous Things and Activities No 32*' (1970) which had taken a negative view of imposing stricter liability for high risk activities. Lord Goff felt it was for parliament to impose statutory controls to regulate these types of practices and that, given the increasing importance of the environment, there would be extensive environmental legislation to control potentially polluting activities in the future. Consequently there was no need to develop the common law principles in this way.

On the question of the natural use of the land, Lord Goff noted that the concept lacked precision, but considered that, in this case, it was not necessary to attempt to redefine it. Rejecting Kennedy J's view that the storage of organochlorines in an industrial village constituted a natural use of land, he remarked, 'I feel bound to say that the storage of substantial quantities of chemicals on industrial premises should be regarded as an almost classic case of non-natural use'.

Comment: This is a leading case on environmental liability at common law. Although it restricts the application of the rule in *Rylands v Fletcher* to foreseeable risks, it may make a defence that a particular use was a natural one less likely to succeed. Historic contamination, as Lord Goff described the escaped pools of solvent, can now be dealt with under legislation, in particular by the contaminated land regime under *Part IIA* of the *EPA 1990*.

Oil Pollution

Landcatch Ltd v The Braer Corporation and Others (11 November 1997) Court of Session (Times Law Reports, 6 March 1998)

[B11.1]

braer; contamination; water; pollution; escape; economic loss

Background: This was a case arising out of the stranding of the *Braer of Shetland* on 5 January 1993. Landcatch reared young salmon at farms in Argyllshire and Wester Ross. Landcatch claimed that, in 1993, it was to sell about sixty five per cent of its salmon to purchasers on the Shetland Islands. The contracts were normally agreed in February, however, the Braer ran aground in January spilling oils into the waters off Shetland. Following the spill, the UK government introduced restrictions on the landing, use and supply of fish from those waters. As a result, the Shetland salmon farmers did not enter into contracts to purchase the young salmon. Landcatch claimed to have sustained losses as a result and sought to recover these losses from the ship owner under *section 1* of the *Merchant Shipping (Oil Pollution) Act 1971* and from the P&I Club under a liability which the purchaser claimed was imposed on that P&I Club by a Norwegian insurance act of 1989.

Test: The main issue in the case was whether Landcatch's losses were 'damage caused ... by contamination resulting from the discharge or escape' of oil under *section 1(1)* of the 1971 Act. Landcatch contended that the 1971 Act imposed strict liability on the ship owner and P&I Club for all losses which would not have occurred but for the escape of oil, and that this liability was not limited by any concept of remoteness or such like.

Decision: The court disagreed, stating that parliament had intended that the normal limitations on recoverability of economic loss would apply, and any contrary intention would have been expressly provided for. In addition, it decided that liability under the 1971 Act should be limited to the area of contamination. The court accordingly held that Landcatch had suffered merely relational economic loss which was therefore not recoverable.

Comment: This decision was appealed by Landcatch. The judge dismissed the appeal stating that if Landcatch's 'but for' approach to the construction of causation under the 1971 Act was correct, it opened up an unlimitless chain of claims which ran counter to the underlying intentions of the 1971 Act and the *Merchant Shipping Act 1974*.

Black v Braer Corporation and Others (3 July 1998) Outer House of the Court of Session (Times Law Reports, 12 October 1998)

[B11.2]

braer; oil pollution; damages; stress; anxiety; depression; mental anguish; shipping; psychological damage; personal injuries

Background: Derrick Black brought an action against the Braer Corporation and others for compensation under *sections 1* and *12* of the *Merchant Shipping (Oil Pollution) Act 1971* for personal injuries suffered as a result of the 1993 Braer Tanker Spill. His injuries included both physical injuries and psychological trauma. The Braer Corporation argued that 'damage' in the statutory provisions did not encompass all types of loss suffered as a result of the spill. Although the Braer Corporation accepted that 'damage' extended to physical injury, it was argued that it did not include stress, anxiety and depression, as these were merely a consequence of other damage suffered rather than themselves being a direct result of the pollution incident. It was asserted that the psychological damage suffered could be directly linked to the pollution and that it was for the person bringing the proceedings, to prove in the circumstances, the exact nature of the conditions suffered and the causes of them.

Test: For the purposes of *sections 1* and *12* of the 1971 Act, 'damage' may include personal injuries such as stress, depression and anxiety, where the person bringing the claim produces proof of the precise conditions suffered and the causes of them. The judge had to determine whether the damage suffered by Mr Black fell within this definition.

Decision: The judge took a systematic approach. He considered that the defendant's concession that physical injury could be included in an action for compensation under the statutory provisions was important. As the Braer Corporation had accepted that physical injury was included and there was nothing in the statutory definition of 'damage' which excluded it, there was no reason why other personal injuries such as stress, depression and anxiety should not also be included (which too were not explicitly excluded from the definition). The judge held that, in any case, it is for the person bringing the action to produce proof of the precise conditions suffered and the causes of them.

Comments: As a result of this decision, it may be possible to seek compensation under *sections 1* and *12* of the 1971 Act for psychological damage incurred as a result of distress suffered following oil pollution incidents such as the Braer Tanker Spill. Whether or not this decision has more general applicability in pollution cases is uncertain as this case was based specifically on a particular statutory cause of action.

R v National Grid Company plc (5 October 1999) Magistrates' Court (Environment Agency News Release, 5 October 1999)

[B11.3]

water pollution

Background: The EA brought an action against the National Grid Company for allowing oil to enter into the Lee navigation canal in December 1998. Little environmental damage occurred due to an early warning of the oil leak and wind conditions.

Test: The National Grid Company was prosecuted under *section 85* of the *WRA 1991* for causing polluting matter to enter controlled waters.

Decision: The company was fined £12,000 and ordered to pay £1,000 in costs. In mitigation, the company had stated that it had fitted a new impermeable bund to the sub-station from where the oil had leaked.

P&O Scottish Ferries Ltd v The Braer Corporation (7 January 1999) Court of Session (Times Law Reports, 10 March 1999)

[B11.4]

braer; oil pollution; damages; economic loss; proximity; direct consequential losses

Background: This case concerned the interpretation of *section 1* of the *Merchant Shipping (Oil Pollution) Act 1971*. P&O brought a claim against the Braer Corporation for compensation under *section 1* of the 1971 Act, for damages caused by oil contamination from the wreck of the Braer. Adverse publicity from the oil spill had effected P&O's passenger and freight ferry services between Shetland and the mainland. Various heads of damage were claimed. P&O argued that *section 1* should be construed in accordance with the underlying *International Convention on Civil Liability for Oil Pollution Damage 1969*, to which the UK was a party and the 1971 Act was intended to implement it in the UK. The Braer Corporation argued that the heads of damage were purely economic in nature and that no circumstances creating a special proximity existed and that such proximity is a requirement to the recovery of such economic losses *(see Murphy v Brentwood DC [1991] 1 AC 398)*.

Test: International treaties do not have the force of law in the UK and where the UK statute implementing such a treaty is clear it shall prevail over the treaty in question. Economic losses can only be recovered under UK law in situations where there exists circumstances creating a special proximity e.g. such losses are a direct consequence of the physical damage itself.

Decision: The claim was dismissed. *Section 1* of the 1971 Act was clear on its terms. The proximity argument also failed. Losses were not the direct consequence of the escape of the oil.

Comment: This case reinforces the principle under English law that economic losses claimed such as the loss of passenger revenue; loss of onboard sales; loss of commercial trailer traffic revenue; loss of land based trailer traffic on Shetland; advertising costs; cost of the loss assessor in preparing the claim and increased agent's commission etc., may only be recoverable in very limited circumstances where they can be shown to be a direct consequence of some physical damage.

R v Milford Haven Port Authority (15 January 1999) Crown Court (Environment Agency News Release, 15 January 1999)

[B11.5]

oil pollution; water pollution prosecution; fines; causing; polluting matter; controlled waters; Sea Empress; environmental offence

Background: On 15 February 1996, the *Sea Empress*, bringing crude oil to Milford Haven in South West Wales, ran a ground at St Anne's Gate at the entrance to Milford Haven waterway as a result of negligent navigation by her pilot. Over a period of seven days while the *Sea Empress* was grounded about 7,200 tonnes of light crude oil and about 250 tonnes of heavy fuel oil was released, mainly at low tide. A further 230 tonnes of fuel oil was released after the tanker had been towed to a jetty within the waterway.

Most of the affected coastline lies within the Pembrokeshire Coast National Park. In the main area affected by this spill there are thirty five sites of special scientific interest, two national nature reserves and one of the UK's three marine nature researches. There are also EC designated SPA's for birds and three special areas of conservation as proposed by the government. The cost of the clean up operation was over £60 million ignoring the impact on tourism and commercial fisheries.

Decision: The Milford Haven Port Authority pleaded guilty to the charge brought by the EA of causing polluting matters to enter controlled waters, contrary to *section 85(1)* of the *WRA 1991*. Milford Haven Port Authority was fined £4 million, and ordered to pay £825,000 in costs, the largest fine ever awarded in a water pollution case. The judge stated that the case was not simply one of a pilot who committed an act of negligent navigation. The pilot system was operated by the Milford Haven Port Authority, who had to reach the highest possible standards in relation to the training and expertise of the pilot. In this case, the pilot had little prior experience of piloting large deeply laden tankers. Since the casualty, pilot training and qualification procedures have been changed by the Milford Haven Port Authority. Restrictions have been imposed preventing large vessels from entering Milford Haven less than three hours before low water and there has been a reclassification of vessels requiring two pilots.

Comment: Milford Haven Port Authority appealed against the level of the fine and, on 16 March 2000, the Court of Appeal reduced it to £750,000. The court ruled that the fine was 'manifestly excessive' in view of the authority's financial means, that the offence was one of strict liability and the authority had not been found to have been negligent. It also considered that greater credit should have been given for the authority's guilty plea. The court referred to the sentencing guidelines set out in the health and safety case, *R v F. Howe & Son (Engineers) Ltd [1999]* and considered that these should be taken into account in sentencing for environmental offences (see paragraph A14.1).

Gray and Another v Braer Corporation and Others (29 December 1998) Court of Session Outer House (Times Law Reports, 10 March 1999)

[B11.6]

oil pollution; limitation periods; braer; water pollution

Background: This case involved a claim for compensation under the *Merchant Shipping (Oil Pollution) Act 1971* in respect of damage from the 1993 Braer Tanker Spill. Mr Stephen Gray and Mr Stanley Gray sought to amend their case to include reference to losses alleged to have been suffered by the partnership of which they had been partners. The amendment to the case was made more than three but less than six years after the oil spill from the Braer. The question therefore arose as to whether *section 9* of the *Merchant Shipping (Oil Pollution) Act 1971* applied to preclude the extension of the claim to cover these further damages. *Section 9* provides that 'no action ... under *section* 1 of this act shall be entertained by any court ... unless the application is commenced not later than 3 years after the claim arose nor later than 6 years after the occurrence ... by reason of which the liability was incurred'. Mr Stephen Gray and Mr Stanley Gray sought to argue that the two prescription periods under *section 9* applied to different categories of loss.

Decision: The court held that the Grays interpretation of *section 9* was unnatural. It took the view that *section 9* creates one prescriptive period of three years which applies to all claims and a long stop provision that after six years from the date of the relevant occurrence no action would be bought to enforce any claim. The court therefore refused Mr Stephen Gray's and Mr Stanley Gray's application to amend their case.

Landcatch Ltd v International Oil Pollution Compensation Fund (19 May 1999) Court of Session, Inner House, Second Division (Times Law Reports, 14 June 1999)

[B11.7]

oil pollution; braer; damages; limitation periods; water pollution

Background: This case was an appeal by Landcatch Ltd against the decision that the loss it suffered as a result of the Braer oil spill was relational economic loss and therefore not recoverable. Landcatch Ltd reared young salmon for the salmon farming industry at farms in Argyllshire and Wester Ross. Landcatch Ltd claimed that in 1993, it was to sell about sixty five per cent of its young salmon to purchasers on the Shetland. The contracts were normally agreed in February. However the Braer ran aground in January spilling oils onto the waters of the Shetland. Following the spill, the UK government introduced restrictions on the landing, use and supply of fish from those waters. As a result the Shetland salmon farmers did not enter into contracts to purchase the young salmon. Landcatch Ltd claimed to have sustained losses as a result and sought to recover these losses from the ship owner under *section 1* of the *Merchant Shipping (Oil Pollution) Act 1971* and from the International Oil Pollution Compensation Fund under *section 4* of the *Merchant Shipping Act 1974*. Landcatch Ltd contended that both the 1971 Act and the 1974 Act imposed strict liability on the ship owner for all loss which would not have occurred but for the discharge of oil, and that this liability was not limited by any concept of remoteness or the like. The court in the first instance disagreed, stating that parliament had intended that the normal limitations on recoverability of economic loss would apply and that any contrary intention would have been provided for expressly. In addition, it decided that liability under the 1971 Act should be limited to the area of contamination.

Decision: In this appeal, the judge said that the main issue depended on the interpretation of *section 1* of the 1971 Act, and whether the losses that occurred were within the scope 'damage' under that section. *Section 20* of the 1971 Act defines 'damage' to include 'loss'. The judge, in dismissing the appeal, stated that if Landcatch's 'but for' approach to the construction of causation was correct, there opened up a limitless chain of claims which ran counter to the underlying intentions of the 1971 and 1974 Acts, which are consistent within the terms of the *International Convention on Civil Liability for Oil Pollution Damage, Brussels 1969*. While 'loss' could include claims of pure economic loss, in the context of the legislation that did not mean that all such claims were admissible and this was clearly so where the claim was secondary or relational. The judge did, however, concede that the location of the claimant was not relevant and stated by way of example that it would be difficult to justify a distinction between claims made by sea fishermen according to the geographical location of their home ports.

Assurenceforeningen Skuld v International Oil Pollution Compensation Fund and Another (15 April 1999) Court of Session (Times Law Reports, 14 June 1999)

[B11.8]

oil pollution; braer; limitation period; water pollution

Background: Assurenceforeningen Skuld had been ordered by the court, pursuant to *section 5* of the *Merchant Shipping (Oil Pollution) Act 1971*, to pay a limitation fund into court to cover claims arising out of the Braer oil spill. The last date for lodging claims was 19 February 1999 and by this date 363 claims had been received. The Lord Advocate sought to have two additional claims lodged on the limitation fund on 17 March 1999, one month late. The question for the court therefore was whether the judge could exercise his discretion to allow further time after the expiry of the period appointed by the court for the lodging of claims. Assurenceforeningen Skuld contended that there was no discretion. Both they and the court needed to know with certainty what claims were being made against the fund and by allowing late claims could reduce the amount available to meet valid claims made on time.

Decision: The court decided that there was nothing in *section 5(3)* of the *Merchant Shipping (Oil Pollution) Act 1971* to imply that further time could not be allowed by the court. If late lodging were to be fatal to a claim, this would have been made explicit in the wording of the section, or at least unmistakably implied. In addition, because the only formal notification that a prospective claimant on the insurer's limitation fund might receive was a newspaper advertisement, it was highly possible that a claimant might not learn of the court's order for claims until the appointed date had passed. As such, the judge decided that the court's discretion should be exercised in favour of the claimant and the late claims should be lodged.

Planning

R v North Yorkshire County Council, ex parte Brown and Another (11 February 1999) House of Lords ([1999] 1 All ER 969)

[B12.1]

environmental impact assessment, development consent

Background: This case concerns the meaning of 'development consent' under *Directive 85/337/EEC on the assessment of affects of certain public and private projects on the environment*, in the context of the imposition of conditions by the local mining authority, pursuant to *section 22* and *Schedule 2* of the *Planning and Compensation Act 1991*, on the operation of a quarry which is subject to an old mining permission. Planning permission had been granted for the quarry in 1947. The planning permission, typically, was indefinite in duration and not subject to any environmental conditions. Under *section 22* and *Schedule 2* of the 1991 Act, the owner of land, which has the benefit of an old mining planning permission, was required to apply to the local mining authority for registration of the permission within a specified period. In default of registration the planning permission would cease to exist. Once a permission was registered, the owner of the land was then required to apply to the local mining authority to determine the conditions for the operation of the planning permission. In accordance with these provisions, the owners of the quarry obtained registration of the 1947 planning permission and then applied for the determination of the conditions for the operation of the quarry. North Yorkshire County Council, acting as the local mining authority, carried out wide consultations before imposing certain conditions. The applicants, who owned houses in the nearby village, were dissatisfied with the conditions and applied for judicial review to quash the council's decision. They contended that the council had made its decision as to the conditions to be imposed on the operation of the quarry without carrying out an EIA as required by *Articles 1.2* and *2.1* of *Directive 85/337/EEC* implemented in the UK by the *Town & County Planning (Assessment of Environmental Affects) Regulations 1988 (SI 1988 No 1199). Articles 1.2* and *2.1* of *Directive 85/337/EEC* required an EIA to be made before 'development consent' was granted for 'projects likely to have significant affects on the environment'. The council contended that the imposition of conditions was not a 'development consent' within the meaning of *Directive 85/337/EEC.* At first instance the judge dismissed the application for judicial review but the Court of Appeal allowed the applicants' appeal. The council appealed to the House of Lords.

Decision: The House of Lords dismissed the council's appeal. It was held that although the source of the right to operate the quarry remained under the permission granted in 1947 even after conditions had been imposed under the 1991 Act, the owner of the quarry nevertheless could not proceed to implement the permission unless the planning authority had determined the appropriate conditions. The determination does not decide whether the quarry operator may proceed only in the manner in which he may proceed. However, the determination is nevertheless a necessary condition for his being entitled to proceed at all. That was sufficient to bring the determination within the European concept of 'development consent' under *Directive 85/337/EEC.* Although the Directive did not apply to decisions which merely involved the detailed regulation of activities for which principal consent had already been given, the procedure created by the 1991 Act was a new and free-standing examination of the issues. The Act gave the power to the local mining authority to assess the likely environmental affects of old mining permissions which had been granted without any serious consideration of their environments at all. As such it could require information to be provided by way of an EIA. It followed that the procedure under the 1991 Act was a 'development consent' and the court therefore dismissed the council's appeal.

Tandridge District Council v Verrechia (31 March 1999) Court of Appeal (Times Law Reports, 16 June 1999)

[B12.2]

waste; enforcement notice

Background: Mr Verrechia had used his land, in breach of planning controls, for both dumping waste and for parking cars. Tandridge District Council issued an enforcement notice in respect of the car parking issue and Surrey County Council issued an enforcement notice in respect of the use of land for dumping waste. Mr Verrechia appealed against Tandridge District Council's enforcement notice but his appeal was dismissed. Mr Verrechia also appealed against Surrey County Council's enforcement notice. On this appeal, a second inspector amended the notice to include the same alleged breach as the district council's notice, namely car parking, but failed to specify any steps to remedy the breach. Mr Verrechia still failed to remove the vehicles and both the district council and the county council brought injunction proceedings. As a result of these proceedings, Mr Verrechia gave an undertaking to the court to remove the vehicles. Two years later, Mr Verrechia applied to the court to have the undertaking discharged. The district council responded by restoring its application for an injunction. In his application, Mr Verrechia contended that *section 173(11)* of the *Town and Country Planning Act 1990*, as substituted by the *Planning and Compensation Act 1991*, applied so as to give rise to a deemed planning permission. *Section 173(11)* provides '(11) Where - (a) an enforcement notice in respect of any breach of planning control could have required ... any activity to cease, but does not do so; and (b) all requirements of the notice have been complied with, then, so far as the notice did not so require, planning permission shall be treated as having been granted ... in respect of ... the carrying out of the activities.'

Decision: The judge, in assessing the appeal, first considered whether a mixed use of land had to be regarded for planning permissions as a single breach of planning control, a proposition supported by both parties by reference to a DoE Circular 10/97. The judge said that DoE Circular 10/97 did not justify this conclusion. It was a question fact and degree whether the activities would constitute a single breach or a number of separate breaches. In this case, the mixed use consisted of two separate uses: the car parking use which was primarily the responsibility of the district council and; the waste dumping which was the sole responsibility of the county council. Next the judge considered whether the second inspector's amendment to the county council's enforcement notice was a valid one. The second inspector had added to the notice a new and separate breach. However, issuing an enforcement notice in respect of this breach was not, unless remedial steps were specified, the function of the district council which the county council could exercise. First, the court held that a second inspector had no power to add by way of amendment something which the county council could not have originally included in the enforcement notice. Second, *section 176(1)* of the *Town and Country Planning Act 1990* makes it a condition that additional remedial steps required do not cause injustice. In this case, the court held that when the amendments to the enforcement notice were made, no remedial steps could have been properly added in respect of the car parking without injustice being caused to the defendant. Therefore, the requirement of *section 176(1)* could not have been satisfied. For these reasons the court dismissed Mr Verrechia's application. It held that *section 173(1)* did not apply so as to grant Mr Verrechia planning permission to use his land for car parking.

Tidman v Reading Borough Council (4 November 1994) High Court, Queen's Bench Division (Times Law Reports, 10 November 1994)

[B12.3]

negligence; duty of care

Background: Mr Tidman sought informal advice over the telephone from Reading Borough Council as to the need for planning permission on land which he was trying to sell. Mr

Tidman alleged that the advice which he received was negligent and gave rise to loss on his part.

Decision: The court rejected Mr Tidman's claim on the grounds that Reading Borough Council did not owe a duty of care to Mr Tidman and therefore was not liable to him. The court said that whilst it was unlikely, it was not inconceivable that a formal approach to a council, which was known by the council to have very serious implications, and to which the council did choose to respond, might generate a duty of care. In the present case, however, quite apart from any questions of public interest, the relationship between Mr Tidman and Reading Borough Council had not come anywhere near to creating a duty of care on the council's part.

Comment: Whilst this case does not appear to have arisen out of an environmental matter, environmental questions are regularly asked of the various regulatory authorities. Thus the principle of the case is of general relevance.

Houghton v Secretary of State for the Environment (12 January 1995) High Court, Queen's Bench Division ([1995] EGCS 2)

[B12.4]

green belt

Background: Mr Houghton made a planning application for the development of (*inter-alia*) a private tennis court on land which was within the metropolitan green belt. The application was refused and he appealed to the secretary of state. The secretary of state's inspector acknowledged that paragraph 13 of the PPG 2 (1988 - Green Belt) allowed a possible exception for development for the purpose of (inter-alia) 'outdoor sport' to the general policy of no development within the green belt. However, he was in no doubt that, for the purpose of that paragraph, public sport was the main thrust of the exception, although that paragraph was not expressly stated as being limited to public sport. He therefore rejected the appeal. Houghton appealed again on the ground that there was no justification for the inspector implying such a qualification to the phrase 'outdoor sport'.

Decision: The appeal was accepted on that point but otherwise rejected on the ground that following the introduction of *section 54A* of the *Town and Country Planning Act 1990*, the first question to ask was whether development conflicted with the development plan. On that basis, the court found that the inspector had correctly first considered the *section 54A* factors, and it was not therefore relevant that he had erred in his interpretation of PPG2.

Delyn Borough Council v Solitaire (Liverpool) Ltd and Another (26 January 1995) High Court, Chancery Division ([1995] EGCS 11)

[B12.5]

consents; permits; injunction

Background: In July 1994, Solitaire (Liverpool) Ltd opened a Saturday market some three miles from a statutory market in Holywell operated by Delyn Borough Council. The council claimed that by opening a Saturday market, the company infringed its market right and sought an injunction to stop Solitaire running it. In opposing the injunction application, Solitaire claimed that the planning permission, given to it to establish its market, conferred on it a positive right to operate such a market.

Decision: Solitaire's argument was rejected. The court held that planning permission merely removed the impediment on the use or development imposed by the planning laws, and did not involve overriding any other rights relevant to the land. It did not confer a positive right beyond the planning laws. Planning permission did not amount to a statutory authority giving immunity from a suit. The court granted the injunction.

Comment: Those involved in the environmental arena are well aware of the various legal consents, permits, authorisations etc.

which may be required to operate a business. It is a popular misconception that such consents amount to a defence against private law claims by third parties. This case, *Wheeler v J J Saunders Ltd and Others 1995* and *R v Dovermoss Ltd (1995)* serve to highlight that point.

Blue Circle Industries plc v Secretary of State for Wales and Another (12 February 1996) High Court, Queen's Bench Division ([1996] EGCS 26)

[B12.6]

waste; landfill

Background: Blue Circle Industries plc owned and worked a quarry site on lands between St. Athan's RAF landing ground and Cardiff/Wales Airport. Blue Circle Industries plc made an application for planning permission to use the quarry site for the disposal of waste. That application was called in by the Secretary of State for Wales under *section 77* of the *Town and Country Planning Act 1990*. The owner and operator of Cardiff/Wales Airport was the second respondent to the planning application. The secretary of state appointed an inspector who was asked to advise particularly on matters which included aviation safety. He advised against the planning permission. The inspector's report was accepted by the secretary of state without qualification. Blue Circle Industries plc appealed. One ground of the appeal concerned the inspector's approach to potential bird strike incidents associated with birds attracted to the proposed development by reason of putrescible waste. The inspector took the view that landfill sites were a major attraction 'for opportunist feeders such as gulls'. Bird strikes, he held, could have a very severe direct consequence for aircraft with catastrophic results. He also found that the proposed schemes of Blue Circle Industries plc to overcome increased bird strike risks were 'fundamentally flawed and could not meet the circumstances of this case'. Blue Circle Industries plc's appeal was rejected. It argued that what the inspector should have done was to have compared the number of birds likely to be attracted to the site if it were to be developed in accordance with the proposed planning permission, with the numbers of birds likely to be attracted if the existing permission were to be carried out (that involved restoring the land to mainly agricultural use).

Decision: The court held that the inspector had clearly come to the conclusion that such comparison could not be made. It was flawed with practical difficulties in establishing the necessary background reference point, not least because it involved a constantly shifting situation over time and in terms of numbers and species. To carry out such a comparison would be an impossible task to force upon the inspector.

H J Banks & Co Ltd v Secretary of State for the Environment (23 October 1996) Court of Appeal ([1996] EGCS 171)

[B12.7]

waste; landfill

Background: H J Banks & Co operated a coal recovery business, recovering coal from waste heaps at the closed Nailstone Colliery in North West Leicestershire. This was operated under a planning permission for tip washing, subject to a condition for restoration to woodlands and grasslands. H J Banks & Co later applied for planning permission to in-fill the redundant site with controlled waste and to restore the land for recreational and industrial use. The local planning authority refused to grant planning permission. H J Banks & Co appealed to the planning inspector. The planning inspector dismissed the appeal, explaining in his decision letter that the new proposals would delay the final restoration of the site by approximately twelve years. The planning inspector believed this would have a serious and deleterious effect on the area and would constitute a breach of policy L/ST1 (designating the area as a priority area). He did accept the need for further landfill sites in the area but did not consider, in this case, that the benefits would outweigh the impact on this priority area. H J Banks & Co appealed to the High Court. The High Court quashed the planning inspectors decision on the grounds that the planning inspector did not take into account all the benefits of the new proposals, in particular, those relating to the eventual restoration of the site. The secretary of state appealed against the High Court's ruling to the Court of Appeal.

Decision: The Court of Appeal found for the secretary of state. Considering the planning inspector's decision letter, the Court of Appeal was of the opinion that the planning inspector had taken into account all the benefits of the new proposals but, in his view and taking into account that the area was a priority area, it was desirable that the area was restored under the conditions of the original planning permission rather than the restoration being delayed twelve years under the new proposals. The Court of Appeal held that this was a matter for the judgement of the inspector and not the High Court judge.

Comment: The Court of Appeal went on to say that although in this case the planning inspector had been entitled to concentrate on the completion of the works, each case must be decided upon its own facts and, therefore, no wide implications could be read into this decision.

Kyte and Others v (1) Secretary of State for the Environment (2) Shepway District Council (3) Rank Holidays and Hotels Development Ltd (25 October 1996) Queen's Bench Divisional Court (LTL, 29 October 1996)

[B12.8]

area of outstanding natural beauty

Background: Kyte appealed to the High Court against a grant of planning permission to develop a holiday village at West Wood, Lyminge, Kent, an area of outstanding natural beauty (AONB). Kyte argued that the decision of the planning inspector relating to the proposed development and a Diversion Order, were not within the powers conferred by the *Town and Country Planning Act 1990*. Kyte also claimed that the *Town and Country Planning (Inquiries Procedure) Rules 1992 (SI 1992 No 2038)* had not been complied with, which substantially prejudiced Kyte.

Decision: The appeal was dismissed. The court found that the decision and Order were within the powers conferred by the 1990 Act and that the *Town and Country Planning (Inquiries Procedure) Rules 1992* had been complied with. The court also found that the planning inspector had relied on the English Tourist Board's strategy when making the decision and that it was not erroneous for him to do so. Further, the planning inspector's report was clear, consistent and rational. The secretary of state admitted there would be some harm to the AONB, and had not identified the nature and extent of this harm. However, this did not flaw the overall decision because the secretary of state found that the harm was outweighed by the advantages of the scheme.

R v Surrey County Council, ex parte Oakimber Ltd (27 June 1995) High Court, Queen's Bench Division ([1995] EGCS 120)

[B12.9]

judicial review; conservation area

Background: Okimber Ltd, a development company which owned a substantial proportion of land and buildings at Brooklands, Weybridge, Surrey wished to develop part of its site. However, the local planning authority had designated Brooklands as a conservation area. Its designation extended to an area of over 370 acres of which Okimber Ltd owned 149.74 hectares. Okimber Ltd sought judicial review of the planning authority's decision, claiming that it was invalid and unlawful. The power of the local authority with regard to conservation areas in 1989 (the material time), was derived from *section 277* of the *Town and Country Planning Act 1971* (now *section 69* of the *Planning (Listed*

Buildings and Conservation Areas) Act 1990 and related to 'areas of special architectural or historic interest, the character or appearance of which it was desirable to preserve or enhance'.

Decision: The court held in favour of the local planning authority. It held that the intention of parliament was that the local planning authority would not be obliged to look at each parcel of land individually and exclude any part on which there was no building, unless that part itself was of historic interest. It must have been parliament's intention that the local planning authority should consider, as an entity, the whole of an area which gives rise to special architectural or historic interest. The court said that the legislation gave a broad discretion to the local planning authority, as to which parts of the area were areas of special architectural or historic interest which ought to be preserved or enhanced. In the present case, the land in question was well known to the planning committee which had received full representations. The planning committee had taken those representations into account. Its decision was not therefore irrational.

Evans v Waverley Borough Council (12 July 1995) Court of Appeal ([1995] EGCS 132)

[B12.10]

tree preservation order

Background: Mr Evans owned property near Farnham. In relation to certain works that he was doing there, the council made a tree preservation order on the grounds that the order was in the interests of the visual amenities of the area. The original order specified an 'area of mixed broad leafed trees (including willow and alder) and conifers'. On confirmation by the council, that order was changed to 'woodland comprising mixed broad leafed trees (including willow, alder, ash and sycamore and a scots pine)'. Mr Evans argued that the change on confirmation by the council, amounted to a change from an 'area' order to a 'woodland' order.

Decision: The court upheld Mr Evans' argument. It said that whilst the council's power to modify a tree preservation order under *section 199(1)* of the *Town and Country Planning Act 1990* should be construed widely, it was unlawful for the planning authority on confirmation to substitute a woodland order for an area order.

Kent County Council v Secretary of State for the Environment and Another (29 April 1997) Court of Appeal ([1997] EGCS 64)

[B12.11]

waste; landfill; enforcement notice

Background: R Marchant & Sons Ltd had a site in Kent used at least since 1945, for extraction of stone and gravel and for the processing and deposit of mainly building and civil engineering contractors waste from demolition of buildings and walls and the break up of paths and roads. In 1977, a waste disposal licence was granted for this site and in 1992 an enforcement notice was issued alleging a breach of planning control. R Marchant & Sons Ltd had allegedly made a change of use without planning permission by depositing and processing waste. The enforcement notice required deposits to stop and the site to be remediated. R Marchant & Sons Ltd appealed against the notice, on the ground that the site had planning permission for its existing use and *Article 3* of the *Town and Country Planning General Development Order 1988 (SI 1988 No 813)* allowed as permitted development the deposit of waste materials from an 'industrial process' on land used for that purpose since 1 July 1948. Industrial process covered the 'breaking up or demolition of any article'.

Decision: The Court of Appeal held that whilst 'demolition' applied mainly to buildings and structures, bricks and concrete did not cease to be articles when used to build a wall or path. The deposit of the waste was therefore permitted development and the appeal against the enforcement notice was upheld.

Comment: This case illustrates the difficulties and conflicts which can arise between planning and environment law.

R v Wicks (21 May 1997) House of Lords (Times Law Reports, 26 May 1997)

[B12.12]

enforcement notice; judicial review

Background: Mr Wicks had been served with an enforcement notice for breach of planning control. His appeal against the enforcement notice on four of the grounds set out in *section 174(2)* of the *Town and Country Planning Act 1990* was dismissed. At the trial, he sought to argue that the council had not considered whether service of the notice was expedient, that it had acted in bad faith and had been motivated by immaterial considerations.

Decision: The court held that these arguments should have been raised by way of judicial review. It held that there was no general right to challenge the power behind every act done under statutory authority, and whether such a right existed would depend on the meaning of the statute in question. The court found that 'enforcement notice' under section 179(1) of the *Town and Country Planning Act 1990* means a formally valid notice which has not been quashed on appeal or judicial review. The arguments by which Mr Wicks had sought to challenge the notice were therefore irrelevant.

Comment: The decision in this case can equally be applied in respect of environment law procedures.

Hammond v Secretary of State for the Environment and Another (30 January 1997) Court of Appeal (Times Law Reports, 20 February 1997)

[B12.13]

enforcement notice

Background: This case concerned two planning decisions which were in effect contradictory and the question of which should prevail. Mr Hammond had built a bungalow on his land and during building had put a mobile home on the land to live in. He appealed against the issue of an enforcement notice, and the inspector found that the use of the mobile home had deemed permission. A later inspector's decision that the building of the bungalow itself was unlawful, meant that the siting of the mobile home could never have had deemed permission.

Decision: The court held that where the planning inspector had reached a decision and subsequently another planning inspector had reached a contradictory decision, the first decision in time should stand.

Donley v Secretary of State for the Environment and Another (10 November 1997) High Court, Queen's Bench Division ([1997] PLSCS 298)

[B12.14]

enforcement notice; waste; landfill; judicial review

Background: Donley owned a site with planning permission which allowed a change of use of the site to rugby and cricket pitches. Donley began using the site for tipping which he claimed was permitted under the planning permission. An enforcement notice was served requiring him to cease the tipping of concrete and subsoil and to remove all the waste tipped. The enforcement notice also required restoration of the site within three months.

Mr Donley appealed under *section 289* of the *Town and Country Planning Act 1990* and applied for planning permission. The inspector refused planning permission on the basis that he did not have sufficient evidence to conclude that the tipping would not cause unacceptable harm to the appearance of the surrounding area. Mr Donley applied to quash the inspector's decision.

Test: The court considered whether the tipping of concrete and subsoil was a secondary use for the primary use of land as rugby and cricket pitches or whether the land was being used for the primary use of tipping in breach of the planning permission.

Decision: The court held that it was clear that Mr Donley was using the land for tipping and not for rugby and cricket pitches and was therefore in breach of the planning permission. Further the court held that the inspector had been correct in refusing planning permission as he had no detailed information about the level of the land after levelling, and therefore was correct in concluding that it would cause unacceptable harm for the appearance of the surrounding area.

Essex County Council, ex parte Tarmac Roadstone Holdings Ltd (29 July 1997) High Court, Queen's Bench Division (LTL, 30 July 1997)

[B12.15]

waste landfill; waste disposal contract; judicial review

Background: The Waste Planning Authority sub-licensed its interest in a tipping agreement it had with Tarmac Roadstone Holdings Ltd to a company which was a subsidiary of Essex County Council. The tipping agreement was due to run out on 8 August 1997. A clause in the tipping agreement allowed Essex County Council to apply for an extension of the agreement for another fifteen years if there had been no breaches of any planning condition in force on the site. Essex County Council applied for such renewal and Tarmac Roadstone Holdings Limited discovered that there had been breaches of the planning permission. Essex

County Council were therefore not entitled to require the extension of the tipping agreement. Essex County Council therefore sought planning permission in order to validate its actions which had breached the original planning permission on the site. Planning permission was granted subject to conditions and a new notice was sent seeking to renew the agreement. Tarmac Roadstone Holdings Ltd sought judicial review on the grounds that the planning permission had been sought for an improper reason, the permission granted was substantially different from that sought and the minutes of the planning committee showed that the purpose of the planning permission was to grant temporary lawfulness to the site.

Decision: The court held that the planning permission could not stand as there was no decision taken on the merits of the application. Granting permission of affording temporary lawfulness was not a planning consideration at all. The planning permission was therefore quashed.

Main v Secretary of State for the Environment and Another (22 May 1998) High Court, Queen's Bench Division ([1998] PLSCS 175)

[B12.16]

waste; waste transfer station

Background: Mr Main operated a scrap metal yard on a unit which he shared with three residential properties. Mr Main made an application for a certificate of lawful use under *section 191* of the *Town and Country Planning Act 1990* for 'a waste reclamation depot and transfer station'. However the inspector recommended that the overall use of the site was as a scrap yard and the other uses were ancillary and Mr Main appealed.

Decision: The court upheld Mr Main's appeal as the inspector had erred in law as regards the application of the term 'ancillary'. He had determined the relatively small use of haulage and skip businesses as being 'ancillary'. This, the court held, was an incorrect assessment. 'Ancillary' did not mean relatively small and the haulage and skip businesses could be an independent primary use.

Armitage v South Oxfordshire District Council (12 March 1998) High Court, Queen's Bench Division ([1998] PLSCS 91)

[B12.17]

tree preservation order

Background: South Oxfordshire District Council feared that woodland was being adversely affected by sales of certain areas to local residents. Following a complaint by the Forestry Commission, South Oxfordshire District Council issued a tree preservation order. Mr Armitage objected to the order as the trees in question had only been planted fourteen years ago following a Forestry Commission grant. A district council committee considered the objection and contrary to the recommendations of the advising officer, it confirmed the tree preservation order. Mr Armitage appealed on the grounds that such an order could only be confirmed with the consent of the Forestry Commission and that Circular 36/78 stated that a tree preservation order should not be confirmed where land is under good management practices.

Decision: The court rejected this appeal. South Oxfordshire District Council had made two errors; consent of the Forestry Commission should have been obtained (the court found there was clear evidence that consent would have been forthcoming), and the council should have had regard to Circular 36/78. However, the court held, that under *section 198* of the *Town and Country Planning Act 1990*, South Oxfordshire District Council had the authority to make the decision. The council had exercised this authority and there was no indication that the decision would have been any different.

Kettering Borough Council v Perkins (5 March 1998) High Court, Queen's Bench Division ([1998] PLSCS 80)

[B12.18]

scrap metal; waste; injunction

Background: Kettering Borough Council served an enforcement notice against Mr Perkins as it believed he was using his site, which had planning permission for the use of car-breaking, for the sale of vehicle components. After the relevant compliance period, the inspector found that the retail activities had continued as the primary use of the site. Kettering Borough Council sought an injunction against Mr Perkins under *section 187B* of the *Town and Country Planning Act 1990.*

Decision: In granting an injunction under *section 173* of the *Town and Country Planning Act 1990*, the court found that this was not an unfair burden on Mr Perkins. Mr Perkins was required to alter his activities to ensure that sales were ancillary to the use of the site, in accordance with the planning permission.

Berkeley v Secretary of State for the Environment and Fulham Football Club (12 February 1998) Court of Appeal ([1998] PLSCS 42)

[B12.19]

environmental impact assessment

Background: Mr Berkeley applied for planning and listed building consents, which had been granted to Fulham Football Club, to be quashed as: (i) the inspector did not take into account the unitary development plan or policy EN27, and (ii) Fulham Football Club were not required to produce an environmental statement in accordance with *Directive 85/337/EEC.*

Decision: The court held that the inspector had 'fully considered' the environmental impact and need not refer to policy EN27 in his decision letter. Moreover, there was a failure to provide an environmental statement, but such a failure would not have any effect on the course of events or alter the decision. Therefore the application was dismissed.

Radioactive Substances

R v Secretary of State for the Environment and Others, ex parte Greenpeace Ltd and Lancashire County Council (4 March 1994) High Court Queen's Bench Division ([1994] 4 All ER 352, [1994] Env. L.R. 401(Part 4))

[B13.1]

judicial review; wednesbury principle; reasonableness; radioactive substances; environmental impact assessment; public consultation; planning permission; radioactive waste; waste; locus standi

Background: In 1983, full planning permission was granted to British Nuclear Fuels plc (BNFL), for the construction of a thermal oxide re-processing plant (THORP) at Sellafield. Construction was completed in 1992 and BNFL applied to the government for authorisations to reprocess spent uranium oxide fuel – a process which would result in the discharge of radioactive waste into both the sea and air. New authorisations drafted by the HMIP and the Ministry of Agriculture Fisheries and Food (MAFF) were made available for public consultation. Following the consultation, HMIP and MAFF approved the draft authorisations to the relevant government ministers. The government, although satisfied with the draft authorisations, arranged a second period of consultation in view of the considerable public interest expressed. No public inquiry was held. Following this second period of consultation, the authorisations were granted. Greenpeace and Lancashire County Council applied to the High Court for judicial review of the Secretary of State for the Environment's decision to authorise BNFL to commission THORP. They argued that the decision making process was flawed because the secretary of state had incorrectly concluded that he was under no legal obligation to justify the granting of the authorisations. In addition, an EIA would be required in accordance with *Directive 85/337/EEC*, the bringing into operation of THORP constituting a separate project to the original construction of the plant (N.B. no assessment was required for the construction of the plant as the project predated the coming into effect of the Directive). Finally, they argued that the secretary of state should have held a public inquiry. The power to grant authorisations is contained in *sections 13 and 16* of the *Radioactive Substances Act 1993* and although under these sections the secretary of state has the discretion to hold a public inquiry, they argued that it should have been held in this case. The judge, on this point, directed that the court could not interfere with the exercise of the discretion unless the decision was one which no reasonable decision maker could have reached on the basis of the facts before him (the *'Wednesbury Principle'*).

Decision: The application for judicial review failed. The judge held that, in accordance with EU legislation, the secretary of state must give reasons to justify the grant of the authorisations. He then went on to state that, although the minister had erred in law in this respect, this was not sufficient to justify the decision being quashed. He was satisfied that the ministers had considered a wide range of factors in their second consultation and as such the court would use its discretion to refuse to grant relief. In respect to the need for an EIA, the judge rejected the applicants argument that the construction and the bringing into operation of the plant constituted two separate projects. As such, the relevant planning permission had been granted prior to the coming into effect of the Directive. In any event, the judge considered that the information provided and made available to the public met the substantive requirements of the Directive. With regard to the final argument, that the secretary of state should have held a public inquiry, the judge was satisfied that all issues relevant to the holding of a public inquiry had been addressed by the ministers and they had not, therefore, acted in a flawed or irrational manner.

Comment: The judge, rather unusually, did not order Greenpeace and Lancashire County Council to pay the costs of the case. The point of law with regard to the justification of decisions by ministers was of great public interest and the applicants had succeeded on this important point.

Environment Agency v UK Atomic Energy Authority (14 May 1996) Magistrates' Court ((1996) ENDS 256, 46–47)

[B13.2]

waste; radioactive substances; radioactive waste; prosecution; fine; jurisdiction of Environment Agency

Background: A leak of radioactive waste occurred from an underground pipeline at the Winfrith site of the UK Atomic Energy Authority. The leakage contaminated ground water with radioactive tritium. It occurred between January 1993 and April 1994. The underground pipeline was part of the liquid waste system for the steam generating heavy water reactor. The UK Atomic Energy Authority admitted the unauthorised disposal of radioactive waste and was fined £5,000 and ordered to pay costs in the sum of £10,678.

Decision: The UK Atomic Energy Authority successfully contested a charge of breaching a condition in its authorisation requiring that the systems used for liquid waste discharges be kept in good repair. The court found that the pipeline from which the leak occurred was not part of the discharge system and was therefore outside of the jurisdiction of the EA.

Statutory Nuisance

R v Highbury Corner Magistrates' Court, ex parte Edwards (1994) High Court, Queen's Bench Division ([1994] Env. L.R. 215)

[B14.1]

statutory nuisance; breach of covenant; procedure

Background: The applicant, Mrs Edwards, lived in a maisonette in a five-storey block of flats owned by the London Borough of Hackney. Her maisonette suffered from dampness, condensation and mould growth. In April 1993, Mrs Edwards instituted proceedings against the council for statutory nuisance under *section 82* of the *EPA 1990*. Further, in May 1993, Mrs Edwards commenced proceedings in the County Court against the landlord, claiming breaches of covenants implied in the tenancy agreement. The Magistrates' Court refused to issue the appropriate summons on the grounds that Mrs Edwards had been granted legal aid to pursue her claim in the County Court, and that proceedings in the Magistrates' Court were unjustified and would amount to duplication. Mrs Edwards appealed.

Test: The extent to which the applicant was precluded, if at all, from pursuing civil and criminal remedies to the nuisance.

Decision: The court upheld Mrs Edwards appeal. The Magistrates' Court order was quashed and the clerk to the magistrates was ordered to issue the summons.

Comment: The statutory nuisance provisions of the *EPA 1990* could require a wider scope of works by the landlord than those required under the tenancy covenants and, consequently, it was permissible for Mrs Edwards to issue both sets of proceedings.

R v Noseley Metropolitan Borough Council, ex parte O'Toole (18 May 1999) High Court, Queen's Bench Division (Times Law Reports, 21 May 1999)

[B14.2]

abatement notice; statutory nuisance; Environmental Protection Act 1990; environmental health officers; expert witness

Background: Ms O'Toole, a council tenant, had sought an abatement notice under *section 81* of the *EPA 1990*, contending that her premises were in such a state as to be prejudicial to her or a nuisance under *section 79* of the 1990 Act. The magistrates found that although the two environmental health officers were sufficiently qualified and experienced to be regarded as expert witnesses, in the absence of medical evidence regarding the state of Ms O'Toole's health the evidence could not be accepted. The magistrates held that Ms O'Toole had failed to discharge the evidential burden to establish a case, and as a consequence Ms O'Toole's application for an abatement notice was refused.

Decision: On appeal, the judge followed the decision in *Southwark Borough Council v Simpson (1998)* (see paragraph B14.30). He stated that it was not necessary for the environmental health officers to have medical qualifications in order to assess whether the premises were prejudicial to health. As there was no contradictory evidence and the issue was one for expert evidence, the justices should have taken its officers evidence into account. The court held that evidence had been improperly excluded and Ms O'Toole's appeal was allowed.

Coventry City Council v Doyle (17 December 1980) High Court, Queen's Bench Division ([1981] 1 WLR 1325)

[B14.3]

statutory nuisance; prejudicial to health; nuisance order; abatement notice; nuisance; public health; enforcement

Background: Three council tenants brought actions against the council under *section 99* of the *Public Health Act 1936* (now section 82 of the *EPA 1990*), alleging that the state of their houses was prejudicial to health and constituted a statutory nuisance. Before the hearing, one of the tenants was moved to alternative accommodation in order that her original house could be modernised. During the hearing, the second defendant was also moved for the same reason and the third tenant, although still in occupation, had repairs carried out to her property. The Magistrates' Court decided that a statutory nuisance had existed when the actions were originally brought and as such, they made nuisance orders requiring the council to repair the houses. The council appealed to the Crown Court. The judge in the Crown Court agreed that the state of the house was prejudicial to health at the date the action was commenced. However, he stated that the relevant date for proving whether a statutory nuisance existed was not the date that the action was commenced but the date of the hearing, and by this date the nuisance had been abated. This decision was appealed by the tenants to the High Court.

Test: The relevant date for determining whether a statutory nuisance exists is the date of the hearing and not the date at which the action was commenced.

Decision: The High Court held that: (i) the date for determining whether or not the premises were prejudicial to health was the date of the hearing in the Magistrates' Court, not the date that the action was commenced; (ii) a nuisance would not have been abated merely because the houses subsequently became unoccupied. As such, the Magistrates' Court, by making nuisance orders, had taken the appropriate course of action; (iii) a nuisance order should only specify the works necessary to abate that nuisance and should not include any additional work, even where the council had indicated that it would carry such additional work out.

Comment: This judgement leaves it open to individuals or companies who are facing a court hearing, in respect of an alleged statutory nuisance, to take action to abate such a nuisance prior to any court hearing. However, in cases where they have already been served with an abatement notice, this may be of little benefit and is unlikely to protect them from criminal liability for failing to comply with such a notice. The decision is likely to have most applicability in cases brought by individuals under *section 82* of the *EPA 1990* in the Magistrates' Court, where the local authority has failed to take action by serving an abatement notice.

Coventry City Council v Cartwright (29 January 1975) High Court, Queen's Bench Division ([1975] 1 WLR 845)

[B14.4]

nuisance; prejudicial to health; statutory nuisance; waste

Background: This case arose from a complaint made against Coventry City Council in the Magistrates' Court under *section 92* of the *Public Health Act 1936*. The complaint concerned the accumulation or deposit of household refuge and building materials on a vacant site owned by the council (in a residential area). Mr Cartwright argued that the accumulation or deposit was prejudicial to health and was a statutory nuisance.

The magistrates found that a statutory nuisance did exist on the basis that the visual impact of the site could constitute a nuisance and that the inert waste on the site could be dangerous to health. The site was not secure and hence the access was relatively easy. The magistrates granted an abatement order. The council appealed.

Test: Whether the visual impact of the inert waste could constitute a statutory nuisance.

Decision: It was held that the visual impact of the inert waste did not constitute a statutory nuisance. The deposit could only be prejudicial to health if it was likely to cause a threat of disease or attract vermin.

Comment: This case reinforces the principle that there can only be a statutory nuisance if the state of affairs complained of constitute a nuisance of is prejudicial to health.

Dover District Council v Farrar and Others (27 June 1980) High Court, Queen's Bench Division (2 HLR 32)

[B14.5]

statutory nuisance; prejudicial to health; nuisance

Background: Houses built by Dover District Council in 1973 and 1974 were heated by either gas or electric warm air systems. All the houses had building regulation approval and the level of insulation was slightly above that required by the regulations. Within three years, however, a number of the houses heated using electric warm air heating became damp. The tenants could not afford to heat the houses to the extent required to prevent the damp. A number of tenants complained to the Magistrates' Court under *section 99* of the *Public Health Act 1936* that the state of their houses were prejudicial to health within the meaning of *section 92(1)(a)* of 1936 Act, and that the council had failed to abate the statutory nuisance. The court established that if heated properly, using the system installed, the dampness would not have been prejudicial to health, but that the tenants could not afford to do so. A nuisance order was made requiring the council to convert the houses to use gas. The local authority appealed.

Test: Whether the council was liable for a statutory nuisance under the 1936 Act.

Decision: The High Court held that a statutory nuisance had been caused by the act or default of the tenants, even though their refusal to use the expensive heating system was understandable. It was not right to make a nuisance order requiring the conversion of the heating systems because this depended on energy pricing policy at one point in time. The council's appeal was allowed and the justices finding was quashed.

Comment: On a practical note, this was an important case as it provided authority for the proposition that, in appropriate cases, condensation-caused dampness could amount to a statutory nuisance. It has since been relied upon in other cases including *Greater London Council v London Borough of Tower Hamlets (1983) 15 HLR 54.*

Hammersmith London Borough Council v Magnum Automated Forecourts Ltd (31 May 1977) Court of Appeal ([1978] 1 WLR 50)

[B14.6]

nuisance; statutory nuisance; noise; abatement notice; injunction

Background: Magnum operated a 24-hour taxi care centre providing fuel, vehicle washing and refreshment facilities. The care centre was situated in a residential road. Following complaints about excessive noise, particularly at night, Hammersmith London Borough Council served an abatement notice under *section 58(1)* of the *Control of Pollution Act 1974* prohibiting activities at the centre between 11 p.m. and 7 a.m. Magnum appealed under *section 58(3)* of the 1974 Act. However, contrary to the wording of the abatement notice, which stated that the notice would not be suspended pending an appeal, the company continued night-time operations. The council applied to the High Court for an injunction under *section 58(8)* of the 1974 Act to secure compliance. In the Magistrates' Court, the company's appeal against the notice was adjourned because of the High Court proceedings. The High Court refused to grant the injunction because the statutory procedures under the 1974 Act had not been exhausted, and the issue should be decided by the magistrates. The council appealed to the Court of Appeal.

Test: The extent to which the authority had the power to seek an injunction under the 1974 Act.

Decision: *Section 58(8)* of the 1974 Act enabled a local authority to seek an injunction to abate, prohibit or restrict a noise nuisance where it considers that proceedings for an offence under *section 58(4)* would not afford an inadequate remedy. The Court of Appeal ruled that Hammersmith London Borough Council was fully justified in seeking an injunction as no attempt had been made by Magnum to comply with the abatement notice. The appeal was allowed.

Comment: This case makes it clear that a local authority has the power to seek an injunction under *section 58(8)*, where it is considered that a prosecution under *section 58(4)* would not be an effective remedy. It should also be noted that *section 58(8)* provides that if an injunction is granted and the courts later find that there is no nuisance, compensation may be payable to the person subject to the injunction.

R v Fenny Stratford Justices, ex parte Watney Mann (Midlands) Ltd (26 February 1976) High Court, Queen's Bench Division ([1976] 1 WLR 1101)

[14.7]

nuisance; noise; statutory nuisance; judicial review

Background: Three neighbours of a public house complained to the Magistrates' Court under *section 99* of the *Public Health Act 1936*, concerning noise from a juke box. The court found that a statutory nuisance existed and ordered that it should be abated. The nuisance order also included a term requiring that the level of noise in the public house should not exceed seventy decibels. Watney, the proprietors of the public house, applied for judicial review to quash that part of the order setting the decibel limit, on the grounds that its inclusion was an error of law (*certiorari*).

Decision: The High Court ruled that the additional term was so imprecise as to be void for uncertainty. The application for judicial review was granted, the relevant part of the order quashed and the matter remitted to the Magistrates' Court.

Comment: *Section 94* of the 1936 Act prescribed the powers of magistrates to make nuisance orders, including the additional terms that may be included in such orders. Justices had wide discretion concerning the terms to be included (*Nottingham City District Council v Newton [1974] 1 WLR 923, 929, 930 and Salford City Council v McNally [1976] AC 379*). They may add any additional term to the simple requirement to abate a nuisance, provided that the term is practical and may be easily understood by both the recipient of the notice and the aggrieved person, and that where appropriate, the action to be taken to comply with the term is specified. In this case, however, the nuisance order failed to specify where the sound meter should be positioned and how noise other than that from the juke box should be taken into account.

AMEC Building Ltd and Another v London Borough of Camden (19 July 1997) Queen's Bench Divisional Court ([1997] Env. L.R. 330)

[B14.8]

nuisance; statutory nuisance; noise; abatement notice; service

Background: Noise, dust and smoke caused a statutory nuisance at a construction site in north London. AMEC Building Ltd (the main site contractor) and Squibb and Davies Ltd (a specialist demolition firm) were served with abatement notices by Camden London Borough Council under section 80(4) of the *EPA 1990* and *section 60(8)* of the *Control of Pollution Act 1974*. Both companies were subsequently prosecuted by the council for failing to comply with the notices. In the Magistrates' Court, AMEC unsuccessfully argued that the notices had not been properly served and were therefore null because they had been sent to AMEC Construction Ltd, a sister company with a registered office at the same address. The notices had been passed to the correct company and the court considered that because AMEC Building Ltd had corresponded with the council concerning the notices and had not appealed, this was proof that the notices had been served. AMEC appealed.

Squibb and Davies Ltd appealed against a conviction by the Magistrates' Court for failing to comply with the terms of the abatement notices requiring certain works to be carried out. The company argued that, as there was no evidence that the nuisance continued to exist after the notices were served, there was no basis to establish non-compliance.

Test: The court had to consider (1) whether the notice had been served correctly pursuant to *section 160* of the *EPA 1990* and *section 233* of the 1974 Act (these sections make no provision for the service of a notice other than directly on the relevant person or body, even if that person or body eventually receives the notice, e.g. if it is passed to them from an associated company. Evidence of receipt is not sufficient to prove service) and; (2) whether in Squibb's case it was necessary to prove the occurrence or recurrence of the nuisance.

Decision: The High Court held that as the abatement notices were not directed to AMEC Building Ltd, they were not properly served and the company was not bound by them. The appeal was allowed.

The appeal of Squibb and Davies Ltd was dismissed. The court ruled that as the prosecution brought by the council was for the failure to carry out the works specified in the abatement notices, there was no need to prove the occurrence or recurrence of the statutory nuisance. It was only necessary to consider whether the notices had been complied with (*A Lambert Flat Management Ltd v Lomas [1981]* (see paragraph B14.20)).

Comment: This case makes an important point concerning the need for abatement notices to identify very specifically the intended recipient. Failure to address a notice to the correct party may result in that notice being invalid. It also emphasises that it is not necessary for the prosecution to prove that a statutory nuisance exists where a summons is for the failure to carry out works specified in an abatement notice. If the alleged contravention is for failure to abate an existing nuisance, the occurrence or recurrence of that nuisance must be proved. This is supported by the wording of *section 80(7)* of the *EPA 1990*: 'Subject to subsection (8) below, in any proceedings for an offence under subsection (4) above in respect of a statutory nuisance it shall be a defence to prove that the best practicable means were used to prevent, or to counteract the effects of, the nuisance'. The use of the words 'statutory nuisance' indicate that offences under *section 80(4)* need not involve the existence of a statutory nuisance.

Morrissey v Galer (20 January 1955) High Court, Queen's Bench Division ([1955] 1 WLR 110)

[B14.9]

nuisance; noise; animals

Background: Mr Morrissey kept greyhounds which created a noise and caused nuisance to his neighbours. A local bye-law made by Kent County Council under the *Local Government Act 1933* provided that: 'No person shall keep within any house, building or premises any noisy animal which shall be or cause a serious nuisance to residents in the neighbourhood'. A notice was served on Mr Morrissey alleging serious nuisance and he was subsequently convicted for the offence under the bye-law. On appeal, he successfully argued that the bye-law was *ultra vires* on the grounds that it covered the same matters as *section 92* of the *Public Health Act 1936*. Kent County Council appealed.

Test: Whether the bye-law was ultra vires on the grounds that it covered the same matter as *section 92* of the 1936 Act.

Decision: The High Court held that the bye-law and the statute did not cover the same issue. Under *section 92* of the 1936 Act, it is the conditions in which animals are kept that may give rise to a statutory nuisance. This section did not deal with nuisance merely caused by noisy animals. The bye-law was not ultra vires.

Comment: Although the provisions of the 1936 Act concerning statutory nuisance have been replaced by the *EPA 1990* (in England and Wales), the description of a statutory nuisance as 'any animal kept in such a place or manner as to be prejudicial to health or a nuisance' used in the 1936 Act, has been carried forward as *section 79(1)(f)* of the 1990 Act.

Chapman v Gosberton Farm Produce Co Ltd (4 June 1993) High Court, Queen's Bench Division ([1993] 1 Env. L.R. 191)

[B14.10]

nuisance; noise; statutory nuisance; best practicable means

Background: Gosberton operated a large vegetable processing depot. Noise generated by vehicles, machinery and plant was considered to be a statutory nuisance. South Holland District Council served an abatement notice on the company under *section 58* of the *Control of Pollution Act 1974*, followed by a summons alleging non-compliance with the notice. There had been discussions and agreement between the parties concerning the type of works required to abate the nuisance, specifically the enclosure of noise-producing activities on the site or the provision of acoustic bunding for which planning permission would be required. The Magistrates' Court found that although the abatement notice had been breached, the company could prove, on the balance of probability, that the statutory defence of using 'best practicable means' to prevent or counteract noise nuisance applied (*section 58(5)* of the 1974 Act). This decision was based on the fact that Gosberton had submitted an application for planning permission to extend its facility. The application included acoustic and visual bunding, although further information requested by the local authority had not been supplied. Mr John Chapman, the environmental health officer concerned, appealed on behalf of the council.

Test: Whether the defence of best practicable means was satisfied.

Decision: The appeal was allowed.

Comment: This case turned on the interpretation of the 'best practicable means' defence provided by *section 58(5)* that may be used where noise is caused in the course of a trade or business. The onus is on the defendant to establish this on the balance of probability.

Botross v London Borough of Hammersmith and Fulham (21 October 1994) Queen's Bench Divisional Court (Times Law Reports, 7 November 1994)

[B14.11]

nuisance; statutory nuisance; criminal proceedings; compensation; prejudicial to health

Background: Mrs Botross rented a flat from Hammersmith and Fulham Borough Council. The flat suffered from damp and mould growth. She complained to the Magistrates' Court that the flat constituted a statutory nuisance by virtue of being 'premises in such a state as to be prejudicial to health or a nuisance' (*section 79(1)(a)* of the *EPA 1990*). She also sought an abatement order under *section 82* of the 1990 Act, compensation under the *Powers of Criminal Courts Act 1973* and costs. Although the magistrates found that a statutory nuisance did exist and an abatement order could be made, Mrs Botross' compensation claim was rejected on the basis that the proceedings were civil and therefore the court had no jurisdiction to make a compensation order under the 1973 Act. Mrs Botross appealed.

Test: *Section 82* of the 1990 Act provides that a Magistrates' Court may act on a complaint made by any person on the grounds that they are aggrieved by the existence of a statutory nuisance. If a statutory nuisance is found to exist, the court can order the abatement of the nuisance and may also impose a fine on the defendant.

Decision: The High Court held that the power to impose fines provided under *section 82(2)*, was sufficient to indicate that proceedings under this section relating to statutory nuisances are intended to be criminal in nature. This was further confirmed by considering the relevant parliamentary debates. The courts are therefore empowered to make orders for compensation in favour of those aggrieved by a nuisance. The appeal was allowed and the case remitted to the justices.

East Northamptonshire District Council v Brian Fossett (18 April 1994) High Court, Queen's Bench Division ([1994] Env. L.R. 388)

[B14.12]

nuisance; noise; statutory nuisance; abatement notice; enforcement

Background: Mr Fossett applied for a public entertainment licence for an all-night rave party. The licence was not granted. Despite this, preparations for the event went ahead. Satisfied that a statutory nuisance was going to occur, East Northamptonshire District Council served an abatement notice on Mr Fossett under *section 80* of the *EPA 1990* on the afternoon prior to the party. This prohibited the occurrence of a nuisance from the event arising from the playing of music and other activities at the rave and required him to control all activities to prevent noise nuisance at residential properties. During the rave, complaints were made to the council about loud music and an information was laid against Mr Fossett by the council under *section 80(4)* of the 1990 Act, alleging that he had contravened the abatement notice. Although the Magistrates' Court found that the notice had been breached, they considered that it was imprecise and void for uncertainty because no sound levels for background noise or decibel limits had been prescribed. The information was dismissed and the council appealed.

Test: The court had to consider whether the notice was void for uncertainty.

Decision: The High Court held that the notice was not imprecise and void for uncertainty. There was no requirement, statutory or otherwise, for decibel levels to be specified in the notice. Further, it was held that the noise levels did amount to a nuisance, despite the fact that the rave was a single event and there was no element of continuity. The appeal was dismissed.

Comment: This case is unusual because the local authority used its powers to abate a potential statutory nuisance.

Sterling Homes v Birmingham City Council (4 July 1995) High Court, Queen's Bench Division ([1996] Env. L.R. 121)

[B14.13]

nuisance; statutory nuisance; abatement notice; enforcement; noise

Background: The occupant of a flat within a building owned by Sterling Homes complained to Birmingham City Council. The complaint concerned noise and vibration coming from a nearby industrial plant which could be felt because of structural defects in the building. The council investigated and served an abatement notice on Sterling Homes, requiring it to abate the nuisance within a specified period and to carry out works and other necessary steps to achieve this. The specific action required was not set out in the notice. Sterling did not appeal against the abatement notice. Ten months later, the noise nuisance had increased and the council brought a prosecution under *section 80* of the *EPA 1990*. Sterling was convicted in spite of its argument that the notice did not comply with *section 80* because it did not specify the works to be carried out. The Magistrates' Court found that it was not necessary to prescribe the works or other steps to be taken and, further, because the company had not appealed against the notice it could not argue that the notice was a nullity. Sterling appealed.

Test: The extent to which an abatement notice needed to specify the steps required to abate the nuisance.

Decision: The High Court held that the interpretation placed on *section 94* of the *Public Health Act 1875*, that an abatement notice must specify the works to be carried out or other steps to be taken for compliance, had been perpetuated in *section 80(1)* of the 1990 Act. This had been the intention of parliament and also follows *R v Wheatley [1885] 16 QBD 34* and *Millard v Wastall [1889] 1 QBD 342*. The appeal was allowed.

Comment: This case makes a further point about the content of abatement notices served by local authorities. A notice may simply require a nuisance to be abated. However, where a requirement is included in the notice for works etc. to be carried out to achieve this, these must be specified. This may prove to be difficult for a local authority in some circumstances. See also *Kirklees Metropolitan Borough Council v Field and Others, Times Law Reports, 26 November 1997.*

Lambeth London Borough Council v Mullings (12 July 1990) Queen's Bench Divisional Court (Times Law Reports, 16 January 1990)

[B14.14]

nuisance; statutory nuisance; abatement notice; service; noise

Background: Lambeth London Borough Council served an abatement notice under *section 58* of the *Control of Pollution Act 1974* on Mr Mullings, the occupant of noisy premises, by posting the notice through the letterbox of his premises. The council then laid an information alleging that Mr Mullings had failed to comply with that notice. The information was dismissed because the Magistrates' Court considered that *section 58(2)* of the 1974 Act requires the prosecution to prove service of an abatement notice. The council appealed against this decision.

Test: Whether the manner of service complied with the requirements of the *Local Government Act 1972.*

Decision: *Section 233(2)* of the 1972 Act allows a local authority notice to be given to or served on the person in question, either by delivering it to him, leaving it at his proper address or posting it to him at that address. The High Court therefore ruled that posting the abatement notice through the letterbox constituted correct service upon the occupier in this case and satisfied *section 58(2)* of the 1974 Act. The council's appeal was allowed.

Comment: This case makes another important point concerning the administration of abatement notices. It also highlights that the more general provisions of the local government Acts should be considered when determining the powers and duties of local authorities.

Stevenage Borough Council v Wilson (6 February 1993) High Court, Queen's Bench Division ([1993] 1 Env. L.R. 214)

[B14.15]

nuisance; statutory nuisance; noise; 'dwelling'

Background: A noise abatement notice was served on the occupier of a property in Stevenage under *section 58* of the *Control of Pollution Act 1974*. This prohibited the recurrence of a noise nuisance at that address caused by the playing of music at an excessively high volume and the noisy behaviour of visitors. The notice also required the occupant to take all steps necessary to prevent the disturbance by noise of neighbours and 'in particular to ensure that the amplified music emanating from the dwelling is not clearly audible outside the house or in adjoining dwellings'. Five months later, the police were called following complaints about loud music coming from the garden of the house. In the subsequent prosecution for breach of the notice, the occupant argued that there had been no contravention. This argument was was based on the premise that because the *section 58* notice required that the music emanating from the dwelling should not be clearly audible outside the house, at the time of the complaint, the music had been played in the garden. The Magistrates' Court held that the wording of the notice was imprecise and dismissed the information. The council appealed.

Test: Whether the notice applied to activities in the curtilage of the premises (i.e. the garden).

Decision: The High Court ruled that the address '13 Tintern Close' on the notice described the premises to which the notice related, and must apply to both the house and garden. The notice was not invalid and the appeal was allowed.

Cunningham v Birmingham City Council (6 May 1997) Queen's Bench Divisional Court ([1998] JPL 147)

[B14.16]

nuisance; statutory nuisance; prejudicial to health

Background: An autistic child with a fascination for doors occupied council accommodation, which included a cramped and poorly designed kitchen with four doors. The child's mother asked Birmingham City Council to remedy what she considered to be a dangerous situation in view of her son's condition. The council offered to carry out abatement of the alleged statutory nuisance, but refused to carry out works which Mrs Cunningham felt were needed due to the particular circumstances of her son. Mrs Cunningham laid an information under, *section 82* of the *EPA 1990*, alleging that the premises were prejudicial to health and that the council had failed to abate the statutory nuisance. In the Magistrates' Court, it was concluded that a statutory nuisance did exist and that the subjective requirements of Mrs Cunningham were relevant in determining this. However, a defect in the notice meant that the case failed. Mrs Cunningham appealed on this point.

Test: Whether an objective test was to be applied when considering whether under *section 79(1)(a)* of the 1990 Act, premises which are 'in such a state as to be prejudicial to health or a nuisance'.

An objective test must apply when deciding whether premises are prejudicial to health (as in *Hall v The Manchester Corporation (1915) Ch 732*, a case concerning the fitness of a house for human habitation).

Decision: In consequence of this decision, the court found it unnecessary to address the issue of the defective notice and the appeal was dismissed.

Comment: This was a common sense judgement as the burden on landlords would be huge if they must take into account the health of individual occupants on a subjective basis.

Kirklees Metropolitan Borough Council v Field and Others (31 October 1997) High Court, Queen's Bench Division (Times Law Reports, 26 November 1997)

[B14.17]

nuisance; statutory nuisance

Background: Abatement notices were served by Kirklees Metropolitan Borough Council under *section 80(1)* of the *EPA 1990*, in relation to a wall which was in imminent danger of collapsing. The notices did not specify the works considered necessary to achieve this. The Crown Court allowed an appeal against the decision of the magistrates that the notices were valid. In turn, the council appealed against the Crown Court's decision.

Test: Whether an abatement notice needed to specify the steps required to be taken to abate the nuisance.

Decision: The High Court held that the interpretation given to the *Public Health Act 1875*, that an order requiring a person to take steps to abate a nuisance had to set out the requisite measures to be taken (*R v Wheatley [1885] 16 QBD 34*; *Millard v Wastall [1889] 1 QBD 342*), should be applied to the 1990 Act. In cases such as this, where a person is required to take positive action to end a nuisance rather than merely to cease causing the nuisance, an abatement notice must inform the recipient of the nature of that action for the avoidance of doubt. As the notices served in relation to the wall did not set out the necessary works and the court could not rectify this, they were therefore invalid. The appeal was dismissed.

Comment: This case was heard by a specially constituted three-judge court to decide the issue once and for all. This ruling is consistent with earlier case law that, where a local authority requires a person to carry out works to abate a statutory nuisance, those works must be specified in the abatement notice. Failure to do so will invalidate the notice, irrespective of whether the nuisance exists or not.

Pollway Nominees v London Borough of Havering High Court, Queen's Bench Division ([1989] 21 HLR 462)

[B14.18]

nuisance; statutory nuisance; abatement notice; prejudicial to health; 'premises'

Background: Pollway Nominees owned a flat leased from the freeholder of the whole building. A bedroom wall in the flat suffered from rising damp caused by a structural defect. This outside wall was not demised to Pollway. However, as the owner of the flat, Pollway was served with an abatement notice by the London Borough of Havering, since the nuisance arose from a defect of a structural nature (*section 93* of the *Public Health Act 1936*). The notice was not complied with, and following an application by the local authority, an abatement order was made by the Magistrates' Court. The court found that the flat was prejudicial to health and a statutory nuisance. Pollway argued that although it was the owner of the flat (as defined by section 343 of the 1936 Act), it was not the owner of the premises referred to by sections 92 and 93. It therefore argued that the abatement notice should have been served on the freeholder of the whole building.

Test: The High Court held that term 'premises' as used in section 92(1)(a) of the 1936 Act ('any premises in such a state as to be prejudicial to health or a nuisance') and section 93 ('... where the nuisance arises from any defect of a structural character, the notice shall be served on the owner of the premises... '), relates to the premises that are prejudicial to health, i.e. in this case the flat, not the outside wall. Further, where a statutory nuisance is caused by a structural defect, this is not limited to defects arising on the premises: the owner must be served with the abatement notice regardless of whether he is responsible for causing the nuisance. The fact that the owner might be unable to gain access to remedy a defect does not preclude the serving of an abatement notice (Parker v Inge [1886] 17 QBD 584).

Decision: The appeal was dismissed.

Comment: In such circumstances, several avenues could have been open to the flats owners, *inter alia*, statutory nuisance proceedings against the freeholder or through contractual rights likely to exist under the terms of the lease.

Wellingborough Borough Council v Gordon (22 October 1990) Queen's Bench Divisional Court ([1993] Env. L.R. 218)

[B14.19]

nuisance; statutory nuisance; noise; reasonable excuse; mitigation

Background: In 1985, Mr Gordon was served with an abatement notice under *section 58* of the *Control of Pollution Act 1974*, prohibiting the recurrence of the playing of loud music at his house. Three years later he held a birthday party at which music was played. The police visited the house and their request that the music be turned down was complied with. No complaints were made by neighbours about the noise. Wellingborough Borough

Council prosecuted Mr Gordon for breaching the notice under *section 58(4)* of the 1974 Act. The Magistrates' Court found that there had been a noise nuisance. However, Mr Gordon was acquitted on the basis that there had been a reasonable excuse: the party was an isolated incident; it was three years since the serving of the notice and there had been no breaches in that time; there had been no complaints by neighbours about the noise and he had attempted to minimise any disturbance by holding the party on a Friday night and inviting his neighbours. The local authority appealed.

Test: The defence of 'reasonable excuse' within the meaning of *section 58(4)* of the 1974 Act, is only available where there is a special difficulty in relation to compliance with a notice, for example, in an emergency or in circumstances beyond the defendants control (*A Lambert Flat Management Ltd v Lomas [1981]*).

Decision: The High Court found that a nuisance can exist, despite the fact that complaints are not made by neighbours. The evidence may come from a different source and not necessarily from those who might have been adversely affected by the nuisance (the authority on this point was provided by *Cook v Adatia and Others [1989] 153 JPL 129*). As such, the nuisance did exist. Further, the mitigating factors cited by the Magistrates' Court did not amount, either severally or jointly, to a 'reasonable excuse' within the meaning of *section 58(4)* of the 1974 Act. Mr Gordon had contravened the notice deliberately and intentionally. The factors described by the Magistrates' Court were relevant however to what penalty should be applied. The appeal was allowed.

Comment: This case follows the judgment in *A Lambert Flat Management Ltd v Lomas [1982]*, that the 'reasonable excuse' defence provided by *section 58(4)* is not intended to give the recipient of an abatement notice a choice of forum for an appeal, i.e. by this defence or by appealing under *section 58(3)* of the 1974 Act.

A Lambert Flat Management Ltd v Lomas (19 December 1980) High Court, Queen's Bench Division ([1981] 2 All ER 280)

[B14.20]

nuisance; noise; statutory nuisance; reasonable excuse; forum

Background: A Lambert Flat Management Ltd ('ALFML') managed a block of self-contained flats. The tenants' leases included a covenant that the company would keep those areas of the building not demised to the tenants clean and in good order. This included the lifts. The tenants of two flats located next to the lifts were seriously disturbed by noise caused by the operation of the lifts. Abatement notices were served on ALFML under *section 58(1)* of the *Control of Pollution Act 1974*, requiring the statutory nuisance to be abated within six months and specifying the works to be carried out to achieve this. Similar steps had to be taken to prevent the recurrence of the nuisance. ALFML neither appealed against the notice using the procedures provided for by *section 58(3)* of the 1974 Act nor took any steps to comply. The local authority then laid an information before the Magistrates' Court, alleging contravention of the notices contrary to *section 58(4)* of the 1974 Act and ALFML was convicted. On appeal, it was found that a nuisance existed and that the company had not complied with the abatement notices. The appeal was however, allowed because the court held that a defence that would have been open to ALFML had the tenants brought a civil action was a valid defence under the section 58 proceedings brought by the local authority i.e. that the tenants had full knowledge of the existence of the lifts before entering into the leases and therefore had implicitly consented to their presence. ALFML also contended that as the notices were not justified by the terms of *section 58*, they could use the 'reasonable excuse' defence under *section 58(4)*. The Crown Court stated a case for the opinion of the High Court at the request of the local authority.

Test: The High Court held that the only relevance of the tort of nuisance to *section 58* proceedings is to act as a standard to establish whether the level of noise that exists is a nuisance. It is not necessary however to show that the nuisance would be actionable at the suit of the party aggrieved. Once the existence of a noise nuisance has been established, the *section 58* procedures take over, and any defence based on duties in tort or contract to the person affected by the nuisance are not available. On the question of the 'reasonable excuse' defence under *section 58(4)* of the 1974 Act, it was ruled that this defence cannot apply where matters could have been raised on appeal under *section 58(3)*, unless these matters have arisen after the appeal was heard or, if there was no appeal, after the time for appeals has expired. As the company had not put forward any special reason for not appealing using the *section 58(3)* mechanism, it could not be permitted to use the reasonable excuse defence as this was not designed to give the recipient of an abatement notice a choice of forum in which to attack a notice. The reasonable excuse defence is only available for instances where there is some special difficulty in complying with a notice.

Decision: The case was remitted to the Magistrates' Court with a direction to restore the conviction.

London Borough of Tower Hamlets v Manzoni and Another (May 1983) High Court ((1984) 148 JP 123)

[B14.21]

noise; statutory nuisance

Background: The London Borough of Tower Hamlets served abatement notices on two people demonstrating against the sale of pets in a street market. The demonstration involved the chanting of slogans using a megaphone during the day. The council made use of the statutory nuisance provisions of *Part III* of the *Control of Pollution Act 1974* because *section 62* of that Act, dealing with noise in the street, only prohibits the use of non-trade or business loudspeakers between 9 p.m. and 8 a.m. The *section 58(1)* notices required the demonstrators to restrict the recurrence of the nuisance, to cease the use of the amplification devices in the street and to ensure that the noise level created by the demonstration activities did not exceed the background noise level in the area.

The demonstrators appealed against the serving of the notices and the requirement concerning the reduction of the noise to the background noise level was deleted. The other terms of the notice were upheld however and the demonstrators appealed to the Crown Court, this time claiming that *section 58* did not apply to nuisance caused by noise in the street. The appeal was allowed and the local authority appealed to the High Court.

Test: Although the plain words of *section 58(1)* do not restrict its ambit to noise from premises, when *Part III* of the Act is read as a whole, *section 58(1)* should be construed as being subject to that restriction. The statutory nuisance provisions do not therefore apply to noise generated in the street, only to noise from premises.

Decision: The appeal was dismissed.

Comment: This case made an important distinction between the types of noise that may be subject to the statutory nuisance procedures of the 1974 Act. These provisions and the corresponding provisions of the *EPA 1990* (which apply in England and Wales) have been amended by the *Noise and Statutory Nuisance Act 1993*, to add noise emitted from or caused by a vehicle, machinery or equipment in a street to the list of activities that may be considered to be a statutory nuisance.

Polychronakis v Richards and Jerrom Ltd (16 October 1997) High Court, Queen's Bench Division (Times Law Reports, 19 November 1997)

[B14.22]

nuisance; statutory nuisance; burden of proof; reasonable excuse; abatement notice

Background: Richards and Jerrom Ltd was acquitted of a charge under *section 80(4)* and (6) of the *EPA 1990* for failing to comply with an abatement notice served under *section 80(1)* of that Act. The company had raised the defence of reasonable excuse. Mr John Polychronakis, prosecutor on behalf of Dudley Metropolitan

Borough Council, appealed against the decision of the Magistrates' Court on the basis that it was for the defendant to prove and not for the prosecution to disprove the defence of reasonable excuse.

Test: The court had to consider on where the burden of proof rested for the reasonable excuse defence.

Decision: The appeal was allowed because of prosecution evidence that had been overlooked by the justices. On the matter of the burden of proof, the High Court ruled that whether it was for the defendants to prove or for the prosecution to disprove, the defence of reasonable excuse depended on the construction of the statute. Unlike the defences in *sections 80(8)* and *(9)* which explicitly place the burden of proof on the defendant, there was nothing in the rest of *section 80* to indicate that this was the case. Therefore, once the defendant had put forward evidence for the reasonable excuse defence, it was for the prosecution to prove beyond all reasonable doubt that the excuse was not a reasonable one.

R v Carrick District Council, ex parte Shelley and Another (3 April 1996) High Court, Queen's Bench Division (Times Law Reports, 15 April 1996)

[B14.23]

nuisance; statutory nuisance; prejudicial to health abatement notice; service

Background: For several years, complaints had been made concerning the presence of sewage-related debris on the beach at Porthtowan. A survey conducted by the National Rivers Authority in 1990-91, placed the beach in the worst of four categories of contamination by sewage. Subsequently, one of two sewage outfalls in the area was screened but no comparable survey had been conducted to allow the effect of this action to be determined. Carrick District Council investigated the problem and evidence was submitted to a council committee, which resolved that no action would be taken save for continued monitoring of the situation. It was not considered appropriate to serve an abatement notice. Following this decision, local residents applied for judicial review of the council's resolution.

Test: Under *section 79(1)(e)* of the *EPA 1990*, any accumulation or deposit which is prejudicial to health or a nuisance is a statutory nuisance. Once a statutory nuisance has been found to exist, a local authority has a duty, not a discretion, to serve an abatement notice. The council did not reach any decision as to whether a nuisance existed, just that it was 'not appropriate' to serve a notice. The use of the word 'appropriate' implied the exercise of discretion rather than judgement of fact.

Decision: The High Court found that the council had not discharged its statutory duty under *Part III* of the 1990 Act to investigate a potential statutory nuisance and its resolution must be reconsidered.

Comment: This case demonstrates the important distinction between the duties of local authorities and those functions where there is a degree of discretion.

R v Liverpool Crown Court, ex parte Cooke (3 April 1996) Queen's Bench Divisional Court, (Times Law Reports, 22 April 1996)

[B14.24]

statutory nuisance; nuisance; compensation; judicial review

Background: This was judicial review by Jacqueline Cooke against an earlier judgement which, whilst convicting Liverpool City Council of a statutory nuisance, restricted compensation merely to the period of the nuisance stipulated in the summons. The summons, which concerned a nuisance under *section 79(1)(a)* and *(e)* of the *EPA 1990,* merely stated that on the date the summons was issued, there was a statutory nuisance. The nuisance had in fact existed for many months before the date of the summons but the summons did not claim compensation for that earlier period.

Decision: The court held that there was no warrant for construing the provisions of the 1990 Act, so as to entitle a court to take account of the whole period for which the nuisance was alleged to have existed in the absence of a proper pleading of that effect in the summons.

Comment: This case emphasises the need to focus very carefully on the technical provisions of summonses and notices in respect of statutory nuisances.

Issa and Another v Hackney London Borough Council (19 November 1996) Court of Appeal ([1996] EGCS 184)

[B14.25]

nuisance; statutory nuisance; civil liability; criminal liability

Background: In June 1989, Hackney London Borough Council pleaded guilty to an offence under *section 99* of the *Public Health Act 1936* of causing a statutory nuisance. The nuisance was in relation to premises which were severely affected with condensation and associated mould growth which was prejudicial to health. The council was fined and ordered to pay compensation to Issa's father. The court also ordered that the nuisance be abated. The necessary abatement works were completed in December 1989. In July 1992, Issa and another, suing by their father, brought an action claiming damages for the ill health which they alleged they had suffered as a result of their occupation of the premises. As a preliminary issue, the judge decided that criminal conviction was enough to establish that the council would be liable for any loss or damage suffered by Issa. At the trial the judge awarded damages to Issa.

Decision: On appeal to the Court of Appeal, the council submitted that civil liability did not arise simply as a result of the commission of a criminal offence under *Part III* of the *Public Health Act 1936.*

Comment: The court allowed the appeal on the grounds that *Part III* of the 1936 Act was simply designed to deal with the abatement of statutory nuisances, and it should not be construed so as to create a civil liability. When a person was found guilty under the 1936 Act, he was not therefore automatically liable in a civil action to any person who suffered loss or damage as a result of the matter which gave rise to the criminal proceedings.

Hollis v Dudley Metropolitan Borough Council; Probert v Dudley Metropolitan Borough Council (25 November 1997) Queen's Bench Divisional Court, (Times Law Reports, 12 December 1997)

[B14.26]

statutory nuisance; private enforcement; costs; abatement order

Background: This case concerned the question of costs incurred by individuals in bringing statutory nuisance proceedings for an abatement order. Mrs Hollis and Mr Probert appealed against the decision of Dudley Magistrates' Court to disallow all the costs they incurred in bringing the statutory nuisance proceedings under *section 82* of the *EPA 1990* against Dudley Metropolitan Borough Council.

Test: *Section 82(12)* of the *EPA 1990* states that where such proceedings are brought, and it is proven that the alleged nuisance existed at the time that the complaint was made 'the court shall order the defendant to pay the person bringing the proceedings such amount as the court considers reasonably sufficient to compensate him for any expenses properly incurred by him in the proceedings'.

Decision: It was held that a court is obliged to award costs to individuals bringing statutory nuisance proceedings seeking an abatement order. Those costs should cover those necessarily incurred, including those incurred in investigating whether a nuisance exists.

Comment: This is an important decision with regard to the access of ordinary individuals to the judicial mechanisms designed to trigger the statutory nuisance enforcement procedures where local authorities themselves have failed to act. Obviously, the costs of so doing may be a significant deterrent to members of the public in many cases.

SFI Group v Gosport Borough Council (28 January 1998) Queen's Bench Divisional Court (NLD, 29 January 1998)

[B14.27]

statutory notice; abatement notice; best practicable means

Background: On 25 August 1995, Gosport Borough Council served an abatement notice on SFI Group under *section 80(1)* of the *EPA 1990*. On 13 September 1995, SFI appealed to the Magistrates' Court under *section 80(3)* of the 1990 Act. The appeal was dismissed. SFI then appealed to the Crown Court. The Crown Court held that there was a statutory nuisance as at 25 August which, at the date of the magistrates' hearing, was likely to recur. Although the best practicable means to prevent a recurrence of the nuisance had not been taken by the date of the hearing, such measures had been taken by the date of the Crown Court hearing. As a result, the nuisance did not exist nor was it likely to recur. The Crown Court therefore quashed the abatement notice. The council appealed to the High Court to determine whether the Crown Court looked at the correct date when assessing the likelihood of occurrence of the nuisance.

Decision: The court held that the date to be taken into account by both the Magistrates' Court and the Crown Courts, was the date when the abatement notice was served.

R v Bristol City Council, ex parte Everett (13 May 1998) High Court, Queen's Bench Division (Times Law Reports, 27 May 1998)

[B14.28]

statutory nuisance; physical injury; judicial review

Background: Ms Everett, the tenant of a nineteenth century house in Bristol, suffered from a back injury. As a result, she had difficulty in negotiating a steep internal staircase at the premises. Ms Everett contended that the staircase gave rise to a statutory nuisance under *section 79(1)(a)* of the *EPA 1990*. Initially, Bristol City Council appeared to share Ms Everett's view. In December 1994, the council served an abatement notice on the landlord pursuant to *section 80* of the 1990 Act, requiring the replacement of the existing staircase. However, in December 1996, the council informed Ms Everett that the staircase could not be considered a statutory nuisance and that the abatement notice had been incorrectly served. Ms Everett applied for judicial review of the council's decision.

Test: The court had to consider the extent to which *section 78* of the 1990 Act applied to physical injuries caused by an accident.

Decision: The court decided that the similar expressions used in earlier statutes related to the direct effect on human health of filthy or unwholesome premises (and in particular the risk of illness), rather than physical injury. The court could not see any reason for widening the scope of the current statutory nuisance provisions. Accordingly, the court held that premises in such a state as to increase the risk of an accident, but not the risk of illness, did not constitute a statutory nuisance for the purposes of *section 79(1)(a)*.

Comment: The decision in this case would seem to make it clear that the statutory nuisance provisions cannot be extended to cases of actual or potential physical injuries.

East Staffordshire Borough Council v Fairless (14 October 1998) High Court, Queen's Bench Division ([1998] All ER (D) 456)

[B14.29]

statutory nuisance; abatement notice; forum; warning notice; abatement order

Background: Mr Fairless, a council tenant, sent a letter to East Staffordshire Borough Council, informing it that the premises occupied by him were prejudicial to the health of the occupants and constituted a statutory nuisance under *section 79(1)* of the *EPA 1990*. He instituted proceedings for an abatement order under the 1990 Act and a summons was issued on 5 January 1998. The magistrates found there had been a statutory nuisance in existence at the date of laying the information but that this had been abated by the 5 January. The information was dismissed but the magistrates made an order that the council pay Mr Fairless' costs. The council appealed on the grounds that the tenant had not served a valid warning notice under *section 82(6)* of the 1990 Act, neither specifying the works required to remedy the complaint, nor identifying the capacity in which the proposed defendant was to be proceeded against.

Test: The court had to consider the form of the notice given under *section 82(6)*.

Decision: The appeal was dismissed. It was held that there was no prescribed form for a notice under *section 82(6)*. The 1990 Act expressly sets out the requirements for an abatement notice and it was not necessary to imply additional requirements. The warning notice must specify the matter which is being complained of but there is no need for it to specify measures necessary to abate the nuisance, nor to state the capacity in which the proposed defendant was being requested to abate the nuisance.

Southwark London Borough Council v Simpson (3 November 1998) High Court, Queen's Bench Division ([1998] PLSCS 283)

[B14.30]

statutory nuisance; structural defect prejudicial to health; expert witness

Background: Ms Simpson was the occupier of premises owned by Southwark London Borough Council. In 1997, she made a complaint against the council that she was aggrieved by a statutory nuisance under *section 79(1)(a)* of the EPA 1990 arising from a structural defect. The nuisance itself resulted from dampness and mould which Ms Simpson claimed was prejudicial to health. In the Magistrates' Court hearing, a chartered surveyor gave evidence on behalf of Ms Simpson. He stated that, although he had no medical experience to confirm the claim that the dampness was prejudicial to health, he had read various articles stating that similar dampness problems had been found to be so. The Magistrates' Court found in favour of Ms Simpson, holding that it had been proved beyond reasonable doubt that the premises were in such a state as to be prejudicial to health. The council appealed, contending that there had not been produced before the court any expert evidence proving the premises were prejudicial to health. It was submitted that the evidence of the surveyor was not sufficient because he was not a medical expert and, in any event, he had no relevant experience but merely relied on articles he had read which he had neither shown nor given details of to the magistrates.

Test: Whether the evidence of the surveyor was relevant and sufficient as to the question of whether or not premises were prejudicial to health.

Decision: The appeal was allowed.

Comment: The court held that although it was not necessary for an expert to have medical knowledge to give evidence as to whether a nuisance is prejudicial to health, he was required to have experience in the relevant field. The surveyor had had no such experience, merely relying on articles he had read. An appropriate person to provide the evidence would have been an environmental housing officer, who would have had the relevant experience.

R v Falmouth and Truro Port Health Authority, ex parte South West Water Ltd (23 April 1999) High Court, Queen's Bench Division (Times Law Reports, 9 May 1999)

[B14.31]

statutory nuisance; duty to consult; abatement notice; water course; judicial review

Background: The case involved an application for judicial review of decisions made on the 11 May and 1 July 1998 by Falmouth & Truro Port Health Authority to serve an abatement notice on South West Water (SWW), under *section 80* of the *EPA 1990.* The abatement notice alleged that sewage discharges into a watercourse which was part of an estuary had caused a statutory nuisance contrary to *section 259(1)(a)* of the *Public Health Act 1936* as amended by the 1990 Act. SWW argued that Falmouth & Truro Port Health Authority had a duty to consult prior to serving the notice.

Test: Whether the authority had a duty to consult prior to service of an abatement notice.

Decision: The court held that an enforcing authority is not under a duty to consult an alleged perpetrator, prior to serving that person with an abatement notice. The authority had, however, in this case, approached SWW to enquire what steps it would take to resolve the dispute. The judge indicated that this gave rise to a legitimate expectation of consultation which, if not carried through, could make the issuing of an abatement notice susceptible to a judicial review. However, the judge agreed with SWW in that *section 259(1)(a)* of the 1936 Act, applied to a limited area of water and could not include an estuary. The abatement notice was invalid as it failed to specify the works necessary to abate the nuisance. On these grounds, SWW's application was granted.

Comment: This case raised interesting questions about the extent of consultation an enforcing authority may wish to undertake prior to serving an abatement notice.

Trespass

Director of Public Prosecution v Barnard and Others (9 November 1999) High Court, Queen's Bench Division (Times Law Reports, 9 November 1999)

[B15.1]

aggravated trespass; environment protestors

Background: A group of trespassers gathered on land in the open air at Doe Hill Quarry, Derby on the 31 October 1997. They unlawfully entered the land with the intention of intimidating persons who were already on the land and about to engage in the lawful activity of open cast mining. Their intention was to deter the miners from engaging in the mining activity or obstructing or disrupting that activity. *Section 68* of the *Criminal Justice and Public Order Act 1994* makes aggravated trespass an offence i.e. to trespass on land in the open air with the intention of (a) intimidating persons so as to deter them from engaging in an activity; (b) of obstructing that activity or; (c) of disrupting that activity. The court then went on to consider whether the acts of the intimidators were sufficient to constitute a trespass. The prosecution brought an application for leave to amend the information which stated that the respondents unlawfully entered on land and committed an act of aggravated trespass.

Test: This case involved the principle that the occupation of land can only constitute the offence of aggravate trespass to those occupying the land with intent to intimidate, obstruct or disrupt. The principle only applies if the occupation is overt and distinct from a mere act of trespass.

Decision: The court cited Lord Justice Shiemann in *Winder and Others v Director of Public Prosecutions (Times Law Reports, 14 August*

1996), which lay three elements required to establish aggravated trespass. These elements are (1) trespass, (2) intention to disrupt any lawful activity and (3) an act done to that end. The judge found that the allegations that the trespassers had committed meant that they had 'unlawfully entered on land' the offence of trespass but not of aggravated trespass. Proof was required of trespassing on land in the open air and doing a distinct and overt act, other than the act of trespassing. The court held that unlawful occupation is sufficient to establish original trespass but is not enough to constitute the second criteria of intention to intimidate.

Waste

R v Canterbury Crown Court, ex parte Kent County Council (16 June 1993) Queen's Bench Divisional Court ([1994] Env. L.R. 192)

[B16.1]

waste; costs; settlement

Background: Kent County Council had served a notice under *section 16* of the *Control of Pollution Act 1974* (the *COPA 1974)*, in respect of the presence and migration of noxious substances from a refuse tip owned by Wakeley Brothers (Rainham Kent) Ltd. The matters which were the subject of that notice were settled by consent between the parties. The only issues remaining for the court related to an order for costs made by the Magistrates' Court. The magistrates ordered that the council pay the costs and the council sought to appeal the decision on the grounds that the costs were not appropriate or reasonable.

Decision: Ordinarily, in proceedings before a Magistrates' Court, it is the magistrates themselves who consider who should pay the costs and in what sum. This is because there are no taxation provisions available for the assessment of costs. No appeal lies against a magistrates' costs order under the general provisions governing the exercise of powers by magistrates. To overcome that hurdle, the council sought to argue that the award of costs was not made by the magistrates solely pursuant to their general powers. They argued that it was also a decision made 'in pursuance' of the *COPA 1974* and that, therefore, there was a right of appeal under *section 85* of that Act. The court rejected that argument.

The court held that a simple costs order was not an order made pursuant to the *COPA 1974*.

Comment: The practical point to be derived from this case is that, bearing in mind that many enforcement disputes are settled prior to trial at court, the parties should properly provide for the payment of costs in their terms of settlement.

Euro Tombesi and Adino Tombesi, Roberto Santella, Giobanni Muzi and Others, Anselno Savini (25 June 1997) European Court of Justice (Joined Cases C–224/95, C–304/94, C–330/94, C–342/94 (25 June 1997) (ECJ), [1997] All ER (EC) 639)

[B16.2]

European Union; definition of waste; recyclable material

Background: These joint cases were the latest in a line of rulings by the ECJ on the meaning of 'waste' under the EC legislation. The cases arose from criminal proceedings brought against Tombesi (and others) for illegally handling and disposing of waste without the appropriate authorisation. The Italian courts referred a number of questions to the ECJ for a preliminary ruling under *Article 177* of the *1957 Treaty*.

Advocate General Jacob, in his opinion dated 24 October 1996, stated that the community rules on waste applied to 'substances or objects which the holder discards or intends or is required to discard, even where they are capable of reuse' or where they have a commercial value.

Decision: The court ruled that it was settled law that the definition of waste under *Directive 75/442/EEC (the Waste Framework Directive)*, was not to be understood as excluding substances and objects capable of economic re-utilisation. It held that the same applies to the definition of waste as set out in *Directive 91/156/EEC* which amends *Directive 75/442/EEC*.

The ECJ held that waste includes all discarded objects, whether or not they have economic value and are collected on a commercial basis for recycling, reclamation or reuse. This applies whether or not the materials may be the subject of a commercial transaction or are quoted on public or private commercial lists.

In his earlier opinion on these cases, Advocate General Jacobs was also of the view that a deactivation process intended to render waste harmless (including incineration), together with landfilling in hollows and embankments, were all disposal or recovery operations and, hence, subject to Community law.

The decision of the ECJ followed the Advocate General Jacob's opinion in all these respects, as well as his views on what which substances the Community rules on waste applied to.

Comment: This case is in a long line of ECJ and UK domestic cases regarding the complex issue of the definition of waste. Later cases have developed the definition further (see *Inter-Environment Wallonie v Region Wallonne (1997), Mayer Parry Recycling Ltd v Environment Agency (1998),* see also *Vesosso & Zanetti*). It was hoped that this case would put an end to the uncertainty which has surrounded this definition. However, as the subsequent cases highlight, this has not happened.

Inter-Environment Wallonie v Region Wallonne (18 December 1997) European Court of Justice (FT, 6 January 1998, [1998] All ER (EC) 155)

[B16.3]

European Union; definition of waste; recyclable material

Background: Inter-Environment Wallonie, a Belgian environmental interest group, commenced proceedings against the Walloon Region of Belgium, alleging that the Walloon Region's implementation of *Directive 75/442/EEC* (the *Waste Framework Directive*) as amended by *Directive 91/156/EEC* was flawed. Under the Directive, any company carrying out the disposal or recovery of waste must be required to obtain a permit. The only exception provided for this is where companies carry out disposal or recovery of their own waste at the place of production. This exception is not to be applied to hazardous waste.

The implementing Order in the Walloon Region exempted from the permitting requirement installations carrying out the collection, pre-treatment, disposal or recovery of toxic or dangerous waste. This applied in the instance where the installation was an integral part of an industrial process. The Belgian Conseil d'Etat considered that the Order contravened EC law but noted that it was adopted during the period allowed for implementation of the Directive. The Conseil d'Etat therefore referred to the ECJ the question of to what extent EU member states could adopt legislation contrary to a Directive, during the period allowed for implementation. The Conseil d'Etat referred a further question to the ECJ asking, in relation to the *Directive 75/442/EEC* definition of waste, whether waste includes substances which directly or indirectly form an integral part of an industrial process.

Inter-Environment Wallonie and the EC took the view that legislation implementing a Directive, which is adopted prior to the end of the period allowed for implementation, has to be consistent with the Directive's provisions. Submissions from Belgium, France and the UK took the stance that, in such circumstances, member states could still adopt legislation which is inconsistent with the Directive's provisions. The UK added the caveat to this that it would be unlawful to adopt national legislation that would prevent or hinder the correct transposition of the Directive into domestic law.

Test: The ECJ worked from the basic rule that EU member states are obliged to take all necessary measures to ensure the intended effect of a Directive is achieved. Directives have legal effect under the *1957 Treaty* from the date of their notification. Where an implementation period is provided, member states are only obliged to ensure implementation by the end of that period. However, they must also take necessary measures during that period to ensure that the Directive is effectively transposed by the end of that period. The ECJ ruled that during the period allowed for implementation, member states could not take measures liable to seriously compromise the aims of the Directive. In assessing any particular case, the national court should look at whether the national legislation fully implements the Directive and whether in practical terms the provisions are incompatible.

Decision: On the second question referred to it, the ECJ stated that the meaning of 'waste' turns on the meaning of the term 'discard' and this covers both the disposal and recovery of a substance or object. The definition of waste does not exclude substances or objects capable of economic re-utilisation. However, it is important to remember that there is a distinction between normal waste recovery and the treatment of substances or objects which are not waste.

Comment: In its decision, the ECJ sought to explain the definition of 'waste' with a different focus, shifting away from the term 'discard'. Instead, the focus was on whether the waste is sent for disposal or recovery. In doing so, it sought to avoid acknowledging that the effect of its decision moved towards making the word 'discard' irrelevant. See also *Euro Tombesi and Adino Tombesi, Roberto Santella, Giobanni Muzi and others, Anselno Savini (1997), Mayer Parry Recycling Limited v Environment Agency (1998), Vesosso & Zanetti.*

R v Gray (February 1995) Crown Court ((1995) 241 ENDS 43)

[B16.4]

fly tipping; chemical waste

Background: Mr Gray was found to have dumped 4.45 gallon drums, along with other smaller drums, of chemicals including formaldehyde, ammonia. acetic acid, sodium pentachlorophenate and hydrogen peroxide in a residential street in Plaistow. The Waste Regulation Authority had served a notice under *section 71* of the *EPA 1990* on Mr Gray, requiring information on where he had taken the chemicals. He did not enter the information correctly.

Decision: Mr Gray was found guilty on three counts and was sentenced to: eighteen months imprisonment for depositing waste in a manner likely to cause harm to human health or pollution contrary to *section 33(1)(c)* of the *EPA 1990*; a further six months imprisonment (running concurrently) for supplying false and misleading information in response to the *section 71* Notice; and to one day's imprisonment or a fine of £100 for failing to supply transfer notices required by *section 34(1)(c)* of the *EPA 1990.*

Renfrew District Council v Gotec Industrial and Environmental Services (1995) High Court ((1995) 242 ENDS 44)

[B16.5]

asbestos; special waste

Background: Gotec Industrial and Environmental Services, whose business included asbestos stripping, was appointed as a sub-contractor to remove certain asbestos lagging from pipework in a church boilerhouse in Paisley in 1993. It removed the asbestos in plastic bags to its premises. Some weeks later the bags were discovered by environmental health officers from the District Council. Gotec was subsequently convicted in the Sheriff's Court of several offences (including offences under *section 3(1)(a) and (b)* of the *COPA 1974* and of not providing consignment notes of the waste contrary to the *Control of Pollution (Special Waste) Regulations 1980 (SI 1980 No 1709)*. Gotec appealed on several grounds, none of which were relevant. These included a challenge to the right of the environmental health officers to enter Gotec's premises. Such officers have rights to enter any 'land' pursuant to *section 91* of the *COPA 1974.*

Test: The court applied a common sense interpretation to the words 'land' and 'producer'.

Decision: The court did not accept Gotec's suggestion that 'land' does not include buildings. More significantly, Gotec argued that the *Control of Pollution (Special Waste) Regulations 1980* did not apply because Gotec was not the 'producer' of the waste asbestos (the producer was either the church or the church's contractors). That again was rejected by the court.

The court held that since Gotec was employed to break up the pipe lagging, they were responsible for producing the waste.

Gotec was also convicted of offences under *section 3(1)* of the *HSWA 1974* for its unsafe handling of the plastic bags of asbestos.

Comment: Whilst the waste aspects of this case were dealt with under the provisions of the *COPA 1974*, the comments of the court relating to the responsibilities for waste, where a chain of persons are involved, may be very pertinent to the duty of care as respects waste posed by the *EPA 1990.*

NRA v Aquaspersions (25 November 1994) Magistrates' Court ((1995) 240 ENDS 43)

[B16.6]

water pollution; trade effluent

Background: Aquaspersions admitted to having washed several hundred litres of Thiram (a vulcanising agent which is highly toxic to fish) into sewers which connect up to the Redacre Sewerage Treatment Works. The incident occurred after a storage tank had been overfilled. A subsequent discharge from Redacre Sewerage Works, which contained Thiram, led to the death of some 30,000 fish in the River Calder. The NRA was forced to bring this prosecution under the waste provisions of the *EPA 1990*, namely *section 33*, which prohibits the unauthorised or harmful treatment, deposit or disposal of waste.

Decision: The NRA was successful. Aquaspersions pleaded guilty and was fined £5,000 and ordered to pay costs of £13,000.

Comment: This case is interesting since the prosecution successfully used legislation relating to waste when the case essentially concerned water pollution.

Devon Waste Regulation Authority v X (26 February 1996) Crown Court ((1996) 254 ENDS 53)

[B16.7]

planning; waste storage; waste disposal; planning

Background: In November 1991 and March 1994, X, a farmer, dumped rubble, stone, sand and mud on a part of his farmland in Kenton. The farmer claimed that the waste was to be used for the foundations and floor of a barn. The Waste Regulation Authority had warned him that it could only be stored for a maximum of three months albeit that it remained there for over three years.

In February 1995, the Waste Regulation Authority secured a conviction of the farmer for offences under the *COPA 1974* and the *EPA 1990*. The farmer was fined £3,000 and ordered to pay costs. The farmer appealed.

In January 1996, the Waste Regulation Authority was consulted by Teignbridge District Council over the farmer's application for a Certificate of Lawfulness for the Deposit. The Waste Regulation Authority objected to the application. However, the authority was not informed that on 23 February 1996 a Certificate of Lawfulness had been issued to the farmer by the district council.

Decision: In an appeal before the Crown Court on 26 February 1996, which was allowed, the conviction was quashed on the basis of the new found Certificate of Lawfulness.

Comment: This case emphasises the close relationship between environmental law and planning law and potential conflict between the two.

The Shanks & McEwan (Midlands) Ltd v Wrexham Maelor Borough Council (18 March 1996) Queen's Bench Divisional Court (Times Law Reports, 19 April 1996)

[B16.8]

landfill; waste management licence; operator; licence holder

Background: Shanks & McEwan (Midlands) Ltd successfully appealed against a conviction by Wrexham Magistrates' Court for breach of a waste management licence concerning a landfill. The waste management licence in question, required the landfill surface to be covered with uncontaminated soil at the end of each working day. Shanks & McEwan (Midlands) Ltd was the licence holder but was not the company operating the site.

Test: The court applied a natural meaning to the words 'a person who contravenes' in *section 33(6)*. It concluded that the site operator had, by its failure to act, contravened the licence and not the licence holder, in this case Shanks & McEwan.

Decision: On the appeal, the court held that *section 33(6)* of the *EPA 1990*, pursuant to which Shanks had been convicted, contemplated the person who was in actual occupation of the site rather than the licence holder (the person in occupation could, of course, also be the licence holder but that was not the case in this instance). For a person to contravene the condition of the waste management licence, it was necessary for that person to be a person by whom the offence was committed. It was not Shanks in this case.

Comment: This case is of importance when analysing actual or potential breaches of waste management licences and when analysing or drafting licence agreements. It is not uncommon for a licence holder and operator to be different companies.

Hunts Refuse Disposals Ltd v Norfolk Environmental Waste Services Ltd (22 May 1996) Court of Appeal ([1996] NPC 88)

[B16.9]

lease; licence; restoration; landfill

Background: Two disputes arose between the parties relating to their respective rights in or about a landfill at Priory Farm, King's Lynn. The dispute centred around two documents labelled 'Licences' and dated 15 May 1974 and 11 August 1986. Neither Hunts nor Norfolk Environmental were party to those licences. A complex contractual relationship existed between the parties. Hunts stood in the position of the owner and Norfolk Environmental stood in the position of licensee/lessee. The licences were expressed to expire on 14 May 1995. On expiry, Hunts planned to commence its own landfilling at the site. Norfolk Environmental, however, claimed that it was occupying the landfill not as licensee but as lessee. It claimed it was entitled to remain at the landfill until after 14 May 1995, pursuant to the protection provided by *Part 2* of the *Landlord and Tenant Act 1954*. The parties agreed that the deciding factor was whether or not Norfolk Environmental had 'exclusive possession' to the landfill.

Test: In establishing whether or not Norfolk Environmental had 'exclusive occupation', the court looked to the wording of the licence and the overall facts of the case.

Decision: Both the court at first instance and the Court of Appeal decided that Norfolk Environmental did not have exclusive occupation. This issue was therefore decided in favour of Hunts and Norfolk Environmental was required to vacate the site.

The second issue related to the calculation of rent payable by Norfolk Environmental to Hunts for landfilling between the years 1993–1994. Clause 2(6) of the relevant licence stated that: 'a rent at the rate of 10p per cubic yard [later adjusted] of dry waste deposited at the site during each year of the period of the Licence

Period the volume to be calculated at the end of each year in accordance with the provisions of clause 3(2) . . .'. Clause 3(2) stated that 'For the purpose of calculating the amount of dry waste so deposited a survey of the available air space shall be taken at the commencement of the Licence Period and at each anniversary thereof by a firm of Chartered Surveyors to be appointed jointly by Grantor and the Licensee the Licensee to be responsible for the Surveyors' charges. In the event of any dispute between the parties as to the amount of dry waste deposited in any year of the Licence Period the decision of such Chartered Surveyors based on the difference between the available airspace at the beginning and end of each year shall be finding and binding upon the parties. In calculating the differences in such airspace the Surveyor can have due regard to any additional airspace created in connection with the extraction of minerals during the relevant year.'

Hunts argued that the effect of these clauses was that any airspace consumed at the site, whether by waste itself or by engineering works such as lining or capping, was subject to the payment of rent. Norfolk Environmental argued that rent was only payable on the volume of air space consumed by waste and not by materials used to contain waste and to restore the site. On this issue, the judge at first instance and two of the three lord justices in the appeal held in favour of Hunts.

Comment: The distinction between licensee and lessee is often litigated in relation to other activities. This case is the first reported decision in the context of a landfill.

Yorkshire Water Services Ltd v Sun Alliance and London Insurance plc and Others (20 August 1996) Court of Appeal (Times Law Reports, 20 August 1996)

[B16.10]

insurance; sudden and accidental damage; flood alleviation; water pollution; land fill; water pollution

Background: Yorkshire Water Services Ltd was the owner/operator of a landfill on the banks of the River Colne. On 12 February 1992, an embankment of the landfill failed and a large quantity of sewage sludge escaped and was deposited in the River Colne and neighbouring sewerage works owned and operated by Yorkshire Water. ICI initiated proceedings against Yorkshire Water, claiming that its neighbouring operations had been damaged. These proceedings were subsequently settled.

Yorkshire Water carried out urgent flood alleviation works costing £4,601,061 in order to prevent further damage to its own property and property of others.

Yorkshire Water claimed against Sun Alliance, London Insurance and others ('insurers'), that it was entitled to recover the amount spent on the flood alleviation works under its insurance policies taken out with them. The insurers rejected this insurance claim on the grounds, amongst others, of material non-disclosure and that in any event Yorkshire Water's losses were irrecoverable under the terms of the insurance policy. The insurers maintained that the costs of flood alleviation works were not recoverable under the terms of the policy.

Decision: At court, the following preliminary issues arose: (1) whether the cost of the flood alleviation works were the subject of any indemnity under the express terms of the insurance policies; and (2) whether Yorkshire water was entitled, by virtue of implied terms of the policies, to recover the costs of the flood alleviation works. The judge found in favour of the insurers.

Yorkshire Water appealed to the Court of Appeal in respect of those issues. In relation to the first issue, the Court of Appeal held that the express terms of the policies did not extend to the cost of flood alleviation works. In relation to the second issue, the Court of Appeal also found for the insurers that there were no implied terms under the insurance policies and, in any event, the cost of alleviation works was excluded by the express terms of the policies.

Comment: Obtaining and claiming under insurance policies in respect of environment related risks has presented difficulties for some years. Although the market for insurance covering environment related risks is improving, it is important to focus carefully on the wording of the policy.

Westminster City Council v John Riding (17 July 1995) Queen's Bench Divisional Court (JPEL, August 1996)

[B16.11]

litter; commercial waste

Background: On 4 August 1994, John Riding was charged with depositing plastic sacks, empty beer and crisp cartons and two empty bread bags, contrary to *section 87(1)* of the *EPA 1990* (offence of leaving litter). In the Magistrates' Court, John Riding made a submission of no case to answer at the conclusion of the prosecution's evidence. He contended, amongst other things, that the litter in question did not amount to litter within the meaning of *section 87(1)*. John Riding claimed that the materials should properly be categorised as 'commercial waste' rather than litter (pursuant to the definition of 'waste' in *section 75* of the *EPA 1990*). It was noted that there was, in fact, no statutory definition of litter.

The magistrates took the view that the word 'litter' was not intended to include street or commercial refuse bagged up and awaiting collection by waste removal contractors. As such, they found that there was no case to answer.

Test: The court held that litter can include household and commercial waste. Whether or not an offence under *section 87* of the *EPA 1990* is committed depends on whether it has been left.

Decision: The council appealed against the magistrates decision. The High Court observed that whilst piles of plastic sacks lining the streets of towns and cities constituted litter of a public place, the issue for the court was to determine whether *section 87* of the *EPA 1990* covered the placing of waste on the pavements for collection. The court considered that the word 'litter' should be given its natural meaning of 'miscellaneous rubbish left lying about'. This definition should include household waste and commercial waste.

Therefore, the rubbish deposited by John Riding was not precluded from being litter. The court went on to say that for an offence under *section 87* of the *EPA 1990* to be committed, proof was required not only of the deposit of such waste in public places but also that the waste had been left there. In relation to the second requirements of the offence, the court referred to the decision in *Vaughan v. Biggs [1960] 1 WLR 622* where it was stated that 'the act . . . is only an offence if it [the waste] is not removed.'

On this occasion, there was no evidence to indicate when the commercial waste was placed on the highway. Therefore, the council had failed to prove that waste was being left there. The appeal was dismissed.

Comment: This case does not resolve how long waste may remain awaiting collection after it has been left. In the event of a dustman's strike would all householders and businesses be committing offences if they put their waste in the street as they normally would?

Rock plc v Alyn and Deeside District Council Planning Authority (The Waste Manager, September 1995)

[B16.12]

planning; landfill; inert waste; active waste

Background: The site in question, a former quarry, had planning permission dating from 1978 for the disposal of sub-soil, rock, topsoil and builders' debris. However, Rock plc was concerned that those materials were in too short supply to allow the site's completion for restoration within a reasonable period. It therefore applied for permission to landfill contaminated soil, together with commercial and industrial waste such as paper, wood and cardboard. The application aroused considerable public reaction. In response, the council suggested a condition controlling the type of waste accepted. Rock plc appealed to the planning inspector.

Decision: The planning inspector was not prepared to accept the council's decision. He said that the question of the type of waste entering a landfill was a question for the Waste Regulation Authority. He argued that the Planning Authority should be concerned with other more traditional matters such as engineering and impact on the local areas.

Comment: This case highlights the legal and practical difficulties of delineating the powers of planning authorities and environmental regulators, particularly in relation to landfill.

Kent County Council v Secretary of State for the Environment and Others (13 July 1995) High Court, Queen's Bench Division ([1995] EGCS 130)

[B16.13]

planning

Background: The site in question was located at Riverhill, Kent. The depositing and processing of inert waste arising from the demolition of walls, buildings etc. and the breaking up of roads, driveways and paths had been taking place at the site since 1945. The planning inspector accepted that planning permission was not required for these activities and therefore that they did not breach planning control. There was, however, no permission for the deposit of waste materials on the land. The plan in question at issue was whether the activities were permitted by the *General Development Order 1988 (SI 1988 No 1813).*

Part 8 of *Schedule 2* of the *General Development Order* allowed for permitted development of 'the deposit of waste material resulting from an industrial process on any land ... use for that purpose on

1 July 1948'. Industrial process meant a process for or incidental to the 'breaking up or demolition of any article'. The local authority disputed the legality of the activities on the basis that waste material deposited on the site did not result from an industrial process as defined in the *General Development Order*. The local authority submitted that the word 'article' was not a term of art and did not include land or realty. The building inspector did not agree.

Decision: The court held in favour of the building inspector. The inspector said that the word 'article' had many meanings and therefore the content of the text in which it occurred was of crucial importance. In the context of the word in the definition of industrial process, it was difficult to see what 'demolition' could refer to if not to a building or a similar thing. Further, there is nothing in the ordinary meaning of the word 'article' that could be taken to exclude parts of buildings such as walls, floorboards and doors etc.

Middleton v Wiggin and Another (14 June 1995) Court of Appeal ([1996] Env. L.R. 17)

[B16.14]

landfill gas; migration; insurance; landfill; disposal

Background: Between 1979 and 1982, Hargreaves Clearwaste Ltd disposed of waste at Loscoe Landfill, Derbyshire, in accordance with the terms of the Waste Disposal Licence. The method of disposal was to build three sided bunds of earth within the site and then to deposit waste into the cells formed by the earth. As each was filled up, it was sealed off with a final wall and then a covering of earth. All waste was covered with soil at the end of each working day.

The natural processes of putrefaction and degradation produce landfill gas. The geological structure of the immediate surroundings of the landfill site enabled some of the landfill gas to migrate laterally, including in the direction of Clarke Avenue.

A bungalow was situated at 51 Clarke Avenue and that bungalow was constructed with an underflow void. Prior to 24 March 1986, a quantity of landfill gas migrated from the Loscoe landfill site and collected below ground level in voids near the bungalow. On 24 March 1986, the landfill gas was released from the void and rode into the underfloor void at 51 Clarke Avenue. The central heating boiler at the property drew air from the underfloor void and, as a result, some landfill gas was drawn into the boiler. The result was an explosion which caused the destruction of the bunglow.

The issue before the Court of Appeal was whether the landfill operator's public liability insurance would cover the liability for the loss suffered by the owners of the property. That issue essentially concerned the legal construction of an endorsement to the policy which stated that: the insurers would not be liable 'in respect of injury, illness, disease, loss or damage arising from the disposal of waste materials in the way the insured or their servants or agents intended to dispose of them unless such claim arises from an accident in the method of disposal'. Analysis of the policy endorsement required the court to enquire into the meaning of the word 'disposal'. In accordance with the usual rules and interpretation of contracts, the court said that the word should be given its ordinary and natural meaning. In that context, it referred to the *Oxford English Dictionary* which defines disposal as 'the action of disposing of, putting away; getting rid of; settling or definite dealing with'.

Decision: The court accepted the dictionary definition of disposal. Having done so, the court rejected the landfill operator's argument that the migration of landfill gas was 'an accident in the method of disposal'. The majority of the judges considered that the disposal by the landfill operator was completed when the waste was buried and covered with soil. As such, the migration of the landfill gas was not an accident in the method of disposal and thus the landfill operator was denied insurance coverage.

Comment: This case underlines the need to carefully analyse and negotiate insurance policy wording in relation to environment related risks. This is still important despite the recent improvement in the market for environment insurance.

Shropshire Waste Regulation Authority v Severn Trent Water (October 1995) Magistrates' Court ((1995) 250 ENDS 45)

[B16.15]

duty of care; waste management licence

Background: Severn Trent Water pleaded guilty to two waste offences under the *EPA 1990,* after illegally disposing of drums of anti-foam liquid at a landfill site. The offences were a failure to provide an accurate written description of the waste contrary to *section 34(c)(ii)* of the *EPA 1990* and knowingly causing liquid waste in containers to be deposited in breach of the relevant waste management licence contrary to *section 33(1)(a)* of the Act.

Decision: Severn Trent Water was convicted of the two offences. It stated that the incident occurred due to a failure to properly instruct workers in the 'duty of care' obligations imposed by *section 34* of the *EPA 1990.*

Comment: This relatively simple case illustrates how a waste producer can have liability for the disposal of waste. This can be both under the duty of care under *section 34* of the *EPA 1990* and under the more direct offence of knowingly causing waste to be deposited in breach of a waste management licence under *section 33(1)(a)* of that Act.

R v Environment Agency, ex parte Dockgrange Ltd and Another (22 May 1997) High Court, Queen's Bench Division (Times Law Reports, 21 June 1997)

[B16.16]

transfrontier; shipment of waste; judicial review

Background: Dockgrange Ltd and Mayer Parry Recycling Ltd applied for judicial review of the decision of the EA, to take enforcement action against them. They sought a declaration on the correct interpretation to be given to *Regulation 259/93* on the transfrontier shipment of waste.

Regulation 259/93 operates on a system of categorising shipments of waste for recovery in red, amber and green lists, according to the risks they impose to the environment. Green list wastes are the least regulated as they pose the lowest risk to the environment. Red list waste and waste unassigned to a list are subject to stricter requirements.

The applicants both imported processed mixed waste, the contents of which would alone all be green list wastes. The EA took the view in 1996 that 'car fragmentiser waste' was not assigned to any of the lists and therefore the red list procedure applied. The delay caused in obtaining prior notification and the reluctance of the German authorities to treat the waste as red list waste, prevented the applicants from importing the materials.

Decision: The court held that there was nothing preventing mixed waste from falling into the green list as long as all the individual constituents were identified in that list.

Whilst the court considered it appropriate for the EA to have a policy on the matter, it took the view that the existing policy did not allow sufficient flexibility. The question of whether the Regulation had been sufficiently complied with in this case, was a matter for the criminal court due to hear the prosecution.

Comment: This was a significant case on the interpretation of *Regulation 259/93*. It demonstrates that the courts are prepared to rule against the EA policies which lack flexibility and are perhaps over cautious.

R v Lloyds Environmental Waste Management Limited (17 January 1997) Crown Court (ELM, 1997, 9(6), 252)

[B16.17]

pollution of the environment; harm to human health

Background: Four charges were brought against Lloyds Environmental Waste Management Ltd. The charges were for disposing of sewerage waste in a manner likely to cause pollution of the environment or harm to human health under *section 33(1)(c)* of the *EPA 1990.*

Decision: The effect of the judges direction of the jury was that the prosecution need only show that there was a reasonable probability that people would be affected and caused offence by the waste, rather than that people were actually caused offence and affected by the waste. The jury convicted the defendant.

Comment: The direction to the jury significantly eased the burden of proof on the prosecution. *Section 33(1)(c)* is a broad offence and a potentially potent weapon held by the EA.

R v Terence Garrett (1997) Court of Appeal ([1997] 1 Cr App R (S) 109)

[B16.18]

waste carrier; fly tipping; pollution of the environment; harm to human health; clinical waste

Background: Terence Garrett traded as a waste carrier. He stored chemical waste at a site without a waste management licence. On one occasion, he disposed of chemical waste in a refuse skip located on private land. On another occasion, he took chemical waste to an incinerator and stated it was waste paper and cardboard.

The chemical waste caused a fire and would have exploded if it had reached the incinerator itself. Terence Garrett was charged with an offence under *section 33(1)(b)* of the *EPA 1990* for the unauthorised or harmful deposit of waste and two offences under *section 33(1)(c)* of the Act for disposal of waste in a manner likely to cause harm. He pleaded guilty to all counts and was sentenced to eighteen months imprisonment. He appealed against the sentence.

Decision: The sentence was reduced by the Court of Appeal to twelve months on the ground that the maximum sentence was two years and the offence was not the worst possible.

Comment: This case shows that the courts are prepared to imprison individuals for flagrant waste offences. Although the worst possible effects did not result, the flagrancy of the offences was high.

Shanks & McEwan (Teesside) Ltd v The Environment Agency (24 January 1997) High Court, Queen's Bench Division ([1997] 2 All ER 332)

[B16.19]

employees; deposit of waste

Background: The site manager of a Shanks & McEwan (Teesside) Ltd waste management facility, decided to discharge the contents of a tanker of controlled waste into a bund. He failed to fill in the requisite waste disposal form advice note to indicate the position of the container into which the load was discharged. Shanks & McEwan argued that it was not guilty of an offence under *section 33(1)* of the *EPA 1990.* They argued that it did not know that the deposit was being made in breach of the conditions of its waste management licence, as the manager of the facility had not filled out the relevant forms.

Decision: Shanks & McEwan was found guilty of an offence under *section 33(1)* of the *EPA 1990.* The court ruled that knowledge of the waste being caused or permitted to be deposited on its land was sufficient for an offence. It was not necessary to show that Shanks & McEwan knew of the particular deposit or that it had knowingly permitted the conditions of the waste management licence to be breached.

Comment: In this case the court's ruling prevented the company, Shanks & McEwan, from hiding behind the acts of its employees.

London Waste Regulation Authority v Drinkwater Sabey Ltd and Another (17 July 1996) High Court, Queen's Bench Division ([1997] Env. L.R. 137)

[B16.20]

waste management license exemptions

Background: Drinkwater Sabey Ltd had a waste management licence allowing it to receive 490 tonnes of waste per day at one of its sites. On one day over 980 tonnes of waste were delivered. Drinkwater Sabey successfully showed that the majority of that waste was of a type exempt from the *Waste Management Licensing Regulations 1994 (SI 1994 No 1056)*. The London Waste Regulation Authority sought to argue that despite the exemption of the material, the waste management licence should still apply to all activities on the site, whether exempt or not.

Decision: It was held that licence conditions do not apply to exempt activities at all and that the waste management licensing requirements only apply insofar as an exempt activity must be registered.

Thames Waste Management Ltd v Surrey County Council (1 November 1996) High Court, Queen's Bench Division ([1997] Env. L.R. 148)

[B16.21]

deposit of waste

Background: Thames Waste Management Ltd was prosecuted under *section 33(1)(a)* of the *EPA 1990,* for disposing of waste otherwise than in accordance with its waste management licence.

Thames Waste argued that the prosecution should have been brought under *section 33(6)* of the *EPA 1990*, for breach of a licence condition instead. The condition of the waste management licence required waste tipped to be covered on the day that it was deposited.

Thames Waste sought to argue on appeal that the deposit was lawful and it was only the failure to cover which breached the licence.

Decision: The court held that the term 'deposit' could include a continuing state of affairs. Therefore, by virtue of not covering the waste in accordance with the waste management licence, an unlawful deposit of waste had been made and Thames Waste had committed an offence under *section 33(1)(a)* of the *EPA 1990.*

North Yorkshire County Council v Boyne (24 April 1996) High Court, Queen's Bench Division ([1997] Env. L.R. 91)

[B16.22]

waste management license exemptions

Background: North Yorkshire County Council appealed against the decision of Harrogate Magistrates' Court that Mr Boyne had a defence to the charge under *section 33(1)(b)* of the *EPA 1990*, of keeping waste at his site without a valid waste management licence.

Decision: The court concurred with the magistrates view that Mr Boyne had successfully established a defence under the exemption in *paragraph 40* of *Schedule 3* of the *Waste Management Licensing Regulations of 1994 (SI 1994 No 1056)*. The quantity of waste at the site never exceeded the limit of fifty cubic metres. The court considered that a bund around the site of soil bricks and rubble was not an adaptation of the site for reception of waste for disposal or recovery elsewhere, but was of merely cosmetic significance. The court was also satisfied that the storage of waste was incidental to the collection or transport of the waste.

Comment: The exemptions to the requirements of the *Waste Management Licensing Regulations 1994* are highly prescriptive and give rise to difficulties in interpretation and application in practice.

Shanks & McEwan (Southern Waste Services) Ltd v Environment Agency (14 October 1997) Queen's Bench Divisional Court (ILR, 17 October 1997)

[B16.23]

special waste; duty of care; waste carriers

Background: Shanks & McEwan was engaged by United Overseas Ltd to collect and dispose of waste. The waste in question fell within the definition of 'special waste' in the *Control of Pollution (Special Waste) Regulations 1980 (SI 1980 No 1709)*. United Overseas Ltd did not inform the Shanks & McEwan driver that the waste was special waste, and did not prepare the consignment note required by *Regulation 4(1)* of the 1980 Regulations to be provided to the carrier and to the local authority. The Shanks & McEwan driver delivered the waste to a Shanks & McEwan disposal site not licensed to take special waste. The waste was identified by a Shanks & McEwan chemist as special waste and was diverted to a landfill site licensed for special waste.

United Overseas Ltd pleaded guilty to charges of failing to prepare the requisite consignment note under *Regulation 4(1)*, breaching the duty of care under *section 34(1)* of the *EPA 1990*, as producer of the waste, to take reasonable measures to prevent another person contravening *section 33* of the *EPA 1990*.

Decision: Shanks & McEwan appealed successfully against its conviction under *Regulation 16* of the *Control of Pollution (Special Waste) Regulations 1980*, for failing as carriers of special waste to complete its part of the consignment note required under *Regulation 4(5)* of the Regulations. They also appealed successfully against the conviction under *section 34(1)* of the *EPA 1990* for breach if its duty of care to take reasonable measures to prevent contravention by another of *section 33* of the *EPA 1990*.

Shanks & McEwan submitted that it was not a carrier of the waste within the Regulations. The 'carrier' was defined as 'any person who transfers special waste from the premises at which it is produced to another person for disposal'. Shanks & McEwan was transferring the waste to its own disposal site not to another person for disposal. The court accepted Shanks & McEwan's submission that it was for parliament and not for the courts to amend this gap in the legislation (as the *Special Waste Regulations 1996 (SI 1996 No 972)* did).

The court rejected the argument that the duty of care did not extend to preventing a breach of *section 33* of the *EPA 1990* by persons who had earlier contact with or control of the waste. The court also rejected the view that without an actual offence being committed under *section 33*, no offence could be committed under *section 34* of the *EPA 1990*. In this case, no offence had been committed under *section 33*, but the court held that there was no evidence that Shanks & McEwan had failed to take all reasonable measures to prevent any breach of *section 33*. Accordingly there was no breach of its duty of care.

Comment: This case involved a number of important legal points and shows that the courts will not always close loopholes in the law by interpretation.

Environment Agency v Green Environmental Industries and John Moynihan (15 September 1997) Crown Court ((1997) 272 ENDS 45)

[B16.24]

clinical waste; waste carriers; waste management licence

Background: A company neighbouring a disused factory on an industrial estate in Hoddesdon complained to Hertfordshire County Council that clinical waste was being handled and repackaged in the disused factory. The council discovered twelve vehicles and containers of clinical waste at the site. The company responsible, Green Environmental Industries, and its director, John Moynihan, agreed to remove the waste for incineration. The council found that Green Environmental Industries did not have a waste management licence for the site and was not a registered waste carrier. Mr Moynihan also failed to provide any waste transfer notes and confirmation that waste had been incinerated.

Some of the waste was located in trailers in a transport cafe car park and later 61,000 bags of clinical waste, 3,000 bins containing sharp instruments and 600 medi-bins containing body tissues and amputated limbs, were located in a warehouse of a former plastics factory in Hertford. The site had been let to Green Environmental Industries in July for waste paper shredding.

Mr Moynihan refused to comply with notices requesting information, claiming that the notices contravened his right not to incriminate himself. Mr Moynihan applied for judicial review but his application was refused.

Decision: Mr Moynihan pleaded guilty to two offences of depositing controlled waste without a waste management licence contrary to *section 33(1)(a)* of the *EPA 1990*. He was sentenced to ten months and eighteen months to run concurrently for the offences. The court refused to award the EA costs of £20,000 and held that the £209,150 costs of the clean up operation would have to be recovered through the civil courts.

Green Environmental Industries, however, was in receivership and Mr Moynihan had been declared bankrupt. Following an investigation by the police, Mr Moynihan pleaded guilty on three charges of conspiracy to defraud and was sentenced to a jail term, adding a further nine months to his sentence.

Comment: Green Environmental Industries obtained the waste from Harrison-Benn Clinical and Security Waste, GBC Clinical Waste and Cleanaway. Despite Mr Moynihan's fraud, the case raised serious questions about these companies' compliance with the duty of care as respects waste under *section 34* of the *EPA 1990*. See also connected cases including the judicial review: *R v Hertfordshire County Council, ex parte, Green Environmental Industries Limited and John Moynihan (1997)* (see paragraph B16.35).

R v Witham (17 March 1997) Magistrates' Court (Waste Planning, 24 September 1997)

[B16.25]

planning; enforcement notice

Background: In September 1993, Mr Witham was granted planning permission by Northamptonshire County Council to tip 3,750 cubic metres of inert waste to restore the land for agricultural use. The site had been a small sand and gravel quarry and then had been used as a tip accepting household and industrial waste. The surface had been covered with inert soil forming material but remained poorly restored and unsuitable for agricultural use. The planning permission issued to Mr Witham allowed tipping of further material to restore another part of the former tip. The permission set certain levels to which the land could be tipped in order to ensure proper restoration. Mr Witham ignored initial warnings that the levels were too high and requirements that he survey the site to check the levels.

The council carried out a survey in March 1995. This indicated that the amount of waste tipped exceeded the authorised level by approximately 5,000 cubic metres. Mr Witham ignored requests for him to remove material and, in August 1995, the council issued an enforcement notice requiring the removal of 5,000 cubic metres by 7 October 1995. Approximately 1,000 cubic metres were removed but the enforcement notice was not complied with.

Decision: On 22 March 1997, Mr Witham was prosecuted in Daventry Magistrates' Court and fined £2,000 for non-compliance with the enforcement notice.

R v Lanstar (August 1997) Crown Court ((1997) 271 ENDS 43)

[B16.26]

duty of care; unlicensed waste

Background: Lanstar operated an industrial waste treatment business. In 1995, Lanstar transported residues from its solidification process in batches of ten to fifteen tonnes from its Cadishead site to UK Waste's disposal landfill in Ruislip. UK Waste sampled the residues and found that several loads exceeded the levels of chlorinated hydrocarbons the site could accept. On 14 July 1995, Lanstar redirected one of the batches to 3C Wastes Arpley landfill site which was not licensed to take chlorinated hydrocarbons. In addition, UK Waste reported to Chester County Council that other batches containing chlorinated hydrocarbons arrived on 14 and 19 September, but the chlorinated hydrocarbon levels were not mentioned in the consignment notes.

Decision: The case was heard over three days by magistrates and the prosecution alleged that Lanstar's documents had been tampered with. The magistrates transferred the case to Warrington Crown Court. Lanstar then pleaded guilty to two offences of breaching the duty of care under *section 34* of the *EPA 1990,* relating to the delivery of waste to the Ruislip site, and to a further offence in relation to the deposit of controlled waste at 3C Wastes site contrary to the site licence.

Lanstar was fined a total of £24,000 and ordered to pay £8,517 in costs.

Re: Mineral Resources Ltd; Environment Agency v Stout (30 April 1998) High Court, Chancery Division ((1998) PLSCS 144)

[B16.27]

waste management licence; insolvency; liquidator

Background: Mineral Resources Ltd held a valid waste management licence and ceased trading in 1997. The liquidator gave notice to disclaim the licence.

The EA applied to the court to obtain a declaration that the liquidator could not disclaim the licence.

Decision: The court granted the declaration. The court found that for the purposes of the *Insolvency Act 1986,* the waste management licence constituted 'property'. Property can be disclaimed under the *Insolvency Act 1986* unless there is a conflict with *section 39* of the *EPA 1990* which prevents waste management licences from being surrendered. The court held that *section 39* should prevail due to the application of the general rules of statutory construction and in the public interest of protection of the environment.

Comment: In this case the court gave precedence to the provisions and intent of the *EPA 1990.* The 1990 Act makes it a requirement that land which is subject to a waste management licence, must be restored to a satisfactory condition prior to surrender. Allowing a waste management licence to be disclaimed would be to allow this requirement to be avoided. (See also the *Re Wilmott Trading Ltd case (1999)* in paragraph B16.38).

Mayer Parry Recycling Ltd v Environment Agency (9 November 1998) High Court, Chancery Division ([1999] Env. L.R. 489)

[B16.28]

judicial review; waste management licence; scrap metal; definition of waste; European Union; recyclable material

Background: Mayer Parry Recycling Ltd is one of the largest scrap metal merchants in the UK. In association with the British Metals Federation, they commenced proceedings by way of originating summons under *Order 28* of the *Rules of the Supreme Court,* seeking declarations as to whether different categories of scrap metals constitute waste and hence whether they are subject to regulation under waste laws. The EA was the defendant in the proceedings.

The definition of waste had several practical and commercial impacts for Mayer Parry. The issues before the court were whether Mayer Parry required a waste management licence under *section 33* of the *EPA 1990* to operate its sites; whether the duty of care as respect wastes under *section 34* of the *EPA 1990* applied to its activities; whether it required registration as a waste carrier under the *Control of Pollution (Amendment) Act 1989* to transport its scrap metal or; whether *Regulation 259/93 on the supervision and control of shipments of waste within, into and out of the EU* applied to its exports and imports of scrap metal.

Decision: The judge, Mr Justice Carnwath, first addressed a point of procedure raised by the EA. The EA originally objected to the case being brought by way of the originating summons procedure, stating that the proceedings should have been brought by way of judicial review under *Order 53* of the *Rules of the Supreme Court.* Mr Carnwath took the view that either procedure was available to Mayer Parry. However, he did consider on balance, the volume of affidavit evidence and the fact that the court was being asked to make findings of facts, the originating summons procedure was, if anything, more appropriate.

It was common ground that the applicable definition of waste is that in *Article 1* of *Directive 75/442/EEC on waste* (as amended by *Directive 91/156/EEC*). This definition is often referred to as 'Directive Waste'.

Article 1 of the Directive provides: '(a) "waste" shall mean any substance or object in the category set out in Annex 1 which the holder discards or intends or is required to discard.' The Directive also refers to 'disposal' and 'recovery' of waste. Disposal and recovery are defined to mean any of the operations provided for in *Annex IIA* or *IIB* to the Directive respectively. One category of recovery operation listed in *Annex IIB* is 'recycling/ reclamation of metals and metal compounds'. Both parties and Mr Justice Carnwath noted the purposive approach to be taken in interpreting an EC directive. They all considered that where the different language versions of a directive diverge, interpretation is to be by reference to the purpose and general scheme of rules of which it forms part.

Mr Justice Carnwath briefly set out the development of the English language version of the definition of 'Directive Waste' and the apparent discrepancy with other language versions of the Directive. Whilst the word 'discard' was introduced on amendment into the English language version of the Directive to try and resolve the discrepancy, the judge suggested that it led to difficulties of its own making. He considered that the term 'get rid of' rather than 'discard' would have more accurately reflected the intention behind the Directive. Two recent decisions of the ECJ in the analysis of Advocate General Jacobs in each of them was central to the dispute. These cases were *Euro Tombesi and Others (1997)* and *Inter-Environment Wallonnie v Region Wallonne (1997).* Mr Justice Carnwath noted from the Advocate General's opinion in the *Tombesi case,* the difficulties being found throughout the EC in interpreting the definition of waste, particularly when applied to residues or by-products of particular processes which are suitable for recycling. The Advocate General took the view that '. . . little is to be gained by considering the normal meaning of the term "discard" which should be taken as having a special meaning encompassing both disposal of waste and its consignment to a recovery operation.' The Advocate General stated that the concept of a 'recovery operation' is a matter for member states and not the national courts to apply on the facts and that there may very well be borderline cases.

In answering the specific question put to it in the *Tombesi case*, the ECJ did not in the end need to address the issue of the word discard. The ECJ did not expressly adopt the reasoning of the Advocate General.

In the subsequent *Wallonnie case,* the question referred to the ECJ which is relevant to this case was as follows: 'Is a substance referred to in *Annex 1* (to the 1991 Directive) which directly or indirectly forms an integral part of an industrial production process, to be considered 'waste' within the meaning of *Article 1A* of that Directive?' On that question, the ECJ ruled that a substance is not to be excluded from the definition of waste merely because it directly or indirectly forms an integral part of an industrial process.

Mr Justice Carnwath took the view that the reasoning of the ECJ in the *Wallonnie case* came much closer to an express adoption of the Advocate General's approach. The ECJ recognised that the scope of the term 'waste' turns on the meaning of 'discard'. However, it adopts the view that the term discard covers both disposal and recovery of substance or objects. Mr Justice Carnwath rejected Mayer Parry's submission that in this context 'covers' means it is capable of applying to, but not necessarily co-extensive with, disposal and recovery operation. Instead he interpreted the ECJ's position to be an adoption of the Advocate General's approach that 'discard' has a special meaning encompassing and limited to not only the disposal of waste but also its consignment to recovery operation.

The judge went on to apply this reasoning to the arguments in the present case. The EA adopted the reasoning of the Advocate General, putting emphasis on the *Annex IIB* list of recovery operations rather than on the term 'discard'. In essence, the EA argued that any substance which is consigned to a recovery operation is waste. The EA contended that the recovery operation 'recycling/reclamation of metals and metal compounds' covers operations which have the purpose of making the metal content of substances or objects reusable as raw material (including any measures which have the purpose of ensuring that the metal is reusable without threat to public health or the environment). This in turn covers all the processes carried out by Mayer Parry.

The EA agreed, however, that scrap metal can be used as furnace feedstock without further processing as a raw material and therefore is not waste. Further, it accepted that scrap metal that is at the stage of furnace feedstock but which is further processed or graded solely for economic reasons (i.e. to make into a more valuable feedstock), is not by such processing or grading subjected to recovery operation and therefore is not waste.

Mayer Parry argued that the concept of 'discard' was central. It suggested that in any particular case, it is necessary to look at all the facts in order to determine whether a discarding intention is reasonably, on objective appraisal of the surrounding circumstances, to be attributed to the disposal.

Mr Justice Carnwath thought that the EA's approach was in principle correct. He proceeded to state what he considered to be a reasonably clear general concept. However, in so doing he may have reintroduced some uncertainty because in some respects this judgement steps back completely from following his interpretation of the ECJ's decision in the *Wallonnie case*.

Mr Justice Carnwath stated that the term 'discard' is to be used in a broad sense equivalent to 'get rid of'. The term is generally concerned with materials which have ceased to be required for their original purpose, normally because they are unsuitable, unwanted and surplus to requirements. In assessing the limits of this category of discarded material, Mr Justice Carnwath stated that it is necessary to assess whether the material is put to a disposal or recovery operation. This is because materials, which are not to be reused but which do not require any recovery operation before being put to their new use, are not waste. Further, materials which are made ready for reuse by a recovery operation, cease to be waste when the recovery operation is complete. The judge observed that all materials referred to in the evidence are capable of being waste as they are 'got rid of' by their original users as not wanted or needed for their original purpose. Whether the materials are waste, in his judgement, turns on the scope of the term 'recovery'. If the discarded materials do not require recovery for their re-use they are not waste. If they do require recovery, they are waste and remain waste until those recovery operations are complete. The judge acknowledged the difficulty drawing a clear line between recovery operations and industrial operations in which recycled scrap is used as a raw material. He did not, however, offer a solution to this difficult issue.

Comment: This case addressed the problematic legal definition of waste. Although the proceedings related in particular to the question of whether different categories of scrap metal constitute waste, the judgement will have significance throughout Europe and the EU of the various industries. See also *Euro Tombesi and Adino Tombesi, Roberto Santella, Giobanni Muzi and others, Anselno Savini (1997), Inter-Environment Wallonie v Region Wallone (1997) and Vesosso & Zanetti.*

R v Collier (18 September 1998) Crown Court ((1998) 284 ENDS 48)

[B16.29]

forfeiture; waste disposal; burning of waste

Background: Kenneth Collier operated an illegal waste business for a number of years. During this time, he had illegally deposited approximately 120,000 tonnes of waste on an unlicensed site.

Decision: In proceedings brought by the EA, Mr Collier pleaded guilty to thirteen offences of illegally disposing of and burning waste contrary to *section 33(1)(a) and (b)* of the *EPA 1990*. He was given a four months prison sentence, suspended for two years and fined £5,000. The court also ordered the forfeiture to the EA under *section 43* of the *Powers of Criminal Courts Act 1973* of Mr

Collier's vehicle fleet, which had been used to conduct the illegal land filling.

Comment: Under the above power of forfeiture, which was used for the first time in this case in relation to a waste defence, the EA has the power to sell the vehicles after six months and retain the proceeds.

R v Metropolitan Stipendary Magistrates and Others, ex parte London Waste Regulation Authority; Berkshire County Council v Scott (1993) High Court, Queen's Bench Division (Times Law Reports, 14 January 1993

[B16.30]

disposal of waste; deposit of waste

Background: These cases relate to the same point of law and were heard together. The first case was an application for judicial review of a decision by the Magistrates' Court not to commit to trial the case brought for the illegal deposit of waste under the *COPA 1974*. The magistrate held that the defendants activities did not amount to an offence because the waste did not remain on site but was removed elsewhere (the disposal of waste was not therefore final).

The second case related to the decision of a magistrate to allow an appeal against a notice pursuant to *section 16* of the *COPA 1974* requiring the removal of waste. The magistrate again relied on the fact that the waste had not been finally disposed of. The council appealed against this decision.

Decision: The court concluded that the idea that the terms 'disposal' or 'deposit' referred to a final resting place was wrong. Lord Justice Watkin considered that the words related to 'getting rid of something'. It was considered that parliament's intention was not to limit the offences to cases of final disposal.

Comment: This followed an earlier judgement in *Leigh Land Reclamation Ltd and Others v Walsall Metropolitan Borough Council (1991) 3 JEL 281(c)*. The court considered that the decision in the *Leigh case* was wrong.

R v Avon County Council, ex parte Terry Adams Ltd ((1994) 229 ENDS 44)

[B16.31]

contracting out; waste disposal authority; local authority waste disposal company (LAWDC)

Background: Under *Schedule 2* of the *EPA 1990*, contracts relating to the keeping, treatment or disposal of controlled waste must be put out to competitive tender. Accordingly, Avon County Council, the waste disposal authority, created an arm's length waste disposal company (Avon Waste Management). In awarding contracts, the waste disposal authority was required to avoid undue discrimination in favour of one proposed contractor. Instead it was required to favour contractors which would minimise environment pollution and maximise recycling.

Six disposal contracts were put out to tender by the waste disposal authority. All of the contracts were subsequently won by Avon Waste Management. Terry Adams Ltd had tendered for a contract with a price approximately half that quoted by Avon Waste Management. Terry Adams Ltd, therefore, issued proceedings on the basis that there had been undue discrimination.

Decision: The Court of Appeal found that part of the disposal contracts were unduly discriminatory. In particular, the contract relating to the transfer of waste contained conditions concerning the use of oil and the existing waste transfer station in the area had previously been transferred to Avon Waste Management. In addition, although the council was permitted to have policies favouring incineration, the proposed contract was discriminatory in that the terms required a tender to provide a new incinerator and a site to operate on. The existing incinerator and site had previously been transferred to Avon Waste Management.

The council argued that it was necessary to award all the contracts to Avon Waste Management on the grounds that the bids were interdependent and in order to achieve economic viability. This was considered by the court to be a valid basis on which to award the contract.

Comment: *Part II* of *Schedule 2* of the *EPA 1990* deals with procedures for the contracting out of waste disposal services. These provisions are supported by DOE Circular 8/91.

Kent County Council v Beaney (22 October 1991) High Court, Queen's Bench Division ([1993] Env. L.R. 225)

[B16.32]

knowledge; disposal of waste

Background: Beaney owned and occupied a farm in Kent. There was considerable evidence to demonstrate that controlled waste was being deposited on the farm and that no disposal licence was in force. Certain waste had also been destroyed and evidence suggested that Beaney was aware of this.

The council appealed the decision of the Magistrates' Court that there was no case to answer, on the basis that the respondent had not known or permitted the deposit of controlled waste.

Decision: The court found that it could be inferred that Beaney had knowingly permitted the deposit of controlled waste. It was a provisional inference which could be rebutted by evidence to the contrary. As such, the justices had incorrectly decided that there was no case to be answered. The appeal was allowed and the matter was remitted to the Magistrates' Court.

Comment: Effectively, the court reversed the burden of proof in this case in relation to knowledge. An interference of knowledge is significant in environment law due to the number of offences and requirements for remedial action turning on terms such as 'knowingly permit'.

Cheshire County Council v Armstrong's Transport (Wigan) Ltd (21 June 1994) Queen's Bench Divisional Court ([1992] Env. L.R. 62)

[B16.33]

definition of waste; waste disposal licence

Background: Armstrong's Transport (Wigan) Ltd was responsible for crushing concrete and rubble for a use as an infill for the footings of new buildings. Following discussions with the council on the legality of processing the concrete and rubble, Armstrong's Transport hired land, transported the rubble to it, crushed it and then transported the rubble back. The council brought a prosecution, alleging that the concrete stored on the temporary site for the processing amounted to waste and, hence, required a waste disposal licence. The magistrates disagreed with its view, finding that the material was not waste. The council appealed its decision.

Decision: The appeal was dismissed. The material was considered to be unwanted, disposed of or discarded.

Durham County Council v Thomas Swan & Co Ltd (23 June 1994) Queen's Bench Divisional Court ([1995] Env. L.R. 72)

[B16.34]

meaning of empty; deposit of waste

Background: Thomas Swan & Co used phenol in an industrial process. It obtained the phenol from 200 kilogram barrels of the substance. Once extracted, less than 100 grams of phenol remained in the barrel. The barrels were sealed and stored ready for transportation to a transfer station or reconditioning plant. Particular barrels were deposited at a transfer station. As a matter of practice, if any barrels were found to contain any waste liquid, they were returned to the waste producer (in this case Thomas Swan & Co) immediately. In 1991, several of the barrels stored outside the licensed site were found to contain a mixture of phenol and water and were traced back to the Thomas Swan & Co. The site operator and Thomas Swan & Co were prosecuted under *section 3(2)* of the *COPA 1974,* for causing controlled waste to be deposited on land which was not licensed. The site operators pleaded guilty whilst Thomas Swan & Co was acquitted before the same magistrates.

The main issue was whether the barrels could be described as empty when they were taken from Thomas Swan & Co's premises. The barrels contained less than one per cent of their original volume.

Decision: The understanding of the term 'empty depended upon the context in which it was being considered. The only realistic standard to be applied was that employed in trade practice (i.e. less than one per cent of the original volume of the barrels). The High Court therefore dismissed the appeal and stated that magistrates were entitled to find that the barrels in this instance were empty.

Comment: Interestingly, even one per cent of certain substances could be harmful to the environment, and how much waste liquid one per cent constitutes depends on the size of the tanks.

R v Hertfordshire County Council, ex parte Green Environmental Industries Ltd and John Moynihan (31 July 1997) Court of Appeal, Civil Division ([1998] Env. L.R. 153)

[B16.35]

clinical waste; waste carriers; waste management licence; investigatory powers

Background: This judicial review arose out of criminal proceedings brought by Hertfordshire County Council in relation to a major illegal clinical waste operation. Moynihan was later convicted of two offences under *section 33* of the *EPA 1990*. The judicial review concerned Hertfordshire County Council's powers of investigation under *Part II* of the *EPA 1990* (now the EA's powers). Under the duty of care as regards waste, established by *section 34* of the *EPA 1990*, the secretary of state was empowered to make regulations requiring the furnishing of documents. The *Environmental Protection (Duty of Care) Regulations 1991 (SI 1991 2839)* are an example of such regulations. *Section 69* of the *EPA 1990* empowers officers to enter premises, sample, take measurements and to require provision of information and documentation. This provision importantly states that no answer provided may be used as evidence in a prosecution case against the person giving the answer. Under *section 71* of the *EPA 1990*, the Secretary of State and Waste Regulation Authorities (now the EA), are empowered to require by notice specified information which they reasonably require. Failure to comply with the notice 'without reasonable excuse' is a criminal offence. Having discovered lorry loads of clinical waste, Hertfordshire County Council wished to investigate the suspected illegal waste operation further. It warned Green Environmental Industries Ltd that it would be inviting a company officer to be interviewed under caution in accordance with the *Police and Criminal Evidence Act 1984*. Hertfordshire County Council subsequently served a notice under *section 71* of the *EPA 1990*, requiring identities of those who had handled, transported and supplied the clinical waste. Green Environmental Industries Ltd refused to comply with the notice without assurance that the information would not be used in a prosecution against it. The basis for its position was that the notice under *section 71* of the *EPA 1990* would otherwise effectively circumvent self-incrimination safeguards and the procedures under the *Police and Criminal Evidence Act 1984*. Hertfordshire County Council went on to threaten prosecution for non-compliance with the notice under *section 71* and served a further notice requiring information under *section 34* of the 1990 Act.

Decision: The court dismissed Green Environmental Industries Ltd's argument that *section 34* of the *EPA 1990* only applied in relation to lawful activities and not where illegal activity is suspected. The case hinged therefore on the court's interpretation of the relationship between *section 69* of the *EPA 1990* which provides express protection against self-incrimination and *section 71* of the 1990 Act which does not. The court interpreted *section 69* narrowly. It held that the self-incrimination provisions were narrow in scope, only protecting the individual concerned and only if the question had been answered. The court ruled further that those provisions could not protect the company and apply only to all answers and not documentation obtained. All statements by other individuals or other documents obtained under *section 71* of the *EPA 1990* are therefore admissible evidence unless the court's discretion to exclude evidence from confessions unfairly obtained under *section 78* of the *Police and Criminal Evidence 1984* is applied. The court therefore held that Hertfordshire County Council was acting within its powers in using *section 71* of the *EPA 1990*. The court went on to consider to what extent, referring to general principles, Hertfordshire County Council could seek to get Green Environmental Industries Ltd and Mr Moynihan to incriminate themselves under the threat of a fine if they refused. Considering English and ECJ case law, the court held that *section 71* of the *EPA 1990* allowed collection of information reasonably required which might go toward bringing a prosecution. The fact that it might incriminate the provider was not a reasonable excuse to refuse disclosure. The court considered that the non-inclusion by parliament of an express self-incrimination provision in *section 71* of the *EPA 1990* was intentional.

Comment: The court felt that parliament had intentionally not provided for self-incrimination in *section 71* as it had in *section 69* of the *EPA 1990*. *Section 71* provides that no answers provided to the EA when exercising its extensive powers to obtain information, can be admitted in evidence against that person in criminal proceedings. This case concerned that relationship between *section 69* powers and *section 71* powers. This case formed part of a series of cases relating to the same illegal clinical waste operation. See also *Environment Agency v Green Environmental Industries and John Moynihan (1997)* (paragraph B16.24).

Black Country Developments Corporation v Wolverhampton Metropolitan Borough Council (APP/WM/96/66/March 1997)

[B16.36]

waste management licence; licence; surrender

Background: Black Country Developments Corporation appealed against the rejection by Wolverhampton Metropolitan Borough Council of an application to surrender a waste management licence. The licence was granted on 31 March 1993 to the development corporation for land reclamation and land landfilling operation in Wolverhampton.

The inspector considered that there was one principle issue in the determination of the appeal. This related to whether the surrender of the licence was premature given the test in *section 39* of the *EPA 1990* and the recommendation in the Waste Management Papers 26A and 27.

Test: The inspector must be satisfied that 'whether it is likely or unlikely that the condition of the land, so far as that condition is as the result of the use of the land the treatment of keeping or disposal of waste ... will cause pollution of the environment or harm to human health.' The inspector felt that this test was ambiguous.

Paragraph 1.5 of Waste Management Paper 26A provides that the Water Resources Authority (now the EA), must be satisfied that the condition of the land is unlikely to cause pollution of the environment or harm to human health.

Decision: The appeal was dismissed. The inspector concluded that although pollution to the environment or harm to human health was unlikely from landfill gas emissions on the site at present, the application to surrender was considered to be premature and further monitoring should be carried out to establish a gas emissions regime.

Vesosso & Zanetti (Joined Cases C–206/88 and C-207/88 (ECJ), (1990) LMELR 2(4))

[B16.37]

definition of waste; European Union; recyclable material

Background: Following the appeal by two Italians against a decision which alleged that they collected, transported or stored waste contrary to Italian law, the Italian court referred a question regarding the meaning of waste to the ECJ.

The question was whether the matter was 'waste' within the meaning of *Directive 75/442/EEC on waste.*

Decision: The argument raised in this case was that the material was not waste but was recyclable matter. In reliance on the definition in *Directive 75/442/EEC*, the Advocate General found the matter to be waste and confirmed that waste must be objectively defined and could not be dependent on the subjective intentions relating to disposal. The court agreed that the Directive definition of waste clearly covered recyclable materials.

Comment: This judgement confirms the view that substances destined for specialised recovery operations are likely to be characterised as waste. See also *Euro Tombesi and Adino Tombesi,*

Roberto Santella, Giobanni Muzi and others, Anselno Savini (1997), Inter-Environment Wallonie v Region Wallonne (1997) and *Mayer Parry Recycling Ltd v Environment Agency (1998).*

Re: Wilmott Trading Ltd (31 March 1999) High Court, Chancery Division, (Times Law Reports, 28 April 1999)

[B16.38]

waste management licence; licence surrender; insolvency; liquidator

Background: Wilmott Trading Ltd held a waste management license, permitting it to store scrap metals and other materials at its recycling facility. In 1997, the company fell into financial difficulty and a liquidator was appointed. The liquidator found that the company had insufficient resources to pay its creditors and therefore decided to prepare an account of winding up in accordance with *section 106* of the *Insolvency Act 1986*, towards dissolution of the company under *section 201(2)* of that Act. The liquidator applied to the court for directions and a declaration on five points of law. The EA was the respondent in this action.

Decision: The first issue was whether for the purposes of *section 106* of the *Insolvency Act 1986*, it could be said that the affairs of a company which still holds a waste management licence 'are fully wound up'. The judge held that the mere existence of the licence would not prevent a liquidator from stating the company's affairs to be fully wound up. Accordingly, continued ownership of the licence by a company does not prevent its dissolution. The court went on to consider whether on dissolution of the company, the licence ceases to vest in anyone or becomes vested in the crown. The judge considered that if the licence ceased to vest in anyone, it would effectively cease to exist. It rejected the argument based on the court's reasoning in *Re: Mineral Resources Ltd [1999]* (see paragraph B16.27), that a company holding a waste management licence could not be dissolved as this would lead to determination of the licence in a manner not permitted by *section 35 (11)* of the *EPA 1990*. In that case it had been held on public interest grounds that as long as a company has some resources with which to comply with the licence, the liquidator should not be able to disclaim the licence. The court distinguished this case on the grounds that Wilmott Trading Ltd was wholly incapable of complying with the licence and there were therefore no good reasons for it to exist. In addition, it was held that in *Re: Mineral Resources Ltd*, the liquidator intended to carry out the specific step of putting an end to the licence by disclaiming it. In this case, however, the liquidator proposed that the licence came to an end as an incidental result of the dissolution of the company. On the question of whether on dissolution of the company a waste management licence would automatically vest in the crown, and whether this should prevent dissolution, the crown had declined to make any representations. The court therefore held that the existence of the waste management licence did not prevent the dissolution of the company. It was unnecessary in this case to grant relief to the liquidator to decide what happened to the licence when the company was dissolved.

Re: Bluestone Chemicals Ltd Re: Celtic Extraction Ltd (14 July 1999) Court of Appeal (NLD, 14 July 1999)

[B16.39]

waste management licence; licence surrender; insolvency; liquidator

Background: Celtic Extraction Ltd and Bluestone Chemicals Ltd both held waste management licences granted under the *EPA 1990*. Both companies were put into compulsory liquidation and the Official Receiver acted as liquidator. The EA wrote to the Official Receiver, requiring remedial measures to be taken at both the licensed sites under the terms of the waste management licences. The Official Receiver wrote to the EA asking for the licences to be terminated on the grounds that the companies had no assets. The Official Receiver then applied to the Companies Court for directions on whether or not he could and should disclaim the licences. The judge in the High Court, applying his own judgement in *Re: Mineral Resources Ltd; Environment*

Agency v Stout [1999], directed that the licences could not be disclaimed. He did, however, acknowledge the public importance of the issues in question and gave the Official Receiver permission to appeal.

Decision: The Court of Appeal agreed with the High Court judge on the first issue of whether the licence constituted 'property' for the purposes of *section 436* of the *Insolvency Act 1986*. It decided that a waste management licence did come within the definition of 'property' (or at least an 'interest ... incidental to property') contained in *section 436* on the grounds that: (1) there existed a statutory framework conferring an entitlement on persons satisfying certain conditions, even though there was an element of discretion exerciseable within that framework, (2) the licence was transferable and (3) the licence had a value. On the second issue of whether a licence could be disclaimed as onerous property under *section 178* of the *Insolvency Act 1986*, the Court of Appeal overruled the High Court judge's decision in *Re: Mineral Resources Ltd; Environment Agency v Stout*. The Court of Appeal disagreed with the High Court judge's decision that *section 35(11)* of the *EPA 1990* and *section 179* of the *Insolvency Act 1986* were mutually inconsistent. The court instead took the view that the *EPA 1990* restricted termination of a waste management licence by act of the parties but did not prevent termination by external statutory force. In addition, the Court of Appeal stated that the High Court judge's decision in *Re: Mineral Resources Ltd; Environment Agency v Stout*, would mean that the costs of compliance with the licence would have priority over provable debts. It would also mean that the assets of the company would have to be set aside to pay for future compliance, rather than being distributed equally among the creditors. The court felt that this would not be a desirable situation. Finally, the Court of Appeal stated that it was unlikely that disclaiming a waste management licence would constitute an offence under *section 33* or *section 34* of the 1990 Act, any more than termination of a licence on dissolution of the company or death of an individual holder under circumstances which the EA accepted were both permissible and unavoidable. The Court of Appeal declined to express a view on the correctness of the decision in *Re: Wilmott Trading Ltd No.2* (see paragraph B16.40), that a waste management licence ceases to exist on the dissolution of a company). For these reasons, the Court of Appeal allowed the appeal by the Official Receiver. The court declared that the Official Receiver was entitled to disclaim the waste management licences and if necessary should remit the matter to the High Court judge, to determine whether in the circumstances he should do so and if so under what (if any) conditions.

Comment: In this case, the Court of Appeal decided that a waste management licence was property within the meaning of the *Insolvency Act 1986* and could be disclaimed as 'onerous property' by a liquidator under *section 178* of the *Insolvency Act 1986.* As a result, it overturned the High Court's decision in *Re: Mineral Resources Ltd; Environment Agency v Stout [1999]* (see paragraph B16.27).

Re: Wilmott Trading Ltd (No2) (8 June 1999) High Court, Chancery Division (Times Law Reports, 17 June 1999)

[B16.40]

waste management licence; licence surrender; insolvency; liquidator

Background: In this second case involving Wilmott Trading Ltd, the liquidator of Wilmott Trading Ltd applied to the court for a declaration that on dissolution of a company, a waste management licence would cease to exist and would not automatically vest in the crown as *bona vacantia* under *section 654* of the *Companies Act 1985.* The judge had, at the time of the first hearing, declined to grant a declaration to this effect in the absence of the Treasury Solicitor, who might have wished to argue against the contention that the waste management licence might vest in the crown. On this occasion, both the BA and the Treasury Solicitor appeared and made representations as to why the declaration should be granted.

Decision: The judge looked first at the decision in *Re: Mineral Resources Ltd [1999]*, in which the court concluded that where the *Insolvency Act 1986* collided with the *EPA 1990*, the latter should prevail. It was consistent with the philosophy that the provisions in *sections 35, 40* and *74* of the *EPA 1990*, governing the way in which licences could be transferred or granted, would prevail over *section 654* of the *Companies Act 1985*. Secondly, the judge decided that the waste management licence would not constitute 'property' for the purposes of *section 654*. Although the definition of 'property' in *section 436* of the *Insolvency Act 1986* might be wide enough to catch waste management licences, a licence would not be property in the way that word was used in *section 654* of the *Companies Act 1985*. The judge reached this conclusion after considering the definitions in *sections 744* and *744(A)* of the *Companies Act 1985* (inserted by *section 145* of the *Companies Act 1989*). These sections omitted any reference to property' and *section 735(A)* of the *Companies Act 1985* (inserted by *section 43 9(1)* of the *Insolvency Act 1986*) which incorporates provisions of the *Insolvency Act 1986* into the *Companies Act 1985*, but conspicuously did not include *section 436* of the *Insolvency Act 1986*). On the basis of this analysis, the judge held that a waste management licence held by a company ceases to exist, but does not vest in the crown, if the company is dissolved.

Re: Leeds City Council v Spencer (6 May 1999) Court of Appeal (Times Law Reports, 24 May 1999)

[B16.41]

waste; household waste; vermin and pests

Background: The case involved an appeal by Gordon Spencer against a decision by the Leeds County Council. The council required Gordon Spencer to pay for the cost of work carried out by the authority to clear accumulated refuse from a communal bin yard shared by three houses, of which he was the landlord. In December 1992, the condition of the bin yard was such that the council was entitled to exercise its power to issue a notice under *section 4* of the *Prevention of Damage by Pests Act 1949*. The council served a notice under that Act, requiring Gordon Spencer to keep the land free from rats and mice and to remove at his own expense waste which had accumulated. Gordon Spencer refused to remove the waste and the council carried out the clearance itself and sought to reclaim the costs of the works from him. Gordon Spencer argued that an important consideration was that the council had failed in its obligations under *section 45* of the *EPA 1990*, to remove household waste free of charge. There exists no general duty on householders to put out household waste for collection in a recepaicle of any kind. Parliament has left it open to each council to decide what dustbin or plastic sack regime it considers appropriate.

Decision: The court held that the council had failed to serve a notice under *section 46(1)* of the *EPA 1990* on the householders, requiring them to place their waste for collection in receptacles of the kind and numbers specified in the notice. The court therefore concluded that there was a mismatch between the obligations the council could require of its waste collection contractors and the duties which were imposed on it by statute under *section 45* of the 1990 Act to remove household waste free of charge. The court held that the unsatisfactory position in the yard had been allowed to arise because of the council's breach of its public duty under *section 45* of the *EPA 1990*. By serving a notice on Gordon Spencer requiring him to clear the yard at his own expense, the council was imposing on him the cost of discharging an obligation that parliament had imposed on it. This was ultra vires.

Re: Mineral Resources Ltd; Environment Agency v Stout (30 April 1998) High Court, Chancery Division ([1999] 1 All ER 746)

[B16.42]

waste; waste management licence; waste management licence surrender; insolvency; liquidator

Background: In this case, the court decided that a waste management licence could not be disclaimed as 'onerous property' by a liquidator under *section 178* of the *Insolvency Act 1986*. The insolvent company held a waste management licence in respect of a landfill site in Hinxton. The liquidator, having decided that the licence was unsaleable, sought to disclaim it as 'onerous property'. The EA sought a declaration that the liquidator had no power to disclaim the licence on the basis that: (a) it was not 'property' within the meaning of the *Insolvency Act 1986* and; (b) even if it was 'property', the power to disclaim would be excluded by the provisions of the *EPA 1990*, which provides that a waste management licence 'shall continue in force' until revoked under *section 38* or surrendered under *section 39* of that Act.

Decision: The judge decided that, because the *EPA 1990* provides for the transfer of waste management licences and that there was a market in them, the waste management licence does constitute 'property' within the meaning of the *Insolvency Act 1986*. However, he went on to state that the waste management licence could not be disclaimed for the following reasons: (1) the *EPA 1990* was enacted after the *Insolvency Act 1986* and therefore as a matter of construction, its terms should be given preference over any conflicting terms in the earlier Act; (2) contrary to the liquidator's submissions; it would not be open to the FA to prove in the liquidation for any loss or damage it suffered as a result of any disclaimer under the *Insolvency Act 1986* and thus this would not provide any remedy to the EA and; (3) the benefit to the public of maintaining a healthy environment should take priority over the interests of the good administration of business and commerce under the *Insolvency Act 1986*.

Water Pollution

Environment Agency v Campbell and Another (8 May 1998) High Court, Queen's Bench Division (Times Law Reports, 18 May 1998)

[B17.1]

sheep dip; procedure

Background: Roy Campbell and Cowall Leisure Ltd were accused of causing sheep dip to enter a stream. Before a hearing on 12 November 1997, the solicitors for Campbell and Cowall Leisure wrote to the EA explaining that their clients would plead guilty. The prosecutor's representative failed to appear at the hearing and the magistrates dismissed the information under *section 15* of the *Magistrates' Court Act 1980*. On 17 December 1997, the EA laid an identical information against Campbell and Cowall. Workington magistrates refused to hear the new information on the basis that, where a charge has been dismissed, the prosecution cannot thereafter institute proceedings on the same or an essentially similar charge. To hear the information would be an abuse of the process of the court. The EA appealed.

Test: The court considered the extent to which the magistrates had a discretion to decide whether the new information should be heard, and whether such a discretion was exercised correctly.

Decision: The court noted that, in the light of *section 15* of the 1980 Act, the only options were to adjourn the case or to dismiss the information. In view of the fact that Mr Campbell and Cowall intended to plead guilty and also that there had been a previous adjournment of the case at their request, it was difficult to see what prejudice they would have suffered had an adjournment been granted. The magistrates did not exercise their discretion to decide whether it would be an abuse of process for the new information to be heard. Had they exercised their discretion when viewed against public interest in the issues being tried, they would have concluded that it could not be an abuse of process of the court to allow the information to be heard.

The appeal was allowed and the magistrates were ordered to hear the new information.

Comment: A court which dismisses an information because a prosecutor fails to appear is not necessarily barred from hearing an identical information subsequently laid against the same defendant.

Losinjska Plovidba v Transco Overseas Ltd and Others (14 June 1995) High Court, Queen's Bench Division (Times Law Reports, 18 July 1995)

[B17.2]

shipping; dangerous substances; hazardous substances; transportation

Background: Losinjska Plovidba was a bare-boat charterer of a ship which operated a liner service. In the incident in question, the ship carried drums of hydrochloric acid and sodium hydrochloride. The first defendant, Transco Overseas Ltd was the shipper. The second defendant, Hays Chemical Distribution Ltd was the supplier of the drums. The containers holding the drums had leaked as a result of damage which had been caused to the drums themselves. Contamination was caused to the vessel and to the containers. The cause of action against Hays was in tort. Hays sought an interlocutory order dismissing the action against it.

Test: The issue was whether the potential claim against Hays was of sufficient merit to warrant going to trial.

Decision: The court decided that the claim against Hays was of sufficient merit.

It was arguable in law that if articles were put into circulation and remained positively dangerous, unless preventative measures were taken to neutralise the danger, a person who was obliged to take such steps did not have the option simply to abandon the article. Therefore, any person subsequently damaged may have a claim in tort against the person who negligently put such articles into circulation.

Comment: Whilst the case is a shipping case, its principles are worthy of note in general in relation to the transportation of hazardous substances.

R v Secretary of State for the Environment, ex parte Kingston Upon Hull City Council, and R v Secretary of State for the Environment, ex parte Bristol City Council and Another (26 January 1996) High Court, Queen's Bench Division (Times Law Reports, 31 January 1996).

[B17.3]

urban waste water treatment directive; judicial review; sewerage effluent

Background: This was an application for judicial review of decisions, dated 18 May 1994, of the Secretary of State for the Environment. The decisions concerned establishing esturine limits of the Humber and Severn estuaries and when designating high natural dispersion areas within those estuaries under the *Urban Waste Water Treatment, England & Wales Regulations 1994 (SI 1994 No 2841)*. These Regulations implemented the provisions of *Directive 91/271/EEC on urban waste water treatment*. The dispute between the parties was whether primary or more stringent and expensive secondary treatment of household and industrial sewage was required under the legislation. All the relevant discharges of water within the council's areas were above certain levels and required secondary treatment if the discharges went into estuaries. The secretary of state had defined the estuary limits by reference to man-made topographical features, namely bridges on the River Severn and Humber. By doing so, the secretary of state effectively redrew the boundary of the estuaries in order to escape the cost requirements of the Directive. The secretary of state argued that as the Directive contained no criteria for ascertaining the outer limit of the estuary, he had a wide discretion and could see nothing wrong in using the man-made topographical features to define the estuary limits.

However, the council argued that in establishing the outer limit of an estuary, it was necessary to apply objective criteria. They said that such objective criteria should be based on the salinity of the receiving waters or otherwise based upon the topographical features of the receiving waters.

Decision: The court concluded that because the Directive did not include any express criteria for determining the limits of estuaries, member states were intended to have a discretion in that regard. The court therefore rejected the argument that salinity or natural topography had to be used in establishing the estuary limits. It also stated that it was important that there had to be genuine and rational assessment in each case as to what actually constituted the estuary. Regard had to be taken to all of the relevant circumstances relating to the characteristics of the area and the water in question for the purposes of the Directive to prevent adverse environmental effects. To that end, the cost of treatment of waste water was not a relevant consideration.

It was clear that the Directive stated that discharges to estuaries over a certain amount had to be the subject of secondary treatment, regardless of whether or not those discharges went into a high natural dispersion areas. Clearly, if costs considerations were allowed to permit boundaries to be redrawn, the result would be the establishment of estuaries which were not really estuaries but merely fictitious bodies of water drawn to avoid obligations imposed by the Directive.

The court held that the decisions of the secretary of state were wrong.

Comment: The court sought to apply the general wording of the Directive which leaves discretion to member states while preventing decisions being made on arbitrary and/or illogical grounds.

National Rivers Authority v Yorkshire Water Services Ltd (17 November 1994) House of Lords ([1994] 3 WLR 1202)

[B17.4]

Water Act 1989; sewerage undertaker

Background: Yorkshire Water Services Ltd had been charged, under *section 107* of the *Water Act 1989* for causing poisonous, noxious or polluting matter to enter controlled waters. The offending matter was ISO-Octanol. It was accepted as a matter of fact that Yorkshire Water, in granting consent to its industrial customers to discharge trade effluent into its sewers, imposed the condition that those customers would not discharge ISO-Octanol. It was also found that, during the night of 13 May 1990, an unknown person unlawfully discharged ISO-Octanol which passed into and through the sewerage system operated by Yorkshire Water. The offending matter then passed into Hunsworth Beck, then flowed into the River Spen, both of which are controlled waters.

Decision: Yorkshire Water had been granted a consent by the NRA to discharge sewerage effluent into Hunsworth Beck subject to conditions. The discharge of ISO-Octanol breached those conditions. Two points of legal principle were raised before the House of Lords. The first was whether in light of the fact that the discharge of ISO-Octanol into the sewerage system of Yorkshire Water was by an unknown third party, it could be said that Yorkshire Water had caused the poisonous, noxious or polluting matter to enter controlled waters. The House of Lords held that that was a question of fact which it could not determine (it would ordinarily be returned to a lower court to determine). However, it held that where a sewerage undertaker's system gathered effluent into the sewers, which was subsequently treated and the resultant liquid discharged into controlled waters, the circumstances under which any poisonous, noxious or polluting matter entered the sewers did not preclude the conclusion that the undertaker caused the polluting matter to enter controlled waters in contravention of the *Water Act 1989*.

Ultimately, however, that question of fact did not have to be decided as the House of Lords held that *section 108(7)* of the *Water Act 1989* provided a complete defence to Yorkshire Water. The defence is attributable to a discharge which another person caused or permitted to be made into the sewer. If that discharge is in contravention of conditions imposed by the sewerage undertaker then the undertaker cannot reasonably be expected to prevent the discharge into the sewer.

Comment: Following the repeal of the *Water Act 1989* and the effective splitting of water regulations into the *Water Resources Act 1991* and the *WIA 1991,* the equivalent wording to *section 198(7)* of the *Water Act 1989* is in section 87(2) of the *Water Resources Act 1991*.

NRA v Dairy Crest (November 1994) Crown Court ((1994) 238 ENDS 41)

[B17.5]

trade effluent; mitigation

Background: 6,000 litres of concentrated caustic soda solution spilled from Dairy Crest's site at Aspatria in May 1994. The NRA charged the company with causing trade effluent to enter a river, contrary to *sections 85(3)(a)* and *85(6)* of the *Water Resources Act 1991*. An alarm sounded but the employee responsible for dealing with it was distracted for half an hour before attending to the problem. A bund temporarily held the caustic soda, but the caustic soda dissolved a protective coating on the bund wall and seeped through a crack into a surface water drain. The subsequent discharge into a river caused the death of some 11,000 fish. Dairy

Crest gave evidence that the crack in the bund had probably been caused by piling operations in the previous year.

Decision: Dairy Crest pleaded guilty to the charges. The judge accepted that there was no suggestion of poor design, defective construction or inadequate maintenance at the Dairy Crest site. These factors reflected in the amount of the fine, namely £2,000. Dairy Crest, however, gave evidence of resultant improvements which it had put into place at a cost of £150,000 and that further costs borne by the company included £20,000 for restocking fish populations, £10,000 for legal and investigation costs and £13,000 to anglers for their loss.

Comment: This is a relatively straight forward case but illustrates the approach of the courts to fines in water pollution cases. It should be noted that since this case, there has been an upward pressure on the courts concerning the levels of fines.

R v Dovermoss Ltd (February 1995) Court of Appeal (Times Law Reports, 8 February 1995)

[B17.6]

watercourse; pollution; pollute; pollutant; controlled waters

Background: The prosecution alleged that Dovermoss Ltd had caused slurry to be put on fields, which in turn gave rise to ammonia pollution of underground springs. The incident took place near a Welsh water treatment works and consumer complaints were received concerning the taste of water. Dovermoss Ltd was convicted of pollution of controlled waters contrary to *section 85(1)* of the *Water Resources Act 1991*, but appealed on various points of law, including the definition of (a) 'watercourse' and (b) 'polluting matter'. Dovermoss Ltd submitted that the offence had not been committed because 'controlled waters' had not been effected. It submitted that the waters in question had most probably (due to siltation of a relevant stream) jumped its normal course and meandered across fields. 'Controlled waters' is defined in *section 104* of the *Water Resources Act 1991* and in particular *section 104(1)(c)* of that Act. The definition of 'watercourse' is explained in *section 221* of the *Water Resources Act 1991.*

Decision: Dovermoss Ltd lost its argument. The court held that a watercourse, such as the one in question, did not cease to be a watercourse merely because it was dry at any particular time. Water which was diverted from its normal course did not cease to be controlled waters. Dovermoss Ltd raised another argument. It contended that pollution had not been caused because the prosecution had not proved that some actual harm had resulted to the water causing harmful effect on animal or plant life. It argued that as the ammonia levels were within regulation levels, no such harm was shown. Again this was rejected by the court. The court said that for the purposes of the *Water Resources Act 1991,* 'pollute', 'pollution' and 'pollutant' etc. must bear their ordinary meanings. The court relied upon the definition of 'pollute' in the Oxford English Dictionary, namely 'to make physically impure, foul or filthy: to dirty, stain, taint, befoul.' It is a question of fact whether pollution occurs but it was not necessary to establish in a case like this that actual harm occurred. The likelihood of causing harm was sufficient. Importantly, the court by implication rejected the suggestion that being within regulatory limits amounted to a defence. Dovermoss Ltd also raised one further ground of appeal which the court reluctantly accepted. That ground was not relevant to this publication.

Comment: This is an important decision in relation not only to water pollution, but also to pollution of other media. In particular, the broad meaning given to the word 'pollution' gives added force to the strict liability offences under the *Water Resources Act 1991.*

Attorney General's Reference No. 1 of 1994, Court of Appeal (ILR, 31 January 1995)

cause; knowingly permit

[B17.7]

Background: This case arose out of attempts to convict three parties, who each had a varying involvement in the running of a sewerage system which caused polluting matter to enter controlled waters contrary to *section 107(1)(a)* of the *Water Act 1989*. The polluting matter had entered the controlled waters due to the sewerage system not being sufficiently maintained. The relevant parties were each acquitted. The matter came before the Court of Appeal so that its opinion could be given on various points of law arising out of the operation of *section 107(1)(a)* of the *Water Act 1989*. *Section 107(1)(a)* states that a person contravenes the section 'if he causes or knowingly permits (a) any poisonous, noxious or polluting matter or any solid waste matter to enter any controlled waters.'

Decision: The court held that the following propositions were applicable to the offence, namely:-

(1) It was a question of fact in each case whether a defendant could be said to have 'caused' the entry of the polluting matter into the controlled waters;

(2) The word 'knowingly' as used in *section 107(1)(a)* of the *Water Act 1989* did not qualify the word 'causes' i.e. it only qualifies the word 'permits';

(3) The word 'causes' should be given its plain meaning;

(4) The word 'causes' involved active participation in the operation or chain of operations which resulted in the pollution of controlled waters in question; and

(5) That merely tacit standing by and looking on was insufficient to amount to 'causing'.

The court considered the situation where a party had undertaken the day to day maintenance of a sewerage system, but failed properly to do so and in fact ran it unmaintained. It concluded that it would be sufficient to entitle a jury to find that party guilty of 'causing' pollution if such pollution resulted from that lack of maintenance.

Comment: Whilst *section 107(1)(a)* of the *Water Act 1989* has been repealed, this reference remains highly relevant for two reasons. The first is that *section 107(1)(a)* of the 1989 Act has been replaced by *section 85(1)* of the *Water Resources Act 1991* in virtually the same terms. The second is that the phrase 'cause or knowingly permit' is a common phrase used in many statutory provisions relating to environmental and other laws, and consequently any judicial pronouncement on that phrase is of interest.

HMIP and NRA v Nipa Laboratories (1 March 1996) Magistrates' Court ((1996) 254 ENDS 52)

[B17.8]

integrated pollution control

Background: In August 1995 the Nant Dowlais stream, Pontypridd, was polluted with alcohols and acetone from Nipa Laboratories' Pontypridd site. Apparently, a process effluent pump failed causing a back up of effluent in a drainage system. That effluent leaked through a cracked pipe in the site's surplus water drains. This was then compounded by another pump failure which allowed the surface water sump at the site to overflow. The pollution killed approximately 450 fish and an unquantified number of invertebrates. HMIP charged the company with failure to maintain the pumps, which was a condition of its IPC authorisation.

Decision: The NRA prosecuted the company for causing polluting matter to enter controlled waters contrary to *section 85(1)* of the *Water Resources Act 1991*. The company pleaded guilty to both counts and was fined £5,000 for each offence and ordered to pay costs in the sum of £11,000.

Comment: Although this is a straight forward case, it illustrates how the regulators (now the EA) seek to prosecute under *Part I* of the *EPA 1990* and the *Water Resources Act 1991,* where water pollution occurs from a plant which is subject to an IPL authorisation.

Environment Agency v Raymond Hake (July 1996) Magistrates' Court ((1996) 258 ENDS 45)

[B17.9]

waste; pesticide

Background: Officers of the former NRA were called to a pollution incident where a stream had turned pink and was full of dead fish. They traced the pollution to a derelict seed mill and discovered approximately 1,000 litres of waste had been emptied down a surface drain. An officer from Somerset's Waste Regulation Authority had previously called at the seed mill and advised that several drums of waste pesticide had been disposed of in an environmentally safe manner. Mr Hake was the demolition contractor responsible for the activities at the mill. He was charged with keeping controlled waste in a manner likely to cause pollution and failing to prevent the escape of waste from his control contrary to *section 33(6)* and *section 34(6)* of the *EPA 1990*. He was also charged with causing polluting matter to enter controlled waters contrary to *section 85* of the *Water Resources Act 1991*.

Decision: Mr Hake was found guilty on all three charges and was sentenced to 200 hours community service for the water pollution offence. He was fined £1,500 in relation to the offences under the 1990 Act.

Comment: This is a straight forward case but illustrates how there can be a connection between waste and water pollution offences and the policy of the EA to prosecute for both where possible.

Environment Agency v Severn Trent Water (August 1996) Crown Court ((1996) 259 ENDS 38)

[B17.10]

Salmon and Freshwater Fisheries Act 1975

Background: Severn Trent Water leaked ferric sulphate into a Welsh salmon river. This leak polluted the river killing ninety eight per cent of the salmon stock.

Decision: Severn Trent Water pleaded guilty to charges of causing polluting matter to enter controlled waters contrary to *section 85(1)* of the *Water Resources Act 1991* and of causing a noxious substance to flow into water containing fish contrary to *section 4(1)* of the *Salmon and Freshwater Fisheries Act 1975*. Severn Trent Water was fined £100,000 for the offence under the 1991 Act and £75,000 for the offence under the 1975 Act. It was also ordered to pay legal costs of £35,296 and re-stocking costs of £8,483.

Comment: This case is included because of the level of the fines imposed.

NRA v Leigh Environmental (20 June 1995) Magistrates' Court ((1995) 246 ENDS 46)

[B17.11]

causation; expert witness

Background: Employees of Leigh Environmental attended to the cleaning out of an oil interceptor of a surface water drainage system at Upper Heyford Airfield. Two independent eye witnesses gave evidence to the effect that they had seen oil and silt in a ditch near the Upper Heyford Airfield in or around the same time as the Leigh Environmental employees were attending to the oil interceptor. The witnesses also stated that they heard a pump running, which the NRA argued was consistent with the Leigh Environmental staff pumping all or part of the interceptor's contents into the watercourse. Leigh Environmental denied a charge by the NRA that it was responsible for causing polluting matter to enter controlled waters contrary to *section 85(1)* of the *Water Resources Act 1991*. Leigh Environmental argued that the pollution could have been caused by a back up of water in the drainage system which had by-passed the interceptor.

Decision: Ultimately the matter came down to a battle of expert witnesses and the magistrates found in a favour of the NRA. The magistrates fined Leigh Environmental £10,000 and ordered that it pay costs in the sum of £2,400.

Comment: This case highlights the point that even in the case of strict liability offences, it is necessary to prove causation and this can give rise to difficulties.

NRA v Biffa Waste Services Ltd (15 November 1995) Queen's Bench Divisional Court (Times Law Reports, 24 November 1995)

[B17.12]

controlled waters

Background: Biffa Waste Services Ltd drove tracked vehicles on a river bed whilst working on the River Roddlesworth. The activity caused mud and silt deposits from the river bed to be churned up in the water, resulting in the river discolouring. Biffa Waste Services Ltd was charged by Chorley justices under *section 85(1)* of the *Water Resources Act 1991* with causing polluting matter to enter controlled waters. It was acquitted and the NRA appealed.

Decision: The appeal was dismissed. The court held that a river bed is part of controlled waters. Therefore, polluting matter had not entered the river contrary to *section 85* as the mud and silt had already been present.

Comment: The court made an important distinction in this case. A number of prosecutions involve the discharge of silt laden water. In terms of the harm to aquatic life, those cases are unlikely to differ significantly with this case where the silt was disturbed in the river.

R v John Barker (20 October 1997) Magistrates' Court ((1997) 273 ENDS 45)

[B17.13]

causation; custodial sentence

Background: John Barker operated a milk bottling business from Moorside Farm at Wrishton, Blackburn and had a gas oil storage tank on the premises. The EA had warned Mr Blackburn that the tank should be bunded and on 23 February 1997, gas oil from the tank polluted a nearby pond and stream.

Decision: Mr Barker pleaded guilty to a charge under *section 85(1)* and *(6)* of the *Water Resources Act 1991* of causing pollution to controlled waters. He pleaded in mitigation that his young son had opened the tap on the tank. The magistrates sentenced him to two months in prison.

Comment: This is thought to be the first case where a custodial sentence was passed for a water pollution offence. This case is also of interest from the point of view of causation.

R v Foundation Developments (21 November 1997) Magistrates' Court ((1997) 275 ENDS 49)

[B17.14]

abuse of process; discharge consent

Background: This case was a relatively simple water pollution prosecution in which Foundation Developments sought to rely on an unusual defence. In December 1996, Foundation Developments was acting as sub-contractor to Alfred MacAlpine in building a new housing estate in Basingstoke close to the River Lodden. Foundation Developments excavated a large hole in the chalk to house a large storm water tank. It pumped clean water from the chalk into the river to keep the hole dry but also had to pump water from the bottom of the hole. This water was laden with silt and when pumped into the river turned it white for approximately two kilometres downstream. The EA brought a prosecution against Foundation Developments for causing pollution of controlled waters contrary to *section 85(3)* and *(6)* of the *Water Resources Act 1991*. Foundation Developments submitted that the EA had shown prejudice against it and therefore that the prosecution constituted an abuse of process and should accordingly be set aside. Foundation Developments' grounds for those arguments were that Alfred MacAlpine had applied for a discharge consent and despite the fact that the discharge went on for several months (much longer than expected) and much more water than expected was discharged, the EA did not process the application. The EA argued that Foundation Developments committed a water pollution offence and that the discharge would have been outside the terms of any discharge consent granted. The EA brought to the court's attention a similar incident three months previously in relation to which a prosecution was not brought.

Decision: The court went on to reject Foundation Developments' arguments based on abuse of process. Foundation Developments also sought to argue that the prosecution should properly have been brought against the contractor, Alfred MacAlpine. However, the court ruled that Foundation Developments had specific responsibility for the discharge and the charges had therefore been properly brought. Accordingly, Foundation Developments was found guilty and fined £1,000 and was ordered to pay £3,000 in costs.

Welsh Water v Gower Chemicals (15 June 1998) Crown Court ((1998) 281 ENDS 51)

[B17.15]

health and safety; trade effluent

Background: In October 1996, two workers of Neith and Port Talbot Council died while working in a chamber at a pumping station in Crymlyn Borrows near Swansea. Following the incident, the HSE prosecuted the local authority under the *HSWA 1974* and the local authority was fined £150,000. It was established following an investigation of the incident that both workers had suffocated from fumes of CFC-11 and a tracer compound methyl styrene. Both substances were tracked back to the Gower Chemicals site. The discharge of these chemicals was not consented under Gower Chemicals trade effluent agreement with Welsh Water. Welsh Water therefore brought four charges under the *WIA 1991*. Three charges were brought under *section 121(5)* of the *WIA 1991* for discharging effluents other than those described in the trade effluent agreement, discharging substances liable to produce toxic vapours, and discharging to sewer at an unauthorised location. The fourth charge was for discharging material likely to prejudicially effect the treatment and disposal of the contents of the sewer under *section 111(1) and (3)* of the *WIA 1991*.

Decision: Gower Chemicals pleaded guilty to discharging substances liable to produce toxic vapours and discharging them to a sewer at an unauthorised location. It transpired that while unloading a tanker containing the CFC liquids, a spill occurred some of which flowed into drains which Gower Chemicals thought went to a soakaway. In fact, the drain led to sewer. In court, Gower Chemicals was criticised for failing to report the loss of the CFCs and was held to be negligent in not knowing that the drain in question led to a sewer. The court fined Gower Chemicals £50,000 for each of the two charges and ordered the company to pay £33,000 in costs.

Environment Agency v Brock plc (16 February 1998) Queen's Bench Divisional Court (NLD, 16 February 1998)

[B17.16]

waste; landfill; leachate

Background: In December 1996, an EA officer found contaminated leachate leaking from the Hooton landfill in Ellesmere Port, Cheshire into a ditch tributary of the River

Dibben. The source of the escape was traced to a leak in a rubber seal in a hose carrying the leachate from the landfill to a treatment lagoon. The landfill operator, Brock plc, was charged with causing polluting matter to enter controlled waters, contrary to *sections 85(1)* and *85(6)* of the *Water Resources Act 1991*. The magistrates acquitted Brock plc on the grounds that (1) the ditch tributary was not controlled water within the meaning of the *Water Resources Act 1991* since Brock plc had extended the ditch itself and, (2) Brock plc did not cause the leachate to escape because the leak was neither within its control nor the result of its negligence on the basis that the rubber seal, which was normally expected to last twelve months, had been installed only two months earlier.

Decision: The magistrates' decision was overturned by the Queen's Bench Divisional Court on appeal by the EA. The court followed the principles in *Empress Car Company (Abertillery) Ltd v National Rivers Authority [1998]* (see paragraph B17.19), which set out how to approach issues of causation in water pollution cases. The first issue to consider was whether there had been a positive act by Brock plc. The court found that the pumping of the leachate constituted a positive act. The second issue was whether the failure of the rubber seal was a normal fact of life or something extraordinary. The court held that such items are often defective and, although the defect may not be detectable, such defects are nevertheless ordinary occurrences. The unforseeably early failure of the seal therefore provided no defence. The remaining question was whether the ditch was controlled water. *Section 104* of the *Water Resources Act 1991* provides that a man-made watercourse can be controlled water. The court held that the ditch was controlled water as water flowed through it into another watercourse which was itself controlled water. Brock plc was fined £2,000 and ordered to pay costs of £3,526.

South v Fairclough (10 March 1998) High Court, Queen's Bench Division ([1998] MPC 36)

[B17.17]

nitrates; nuisance; foreseeability

Background: Mr Savage farmed land adjacent to Mr Fairclough's farm and obtained water from a spring. The court found as fact that the water supply was contaminated with nitrates. The court also accepted that a substantial cause of this contamination had been the farming practices of Mr Fairclough. Mr Savage sought to recover damages for nuisance by applying *Cambridge Water v Eastern Counties Leather plc [1994]* (see paragraph B10.10). Mr Fairclough had used chemical fertilisers since 1979 and deposited pig and other manure from 1980. His practices had altered over time following good practice guidance until 1991 when there were no pigs left on the farm.

Decision: The court held that Mr Fairclough was not liable for nuisance. Applying *Cambridge Water v Eastern Counties Leather plc,* the court held that a 'reasonable user' was a farmer who complied with good practice guidance available at the time. The court found that Mr Fairclough had operated his farm in accordance with such guidance. Moreover, Mr Savage had to establish that the harm was foreseeable. Following *Cambridge Water v Eastern Counties Leather plc,* the test was whether an appropriate notional person fit to run the business would have foreseen the harm of his practices at the time (in this case 'a good farmer'). Although the effects of nitrates were generally known in the mid-1980s, a good farmer would not have known of this before 1991. The court held that the harm was not foreseeable and that Mr Fairclough was not liable for nuisance.

R v Yorkshire Water (20 March 1998) Magistrates' Court ((1998) 279 ENDS 48)

[B17.18]

supply water unfit for human consumption

Background: Yorkshire Water were found guilty of supplying water unfit for human consumption contrary to *section 70* of the *WIA 1991,* after residents of four villages near Boroughbridge found their water running black. One of the two boreholes used to abstract water for these villages had been closed for tests and so there was less water in the storage tower than usual. When the water from the operating borehole became turbid with suspended sediment, the treatment plant was shut down. As there was insufficient water in the water tower to flush the system clean, dirty water was supplied to these villages without warning.

Decision: The water was not a threat to health but Yorkshire Water were fined £4,000 for each of the three charges.

Empress Car Company (Abertillery) Ltd v National Rivers Authority (6 February 1998) House of Lords ([1998] 1 All ER 481)

[B17.19]

causation; positive act; vandalism

Background: Empress Car Company (Abertillery) Ltd maintained a diesel tank on its premises in Abertillery. In March 1995, the outlet from the tank was opened by an unknown person and the contents of the tank flowed into the yard and drained into the River Ebbw Fach. The company was charged under *section 85(1)* of the *Water Resources Act 1991*, which provides that it is an offence to cause or knowingly permit any poisonous, noxious or polluting matter or solid waste to enter controlled waters. The company was convicted, and it's appeals to the Crown Court and Queens Bench Divisional Court were both dismissed. On appeal to the House of Lords, the company submitted that the cause of the escape was not the keeping of the oil and the opening of the tap by an unknown person. The company further submitted that 'causing' for the purposes of *section 85(1)* of the *Water Resources Act 1991* required a positive act and the escape had not been caused by any such positive act by the company. The first issue before the court was whether there must have been some 'positive act' by the company and, if so, whether the company had carried out such an act.

Decision: The House of Lords held that the maintenance of the diesel tank constituted something which the company had done to 'cause' the pollution and, as such, this constituted a positive act by the company. The second issue before the court was whether the maintenance of the diesel tank did, in fact, 'cause' the oil to enter the river. The House of Lords held that in circumstances where a company's actions produced a situation in which polluting matter could escape, but a necessary condition of the actual escape was the act of third party or a natural event, it must be considered whether that act should be regarded as an ordinary occurrence of something extraordinary. If the act was an ordinary occurrence, it would not sever the causal connection between the company's actions and the pollution. However, if the act was something extraordinary, this would break the causal connection. The court noted that the distinction between 'ordinary' and 'extraordinary' is one of fact and degree, and that, regrettably, there was nothing unusual about ordinary vandalism. Applying those principles, the court at first instance was justified in finding that the Empress Car Company (Abertillery) Ltd had caused the pollution, and therefore the company's appeal was dismissed.

Comment: The case indicates that the presence of an intervening act in the chain of causation does not necessarily provide a defence to proceedings brought under *section 85(1)* of the *Water Resources Act 1991*. It also demonstrates a potential distinction between criminal and civil liability concerning the question of the foreseeability of harm caused.

R v North West Water Ltd (November 1998) Magistrates' Court ((1998) 286 ENDS 50)

[B17.20]

supply water unfit for human consumption; drinking water inspectorate

Background: Following a recommendation by the Drinking Water Inspectorate, North West Water was charged with two offences of supplying water unfit for human consumption contrary to *section 70* of the *WIA 1991*. The incident occurred following a major burst in a water main. This resulted in water being supplied which exceeded statutory limits for iron, manganese, aluminium and turbidity. The magistrates heard that about 1,000 people may have been affected by the supplies, which were linked to a service reservoir.

Decision: North West Water pleaded guilty to the two charges and was fined £3,000 and ordered to pay costs of £2,842.

L Nederhoff & Zn v Dijkgraaf en hoogheemraden van het Hoogheemraadschap Rijnland (29 September 1999) European Court of Justice (Case C–232/97 (29 September 1999) (ECJ))

[B17.21]

discharge; water; dangerous substances; European Union

Background: In this case, the ECJ redefined the scope of the meaning of 'discharge' as referred to in *Directive 76/464/EEC on combating water pollution*. The court ruled that particles of arsenic, chromium and copper should be considered to have been discharged for the purposes of *Directive 76/664/EEC,* when they have exited a process into a dry ditch that later fills with water. Nederhoff had originally brought proceedings in June 1997 against the competent water authority for refusing to grant an authorisation to place posts treated with creosote in surface water. Six questions on the interpretation of *Directive 76/769/EEC on restricting the use of certain dangerous substances* were referred to the ECJ.

Decision: The court referred to *Article 1(2)(d)(e)* of *Directive 76/464/EEC. Directive 76/464/EEC* defines 'discharge' as the introduction into waters of certain substances and defines 'pollution' as the discharge by man, directly or indirectly, of substances or energy into the aquatic environment that cause hazards to human health, harm to living resources and aquatic ecosystems and damages to legitimate users of water. The Netherlands transposed *Directive 76/464/EEC* into Dutch law by its law on *Pollution of Surface Waters 1981. Article 1* of that legislation prohibits the unauthorised introduction into surface water of waste or polluting or harmful substances. Nederhoff used wooden posts treated with creosote for shoring up banks. Creosote is classed as a dangerous substance under Dutch law. Nederhoff was placing the wooden posts in surface water in a ditch without authorisation and contaminating it with creosote. It eventually made an application for authorisation but it was rejected on the ground that it would be preferable to find an alternative solution less harmful to the environment. The Dutch authorities took a 'source approach' to the problem, which means that the emission of dangerous substances should be combated above all at the source by the use of alternative materials. Nederhoff appealed arguing that *Article 1(3)* of *Directive 76/464/EEC* applies to discharges, not to diffuse sources of pollution. It also argued that the policy effected a general prohibition and that there already exists sufficient provisions for dangerous substances in the Dutch law of pesticides. The Dutch court applied a broad interpretation of 'discharge' without distinguishing between the sources. The Dutch court referred several questions to the ECJ for a preliminary ruling. The ECJ concluded that the escape of creosote on wooden posts placed in surface water constitutes a 'discharge'. It decided that *Directive 76/464/EEC* permits member states to make an authorisation for a discharge, subject to additional requirements not provided for in that Directive, in order to protect against pollution by dangerous substances. Therefore, the result of this decision is that even though the placing of creosote posts in surface water is not a significant source of pollution, the ECJ considers that this should be included in the meaning of 'discharge'.

AML Van Rooij v Daeglijks Bestuur Waterschap Dommel (29 September 1999) European Court of Justice (Case–231/97 (29 September 1999) (ECJ))

[B17.22]

European Union; discharge; water; dangerous substances

Background: In this Dutch case, the ECJ also interpreted the meaning of 'discharge' in *Directive 76/464/EEC on combating water pollution*. The case involved another Dutch company, Crebr Van Aarle VC, a wood treatment business. It held an authorisation for a method of steam fixation, where steam is released onto nearby surface water into a ditch. Mr Van Rooij who lived next to Van Aarle's premises, complained about pollution to the ditch by arsenic, copper and chromium which was emitted from the steam. He argued that the direct and indirect precipitation of the polluted steam into surface water and onto land and roofs of buildings, is a discharge which must be authorised by the Dutch Law on *Pollution of Surface Waters 1981*. The Dutch court referred several questions to the ECJ for a preliminary ruling.

Decision: The ECJ held that the term 'discharge' in *Article 1(2)* of *Directive 76/464/EEC* is to be interpreted as covering contaminated steam precipitated onto surface water. The place of steam emission is only relevant in relation to determining the foreseeability of the pollution. 'Discharge' is interpreted to cover the emission of contaminated steam onto surface water. It was not thought relevant as to who the owner of the drain is. The court drew a distinction between direct and indirect steam pollution although it regarded both as discharges.

Tables of Prosecutions brought by the Environment Agency for Waste and Water Related Offences between 1997 and 1999

The following tables provide details of prosecutions brought by the Environment Agency under the main statutory environmental provisions relating to waste and water together with a summary of the level of fines imposed. For ease of reference, the statistics have been broken down into regions.

The tables are based upon statistics provided directly by each region of the Environment Agency. As a result, in some cases, the periods in which the statistics have been compiled may differ.

Tables index

Table 1 waste related offences 1997–1999

Table 2 water related offences 1997–1999

Table I(a) – Anglian region

Statutory provision	Number of successful prosecutions	Penalty	Average fine imposed (£)[1]	Minimum fine imposed (£)	Maximum fine imposed (£)
1997	24		2,045	49,080	
April 1998 to March 1999					
Section 33(1)(a) EPA 1990[2]	15	11 fines 4 other[3]	1,795	100	5,000
Section 33(1)(b) EPA 1990[4]	5	5 fines	1,900	100	5,000
Section 33(1)(c) EPA 1990[5]	1	1 fine	3,500	3,500	3,500
Section 33(1) EPA 1990 (unspecified)	6	6 fines	2,285	500	6,000

Table 1(a) – continued

Mixed offences[6]	4	4 fines	5,975	900	18,000
April 1999 to December 1999					
	46	-	915	-	42,044

1 Figures approximated to the nearest £5.

2 Section 33(1)(a) of the EPA 1990 – a person shall not deposit controlled waste or knowingly cause or knowingly permit controlled waste too be deposited in or on any land unless a waste management licence authorising the deposit is in place and the deposit is in accordance with the licence.

3 This may include custodial sentences, community service, conditional discharges, probation orders etc.

4 Section 33(1)(b) of the EPA 1990 – a person shall not treat, keep or dispose of controlled waste or knowingly cause or knowingly permit controlled waste to be treated, kept or disposed of except under and in accordance with a waste management licence.

5 Section 33(1)(c) of the EPA 1990 – a person shall not treat, keep or dispose of controlled waste in a manner likely to cause pollution of the environment or harm to human health.

6 This includes prosecutions under more than one statutory provision where information on the breakdown of the penalties was not available.

Table 1(b) – North West region

Statutory provision	Number of successful prosecutions	Penalty	Average fine imposed (£)	Minimum fine imposed (£)	Maximum fine imposed (£)
April 1998 to March 1999					
Section 33(1)(a) EPA 1990	20	6 fines 14 other	785	200	1,500
Section 33(1)(b) EPA 1990	36	28 fines 8 other	1,955	750	10,000
Section 33(1)(c) EPA 1990	14	9 fines 5 other	3,140	250	15,000
Section 33(6) EPA 1990	5	5 fines	9,880	400	15,000
Section 34 EPA 1990[7]	7	5 fines 2 other	1,500	500	3,500
Section 71 EPA 1990[8]	4	1 fine 3 other	500	500	500

Table 1(b) – Continued

Special Waste Regulations 1996	1	1 fine	2,000	2,000	2,000
Regulation 18(6) Waste Management Licensing Regulations 1994	5	5 fines	10	10	10
Unspecified waste offence[9]	20	10 fines 10 other	4,250	4,000	30,000[10]

[7] Section 34 EPA 1990 imposes a general duty of care on those persons which import, produce, carry, keep, treat or dispose of controlled waste or, as a broker, have control of such waste.

[8] Section 71 EPA 1990 sets out the powers of the Environment Agency to obtain information.

[9] Includes cases involving a number of offences on which individual details are not available.

[10] This fine was imposed in respect of three offences. Information on the breakdown of fines was not available.

Table 1(c) – North east region

Statutory provision	Number of successful prosecutions	Penalty	Average fine imposed (£)	Minimum fine imposed (£)	Maximum fine imposed (£)
1998					
Section 33(1)(a) EPA 1990	9	6 fines 3 other	2,910	200	7,000
Section 33(1)(b) EPA 1990	4	4 fines	1,025	300	2,500
Section 33(1)(c) EPA 1990	1	1 other	-	-	-
Section 33(1) EPA 1990 (unspecified)	21	15 fines 6 other	2,560	75	10,000
Section 33(5) EPA 1990[11]	2	1 fine 1 other	100	100	100
Section 34 EPA 1990	16	13 fines 6 other	835	100	2,500

Table 1(c) – Continued

Mixed waste offences	11	9 fines 2 other	2,845	50	7,000
Unspecified waste offences	9	5 fines 4 other	2,500	1,000	6,000
January 1999 to June 1999					
Section 33(1)(a) EPA 1990	2	1 fine 1 other	100	100	100
Section 33 EPA 1990 (unspecified)	1	1 fine	600	100	100
Section 34 EPA 1990	6	5 fines 1 other	2,100	100	7,000
Mixed offences	26	22 fines 4 other	1,690	20	5,000

Table 1(c) – Continued

July 1999 to December 1999					
Section 33 EPA 1990 (unspecified)	32	-	4,420	-	-
Section 34 EPA 1990 (unspecified)	10	-	1,185	-	-

11 Section 33(5) Environmental Protection Act 1990 – where controlled waste is carried in and deposited from a motor vehicle, the person who controls the use of the vehicle (or is in a position to do so) shall be treated as knowingly causing the waste to be deposited whether or not he gave any instructions for this to be done.

Table 1(d) – Welsh region

Statutory provision	Number of successful prosecutions	Penalty	Average fine imposed (£)	Minimum fine imposed (£)	Maximum fine imposed (£)
1997					
Section 33(1)(a) EPA 1990	2	1 other	750	750	750
Section 33(1)(b) EPA 1990	2	2 fines	200	125	200
Section 33(6) EPA 1990	3	3 fines	500	500	500
Section 34(1)(a) EPA 1990	3	3 fines	200	125	7,000
Section 34(1)(c)(i) EPA 1990	1	1 fine	125	125	125
Section 34(1)(c)(ii) EPA 1990	1	1 fine	125	125	125

Table 1(d) – Continued

April 1998 to March 1999					
Section 33(1)(a) EPA 1990	12	10 fines 2 other	985	50	5,000
Section 33(1)(b) EPA 1990	10	8 fines 2 other	600	100	1,500
Section 33(1)(c) EPA 1990	2	1 fine 1 other	150	150	150
Section 33(1) EPA 1990 (unspecified)	2	2 fines	6,250	5,000	7,500
Section 33(6) EPA 1990	2	2 other	-	-	-
Section 34(6) EPA 1990	1	1 other	-	-	-
Section 34 EPA 1990	4	4 fines	810	250	1,500

Table I(d) – Continued

March 1999 to December 1999					
Section 33(1)(a) EPA 1990	14	7 fines 1 other	2,000	50	2,000
Section 33(1)(b) EPA 1990	8	4 fines 4 other	500	200	2,000
Section 33(1)(c) EPA 1990	3	2 fines	1,000	1,000	1,250
Section 33(1)(c)(ii) EPA 1990	2	1 fine	200	200	200
Section 36(1)(b) EPA 1990	1	1 other			

Table I(e) – Midlands region

Statutory provision	Number of successful prosecutions	Penalty	Average fine imposed (£)	Minimum fine imposed (£)	Maximum fine imposed (£)
April 1998 to March 1999					
Section 33(1)(a) EPA 1990	40	30 fines 10 other	1,300	100	15,000
Section 33(1)(b) EPA 1990	13	11 fines 2 other	2,325	200	15,000
Section 33(1)(c) EPA 1990	13	10 fines 3 other	1,480	250	2,500
Section 33(1) EPA 1990 (unspecified)	10	7 fines 3 other	4,515	500	14,000
Section 34 EPA 1990	34	24 fines 10 other	455	50	3,000

Table 1(f) – South west region

Statutory provision	Number of successful prosecutions	Penalty	Average fine imposed (£)	Minimum fine imposed (£)	Maximum fine imposed (£)
1997					
Section 33(1)(a) EPA 1990	36	28 fines 8 other	1,420	50	10,000
Section 33(1)(b) EPA 1990	10	9 fines 1 other	4,650	600	10,000
Section 33(1)(c) EPA 1990	2	2 fines	23,500	2,000	45,000
Section 34 EPA 1990	4	4 fines	610	125	2,000
1998					
Section 33(1)(a) EPA 1990	3	3 fines	2,915	2,750	3,000

Table 1(f) – Continued

Section 33(1)(b) EPA 1990	4	4 fines	2,400	600	3,000
Section 34 EPA 1990	1	1 fine	2,000	2,000	2,000
January 1999 to March 1999					
Section 33(1)(b) EPA 1990	1	1 fine	200	200	200
Section 34 EPA 1990	1	1 fine	2,000	2,000	2,000
April 1999 to December 1999					
Section 33(1)(a) and (6) EPA 1990	14	6 fines 8 other	2,000	100	3,000
Section 33(1) EPA 1990	3	3 other	–	–	–

Table 1(f) – Continued

Section 33(5) and (6) EPA 1990	1	fine	250	250	250
Section 33(1)(b) and (6) EPA 1990	9	4 fines 5 other	300	300	300
Section 34 EPA 1990	2	2 other	-	-	-
Section 59(5) EPA 1990	1	1 fine	200	200	200
Section 62 EPA 1990	3	fine	100	100	100
Regulation 5(2)(b) Special Waste Regulations 1996	1	1 other	-	-	-
Section 1 COPA 1974	3	3 other	-	-	-
Section 71(2) and (3) EPA 1990	1	1 fine	50	50	50

Table 1(f) – Continued

Section 6(1) EPA 1990	1	1 fine	4,000	4,000	4,000
Section 32 RSA 1993[12]	1	1 other			

[12] Section 32 of the Radioactive Substances Act 1993 sets out the main offences relating to registration or authorisation under the Radiactive Substances Act 1993.

Table 1(g) – Southern region

Statutory provision	Number of successful prosecutions	Penalty	Average fine imposed (£)	Minimum fine imposed (£)	Maximum fine imposed (£)
April 1998 to March 1999					
Section 33(1)(a) EPA 1990	10	7 fines 3 other	1,545	150	6,000
Section 33(1)(b) EPA 1990	3	3 fines	2,600	200	7,000
Section 33(1)(c) EPA 1990	1	1 fine	1,500	1,500	1,500
Section 33(1) EPA 1990 (unspecified)	5	5 fines	2,240	250	5,000
Section 34 EPA 1990	6	6 fines	885	200	2,000

Table 1(h) – Thames region

Statutory provision	Number of successful prosecutions	Penalty	Average fine imposed (£)	Minimum fine imposed (£)	Maximum fine imposed (£)
1997					
Section 33(1) EPA 1990	5	5 fines	2,555	25	5,750,000
Section 34 EPA 1990	2	2 fines	1,750	1,500	2,000
Section 7(3) COPA 1974	1	1 fine	1,000	1,000	1,000
Section 59 EPA 1990	1	1 fine	5,000	5,000	5,000
Mixed waste offences	4	4 fines	1,340	1,000	1,000

Table I(h) – Continued

1998					
Section 33(1) EPA 1990	32	25 fines 7 other	1,025	50	11,000
Section 34 EPA 1990	8	7 fines 1 other	925	50	4,000
Mixed waste offences	5	5 fines	990	450	1,700
1999					
Section 33(1)(a) EPA 1990 (unspecified)	24	23 fines 1 other	4,005	30	50,000
Section 34 EPA 1990	1	1 fine	400	400	400

Table 2(a) – Anglian region

Statutory provision	Number of successful prosecutions	Penalty	Average fine imposed (£)	Minimum fine imposed (£)	Maximum fine imposed (£)
1997					
Section 85(1) WRA 1991[13]	32	30 fines 2 other	3,215	200	12,000
1998					
Section 85(1) WRA 1991	47	47 fines	3,380	500	15,000
Section 24 WRA 1991[14]	34	33 fines	655	500	2,500
January 1999 to June 1999					
Section 85(1) WRA 1991	17	15 fines 2 other	2,785	250	9,000

Table 2(a) – Continued

Section 85(3) WRA 1991[15]	1	1 fine	2,000	2,000	2,000
Section 24 WRA 1991	5	5 fines	1,000	1,000	2,500
July 1999 to December 1999					
	23	-	4,980		

[13] Section 85 of the WRA 1991 – provides that it is a criminal offence to cause or knowingly permit any poisonous, noxious or polluting matter or any solid waste matter to enter controlled waters.

[14] Section 24 of the WRA 1991 – provides that it is an offence to abstract water from any source or cause or knowingly permit any person to abstract water from any source without a licence and makes it any offence to install or extend any well or borehole or install or modify machinery for further abstraction except where permitted by a licence.

[15] Section 85(3) of the WRA 1991 – provides that it is an offence to cause or knowingly permit any trade efficient or sewage effluent to be discharged into any controlled waters or into the sea beyond the limits of controlled waters.

Table 2(b) – North west region

Statutory provision	Number of successful prosecutions	Penalty	Average fine imposed (£)	Minimum fine imposed (£)	Maximum fine imposed (£)
1997					
Section 85(1) WRA 1991	51	49 fines 2 other	3,095	250	20,000
Section 85(3) WRA 1991	2	2 fines	4,000	3,000	5,000
Section 85 WRA 1991 (unspecified)	6	6 fines	1,665	1,000	4,000

Table 2(c) – North east region

Statutory provision	Number of successful prosecutions	Convictions	Average fine imposed (£)	Minimum fine imposed (£)	Maximum fine imposed (£)
1997					
Section 85(1) WRA 1991	9	8 fines 1 other	-	-	-
Section 85(3) WRA 1991	4	4 fines	2,000	1,000	12,000
Section 85 WRA 1991 (unspecified)	16	16 fines	-	-	-
1998					
Section 85(1) WRA 1991	7	-	-	-	-
Section 85(3) WRA 1991	3	25 fines 2 other	2,090	600	7,500

Table 2(c) – Continued

Section 85 WRA 1991 (unspecified)	16	-	3,390	-	-
January 1999 to July 1999					
Section 85(1) WRA 1991	2	2 fines	1,340	700	3,000
August 1999 to December 1999					
Section 85 WRA 1991 (unspecified)	10	-	6,200	-	-

Table 2(d) – Welsh region

Statutory provision	Number of successful prosecutions	Penalty	Average fine imposed (£)	Minimum fine imposed (£)	Maximum fine imposed (£)
1997					
Section 85(1) WRA 1991	9	8 fines 1 other	1,730	150	4,000
Section 85(3) WRA 1991	2	2 fines	2,000	1,000	3,000
Section 85 WRA 1991	5	5 fines	4,240	200	8,000
1998					
Section 85(1) WRA 1991	9	7 fines 2 other	1,460	200	5,000
Section 85 WRA 1991 (unspecified)	2	2 fines	1,625	1,250	2,000

Table 2(d) – Continued

January 1999 to March 1999					
Section 85(1) WRA 1991	9	9 fines	1,240	250	4,000
Section 85(3) WRA 1991	2	2 fines	875	250	1,500
Section 85 WRA 1991 (unspecified)	1 fine	1,000	1,000	1,000	
April 1999 to December 1999					
Section 85(1) WRA 1991	19	12 fines 7 other	2,000	250	10,000
Section 85(3) WRA 1991	8	3 others 5 fine	2,000	2,000	3,000
Section 85(6) WRA 1991	7	5 fines 2 other	2,000	1,000	2,000

Table 2(d) – Continued

SFFA 1975 (unspecified)[16]	2	2 fines	1,500	1,500	1,500
Section 4 SFFA 1975	4	3 fines 1 other	500	200	1,750

[16] Salmon and Freshwater Fisheries Act 1975.

Table 2(e) – Midlands region

Statutory provision	Number of successful prosecutions	Penalty	Average fine imposed (£)	Minimum fine imposed (£)	Maximum fine imposed (£)
1998					
Section 85(1) WRA 1991	23	22 fines 1 other	4,500	250	14,000
January 1999 to March 1999					
Section 85(1) WRA 1991	10	10 fines	3,550	500	8,000

Table 2(f) – South west region

Statutory provision	Number of successful prosecutions	Penalty	Average fine imposed (£)	Minimum fine imposed (£)	Maximum fine imposed (£)
1997					
Section 85(1) WRA 1991	3	3 fines	1,835	1,000	2,500
Section 85 WRA 1991 (unspecified)	21	20 fines 1 other	1,985	150	10,000
1998					
Section 85(1) WRA 1991	7	7 fines	2,610	100	6,000
Section 85 WRA 1991 (unspecified)	44	39 fines 5 other	375	100	15,000

Table 2(f) – Continued

January 1999 to March 1999					
Section 85(1) WRA 1991	1	1 fine	13,500	13,500	13,500
Section 85 WRA 1991 (unspecified)	3	3 fines	1,500	500	3,000

Table 2(g) – Southern region

Statutory provision	Number of successful prosecutions	Penalty	Average fine imposed (£)	Minimum fine imposed (£)	Maximum fine imposed (£)
1997					
Section 85 WRA 1991	17	17 fines	3,405	500	6,000
Section 24 WRA 1991	1	1 fine	200	200	200
Section 201 WRA 1991	1	1 fine	50	50	50
April 1998 to March 1999					
Section 85(1) WRA 1991	15	14 fines 1 other	7,125	200	70,000
Section 85 WRA 1991 (unspecified)	4	3 fines 1 other	3,835	500	10,000

Table 2(g) – Continued

Section 24 WRA 1991	3	3 fines	1,750	750	2,500
April 1999 to February 2000					
Section 85 WRA 1991	29	26 fines	4,195	250	25,000
Section 24 WRA 1991	3	2 fines 1 other	4,500	3,000	6,000

Table 2(h) – Thames region

Statutory provision	Number of successful prosecutions	Penalty	Average fine imposed (£)	Minimum fine imposed (£)	Maximum fine imposed (£)
1997					
Section 85(1) WRA 1991	22	22 fines	3,637	500	12,000
Section 85(3) WRA 1991	6	6 fines	5,250	500	12,000
Section 24 WRA 1991	1	1 fine	1,000	1,000	1,000
1998					
Section 85(1) WRA 1991	5	5 fines	4,160	300	10,000
Section 85(3) WRA 1991	4	4 fines	6,750	6,000	7,000

Table 2(h) – Continued

Section 85 WRA 1991 (unspecified)	16	16 fines	3,590	250	11,000
1999					
Section 85(1) WRA 1991	21	21 fines	6,190	2,000	12,000
Section 85(3) WRA 1991	3	3 fines	6,000	6,000	6,000
Section 24 WRA 1991	6	6 fines	3,542	500	7,000
Section 32 RSA 1993[17]	2	2 fines	7,000	7,000	7,000
Section 34A RSA 1993[18]	1	1 fine	3,500	3,500	3,500

17 Section 32 of the Radioactive Substances Act 1993 sets out the main offences relating to registration or authorisation under the Radioactive Substances Act 1993.

18 Section 34A of the Radioactive Substances Act 1993 sets out the offence of knowingly or recklessly making false or misleading statements.

Table of Cases

This table is referenced to paragraph numbers in the book.

Imperial Chemical Industries Ltd v Shatwell [1964] 2 All ER 999 A35.4
Issa and Another v Hackney London Borough Council [1996] EGCS 184 B14.25

Jackson v NCB [1955] 1 All ER 145 A27.2
Jameson and Another v Central Electricity Generating Board, Times Law Reports, 17 December 1998 A8.1
Jennings v Norman Collison (Contractors) [1970] 1 All ER 1121 A5.2
John Summers and Sons Ltd v Frost [1955] 1 All ER 878 A13.1
Johnson v Coventry Churchill International Ltd [1992] 3 All ER 14 A2.1

Kahl and Another v Holderness Borough Council and Another, NLD, 23 November 1998 B8.6
Kay v ITW Ltd [1968] 1 QB 140, [1967] 3 All ER 22 A31.7, A31.9
Kelly v Pierhead Ltd [1967] 1 WLR 65 A6.1
Kent County Council v Beaney [1993] Env. L.R. 225 B16.32
Kent County Council v Secretary of State for the Environment and Others [1995] EGCS 130 B16.13
Kent County Council v Secretary of State for the Environment and Another [1997] EGCS 64 B12.11
Kettering Borough Council v Perkins [1998] PLSCS 80 B12.18
Kincardine and Deeside District Council v Forestry Commissioner [1992] Env. L.R. 151 B3.2
Kirby v National Coal Board [1958] SLT 47 A35.1
Kirklees Metropolitan Borough Council v Field and Others, Times Law Reports, 26 November 1997 B14.13, B14.17
Kuwait Airways Corporation v Iraqi Airways Co [1995] 1 WLR 1147 A8.2
Kyte and Others v (1) Secretary of State for the Environment (2) Shepway District Council (3) Rank Holidays and Hotels Development Ltd, LTL, 29 October 1996 B12.8

Ladds v Coloroll (In Liquidation), Current Law, October 1995 A28.2
Lamb (W) Ltd v J Jarvis & Sons plc [1998] 60 Con LR 1 B8.5
Lambert (A) Flat Management Ltd v Lomas [1981] 2 All ER 280 B14.8, B14.19, B14.20
Lambeth London Borough Council v Mullings, Times Law Reports,16 January 1990 B14.14
Landcatch Ltd v The Braer Corporation and Others, Times Law Reports, 6 March 1998 B11.1
Landcatch Ltd v International Oil Pollution Compensation Fund, Times Law Report, 14 June 1999 B11.7
Latimer v A.E.C. Ltd [1953] AC 643 A1.3, A1.4
Leaky and others v National Trust for Places of Historic Interest or Natural Beauty [1980] 1 QB 485 B9.7
Leeds City Council v Spencer, Times Law Reports, 24 May 1999 B16.41

Table of European Cases

This table is referenced to paragraph numbers in the book.

Table of Statutes

Table of Statutory Instruments

Table of EU Legislative Material

Directives

Regulations

Council Regulation (EC) 307/97 amending Regulation (EEC) 3528/86 on the protection of the Community's forests against atmospheric pollution B4.12

Council Regulation (EC) 308/97 amending Regulation (EEC) 2158/92 on protection of the Community's forests against fire B4.12

Treaties

Treaty of Rome 1957 B4.2, B4.11, B4.15, B16.3
art 5 B4.6
art 30 B4.2
art 34 B4.3, B4.7
art 36 B4.3
art 43 B4.12
art 52 B4.2
art 86 B4.7
art 90(1) B4.7
(2) B4.7
art 130 B4.12
art 130r B6.1
art 130r(2) B6.1
art 130s B4.7
art 130t B4.7
art 169 B4.9
art 173 B3.6
art 177 B16.2
art 189(3) B4.6
art 215 B4.2

Conventions

European Convention on Human Rights B6.5

International Convention on Civil Liability for Oil Pollution Damage 1969 B11.4, B11.7

Vienna Convention on Civil Liability for Nuclear Damage 1963 art I(k)(i) B2.2

Index

This table is referenced to paragraph numbers (with the exception of the Introduction which is referenced to page numbers).